TRAVELLER'S ATLAS
OF THE
WORLD

GEDDES&
GROSSET

PHOTOGRAPHIC CREDITS

The publishers wish to acknowledge the following photographic sources:

PhotoDisc, Inc.

Pages 2, 3, 6, 7, 8 (all 6 pics), 10 (4 pics – 1st col, top; 2nd col, bottom;
3rd col, middle & bottom), 12 (4 pics – 1st col, bottom; 2nd col, top & middle;
3rd col, bottom), 13 (both pics), 14 (both pics), 15, 23 (3rd col, bottom),
25, 26 (both pics), 27, 28, 30 (both pics), 32 (both pics), 33 (both pics), 35 (all 4 pics),
36, 37 (both pics), 38 (2 pics – 2nd col, top; 3rd col, middle), 40 (all 3 pics),
43, 44 (both pics), 45, 46 (3rd col, middle), 47, 48, 49 (2), 50, 51, 52, 53, 54, 55,
56, 59 , 61, 65, 66 (2), 67, 69, 70, 71, 72, 73, 74, 75, 76, 77, 78, 79, 90, 91, 92

The Corel Corporation

Pages 9 (both pics), 10 (2 pics – 1st col, bottom; 2nd col, top), 11, 12 (3rd col, middle),
17, 31, 39 (3rd col, midddle), 60, 68, 83, 84

DigitalVision

Pages 1, 4,16, 18 (all 3 pics), 19 (all 3 pics), 20, 21 (2), 22 (both pics), 23, 24 (all 4 pics)

Keith Whittles

Pages 39 (3rd col, bottom), 46 (1st col, bottom), 57, 58

DC Williamson, London

Pages 62, 63, 64

Stockbyte

Pages 41, 42 (1st col, bottom)

Westock

Page 34

The Image Bank, Inc.

Page 38 (1st col, bottom)

Roger Kinkead

Page 42 (3rd col)

Cover images courtesy of DigitalVision, Corel and PhotoDisc, Inc.

First published 2000 by Geddes & Grosset, an imprint of
Children's Leisure Products Limited

© 2000 Children's Leisure Products Limited,
David Dale House, New Lanark, Scotland

ISBN 1 85534 899 3

Printed and bound in Indonesia

Contents

Using the Traveller's Atlas

The Traveller's Atlas of the World places at your fingertips up-to-date facts and figures reflecting our fast-changing world as well as information on individual countries to be enjoyed by anyone who travels the world. It does so in four complimentary ways:

- by providing basic geographical information about our world
- by supplying up-to-date physical and political world maps
- by giving some basic facts about each country with full-colour illustrations and short notes and information boxes on places and points of interest
- by including a comprehensive Gazetteer and an Index with detailed information on each country including the latest data and statistics.

Geographical information

This introductory section concisely summarises geographical facts about our physical world, including our place in the universe, our neighbours in space, the origin, structure and dynamics of our planet, its enveloping atmosphere and its vast oceans of water.

World maps

The world maps bring alive in full colour the 3-D art of the cartographer with a map coverage that extends to every part of the world. Each continent is treated systematically. Each double-spread or single-page map has been planned carefully to include an entire physical region or political unit. Generous overlaps allow for continuity between maps. Maps consist of different kinds of symbols which are explained below (and further illustrated in the *Map Contents and Legend* on page 5).

Area symbols in one colour, indicate the shape and size of a country on a map of a continent, or a natural feature such as a sea. Coloured area symbols show the height of the land above sea level.

Line symbols show features such as roads, railways, rivers and boundaries.

Point symbols show features (e.g. mountain peaks, heights in metres) and towns.

The International boundary tells you where one country meets another one. The boundary often follows the line of a physical feature, such as a river.

A capital city is shown on the map by an underlining in red. This distinguishes it from the other towns and cities on the map.

Map colour is used on the maps to show various things. Each country is given a different colour from its neighbour on political maps. In the regional maps, colour is used to show the height of land above sea level.

Latitude and longitude lines help to indicate how far north or south of the Equator or how far east or west of Greenwich, London, a place is located.

Cities and towns that are not capitals are shown by an open black circle or square, corresponding to the population size group of each location.

Mountain peaks in mountain ranges are shown by a small black triangle. The name of a mountain and its height in metres are sometimes shown beside the triangle.

Rivers are shown on the map by a fine blue line. The name of the river will be found printed along this line.

Grid letters and numbers at the edges of a map make it easy to find places. These are needed when using the Index.

Map scales are a way of showing an area at a reduced scale, since it is impossible to show a country at its true size on a map. All maps in this atlas are therefore drawn at a reduced scale. To fit the area to be shown on one page, many different scales are used. The amount of information given and the area covered by each map are affected by the scale of the map. For example, at a large scale (1: 2 600 000) England and Wales are shown. At a medium scale (1: 8 000 000) the British Isles are covered. At a small scale (1: 25 000 000) we are able to map the continent of Europe.

There are different ways of expressing the scale of a map: the *scale bar* gives a graphic linear measure and the *representative fraction* gives the scale ratio (for example 1: 8 000 000).

Abbreviations are used if there is not enough space on a map to name a feature in full. The following abbreviations are commonly used in the *Traveller's Atlas*

Arch.	Archipelago
L.	Lake, Loch
C.	Cape
Mt.	Mont, Mount
Hd.	Head
Mts.	Mountains
I.	Island, Isle
Ra.	Range
Is.	Islands
Str.	Strait

Abbreviations used for the country names are listed on the world map or on individual continent maps.

Countries of the world

Information about any given country, together with full-colour illustrations and short notes on some specific places and points of interest, appears after the map in which the country is located.

Gazetteer and Index

The gazetteer lists (in alphabetical order) and describes the countries included in this atlas with facts on climate, economy, government, religion and currency.

Finally, there is an index to most of the place names to be found on the maps. Each entry in the alphabetised index starts with the name of the place, followed by the country in which it is located in italic script. Then, in a column alongside, is first the number of the most appropriate page on which the name appears, usually the largest scale map. Next comes the alphanumeric reference of the map grid on that page. For example, the index entry for Berlin reads:

Berlin *Germany*   52C2

THE PLANET EARTH

Earth is the planet we inhabit, a nearly spherical body which rotates every twenty-four hours from west to east round an imaginary line called its axis. The planet Earth, one of nine planets which circle around the Sun, completes its revolution in about 365 days and 6 hours. It is the third planet from the Sun and the only one we know that supports life. The planet Earth is nearly 4,600 million years old and most probably took over 100 million years to form into a ball of rock. The first tiny signs of growth appeared some 3,500 million years ago and life as we know it has evolved over the last 40 to 50 million years.

Volcanic eruptions produced gases which formed the Earth's atmosphere – a layer of air approximately 1,000 kilometres or 620 miles thick which contains mainly gases (oxygen, nitrogen and carbon dioxide) and water vapour. This layer shields the Earth from the harmful ultraviolet rays emanating from the Sun and protects it from extremes of temperature. The Earth's seas and oceans were formed when the same eruptions also produced huge volumes of water vapour which condensed to fill the hollows in the Earth's crust.

The Earth is regarded as divided into two halves – the northern and the southern hemispheres – by the equator, an imaginary line going right round it midway between the poles. To indicate with precision the position of places on the Earth, additional circles are traced upon the surface so that those of the one set all pass through both poles (meridians), while those of the other are drawn parallel to the equator (parallels of latitude). By reference to them, we can state the latitude and longitude, and thus the exact position, of any place.

The surface of the Earth covers 510,069,120 square kilometres or 196,938,800 square miles of which about 30 per cent is dry land, the remaining 70 per cent being water. The land is arranged into masses of irregular shape and size. The chief masses are called continents while detached masses of smaller size are islands. The surface of the land consists of mountains, valleys, plains, plateaux and deserts. The water area of the Earth is divided into oceans, seas, bays, gulfs and so on, while rivers and lakes are regarded as features of the land surface. The Earth's seas and oceans have an average depth of 3.5 kilometres or 2.2 miles. The great phenomena of the oceans are their currents and tides.

The Earth's daily motion about its own axis takes place in 23 hours, 56 minutes and 4 seconds of mean time. This revolution brings about the alternation of day and night. As the axis on which the Earth rotates is inclined towards the plane of its path about the Sun at an angle of 66.5° and the angle between the plane of the ecliptic and the plane of the Earth's equator is therefore 23.5°, the Sun ascends, as seen from our northern latitudes, from 21st March to 21st June (the summer solstice) to about 23.5° above the celestial equator and descends again towards the equator from 21st June to 23rd September. It then sinks till 22nd December (the winter solstice), when it is about 23.5° below the equator and returns again to the equator by 21st March. This arrangement is the cause of the seasons and the unequal measure of day and night during them.

For all places removed from the equator, day and night are equal only twice in the year (at the equinoxes). At the summer solstice in the northern hemisphere, the North Pole of the Earth is turned towards the Sun and the South Pole away from it. For places within 23.5° of the North Pole there is a period of longer or shorter duration during which the Sun is continually above the horizon throughout the 24 hours of each day. Round the South Pole there is an equal extent of surface within which the Sun for similar periods is below the horizon. The reverse occurs at the winter solstice. The circles bounding these regions are called respectively the Arctic and the Antarctic Circles and the regions themselves, the polar or frigid zones. Throughout a region extending to 23.5° on each side of the equator the Sun is directly overhead at any place twice in the year. The circles which bound this region are called the tropics – the Tropic of Cancer in the northern hemisphere and the Tropic of Capricorn in the southern hemisphere, while the region between is the torrid zone. The regions between the tropics and the polar circles are the north and south temperate zones respectively.

The term 'earth sciences' has entered our vocabulary, covering a synthesis of the traditional disciplines of geology, geophysics, geochemistry, oceanography and meteorology. This new focus reflects worldwide concern as to how the Earth's resources can be best sustained.

In comparison to the age of the Earth, man's relatively short existence has caused alarming levels of pollution, and the environment is under increasing stress. Ozone forms a key layer in the upper atmosphere and there is concern over damage to it, caused by chlorofluorocarbons, chemicals used by man that release chlorine into the upper atmosphere, destroying the ozone. The World sustains more than 5,000 million people. The population has doubled since the early 1950s. Many experts believe that the population could double again within the next half-century. We must learn to sustain this growth and face the growing ecological crisis.

THE SOLAR SYSTEM

All the planets visible in the night sky are members of the Sun's family or the solar system. Planets shine with a steady light while real stars often twinkle. This is because a planet is a disc of light, whereas a star is so distant that it is always just a point of light. The Sun is a typical star in that it radiates heat and light of its own but the planets shine only by the light they reflect from the Sun. Most stars are much larger than planets. The five planets that can be seen without the aid of a telescope are Mercury, Venus, Mars, Jupiter and Saturn. After the invention of the telescope, astronomers discovered three more distant planets – Uranus in 1781, Neptune in 1846 and Pluto in 1930.

The nine planets in the order of their distance from the Sun are Mercury, Venus, Earth, Mars, Jupiter, Saturn, Uranus, Neptune and Pluto. All nine planets travel in the same direction as they orbit around the Sun. The planets closest to the Sun take the least time in orbit. For example Mercury, nearest to the Sun, makes a circuit in only 88 days, Earth takes a year and Jupiter almost 12 years.

The Sun's family has other members apart from planets. Swarming between Mars and Jupiter are

EARTH FACTS AND FIGURES

Surface area: 510,069,120 square kilometres or 196,938,800 square miles

Land area: 150,000,000 square kilometres or 57,500,000 square miles

Seas and oceans area: 361,000,000 square kilometres or 139,400,000 square miles (70.9 per cent of the Earth's surface)

Mass: 6,000 billion, billion tonnes

Diameter: 12,756 kilometres or 7,926 miles at the equator and 12,714 kilometres or 7,900 miles at the poles

Circumference: 40,075 kilometres or 24,901 miles at the equator

Distance from the Sun: 149,500,000 kilometres or 93,000,000 miles

Rotation period: 23 hours 56 minutes 4.1 seconds

Year: 365 days 5 hours 56 minutes 4.1 seconds

Age: 4,600 million years

The Earth as viewed from space

THE PLANETOI

The first astronomers, long ago, noticed five special 'stars' that gradually moved through the constellations. The Greeks called them planetoi (the wanderers) from which came our word 'planet'.

EARTH'S INNER STRUCTURE

This cut-out diagram shows the inner structure of the Earth. The thickness of the Earth's crust may be likened proportionally to the skin of an apple. Beneath it lie the rocks of the mantle and the two-layered core, which is mostly liquid iron.

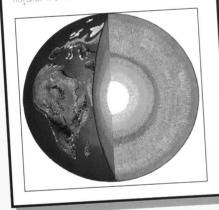

Eruption of Mount St Helens, USA

thousands of asteroids or minor planets. Comets with their streaming tails approach the Sun from the farthest parts of the solar system. In addition, dust and stones called meteoroids are scattered in the space between the planets. Meteoroids burn up if they crash through the Earth's atmosphere, creating meteor trails or shooting stars.

The exploration of most of the planets in the solar system is a major scientific achievement of the twentieth century. Men in space have landed on the Moon and brought back samples from its surface. The five planets that are visible to the naked eye – along with other Moons from those of Mars to the satellites of Saturn – have been investigated and photographed by unmanned spacecraft.

THE EARTH'S STRUCTURE

Man has been able to study the surface of his own planet for as long as the Earth has been inhabited. Yet it is strange to think that nobody had predicted accurately what it would look like from space. Now the Earth can be seen and photographed from space as a beautiful blue and white planet.

Many factors make the Earth unique in the solar system. It is the only planet with substantial amounts of liquid water (oceans cover almost three quarters of the Earth's surface). This vast quantity of water is a powerful force of erosion, the wearing away of the Earth's surface. Mountains are eroded by glaciers, wind and rain. Rivers etch channels through rocks and lowland plains, carrying sediment away from one place and depositing it in another.

Unlike the older rocky planets, the Earth has layers containing tremendous forces that are very active, namely the crust, mantle and two inner cores, one of liquid iron and one of, possibly, solid iron. Magnetism is generated by electric currents flowing through the liquid iron core, which is why a compass needle lines up with the Earth's magnetism and points to the north.

Compared with most of the other rocky worlds in the solar system, Earth is a hive of geological activity. Mountains are constantly being thrust up, earthquakes make the globe tremble and volcanoes cough out liquid rock. This all happens because the crust of the Earth consists of several large plates that will not keep still. According to theory, heat (partly from the decay of radio active rocks) flowing from underneath the plates causes this motion. In certain places, the plates push into each other and cause tremendous buckling. This crumpling of two continental plates has caused the formation of the Alps and Himalayas. Along the west coast of North and South America the continental plates are being forced against the oceanic plates and this has formed a great range of coastal mountains from Alaska to southern Chile. Another effect of these rock movements is to generate friction. This may melt the rock below the surface and this molten material works its way upwards through cracks and erupts as a volcano.

THE ATMOSPHERE

The atmosphere, which surrounds and sustains life, is the stage setting within which the drama of weather is played. Extending from the Earth's surface to perhaps 965 kilometres or 600 miles or

more into space, the atmosphere divides into several layers, each comprised of gases in varying quantities and densities, namely the troposphere, the stratosphere, the mesosphere and the thermosphere.

The predominant gases in the lowest layer, the troposphere, are oxygen, nitrogen, traces (about 0.03 per cent) of carbon dioxide and, most important for the weather, water vapour. Virtually all of our weather, as we know it, takes place in the troposphere. This is mainly because all but the tiniest traces of water vapour – the stuff of which fog, clouds, rain and all other forms of precipitation are made – occur in the troposphere. Without this water vapour there would be no life. The troposphere varies in thickness, from about 8 kilometres or 5 miles over the Poles to about 16 kilometres or 10 miles over the Equator.

There is very little water vapour in the next atmospheric layer, the stratosphere. The stratosphere contains almost no clouds and oxygen and most of the other life-sustaining gases thin out. As the altitude changes, so too does the temperature. This happens because the Earth and the water vapour in the troposphere act as radiators, absorbing and giving off the Sun's heat, but beyond the troposphere, neither the Earth's heat nor water vapour is a factor in determining atmospheric temperature.

In the stratosphere, the temperature becomes warmer with increased altitude because of the dominance of solar radiation. Then in the next layer, the mesosphere, the temperature turns cold again, in part because of the reaction of a gas called ozone that blocks out the Sun's ultraviolet rays. The temperature continues to drop until it reaches 85°C or more below zero. Then, at perhaps 80 kilometres or 50 miles over the Earth, where the thermosphere begins, the gases, under the direct influence of the Sun, become so thinly concentrated that they all but disappear.

These upper layers affect events in the troposphere by shielding the Earth from the searing rays of the Sun. In addition these upper layers together contribute about 25 per cent of the atmospheric weight that presses down upon the Earth's surface. The troposphere contributes the other 75 per cent of the atmosphere's weight through the presence of its relatively dense gases, including water vapour.

Vapour enters the atmosphere by evaporation from oceans, seas, and lakes and, to a lesser extent, from wet ground and vegetation. Heat is needed for evaporation to occur and this heat is taken from the surrounding atmosphere and the surface of the Earth, which therefore becomes cooler. This heat is not lost but is stored in the vapour as hidden or latent heat. The vapour is carried by winds to higher levels of the atmosphere and to different parts of the world. As a result, water vapour may be found throughout the troposphere and over all regions, oceans and continents. Eventually, water vapour condenses into liquid water or solid ice and falls to the ground as precipitation – rain, snow or hail.

In condensing, it also releases its latent heat to the atmosphere. Thus, if water evaporates into the air from a tropical ocean and winds then carry it to a temperate continent, where it condenses and falls as rain, this provides a very effective means of carrying not only water but also heat from places that have plenty to places that are short of both.

In the air around us, the temperature, pressure and moisture content are affected by the fourth critical ingredient that makes up our weather – the wind. As we know, wind is the name for a moving mass of air. Nearly everyone is familiar with winds that blow from north, south, east or west – that is across the Earth's surface or horizontally. But winds also blow vertically – as birdwatchers know from seeing gulls or crows sail upwards on rising currents of warm air or from watching a hawk sink down rapidly on a descending cold current.

Most vertical air currents are much gentler than horizontal winds but they are vitally important because they can generate many different types of weather. When air rises it expands, because the pressure on it becomes less. As it rises, the air cools. Because it cools, its moisture content increases. Eventually the rising air may reach a level at which it becomes saturated with moisture. If it rises still further, water vapour starts condensing to form clouds. Nearly all clouds and rain originate in up-currents of air.

One reason why air starts to rise is because of temperature differences from place to place. Such differences are very marked on sunny days over land, when the air above some surfaces, such as asphalt or bare soil, becomes warmer than that over adjacent surfaces, such as trees or lakes. The warmer masses of air, which can be called bubbles, then start to rise. The air between the rising bubbles sinks to compensate. This type of air movement is called convection.

Once a bubble of air has started to rise, it will continue to do so as long as it remains warmer than its surroundings. As it rises, it cools, initially at a rate of 15°C per 90 metres, but its surroundings also cool with height. Eventually the bubble will reach its condensation level and clouds will start to form. The condensation in such clouds releases latent heat, making the rising air even warmer. This increases the difference in temperature between the rising air and the surrounding air. The atmosphere is then said to be unstable. As long as the atmosphere remains unstable, the bubble of air will grow bigger and rise further, producing a tall cloud. This cloud may become so saturated with moisture that rain or snow begins to fall from it.

On the other hand, if the rate of decrease of the temperature in the air surrounding the bubble is quite small or if the temperature actually rises with height, as it sometimes does, then the rising air bubble will soon become colder than its surroundings. The bubble will then stop rising. In this situation the atmosphere is said to be stable. Bubbles may never reach their condensation level, in which case no clouds will form or the bubble will produce only small, shallow clouds. When clouds do form, condensation may stop before the air becomes so saturated that precipitation begins. This is typically the case in stable air.

THE SEAS AND OCEANS

The water on the Earth's surface that now fills our seas and oceans got there as part of a process that started with the origin of the Earth itself. The material from which the Earth and the other planets were later to be formed probably began as a cloud of gases spinning around the Sun. These gases gradually condensed, making solid particles. Many of them collided and built up larger and larger concentrations of matter.

The part that was eventually to become the Earth seems to have cooled and begun solidifying about 4.6 billion years ago and as the spinning movement shaped matter into a ball, it contracted even further. Under these pressures, matter at the centre of the newly formed Earth began to heat up again and became molten. When this happened, water that had been contained inside the Earth was released to the surface as vapour and was added to the primitive atmosphere. When it cooled and condensed, it fell to the surface as rain and eventually formed the first oceans.

We do not know how much of the water in the oceans came from this source but estimates range from a third to almost all of it. Neither can we tell when this happened but some indication comes from rocks. The oldest rock discovered so far on the Earth's surface is from Greenland and is 3.8 billion years old. It is a kind of rock formed from pebbles laid down under water and later compressed. This shows that water must already have condensed and fallen to Earth during the 800 million years that had passed since the Earth was formed.

The rest of the water in the oceans also came from the interior of the Earth but it was forced to the surface by volcanic eruptions and hot springs. There are many volcanoes and hot springs on land and even more in parts of the ocean and they are still spewing out water. Only a small proportion of this water is new or juvenile water coming from deep inside the Earth for the first time. Most of it is groundwater or seawater that has seeped down into the Earth, heated up through contact with hot rocks and then returned to the surface in a volcanic eruption or a hot spring.

Was the water that came from the Earth's interior to fill the oceans the same salty seawater we know today? As far as we can tell, the oceans have never contained fresh water. Salt, or salinity, comes from gases and other substances dissolved in the water. When water first rose to the surface of the Earth as steam, it contained gases, some of which dissolved in the original oceans. Since then, volcanoes have continued to produce other gases along with water and added them to the oceans. Some of the other substances in seawater reached and still reach the ocean by a different process. They come from rocks on land which slowly break down to produce tiny fragments that flow in rivers into the oceans. The seawater in our oceans reached a composition very similar to what it is today about one billion years ago.

Just as substances are being added to seawater, so also are they being removed. If they were not,

THE PACIFIC OCEAN AND EL NINO

The Pacific Ocean is the world's largest and deepest ocean. It stretches from Australia to Easter Island and from Hawaii to New Zealand. Every two to ten years, the weather throughout the southern Pacific Ocean shifts wildly. The normally wet Far East becomes dry and the arid western coast of South America receives heavy rains. This phenomenon is called El Nino.

Scientists cannot fully explain the subtle interactions between the ocean and the atmosphere that produces El Nino but they do know that the process involves a weakening of the southeasterly trade winds that usually dominate the area's weather and a corresponding redistribution of warm water throughout the Pacific Ocean. The other extreme of this phenomenon, La Nina, brings torrential rains to the Far East and causes severe droughts in South America.

Islands in the Pacific Ocean are either the tips of volcanoes or coral atolls like this one

Geographical Information

Walking on the surface of the moon

the concentration would go on building up. Water is still being added to the oceans by volcanoes, rain and rivers, and is being lost again by evaporation. The salinity of seawater remains at the same level because some of the solids sink to the bottom or are thrown into the air in sea spray. Salt particles attract water in the atmosphere and droplets grow on them, some of which are blown away over the land as rain. By these means, water and solids are recycled through the atmosphere, rivers, sediments, seawater, rock and the Earth's interior to maintain the overall composition of the oceans.

THE MOON

The Moon is Earth's next-door neighbour in space. Moon rocks are distinctly different from Earth rocks and this difference suggests that the Moon was once hotter than the Earth has ever been and emphasises that the Moon has no air and no water. The oldest rocks found on the Moon are 4.6 billion years old. The oldest rock yet discovered on Earth dates from only 3.8 billion years ago.

Moon soil is not at all like Earth soil. It is made entirely from finely pulverised rock – the dust from meteoroid crashes. Moon soil has no water, decaying plant material or life but it does contain some beautiful and unusual glass beads. Emerald green and orange-red in colour and shaped like jewels and teardrops, they are made when a meteoroid impact sprays liquid rock in every direction. As the droplets of rock solidify, they turn glassy.

It was once feared that if a spacecraft landed on the Moon it would rapidly sink without trace into the deep dust layers. However, the lunar soil is well packed into a reasonably firm surface. The main hazard of Moon travel is finding a smooth place to land. At close quarters, the surface looks much like a bomb site with small craters everywhere.

Geological maps of most of the Moon's surface are now available, a possibility undreamed of before about 1960. Samples mainly from the Apollo space programme, have been sent to laboratories throughout the world for very detailed examination. Astronauts left scientific apparatus on the Moon, including sensors that have detected numerous 'moonquakes' as well as the impact of meteoroids, some spacecraft and man-made debris slamming into the Moon's surface. Several small reflectors, like those on a car or bicycle, were placed on the Moon. Scientists can now measure the Moon's distance to within an inch or so by aiming a powerful laser beam at these reflectors and timing the beam's round trip from Earth to Moon and back again. On average, this distance is 385,000 kilometres or 240,000 miles.

Two or three times a year, the full Moon moves into the Earth's shadow, and the Moon is eclipsed. During this so-called lunar eclipse, the shadowed part of the Moon looks dimly red because Earth's atmosphere scatters reddish sunlight into the Earth's shadow. Eclipses do not take place every month because the Moon's orbit is tilted at an angle to the Earth's path around the Sun.

On the surface of the Moon, a man weighs only one sixth of his Earth weight. This is because the Moon's mass is a mere one eightieth of the Earth's, so the gravitational pull is considerably smaller. The Moon's gravitational pull has the important effect of creating ocean tides on Earth. The water

surrounding the solid Earth is distorted into the shape of a squashed ball under the influence of the Moon's attraction. As the Earth spins on it axis, the bulges in the water seem to sweep around the Earth, causing two tides each day in most places. The Sun, too, influences the tides and the highest tides are formed when the Moon and the Sun are both pulling from the same direction.

THE SUN

To the planets, animals and peoples of the Earth, the Sun is a unique and vital star. Every living thing on the Earth owes its existence to the fact that the Sun is nearby and keeps shining and has done so for about 5 billion years. The energy that comes from the burning of coal, oil and natural gas was once sun-energy. These fuels are the remains of plants and animals that grew in the warmth of sun-energy millions of years ago. The nearest star, apart from the Sun, is 300,000 times farther away and the weak star energy we receive from it cannot possibly replace sun-energy.

The Sun is far larger than the Earth – one hundred and nine Earth-planets placed side by side would stretch from one side of the Sun to the other. Its volume is 1.3 million times greater than the Earth and its mass 330,000 times as much. The Earth is about 150 million kilometres or 93 million miles from Sun. Light and heat take eight minutes and twenty seconds to race across interplanetary space and reach the Earth from this distance.

The Sun's gravity pulls much harder than the Earth's. A person who could venture to the surface of the Sun would weigh about one and a half tons. However, this is an impossible adventure since the Sun has no solid surface and the temperature there is about 10,000°F or 5,537°C. This exceeds the melting temperature of every known substance. The temperature of the surface seems high, but inside the Sun it is much hotter. Its entire globe is a glowing mass of gas. At the centre the temperature is about 27 million degrees Fahrenheit or 15 million degrees Celsius.

The gas inside the Sun is three quarters hydrogen, the lightest gas. Deep inside the Sun, hydrogen atoms crowd together, a group of them collides so violently with another group that they fuse together and make a completely different substance: helium. Each second, 650 million tons of hydrogen become helium. A small part of this mass of material is transformed in the process and reappears as pure energy, as Einstein has predicted would be the case. In one second, the Sun's mass falls by 4 million tons. In 50 million years, the lost mass is equal to the mass of the Earth.

Flashes of energy burst forth as the hydrogen turns to helium. The great density of matter traps the energy flashes inside the Sun. They wander through the interior for a million years or so before reaching the surface and streaming off into space.

Along with heat and light, the Sun emits radiation that can be harmful to living creatures. Ultraviolet rays and X-rays damage the cells in plants and animals. The Earth's blanket of atmosphere soaks up almost all of this radiation although the small amount that reaches the ground on a fine day will make fair skin tan or cause painful sunburn if exposure is too long. Astronauts journeying into space have to be protected from the Sun's harmful rays.

Roads – *at scales larger than 1:3 million*
Motorway/Highway
Other Main Road
– *at scales smaller than 1:3 million*
Principal Road: Motorway/Highway
Other Main road
Main Railway

Towns & Cities
☐ Population > 5,000,000
☐ 1–5,000,000
○ 500,000–1,000,000
○ < 500,000
☐ **Paris** National Capital
✈ Airport
International Boundary
International Boundary – not defined or in dispute
Internal Boundary
River
Canal
Marsh or Swamp

Relief
▲ 1510 Peak (in metres)
5,000 metres (16,405 feet)
4,000 (13,124)
3,000 (9,843)
2,000 (6,562)
1,000 (3,281)
500 (1,641)
200 (656)
100 (328)
0
Land below sea level

Note:
The 0–100 contour layer appears only at scales larger than 1:3 million

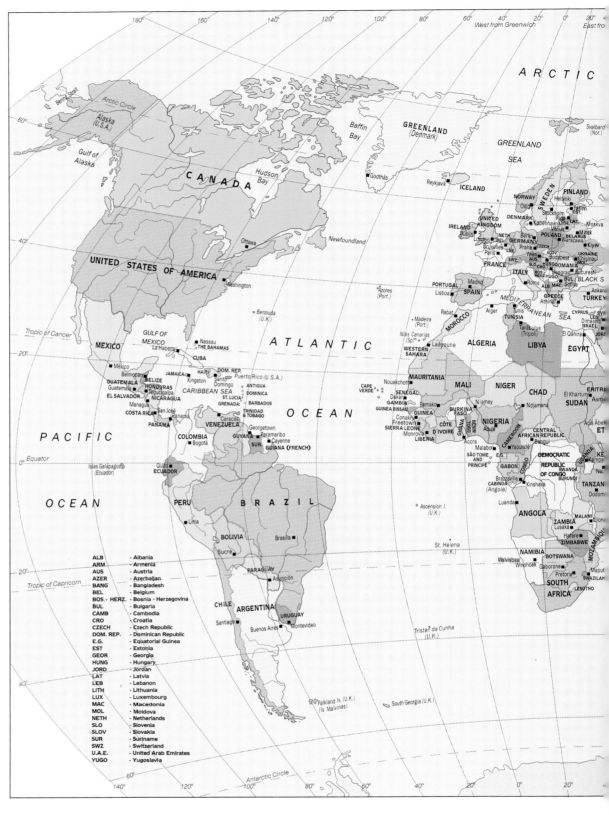

Flags of the world

FACTS AND FIGURES

The selection of world facts and figures that follow provide the traveller with some background information on a world that seems to be more within our reach every day and a chance to look at this world as a whole before becoming engrossed in the more detailed country-by-country descriptions in the pages that follow.

Geography

The world's total surface area is 510,069,120 square kilometres or 196,938,800 square miles. Water covers a substantial 70.9 per cent of the world's surface and the world's four largest water areas are its oceans – the Atlantic, Arctic, Indian and Pacific Oceans. A mere 30 per cent of the world's area is land and the largest land masses are its six continents: Asia, Africa, Oceania, Europe, Antarctica and America (America is often divided into North America and South America).

Each individual continent, with the exception of Antarctica, consists of different countries. The largest of the world's countries is the Russian Federation which spans the continents of Europe and Asia with an area of 17,075,400 square kilometres or 6,592,850 square miles. The smallest country is the Vatican City with an area of only 0.44 square kilometres or 0.2 square miles.

The world's terrain is very diverse, ranging from its highest mountain, Mount Everest (8,848 metres or 29,028 feet), to its lowest land depression, the Dead Sea (408 metres or 1,338 feet below sea level). Approximately 11 per cent of the world's land is permanently covered with ice, while hot and cold deserts cover 40 per cent of the world's surface.

The World, Political
Scale 1: 85 500 000
© Geddes & Grosset

Population

The estimated world population for the year 2000 is 6,082,966,429. The current ten-year growth rate is 12.6 per cent. The world birth rate is 22 births per 1,000 population (1998) and the corresponding death rate is 9 deaths for every 1,000 live births. The life expectancy figure for the world in general is 63 years (61 years for males and 65 years for females).

There is considerable variation between the world's 196 countries in terms of population growth. The most populous country is China with a population of 1,246,871,951. Developed countries, such as the UK, have populations that are evenly distributed across the age groups and usually a growing percentage of the population is elderly. By comparison, a large proportion of the population in developing countries is in the younger age group and about to enter their most fertile years. This factor accounts for the trend of higher levels of population in developing countries.

Countries within the six continents vary greatly in the standard of living they offer. The Human Development Index (published in 1999 by the United Nations) ranks countries according to their quality of living, from the most to the least livable. Canada, Norway and Japan were ranked as the top three most livable countries while at the opposite end of the scale, Sierra Leone, Niger and Ethiopia were rated the least livable countries. Levels of literacy also vary greatly throughout the world. According to UN figures, 79.4 per cent of the world's population over the age of 15 can read and write. Of this total, only 73.6 per cent of women, compared to 85.2 per cent of men, are literate.

Most urban transport systems in China, the world's most populous country, are overcrowded and confusing but the roads are set up for the country's millions of cyclists with plenty of bike lanes, bike parking lots and bike repair shops.

SOME OF THE WORLD'S NATURAL ATTRACTIONS

The snow-capped peak of Mount Fuji (Fujiyama) is both an extinct volcano, which last erupted in 1708, and Japan's highest mountain, at 3,776 metres or 12,388 feet, and is found 100km (62 miles) south-west of Tokyo. It is a highly popular natural landmark which attracts some 400,000 climbers annually.

The Sahara Desert in North Africa is the largest desert in the world. It spans a total of 8,400,000 square kilometres or 3,250,000 square miles from the Atlantic to the Red Sea, and from the Mediterranean to Mali, Niger, Chad and Sudan. A mere one sixth of its total coverage is sand, the remaining areas being rocky and stony.

The striking red stone of Ayers Rock rises sharply from the plains of Uluru National Park in Australia's Northern Teritory, near the resort town of Yulara. It is the world's largest monolith consisting of a 350-metre or 1,148-feet-high sandstone rock. It is owned by the Aborigines and is considered by them to be a sacred place.

The Alps are situated in southern Europe and are Europe's longest and highest range of mountains. Originally formed by the collision of the African and European tectonic plates, they provide a natural separation between central and southern Europe, spanning the borders of Switzerland, France, Germany, Austria, Slovenia, Italy and Liechtenstein.

The Iguazú Falls, in Iguazú national park in Argentina, consist of a total of 275 individual water-falls and in the rainy season this number increases to about 350. With a height greater than Niagara by around 20 metres (65.6 feet), the falls provide a spectacular audiovisual experience that few other waterfalls can match.

Alaska has an area of 58,800 square kilometres or 22,700 square miles and is permanently covered with ice. It is the largest glaciated area after the north and south polar regions. The unspoiled wilderness of Prince William Sound, resting between the Chugach Mountains in the north and the Kenai Peninsula in the west is pictured here.

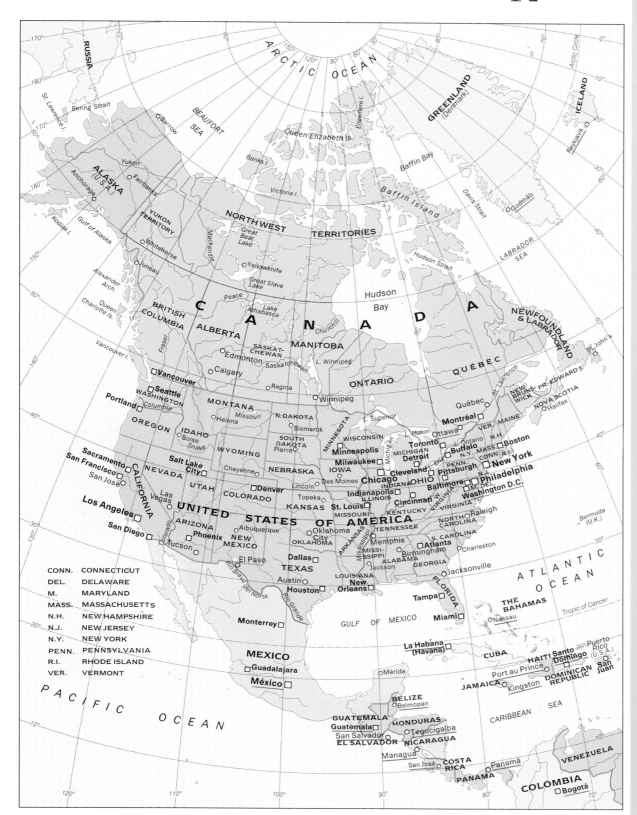

**North America, Political
Scale 1: 41 600 000**

| 0 | 500 | 1000 | 1500 km |

| 0 | 250 | 500 | 750 | 1000 miles |

© Geddes & Grosset

CONN.   CONNECTICUT
DEL.   DELAWARE
M.   MARYLAND
MASS.   MASSACHUSETTS
N.H.   NEW HAMPSHIRE
N.J.   NEW JERSEY
N.Y.   NEW YORK
PENN.   PENNSYLVANIA
R.I.   RHODE ISLAND
VER.   VERMONT

Two of the extremes found in the USA –
the towering buildings in the
financial district of New York and the
rugged beauty of the Arizona desert.

NORTH AMERICA

North America consists of the United States of America (USA), Canada and Mexico. Surrounded by the Arctic to the north, the Pacific to the east, the Atlantic to the west and the Gulf of Mexico to the south, it is a continent of immense contrasts.

These not only encompass its climatic and vegetational zones, that range from lush, green tropical forests in the south to Arctic tundra in the far north and its landscapes, varying from high, rugged mountains to flat prairies, but also its peoples, who include members of every race, nationality and religion.

There is contrast even in terms of economic stability. While the USA and Canada have emerged as powerful and wealthy industrial nations, Mexico is only just embarking on that path despite an expanding industrial base.

North America's First Inhabitants

The ancestors of the original inhabitants of the continent are believed to have migrated to North America from Asia, between 40,000 and 12,000 years ago. Moving east and south, these peoples developed into the many distinctive Indian tribes of North America.

European settlers, who arrived in increasing numbers from the early 17th century onwards, drove many American Indians from their tribal homelands as they spread across the land. Eventually the remaining Indian peoples, their numbers depleted by war, poverty and disease, were forced to live in reservations a fraction of the size of their traditional homelands. In recent years, strenuous efforts have been made to redress some of the past injustices and to re-establish the rights of North America's first inhabitants.

The Inuit

Most of the Inuit people of Canada live in communities in villages provided by the Canadian government but some groups still prefer to live in the High Arctic, braving the icy weather and Arctic blizzards to follow a more traditional way of life. Nunavet, a new territory for the Inuit people in the Northwest Territories, was officially recognised in 1999.

Auyuittuq National Park, Canada

Auyuittuq Park on Baffin Island is the only national park inside the Arctic Circle. The park entrance is at the peaceful Inuit town of Pangnirtung on the Cumberland Sound where harbour seals and beluga whales can be seen. The park can be explored by dog-sleigh or on foot and there are plenty of opportunities to see the Arctic's flora and wildlife, including polar bears and white foxes.

Polar bears are an attraction at Auyuittuq Park

Costa de Oro, Mexico

Some of Mexico's finest beaches are to be found along this mountainous stretch of coast. Rivers spill down into the sea from high green mountains and cool mountain breezes help to keep tourists happy as they enjoy a combination of sun and sea on one of the coast's many beaches. Travelling between beaches, there is much to see in the tropical countryside such as mango and avocado orchards and iguanas, wild and tame. Near the town of Manzanillo, at the southern end of the Costa de Oro, a huge 'green wave' – a swell of some 10 metres or 30 feet – can sometimes be seen rolling in from the Pacific during April and May.

Mount Rushmore National Memorial, USA

Mount Rushmore, South Dakota

The four stone carvings of the faces and heads of American presidents George Washington, Thomas Jefferson, Abraham Lincoln and Theodore Roosevelt that go to make up this national memorial were the inspiration of the sculptor, Gutzon Borglum.

Half a million tons of rock were removed from Mount Rushmore to reach the softer granite from which the heads were dynamited, drilled and chiselled over a period of 14 years. Each head is about 18 metres or 60 feet from chin to crown.

Los Angeles, USA

Los Angeles is a relatively young city that has grown from a community of less than 50,000 just over a century ago to today's huge metropolis, sprawling across a thousand square miles of desert basin between the sea and the mountains of Southern California. Home of Hollywood and Disneyland and of the opulent Beverly Hills, Los Angeles has come to represent the 'American Dream' of glamour, money and overnight success to many people.

Many guided tours focus on brief views of the homes of the stars but the city boasts many unique museums and art galleries, such as the colourful Museum of Contemporary Art, the Natural History Museum of Los Angeles County, which houses a tremendous stock of dinosaur skeletons, and the Getty Center, where a large collection of international art has been amassed thanks to funding from the estate of oil magnate, John Paul Getty.

The Los Angeles skyline

Chichen Itza, Mexico

Chichen Itza is one of the best preserved Mayan cities in Mexico. The Mayan people are thought to have originated in Asia along with the American Indians. By around 600 BC, the Maya had settled in an area that today includes Yucatan and Chiapas in Mexico. They flourished between AD 300 and 900 when many imposing sacred cities were built by a society ruled by priest-kings. The city of Chichen Itza was one of the last great achievements of the Mayan builders and includes many interesting features including a well where human sacrifices were made to please the rain god in times of drought.

Chichen Itza, Mexico

CANADA

Language/s spoken: English, and French in Quebec

Currency: Canadian Dollar

Travel requirements: return ticket and valid passport required, best to contact relevant authority before departure

Major cities: Ottowa (capital), Toronto, Montreal, Quebec, Vancouver

Climate: mild summers and long, cold winters

Crime and safety: take sensible precautions

Grey wolves, the largest members of the dog family, once inhabited the whole of the North American continent except for the extreme south and southwest. Although they are currently only found in northern Canada and parts of Mexico, conservation plans are helping in the recovery of the species.

CANADA

Canada is a vast country covering an area of 9,970,655 square kilometres or 3,849,674 square miles and encompassing six time zones. It consists of ten provinces and two territories held together as a confederation and has a population of nearly 30 million people.

In the west, a broad belt of mountains, including the Rocky Mountains, forms a huge natural barrier of peaks, many of which reach a height of over 3,048 metres or 10,000 feet. Mount Logan in the Yukon is the highest mountain in Canada at a height of 6,050 metres or 19,524 feet.

In the north, the tundra lands and vast tracts of coniferous forest remain thinly populated but they are home to some of Canada's most spectacular wildlife, including bears, wolves, beavers, caribou, moose and musk ox.

Although most of Canada is unsuitable for farming, the southern Prairie Provinces of Manitoba, Saskatchewan and Alberta are one of the world's 'granaries', particularly in wheat production but also in the production of other cereals. Livestock rearing, especially cattle ranching and the rearing of pigs, is the other main area of farming. Fruit and vegetable production is important on some farms, especially in Quebec, British Columbia and Ontario.

Manitoba farmland

Fish from the rich grounds of the northeastern Pacific Ocean and northwestern Atlantic Ocean have always been an important part of the Canadian economy. In addition, the vast lakes and rivers are valuable sources of freshwater fish. Canadian fish products are exported to the USA, Japan and Europe and the industry employs over 100,000 people.

The production of timber and paper is a very important part of the Canadian economy. However, there are increasing environmental concerns about logging operations in hitherto untouched areas of temperate forest in Vancouver.

Logging in Quebec

Canada is rich in mineral resources, including petroleum, natural gas, coal, iron ore, nickel, gold, uranium, copper, lead and zinc. As a country of lakes and rivers that flow from mountainous terrain, Canada has also had great opportunities for the development of hydroelectricity. This cheap and renewable source of energy has contributed greatly to industrial development throughout the country and has been especially important in the more remote areas.

Montreal, Quebec

Quebec is where the first French fur traders and farmers made their home and where to this day the public signs are all in French. Quebec has remained part of the Canadian federation by only the slimmest of electorial margins. Montreal is the largest city in Quebec with over three million inhabitants. It is built on an island at the confluence of the Ottowa and St Lawrence rivers. Much of the history of the city can still be seen in the form of old buildings, such as the Chateau Ramezay which was the home of the French Governor, Claud de Ramezay from 1705–1724 and is now a museum showing the more comfortable side of 18th-century frontier life.

Devon Island, Northwest Territories

Lying south of Ellesmere Island within the Arctic Circle, Devon Island is a land of ice and snow for three quarters of the year. While the sub-surface always remains frozen (permafrost), for a few brief weeks in summer, higher temperatures enable the specially adapted tundra plants to bloom and flourish before winter sets in once more.

Devon Island

Toronto

Toronto is Canada's largest city and the capital of Ontario. It is a city of tall skyscrapers dominated by the Canadian National Communications tower and is a hub of business, commerce and manufacturing industries. It hosts many international events and conferences and has a vibrant atmosphere and cosmopolitan population.

Toronto, Ontario

MEXICO

Mexico, as shown on the next page, forms the southern region of North America and is a large, densely populated country whose people are Spanish-speaking. It is bounded in the north by its long border with the USA. In the south, it shares a longer border with Guatemala and a shorter one with Belize. The Gulf of Mexico and the northern Caribbean Sea lie to the east, the Gulf of California to the northwest and the Pacific Ocean to the southwest.

Mexico is a land of great geographical contrasts and includes most vegetational zones. It is dominated by a vast, central plateau that lies between two great mountain ranges running from northwest to southeast, the Sierra Madre Oriental in the east and the Sierra Madre Occidental in the west. In the south, they unite to form an impressive range of volcanic mountains, the Sierra Madre del Sur. In this area are situated Mexico's greatest peaks, some of which are still active volcanoes. The highest of these, Citaltepetl, reaches a height of 5,699 metres or 18,697 feet. Mexico City, the capital, is also situated in this area.

The northern part of the country is arid semi-desert where cacti and yucca, wolves and coyotes can be found. The coastal plains, lower mountain slopes and the narrow Tehuantepec Isthmus support lush, tropical vegetation and are inhabited by such animals as jaguars and peccaries. Higher up the mountain slopes, temperate forests of oaks and conifers, in which may be found bears and pumas, give way to sparse Arctic vegetation at the highest altitudes. The northwest coast along the Gulf of California lies opposite the narrow, mountainous peninsula of Baja California where beautiful beaches abound. Similar conditions occur in the southeast along the coast of Campeche and Yucatan, where the popular Cancun resort can be found.

Mexico has few rivers or lakes of any size except the Rio Bravo del Norte (Rio Grande) which runs from northwest to southeast along the border with the USA. Much of Mexico receives relatively little rainfall, with about 75 per cent falling in the regions east of the Sierra Madre Oriental, the Gulf coast and the Yucatan Peninsula. The Tehuantepec Isthmus also receives a reasonable amount of rain.

Mexican graffiti

The arid and mountainous conditions mean that only about 15 per cent of the land is suitable for farming, which relies heavily on irrigation schemes. Crops include maize, sorghum, sugar cane, wheat, coffee, oranges, bananas, tomatoes, cotton and potatoes. The most important domestic animals are goats, sheep, horses, donkeys and mules and poultry. Forestry is an important natural resource, the exploitation of which is now strictly regulated. Mexico also has valuable mineral reserves of industrial and precious commodities, including petroleum, natural gas, silver and gold as well as a successful tourist industry.

MEXICO CITY

Mexico's capital is the largest city in the world with over 15 million inhabitants. It is built on the ancient site of the capital city of the Aztecs, Tenochtitlan, which was destroyed by the Spanish conquest. Mexico City preserves some Aztec remains but most lie buried beneath the surface. The modern city suffered a serious earthquake in 1985 which caused the death of about 7,000 people. All new buildings now incorporate construction features designed to withstand the effects of earthquakes.

MEXICO

Language/s spoken: Spanish is official language, English widely spoken
Currency: Nuevo Peso
Travel requirements: return ticket and valid passport required, best to contact relevant authority before departure
Major cities: Mexico City (capital), Guadalajara, Monterey, Puebla, Tijuana, Acapulco
Climate: varies from hot and humid to cooler and more temperate
Crime and safety: take sensible precautions and particular care on public transport

Cancun holiday resort, Yucatan, Mexico

THE STATUE OF LIBERTY, NEW YORK

The Statue of Liberty was the creation of French sculptor, Frederic Auguste Bartholdi. Standing high above southern Manhattan and overlooking Ellis Island, it depicts Liberty throwing off her shackles and showing a beacon of light to the world. Formally dedicated by President Cleveland in 1886, the Statue of Liberty has become a symbol for generations of immigrants of New York's role as the gateway to the USA.

California Poppy Reserve

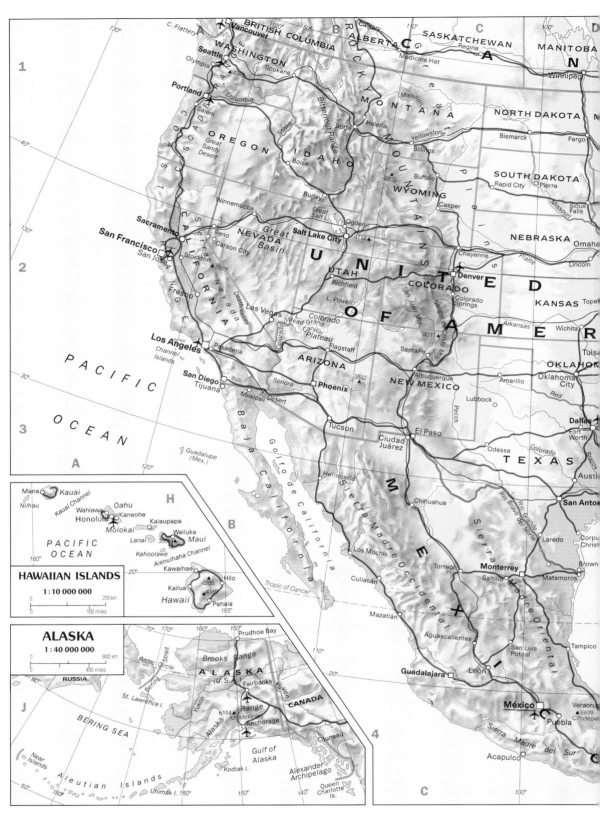

USA

The USA is the fourth largest country in the world, stretching from the vast ice fields and sweeping tundra of Alaska, to the palm-fringed beaches and lush valleys of the Hawaiian Islands.

The USA is bordered by the Atlantic Ocean in the east and the Pacific Ocean in the west, by Canada in the north and Mexico and the Gulf of Mexico in the south. (The Bermuda Islands, Britain's oldest overseas territory, are situated in the Atlantic Ocean some 970 kilometres or 570 miles east of the USA.) Two great mountain ranges dominate the country, the Rocky Mountains in the west and the Appalachians in the east. Between them lie the Great Plains – fertile, flat lands crossed by many rivers. The largest of these rivers, the Mississippi, together with its main tributary, the Missouri, is the third longest river in the world. In the northeast, the Great Lakes (Superior, Michigan, Huron, and Erie) form part of the border with Canada.

The climate in the USA varies a great deal and weather patterns can shift quite dramatically mainly due to the westerly winds sweeping across the country from the Pacific. One or two hurricanes a year can rage across Florida and on a more local scale, tornadoes can cut a path of destruction in the wake of a spring or summer thunderstorm.

The main industries are in iron and steel, chemicals, motor vehicles, aircraft, telecommunications, information technology, electronics and textiles. Although agricultural production is high, it employs only a small percentage of the work force primarily because of its advanced technology. The USA has used both its human resources and its wealth of natural resources, including vast mineral reserves, to turn the country into the world's most developed nation.

CONN.   CONNECTICUT
MASS.   MASSACHUSETTS
R.I.   RHODE ISLAND
N.J.   NEW JERSEY
DEL.   DELAWARE

USA

Language/s spoken: English, many other languages spoken
Currency: US Dollar
Travel requirements: return ticket and valid passport required, best to contact the relevant authority before departure
Major cities: Washington, D.C. (capital), New York, Chicago, Detroit, Houston, Los Angeles, Philadelphia, San Diego, San Francisco
Climate: varies from hot and humid to polar
Crime and safety: crime varies from state to state, take sensible precautions against mugging, burglary of hotel rooms and car hijacking

A cruise ship in Glacier Bay, Alaska

The Hawaiian Islands

Despite being so far out in the Pacific Ocean, the islands of Hawaii have belonged to the USA since 1959 when Hawaii became the fiftieth state of the United States. Each of the Hawaiian Islands has come about as the result of sub-marine volcanic action. Big Island's Kilauea volcano continues this process to this day with lava exploding into the sea.

The islands of Hawaii can boast some of the most beautiful scenery on earth with their volcanoes, palm-fringed beaches, lush valleys and high cliffs and this is what over six million tourists a year come to see and enjoy. The result is that much of what was once unspoilt is now greatly overdeveloped with the islanders now almost totally dependent on the mass tourism market. Inevitably, because so many basic commodities have to be imported, the cost of living is very high.

Alaska

The USA purchased Alaska from Russia in 1867 at a cost of over seven million dollars and thereby acquired its largest state and its highest mountain, Mount McKinley, located near Anchorage and reaching a height of 6,194 metres or 20,320 feet. Alaska's half a million inhabitants live mainly in the cities of Anchorage, Fairbanks, Valdez and Juneau, the state capital.

The exploitation of petroleum reserves in the north around Barrow has brought great riches to Alaska. Long pipelines transport the oil to the Gulf of Alaska.

The state was the scene of a gold rush in the late 19th century and tourists can still pan for gold today. Fishing and fish canning, forestry, hunting and limited farming are the other important contributors to the economy.

ATLANTIC CITY'S BOARDWALK

This wooden boardwalk was originally built as a temporary walkway above the beach so that holidaymakers could walk along next to the sea without taking sand into their grand hotels. Some of the lovely Victorian buildings have survived despite being dwarfed by casinos and fast-food outlets and an early morning walk along the boardwalk still provides a peaceful seaside stroll.

Possessing what is arguably the most famous skyline in the world, the borough of Manhattan is built on an island and is the important heartland of New York City. It contains the busy financial district of Wall Street in which is located the US Stock Exchange. Also in Manhattan are Times Square (named after the New York Times), the theatre land of Broadway, the musical and artistic centre of Greenwich Village and the exclusive and expensive shops of Fifth Avenue. One of the world's most famous skyscrapers, the Empire State Building can also be found on Fifth Avenue. Completed in 1931, it has 102 floors and reaches the immense height of 381 metres or 1,250 feet.

EASTERN STATES

The Eastern States of the USA encompass some of the most populated and industrialised areas in the country but also include rich, varied and beautiful countryside. Fertile farm lands, a coastline that saw much of the early history of the country unfold, great stretches of forest and mountain, the Florida Everglades – all of this and much more provide sharp contrast to the great cities of Washington DC, New York, Detroit, Baltimore, Philadelphia, Atlanta, and Charleston to name but a few.

New York City

New York City is one of the most exciting cities in the world. It comprises the central island of

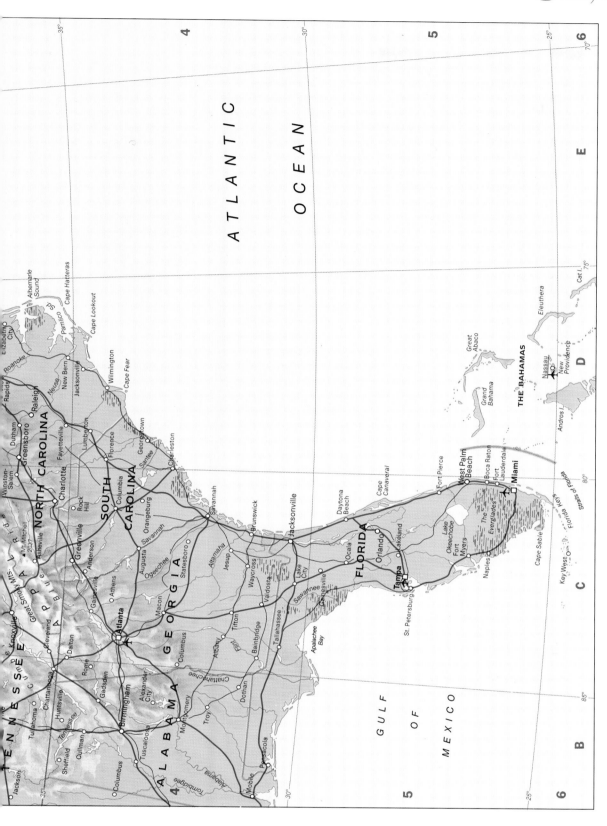

USA, Eastern States
Scale 1: 8 600 000

0   100   200   300 km

0   100   200 miles

© Geddes & Grosset

WALL STREET

Wall Street is situated in the borough of Manhattan in New York City. It is the home of the United States Stock Exchange where the country's premier banks and financial institutions are to be found. On 24 October 1929, the price of stocks on Wall Street plummeted, which led to the catastrophic worldwide depression of the 1930s. This event – called The Wall Street Crash – is still referred to with fear today, especially by those who wheel and deal on the international money markets and particularly when prices begin to tumble.

Manhattan and the four outer boroughs of Brooklyn, Queens, the Bronx and Staten Island. Manhattan alone can offer the visitor the Statue of Liberty and Wall Street, Fifth Avenue and Greenwich Village but for many it is the cultural life of this city which is the main attraction. There are opportunities to enjoy dance, theatre and music from grass-roots productions to state-of-the-art performances and to visit two art museums that are renowned throughout the world – the Museum of Modern Art and the Metropolitan Museum of Art The Museum of Modern Art holds one of the finest and most complete collections of late 19th and 20th century art.

For those wanting some fresh air and exercise, Central Park provides a refuge from the noise and crowds of big city life. Central Park can be explored by bicycle, on foot or even by horse-drawn carriage

East River, New York

WILDLIFE IN THE EVERGLADES

The alligator is probably the most familiar animal to inhabit the swamps and mangroves of the Everglades. However, caimans introduced from South America and the rare American crocodile can also be seen along with 27 species of snake and 16 types of turtle and terrapin.

Although threatened by human activities, the manatees in Florida Bay are one of the more endearing species of mammals. They share their home with the far more common Atlantic bottle-nosed dolphins. The Florida panther is a much more elusive animal. A few of these rare cats are known to inhabit the Everglades and great efforts are being made to conserve them. The bobcat is a more abundant predator and racoons, white-tailed deer, opossum, several species of rodents, marsh rabbits and frogs and toads are other common animals. The Everglades are also rich in birds, particularly waders and other species that favour a marshy and estuarine habitat.

Baltimore, Maryland

Baltimore, Maryland

Baltimore is the largest city in Maryland and has always been a flourishing port, favourably situated in the northwestern extremity of Chesapeake Bay. Baltimore was one of the early destinations for Europeans and was also a departure point for the new territories in the west. The city boasts many fine old buildings, reflecting its early origins and is noted for its beautiful parks and trees. Modern Baltimore has many eminent educational and research establishments, such as the John Hopkins University, as well as manufacturing and industrial developments.

Washington DC

The capital city of the United States of America was built on land bought especially for this purpose from Virginia and Maryland in 1788–89. This land is called the District of Columbia (hence DC) and was a romantic early name for the country, derived from Christopher Columbus. It does not lie within any state but is an independent territory under federal control.

The city's most famous and imposing building is the Capitol, constructed from white marble and housing Congress – the members of the government of the United States. It stands on Capitol Hill at one end of the Mall, a beautiful, tree-lined park that also contains the official residence of the President, the White House. At the opposite end of the Mall stands the Lincoln Memorial, an impressive monument to President Abraham Lincoln (1809–65) containing a statue that is 5.8 metres or 19 feet high.

Modern Washington DC is a city of extremes, in that there are areas of severe poverty, high unemployment rates and the associated problems of drug abuse and crime in marked contrast to the power and glamour of Capitol Hill.

The Everglades, Florida

Florida is known as the 'Sunshine State' and forms the southeastern extremity of the USA, bounded on the western side by the Gulf of Mexico and on the east by the Atlantic Ocean.

The Everglades is a large area of marshes and lakes at the southernmost tip of Florida. It is formed by a slow-moving river, which drops only 4.5 metres or 15 feet along its entire course and which supports dense, natural grass called sawgrass. On slightly raised ground above the water level, other plants can grow, including islands of trees called hammocks. On yet higher ground, there are remnants of a once extensive pine forest.

Where the river meets the coast, the mixing of salt and fresh water enables mangroves to grow which are specially adapted to this habitat. Their tangled roots provide a home for some of the Everglades' abundant wildlife.

The Everglades, Florida

Washington DC

CENTRAL STATES

The Central States of the USA are dominated by the Great Plains States but they also include some of the Great Lakes States and some of the states in the South. Such a vast area has landscapes of infinite variety and an endless choice of exciting places to visit and explore.

The Great Plains States produce two thirds of the world's wheat but for many their appeal lies in the fact that they were the original home of the cowboy – the Wild West, whose plains were covered by wagon-trains and herds of wild bison as the early pioneers made their ways further and further west. Echoes of the old Wild West can be found in the real cowboy and cattle country of the sandy scrublands of northern Nebraska and North Dakota.

The shores of the Great Lakes are inevitably affected by industrialisation but this region can also boast wilderness areas of great beauty. In the states to the south, music draws thousands to the country and blues meccas of Nashville and Memphis and the jazz bars of New Orleans.

Cowboys herding buffalo

New Orleans

New Orleans has grown from a few shacks in 1718 to the vibrant city it is today, with people from many different races and cultures contributing to its growth. The original French and Spanish colonists and the millions of Africans who were imported as slaves to work on the cotton and tobacco plantations were among these people, as well as American settlers who moved into the city after it was sold to America in 1803 and immigrants from Europe who came to New Orleans in the mid-1800s. There has always been tension between the original French inhabitants of the city and the Americans, and the city is still divided into two sections – the French Quarter and the Central Business District and Garden District.

New Orleans had its heyday in the mid-1800s when the cotton and tobacco industries were at their height but the oil and petrochemical industry of today have played an important role in sustaining the economy of the city.

Tourists who come to listen to jazz, to watch the colourful Mardi Gras festival and to explore the world of voodoo, can also enjoy exploring the French quarter and the wonderful food on offer from restaurants specialising in Creole or Cajun cooking.

Chicago, Illinois

Chicago, Illinois

Chicago is located at the southern end of Lake Michigan and developed as an industrial city, where cattle from the Midwestern ranches were brought for slaughter and from where goods were transported by rail throughout the USA. It became known as 'the Windy City' but this may not have been a reference to the weather but rather to its citizens' reputation for boastfulness!

During the time of prohibition in the 1920s, the city's most infamous resident was the gangster, Al Capone, who was involved in many criminal activities, including illegal traffic in liquor. Chicago has long been renowned for its impressive architecture and this continues to this day with several innovative, modern developments. Present-day Chicago is home to important educational, academic and artistic institutions, tourist and sporting attractions and designer shops. It is surpassed in size only by New York City and Los Angeles.

The Mississippi

The Mississippi is the most famous of the great rivers of the USA, arising in Minnesota in the north and flowing for 3,782 kilometres or 2,350 miles before finally entering its delta on the shores of the Gulf of Mexico. Affectionately known as 'Old Man River', the Mississippi has always been important as a navigable waterway, connecting towns that grew up along its length.

The most famous boats on the Mississippi were the paddle steamers that once carried many passengers up and down the river. Today, the Mississippi continues to be used to transport large quantities of freight. A complex system of flood controls is in place to contain the river within its banks. Occasionally, these defences are overwhelmed, particularly after periods of prolonged, heavy rainfall and there may then be considerable problems with flooding as happened in 1993.

GRACELAND, TENNESSEE

The home of Elvis Presley (1935–1977), Graceland lies some ten miles from downtown Memphis. Tours (reservations are recommended) start opposite the house in Graceland Plaza where visiting fans can find souvenirs and other related attractions. Tours of the house allow visitors to explore the downstairs rooms (such as the Jungle Room, where Elvis recorded Moody Blue). Elvis is buried beside the swimming pool in the Meditation Garden.

A Mississippi paddle steamer

'OLD FAITHFUL'

Yellowstone's remarkable geysers, hot springs, mud pools and fumaroles (gushes of steam) are perhaps best appreciated in winter when a thick blanket of snow and ice is punctured periodically by the gurgling and hissing of hot water, steam and mud. This provides welcome winter warmth for the park's wildlife, which includes buffalo, elk, moose and bears. Among the geysers, the most well known is 'Old Faithful', which erupts about every 78 minutes, sending a fountain of steaming water into the air to a height of 30–55 metres or 100–180 feet .

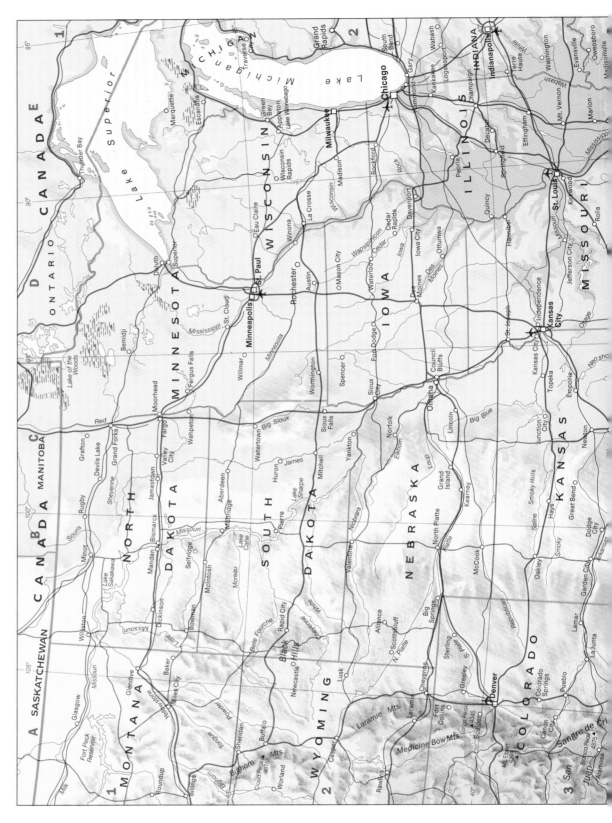

Yellowstone Park

Yellowstone National Park

Designated as a national park in 1872 by the American government, Yellowstone is the oldest national park in the world. Most of its 8,992 square kilometres or 3,472 square miles are situated in Wyoming with a slight overlap into Idaho and Montana.

The famous geysers, mud pools, hot springs and fumaroles of Yellowstone reveal that this is an area of simmering volcanic activity. They occur within the caldera of a huge volcano which erupted over half a million years ago and now forms a vast plateau rising to a height of 2,286 metres or 7,500 feet.

Other spectacular features include the Grand Canyon, the Falls of the Yellowstone River and Yellowstone Lake, which is frozen in winter but surrounded in spring by meadows of alpine flowers.

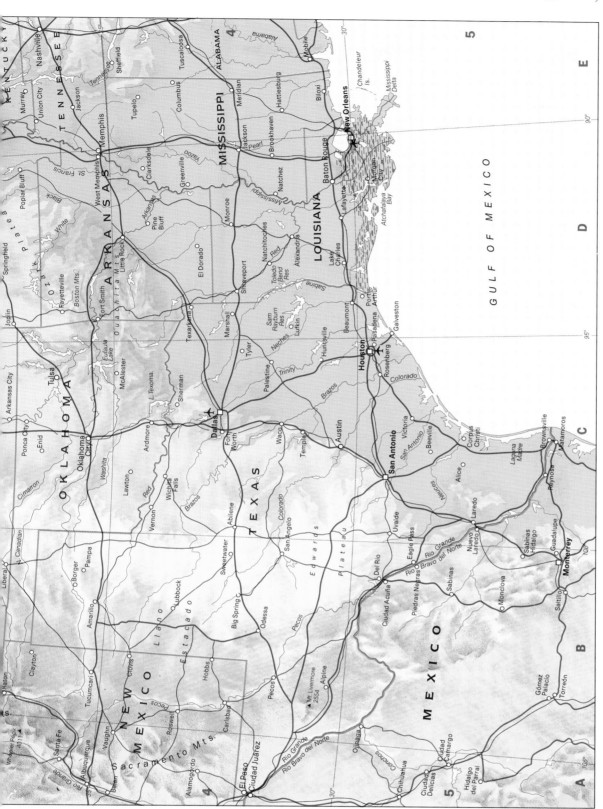

USA, Central States
Scale 1: 8 600 000

| 0 | 100 | 200 | 300 km |

| 0 | 100 | 200 miles |

© Geddes & Grosset

NASA, HOUSTON

Under the control of the National Aeronautics and Space Administration (NASA), the Space Center in Houston, Texas, has been the home of space flight since the launch of Gemini 4 in 1965. NASA allows behind the scenes tours and at the Space Center, Houston, people are given the opportunity, among other things, to try on space helmets and inspect moon-rocks.

St Louis, Missouri

St Louis was founded as a fur-trading post by a French trapper, Pierre Laclade, in 1764. Sold to the USA in the early 19th century, St Louis was soon attracting thousands of immigrants eager to join the wagon trails heading into the west. Its location, at the confluence of the Mississippi and Missouri rivers, has meant that it has always been an important route centre and modern St Louis is a thriving centre of business and commerce.

Two famous citizens are the poet, T S Eliot, and the musician, Chuck Berry, but St Louis' musical heritage is founded on jazz. The Mississippi waterfront was extensively redeveloped in the 1960s to include the Jefferson National Expansion Memorial and the parabolic Gateway Arch. This huge, stainless steel arch has been adopted as the city's emblem and commemorates its pioneering history.

Gateway Arch, St Louis

USA, Western States

Adobe buildings are constructed from bricks made of clay or mud, often containing chopped straw, which have been dried in the sun but not fired. This was a common building method in Mexico and Central and South America and is still sometimes used today. It was used in southern parts of the USA, in places where there were close links with the countries to the south. The influence is particularly strong in Santa Fe, the state capital of New Mexico and the USA's oldest state capital, which has many fine adobe buildings.

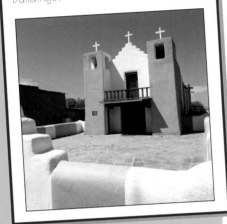

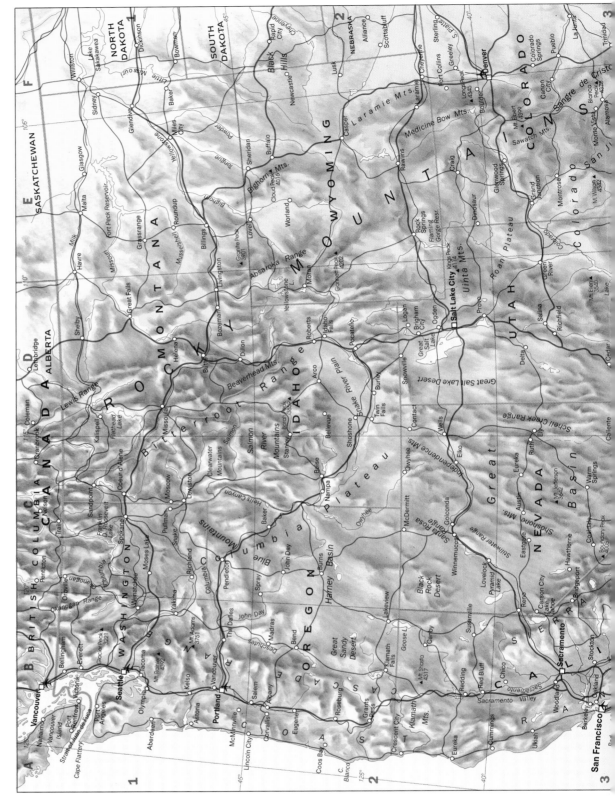

The Rocky Mountains

WESTERN STATES

Much of the USA's Western States is taken up with the Rocky Mountains, which cover a distance of over 1,610 kilometres or 1,000 miles from the Canadian border to the desert of New Mexico. The wide variety of landscapes within the four Rocky Mountain States of Colorado, Wyoming, Montana and Idaho support an equally varied amount of wildlife including bison, bears, moose, elk, beaver, wolves and coyotes. For the tourist who is interested in the outdoors, there are many activities to choose from, such as hiking, cycling, fishing, whitewater rafting and skiing.

To the southwest lie the four desert states of New Mexico, Arizona, Utah and Nevada. The scenery varies from deep canyons and snowcapped mountains to the high plateau deserts, from red and gold autumn leaves in the canyons and mountains to the wild flowers blooming in spring in otherwise barren deserts. Southern Utah has more national parks than anywhere else in the US and it has been suggested that the area be one vast national park.

Over a third of the state of Arizona belongs to American Indian tribes such as the Apache, the Hopi and the Navajo and the state is imbued with the history of these and other tribes and the white settlers with whom they fought. For many visitors to New Mexico, the most obvious feature of the state is its adobe architecture to be seen on homes, churches and even shopping malls.

The state of California is famous for its beautiful beaches, high mountain ranges, hot deserts and for the glitz and glamour of its cities such as Los Angeles. There is something for everyone to enjoy in California from a wide selection of outdoor activities to visiting the many beautiful national parks and places of historical interest.

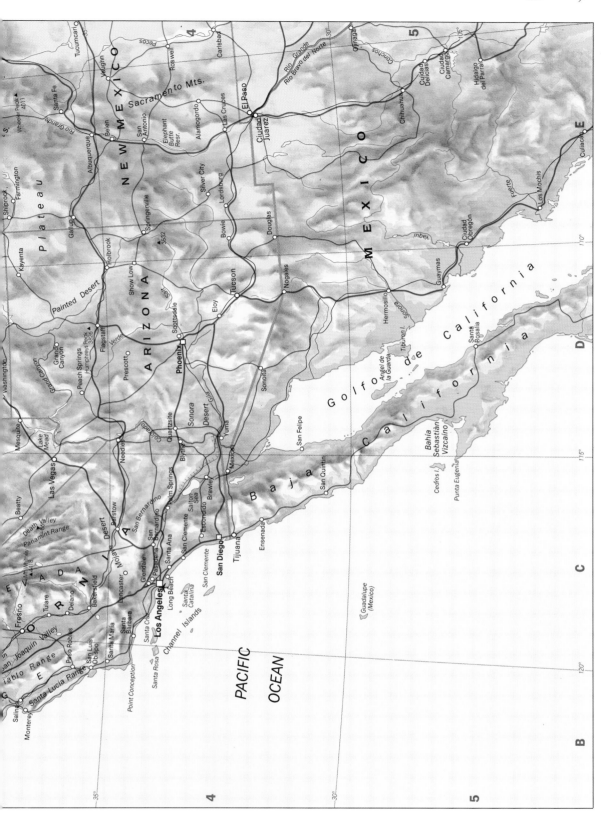

USA, Western States
Scale 1: 8 600 000

| 0 | 100 | 200 | 300 km |

| 0 | 100 | 200 miles |

© Geddes & Grosset

LAS VEGAS

Las Vegas did not exist at all a hundred years ago but now boasts a population of over a million people with some of the largest hotels in the world. Its hotel-casinos attract 30 million visitors every year and, with many offering live entertainment for their customers, it has also become the USA's live entertainment capital.

Las Vegas is also renowned for the fact that over 100,000 weddings a year are performed there in a wide variety of settings, including the Graceland Wedding Chapel where an Elvis impersonator acts as the best man or gives the bride away.

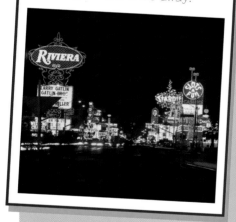

The Grand Canyon, Arizona

The spectacular Grand Canyon, the towering cliffs of which form the gorge of the Colorado River, extends for a distance of 450 kilometres or 280 miles and, in some places, is nearly 1.6 kilometres or one mile deep. The formation of the canyon remains something of a mystery as geologists now believe that the river itself could not have been solely responsible. Whatever forces were involved, layer upon layer of different coloured rocks have been revealed, each containing its own collection of fossils. These enable valuable information to be gained about the conditions and environments of the past. Erosion by wind, water, freezing and thawing have carved the amazing rock formations for which the canyon is famous.

The Grand Canyon has always been a difficult place for people although there is archaeological evidence of human activity from as early as 2000 BC.

Later, throughout many centuries, it was home to native Indian peoples, including the Havasupai, who traditionally occupied the base of the canyon in summer but spent the winter on the high ground above.

The canyon was discovered by Europeans in 1540 during a Spanish expedition but was little disturbed in the years that followed. By the late 19th century, following a few unfruitful attempts at mining, the tourism potential of the Grand Canyon was starting to be realised.

The Bright Angel Trail was constructed in the 1890s and remains the most popular route for tourists today. Even in the late 20th century, however, a trip down into the canyon can still only be accomplished by a long hike on foot or on the back of a mule, with an even more gruelling climb back out again – a round trip of at least 14 or 15 hours. The non-human inhabitants of the canyon include mountain lions, eagles, vultures, snakes and scorpions.

The Grand Canyon National Park

San Francisco

For many people, the world-famous Golden Gate Bridge has come to symbolise the city of San Francisco. The bridge spans the Golden Gate Straits at the approach to San Francisco Bay, a treacherous stretch of water subject to strong currents, which previously could only be crossed by ferry boat. The bridge was opened in May 1937 and it has proved to be a spectacular success. Not only does it provide easy access for commuters and travellers, it has also, from the day that it was opened, attracted countless numbers of visitors, becoming a major tourist attraction in its own right.

San Francisco

The beautiful and vibrant city of San Francisco is a place of steep, hilly streets, sunshine and cable cars but is also occasionally enveloped in dense swirls of fog. A settlement began to develop in the 1830s but it expanded rapidly as people flooded into California during the Gold Rush of 1848. By the turn of the century, San Francisco was a bustling, booming city in which the theatre, music and commerce thrived and which had a cosmopolitan mix of people, particularly a significant Chinese population in Chinatown. San Francisco has always been a city living on the edge as it is built over the great San Andreas geological fault where two of the Earth's vast, tectonic, crustal plates meet and rub together. In 1906, movement along the fault caused an enormous earthquake and this, and a resultant devastating fire, all but destroyed San Francisco, killing thousands of people. Although the city was quickly rebuilt and remains as popular as ever, its people live with an ever-present danger and suffered further severe earthquake damage in 1989. San Francisco, with its Golden Gate and Oakland Bay Bridges, thrives on tourism and is renowned for its Chinatown, excellent seafood and rich musical, cultural and artistic heritage.

Crater Lake, Oregon

Situated in southern Oregon, the Crater Lake National Park lies within the Cascade mountain range and is an area of outstanding beauty and natural wilderness.

Crater Lake

The lake itself lies within the collapsed peak, or caldera, of an ancient volcano, Mount Mazama, which last erupted over 7,500 years ago. Solidified lava sealed the base of the caldera, enabling it to be filled by meltwater and streams to form a deep, azure-blue lake. Because of its high altitude (1,981–2,133 metres or 6,500–7,000 feet) with peaks rising to 2,743 metres or 9,000 feet), the park is subject to frequent heavy snowfalls for much of the year. In the summer months, however, wild flowers and glimpses of the park's birds and animals along with spectacular scenery are enjoyed by many visitors to Crater Lake.

San Diego

A Spanish expedition under the captaincy of Juan Rodriguez Cabrillo set foot on the shores of San Diego Bay in 1542. It was not until 1769, however, that Father Junipero Serro established a fortified mission on Presidio Hill with the aim of converting the American Indian population to Roman Catholicism. Dwellings made of adobe, some of which can still be visited today, were erected around the base of the hill but the mission itself was soon moved (in 1774) ten kilometres or six miles to the north to a more convenient location near fresh water. Over the following years, the settlement came under Mexican and, eventually, American control but modern San Diego began to grow and expand in the years after 1867. Balboa Park with its fine buildings in the Spanish Colonial style, tree-lined promenades and gardens, was established and today it houses an impressive collection of museums and art galleries. Modern San Diego is a renowned tourist resort, with beautiful beaches and a world-famous zoo and sea world. It is also the home port for some of the ships of the American navy and is the second largest city in California.

Sequoia National Park

The Sequoia National Park in California was created in the 1880s in order to protect the giant sequoia trees from being cut down by loggers. In the 1940s, the park was merged with the adjacent King's Canyon National Park. The area includes magnificent deep canyons and the high peaks of the Sierra Nevada mountains as well as groves of giant sequoia trees. It provides a home for many types of animals, including mountain lions, marmots, bears, pine martens, coyotes, racoons, deer and squirrels.

The most famous trees are the General Sherman and the General Grant Sequoias. The General Sherman is the greatest living organism on the Earth today. It is 84 metres or 275 feet tall and still growing fast. The circumference at the base is 31 metres or 103 feet. It was given its name in 1879 by a survivor of the American Civil War and is believed to be between 2,300 and 2,700 years old. Almost as large is the General Grant Sequoia, which is a national monument dedicated to Americans who have lost their lives in war.

Sequoia National Park

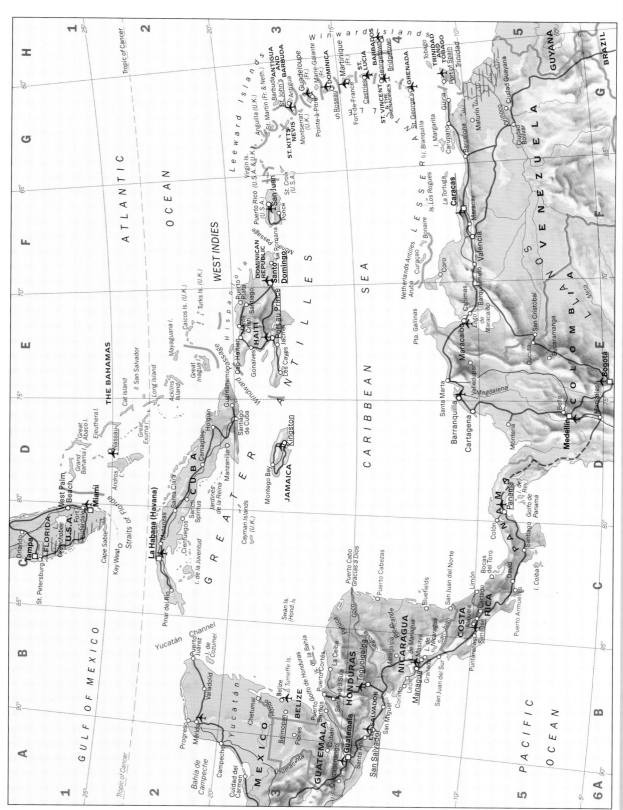

Central America and the Caribbean
Scale 1: 17 000 000

| 0 | 200 | 400 | 600 | 800 km |

| 0 | 250 | 500 miles |

© Geddes & Grosset

Hurricane Mitch

In early November 1998, a devastating storm, nicknamed 'Hurricane Mitch', struck the countries of Central America. Its effects were particularly severe in Honduras and Nicaragua where thousands of people lost their lives and millions more were made homeless and left without food, drinking water or shelter.

The international community mounted one of the biggest relief efforts that the world has ever seen but faced severe difficulties in getting aid to the places where it was most needed because of the extent of the devastation and flooding. It has been estimated that 70 per cent of the landscape of Honduras was ruined and this included man-made structures as well as natural features, such as forests and plantations, that were buried beneath the mud.

St Thomas, Virgin Islands

CENTRAL AMERICA AND THE CARRIBEAN

Central America comprises the southern part of Mexico and a group of small countries that form a narrowing neck of land between North and South America, separating the Caribbean Sea from the Pacific Ocean. The hundreds of islands, in the Caribbean Sea and the Atlantic Ocean, which stretch in a chain from the Bahamas, just off the the coast of Florida, to Trinidad, just off the coast of South America, are sometimes known as the West Indies.

BELIZE

Belize, formerly British Honduras, is one of the smallest and most sparsely populated of the Central American countries with a damp, warm climate and a Caribbean coastline of sandy beaches protected by coral reefs. It is becoming increasingly popular as a tourist resort and has a rich archaeological heritage of Maya sites. Hurricanes pose a considerable threat to the coast.

GUATEMALA

Guatemala is a largely mountainous country with areas of dense jungle and towering volcanic peaks flanking the Pacific Ocean. Three of the volcanoes are still active and the country is also subject to earthquakes. In the northwest, there is a large, low-lying forested area called El Peten in which are located many archaeological remains of the Maya civilisation. Most of the population of nine million people are concentrated in the cities.

THE PANAMA CANAL

The Panama Canal links two great oceans, the Atlantic and the Pacific, across the narrowest point of an isthmus. Construction began in 1903, following a treaty signed with the USA, who agreed to undertake the project in return for control of a 16-kilometre or 10-mile wide zone extending on either side of the canal. Despite being a considerable engineering feat, the construction of the canal took only ten years to complete and was opened to shipping in August 1914.

The Panama canal is 82 kilometres or 151 miles long and has proved to be an economic boon for many countries, saving many thousands of ocean miles and hence both time and money. In 1977, management of the canal was renegotiated so that it was organised jointly by the USA and Panama. On the last day of the 20th century, control of the canal returned fully to Panama.

Scuba diving in the Carribean Sea

HONDURAS

Honduras is a mountainous country with a population of about five million people. Bananas and cotton are grown along the Caribbean coast. Cattle ranching, forestry and pulp and paper production are carried out in some areas but the difficult terrain limits communication and economic activities. The mountains' gold and silver mineral resources attracted the Spanish conquistadors during the 16th century.

EL SALVADOR

El Salvador lies along the Pacific Ocean and is bounded inland by Guatemala and Honduras. It is the smallest of the central American countries with a population of about five and a half million people. Most of the central region is occupied by a range of volcanic peaks, some of which are still active. Past eruptions have deposited a fertile layer of material on a high, central plain providing excellent conditions for coffee plantations. Coffee is El Salvador's main crop but tobacco, maize, beans, rice and sugar are also grown.

NICARAGUA

Nicaragua, sandwiched between Honduras to the north and Costa Rica to the south, is the largest of the Central American countries. The dense forests and sandy beaches of the Mosquito Coast in the eastern part of the country are home to a variety of wildlife including jaguars, monkeys, pumas and crocodiles. The land rises inland to become mountainous interspersed with fertile valleys. In the southwest, there is large basin that contains two vast lakes, Nicaragua in the south and Managua in the north. These are bordered in the north by volcanoes, many of which are still active. Most of Nicaragua's four and a half million people live in the region of the lakes or towards the Pacific coast in the west. Coffee, cotton, bananas and sugar cane are grown, with cattle ranching in some of the upland areas. Nicaragua is subject to earthquakes and the capital, Managua, was severely damaged by tremors in 1931 and 1972.

COSTA RICA

Costa Rica is a small country bounded by Nicaragua to the north and Panama to the south. Three mountain ranges, including some active volcanoes, form the backbone of the land. The Meseta Central is a fertile plateau on the western side of the country where about half the population of three million people are concentrated. Agricultural activities – coffee, bananas, sugar, coconuts and cattle ranching – along with some new manufacturing industries are the mainstay of the economy.

PANAMA

Panama is a narrow, S-shaped isthmus that links Central and South America. It is only about 177 kilometres or 110 miles across at its widest point. Most of the country is mountainous although the peaks are modest by Central American standards.

The economy depends on a wide variety of industries including the production of coffee, sugar cane, bananas, maize, beans, rice, some cattle ranching, fishing, timber production, manufacturing and oil refining. The Panama Canal, which provides a route for ships between the Caribbean and Atlantic and the Pacific, has ensured the strategic importance of the country, particularly to its powerful neighbour, the USA.

THE BAHAMAS

Some 700 beautiful coral islands and keys in the Atlantic Ocean, only a few of which are inhabited, make up the Bahamas. The Turks and Caicos Islands form the southeast archipelago of the Bahamas, which extend for 966 kilometres or 600 miles southeastwards from the coast of Florida. The islands are all low-lying with a subtropical climate and most islanders live on Grand Bahama or New Providence. The British colonised the Bahamas in the 17th century but the islands have been independent since 1973. Tourism is the mainstay of the economy but fishing and limited agriculture, along with international banking, are also important.

CUBA

Cuba is the largest of the Caribbean islands, forming the western end of the Greater Antilles group. The Greater Antilles group of islands includes Cuba, Jamaica, Haiti, the Dominican Republic (formerly Hispaniola) and Puerto Rico. The Cayman Islands lie to the south of Cuba.

Parts of Cuba are quite mountainous with forested slopes of mahogany and pine. Sugar has long formed the mainstay of the economy but other important and developing economic activities are tobacco (Havana cigars), citrus fruits, light manufacturing and tourism.

MARTINIQUE

The rocky, volcanic island nation of Martinique is one of the Windward Islands of the Lesser Antilles group. Renowned for its great natural beauty, Martinique has sandy beaches of black, white and peppered sand, a tropical climate and a mountainous interior. The island's economy relies mainly on tourism with sugar, bananas, pineapples, citrus fruits, nutmeg and spices being grown in some parts of the island.

The Lesser Antilles group consists of the smaller islands to the east and south of the Greater Antilles and they are further divided into the Leeward Islands, the Windward Islands and the Netherlands Antilles.

The British and the US Virgin Islands lie at the northwest end of the Lesser Antilles. Antigua and Barbuda, Dominica, St Kitts and Nevis, Anguilla, Grenada, Guadeloupe, Montserrat and the tiny island of Redonda are part of the Leeward Islands and Aruba is one of the Netherlands Antilles group. Barbados is the most easterly and Grenada the most southerly of the Windward Islands (although Trinidad and Tobago, lying just off the coast of Venezuela, look like the tail end of this island group), which also includes St Lucia and St Vincent and the Grenadines.

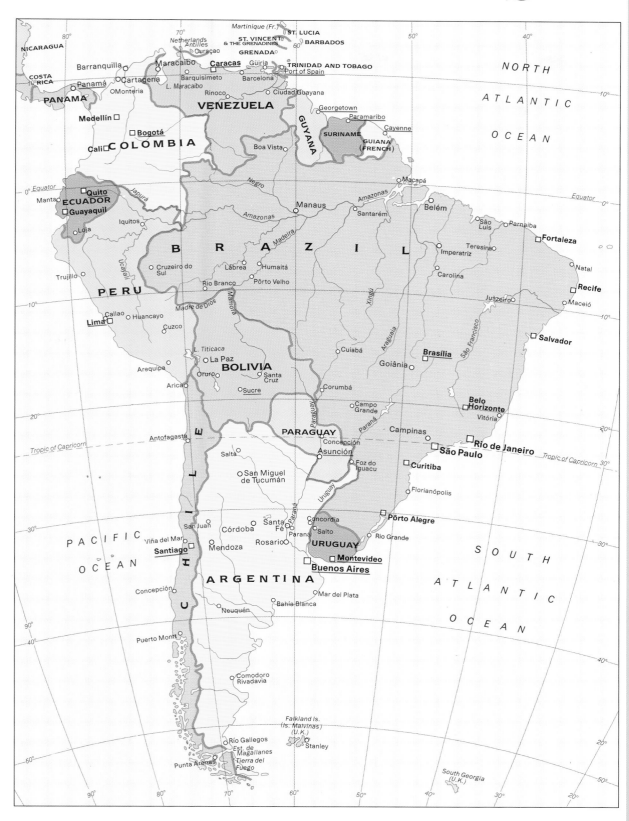

LAKE TITICACA

Lake Titicaca in Bolivia is the highest navigable lake in the world. This huge inland sea was once at the centre of the ancient Tiahuanaco civilisation and near the southeast end of the lake can be seen the ruins of the Gate of the Sun, once part of an elaborate observatory and courtyard built by a civilisation that surfaced around 600 BC and disappeared around AD 1200. Today modern speedboats skim over this deep blue lake alongside traditional gondola-shaped boats made of reeds.

The River Amazon is the second longest river in the world. The vast Amazon Jungle, an almost unbroken carpet of green tropical forest is home to thousands of plant species and exotic bird life. There is much to be seen along the banks of the Amazon River from people fishing from canoes and small river settlements to the huge, almost impenetrable trees of the Amazon Jungle. In recent years, two things have threatened the jungle, arguably one of the world's most ecologically sensitive areas – an influx of settlers from urban centres in Brazil, who are clearing the forest to set up small homesteads, and major projects seeking to exploit the area's mineral resources.

SOUTH AMERICA

South America is a region of immense variety and beauty. The archaeological remains of ancient civilisations can be found among its jungles and mountains. Geographically there are three main regions: the immense mountain range of the Andes, the central, vast river basins and the geologically ancient northern Guiana Highlands and Brazilian Highlands.

The highest navigable lake in the world is found in the Andes on the border of Peru and Bolivia and the largest tropical forest in the world can be found in the Amazon Basin. In the north of Chile, the Atacama Desert contains some of the driest places on earth. Parts of the desert have been without rain for 400 years. Even within its great cities, there is a huge gulf between the opulent lifestyle of the rich and the extreme poverty of the poor.

Bogota, Colombia

COLOMBIA

Columbia is situated in the northwestern part of South America and is unique in having a coastline that borders both the Pacific Ocean and the Caribbean Sea. The dominant topographical feature is the Andes mountain chain. However, Colombia's highest mountain, Pico Cristobel Colon, is not in the Andes but in a separate group of mountains called the Sierra Nevada de Santa Marta, situated just behind the Caribbean coast. The northern part of Colombia, to the east of the Andes, comprises a region of grassy plains or Llanos which is drained by many tributaries of the Orinoco river. Farther south, this gives way to dense rainforests drained by tributaries of the Amazon.

Colombia has a wealth of habitats that provide a home for many different types of plants and animals. Colombia's most important crop is coffee,

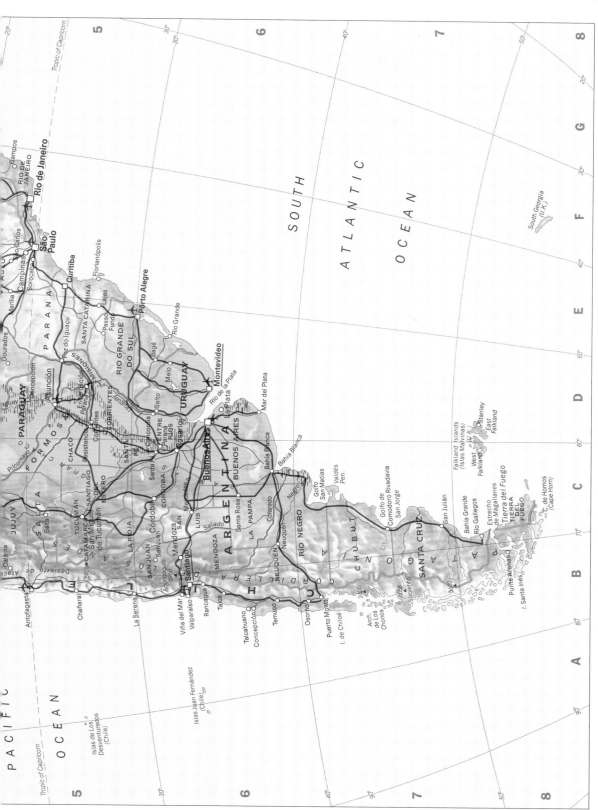

THE RIVER BASINS OF SOUTH AMERICA

Of all the South American river basins, the greatest is that of the mighty Amazon, which, with its tributaries, is the largest river system in the world. The Amazon flows for 6,751 kilometres or 4,195 miles from its source in the high Andes in Peru and is joined by many other large rivers as it proceeds towards the sea. The Amazon basin encompasses 40 per cent of the land area of South America.

In Venezuela, the Orinoco and its tributaries form a second large river basin draining an area known as the Llanos. Farther south, in Paraguay, Uruguay and Argentina, lies the great river system of the Parana, Paraguay and Uruguay rivers, which join to form the vast estuary of the Rio de la Plata and South America's third great river basin.

THE GUIANA HIGHLANDS

The Guiana Highlands straddle Venezuela, Brazil and Guyana and are formed from ancient, hard, crystalline pre-Cambrian rocks, among the oldest in the world. This region, with its sheer cliffs and flat-topped peaks rising from the forests below, was the inspiration for Sir Arthur Conan Doyle's *The Lost World*.

From the largest of these mountains, the world's highest waterfall, the Angel Falls cascades down a drop of 979 metres or 3,212 feet and takes 14 seconds to reach the bottom of the gorge.

Because they have sheer, rocky cliffs on all sides, the table-top mountains or *tepuis* are like islands that have been isolated for millions of years, making them home to some rare plant species that have evolved in an entirely unique way.

but bananas, sugar cane, rice, cacao beans, flowers, cotton, tobacco and potatoes are also cultivated. The country has important natural reserves of minerals and precious stones, particularly emeralds, silver, gold, petroleum, coal, natural gas, platinum, nickel and copper.

VENEZUELA

Venezuela has four distinctive topographical regions: the Guiana Highlands in the south; the plains or Llanos drained by the Orinoco river to the north; the Maracaibo lowlands; and two mountain ranges, separated by the Maracaibo lowlands, called the Venezuelan Highlands. Over two thirds of Venezuela is forested, providing a home for animals such as anacondas and boa constrictors, crocodiles, ocelots, jaguars, monkeys, bears, deer, sloths, armadillos and anteaters.

Venezuela's economy is built on its oilfields locat-

ed in the Maracaibo region, but it also has other important mineral reserves.

Agricultural activities include cattle ranching and the rearing of pigs, sheep and goats while crops include sugar cane, bananas, oranges, maize, sorghum, rice, plantains, coffee and cassava. There are also rich fishing grounds around the coast and off Venezuela's 72 islands.

GUYANA, SURINAME, FRENCH GUIANA

Inland from Guyana's coastal belt there lies a densely forested region that covers about four fifths of the total land area. In the north and in the southwest, the forests give way to the high savannah of the Rapununi and Kanaku regions. In the western, central part of the country lie the Guiana Highlands with their table-top peaks.

Suriname is a country of upland plateaux and highlands that are covered with forests and traversed by numerous rivers and streams, many of which are important navigable waterways. The mangrove swamps of the coastal plain give way inland to a strip of sandy savannah. In the south, the land becomes mountainous and is covered with tropical jungles. The central area is occupied by a low plateau region with savannah and forest.

As the name suggests, French Guiana remains an overseas department of France and the country's inhabitants have enjoyed a relatively high standard of living thanks to support from France.

The coastal belt is a narrow strip of marshy mangrove swamps and then the land gradually rises inland towards the Tumac-Humac Mountains. Behind the coast there is some savannah but 90 per cent of French Guiana is covered with hot, humid, tropical forest where animals such as tapirs, monkeys, anteaters, jaguars, ocelots, caimans and exotic birds can be found.

Most of the population are engaged either in agriculture, fishing, forestry or mining. French Guiana has one extremely modern development – the satellite launch base at Kourou, jointly run by the European Space Agency, the French Space Agency and Arianespace, a company responsible for the Ariane rocket.

ECUADOR

Ecuador means 'Equator' in Spanish and the Equator divides the country into a large southern region and a small northern portion. Although it is a relatively small country, Ecuador has great topographical and climatic variation. It rises inland from the coastal plain to form the Sierra or Central Highlands, consisting of the Western and Eastern Cordillera ranges of the Andes. These are separated by a long, narrow valley forming a high plateau.

Lying to the east of the Andes and comprising about one third of the total land area is the region known as the Oriente. Drained by rivers which form some of the headwaters of the mighty Amazon, this region is covered by dense tropical rainforest and is well known for its biodiversity. The Galapagos Islands, which lie 965 kilometres or 600 miles west of the coast, are also part of Ecuador. Much of Ecuador's coastal plain has been cleared of forests to make way for the cultivation of bananas, sugar cane, coffee, rice, manioc and maize.

PERU

Peru, the 'land of the Incas', is one of the largest of the South American countries and has four topographical regions that run largely north to south. The Costa, a narrrow coastal belt, is a dry, desert region except where it is traversed by rivers flowing westwards to the Pacific. The valleys of these rivers are cultivated for rice, cotton and sugar cane.

Behind the coastal belt, the land rises to the high peaks of the Andes, which are cut by steep-sided gorges interspersed with plateaus. Most of Peru's native Indian peoples live in this region. On the lower western slopes of the Andes, some cultivation is possible, and the higher regions provide grazing for llamas, alpacas, guanacos and vicunas. On the eastern side of the Andes lies the Montana region, an area of subtropical jungle and cloud forest that remains virtually impenetrable in some places. To the east and north, the land flattens to form the Selva, a part of the Amazon basin covered with dense tropical jungle.

BOLIVIA

Bolivia is one of only two South American countries to be surrounded by land on all sides. The dominant topographical feature is the Andes mountain chain. This forms two main ranges, the Cordillera Occidental and the Cordillera Oriental running from north to south in the southwestern third of the country. Between them is a high, treeless plateau called the Altiplano, which is where most Bolivians live. Lake Titicaca, which straddles the border with Peru, is in the northern part of the Altiplano. The lower, eastern slopes of the mountains form a region of forested, fertile valleys called the Yungas.

This gives way to an extensive, low-lying tropical region that comprises about 70 per cent of the total land area. In the southeastern corner of this region, separated from the rest of the region by the Chiquitos Highlands, are the arid plains known as the Chaco. Farther north there are hot savannah lands or Llanos and dense tropical jungles blanketing the river valleys that traverse the region. Much of the land becomes swamp during the rainy season but the higher grasslands are not affected.

Most people live in rural areas and are engaged in fairly basic agriculture. Until quite recently, Bolivia's leading product was tin, but natural gas is now of much greater importance to the Bolivian economy along with timber, soya beans and sugar.

CHILE

Chile is a long, narrow ribbon of a country on the western side of South America. It extends from Peru in the north right down to Cape Horn on the southern tip of Tierra del Fuego. The dominant topographical feature is the Andes mountain chain in the east, which runs the whole length of the country. The highest peaks are in the northern half of the

The Incas were a South American people who established a vast empire encompassing large parts of Ecuador, Peru, Bolivia and Argentina from AD 1200 to 1572 when they were conquered by the Spanish. The Inca civilisation was an extremely advanced one, producing many fine artefacts, although they had no system of writing. Several Inca settlements have been studied including the one at Machu Picchu. This spectacular fortified Inca city is located in the Peruvian Andes at a height of 2,280 metres or 7,480 feet and was unknown to Western archaeologists until 1911.

country and many are active volcanoes. A second, lower range of coastal mountains extends from north to south along the coast.

The two ranges are linked in the north by mountains running transversely from west to east to form a region of peaks and plateaux. This extremely arid land is occupied by the Atacama Desert. One of the world's driest places, the Atacama Desert is also rich in mineral resources.

South of the Atacama Desert lies a fertile, central valley, where grapes, tomatoes, apples, maize, sugar beet, wheat, potatoes and other vegetables are grown. There is a significant winemaking industry in this region. Farther south, a region of forests gives way to steppe-like grasslands

ARGENTINA

Argentina is a large country which also includes the eastern part of Tierra del Fuego. The dominant topographical feature is the Andes mountain chain occupying the western part of the country, which is broader in the north than in the south. The northern Andes consist of peaks, ridges and valleys. Some of these peaks are active volcanoes and others have slopes covered with glaciers surrounding icy, alpine lakes. East of the Andes the land falls away to form undulating plains sloping towards the sea.

In the north, the plains form part of the subtropical region known as the Gran Chaco. In the northeast, in the low-lying Parana river basin, there are tropical swamps and forests inhabited byanimals such as monkeys, peccaries, anteaters, snakes, raccoons, tapirs and the large cats – pumas, jaguars and ocelots. Birds include colourful parrots and hummingbirds.

South of the Chaco is Argentina's rich and productive agricultural region in the grassy plains known as the Pampas. Farther south is Patagonia, a region of dry, cold steppes with few trees but supporting grasslands that are eminently suitable for the rearing of sheep.

Argentina is relatively wealthy by South American standards, with an economy based on agriculture including a modest wine-making industry. Mineral exploitation, particularly of petroleum, is of growing importance to the economy, as is the development of hydroelectric power.

BRAZIL

Brazil is a vast country that occupies nearly half the land mass of South America. There are two dominant topographical features – the great Amazon river basin and the ancient plateau region of crystalline rocks called the Brazilian Highlands. In the central interior, the Highlands form a raised tableland called the Mato Grosso and throughout their extent they are cut by deep river valleys and ridged by mountain ranges.

In the far north, beyond the Amazon basin, lies the southern upland extremity of the Guiana Highlands, another region of very ancient rocks. The Amazon system is navigable by large ocean-going vessels for about 3,700 kilometres or 2,300 miles, a factor that has been of immense importance to the development of Brazil.

Agriculture has always played a leading part in the Brazilian economy but Brazil's mineral resources of iron ore, gold, bauxite, tin, petroleum and natural gas, copper, manganese, silver, titanium, zinc, chromium and quartz have been increasingly exploited since the 1970s. Brazil has valuable timber reserves but there has been worldwide concern over the ruthless and unregulated felling and clearing of vast sections of rainforest.

PARAGUAY

A small country, Paraguay is bounded by land on all sides and divided into two distinctive regions by the River Paraguay. Paraguay Occidental is the larger region to the west of the river. It consists of a marshy, alluvial plain which is also part of the Gran Chaco. In the south and east, much of this area is waterlogged swamp but the land rises gradually and gives way to grassy areas and arid, scrub forest towards the northwestern border.

Paraguay Oriental lies to the east of the Paraguay river and consists mainly of an upland plateau called the Parana Plateau. Paraguay has a subtropical climate and much of the Oriental region is covered with thick forests containing numerous varieties of plants and animals.

With three important rivers, the Paraguay, the Parana and the Pilcomayo, the country has many impressive waterfalls, such as the Guaira Falls, and, in cooperation with its neighbours, it has developed its potential for hydroelectric power to the extent of fulfilling all its energy needs. The Itaipu Hydroelectric Dam on the (Alto) Parana river, opened in 1991 and developed with Brazil, is the largest in the world. Other schemes include the Yacyreta Dam, developed with Argentina and opened in 1994.

URUGUAY

Uruguay is the second smallest South American country, with its western boundary formed by the river from which it takes its name. The Negro river, which rises in Brazil, crosses the country from northeast to southwest, dividing Uruguay almost into two halves. It joins with the Uruguay river in the southwest before opening out into the large estuary of the Rio de la Plata.

Uruguay is a country of low-lying, grass-covered, rolling hills and plains. There is a plateau with hills in the northwest and a second area of higher ground along the Atlantic coast. The climate is temperate and rainfall plentiful and the natural vegetation is prairie grassland. Some of the river valleys are wooded but Uruguay lacks the dense forests of other parts of South America.

THE FALKLAND ISLANDS

The Falkland Islands, or Islas Malvinas, which lie 483 kilometres or 300 miles offshore from Argentina's south Atlantic coast, are claimed by Argentina as part of their territory but belong to Britain. In the 19th century, both countries had settlements on the Falklands but the islands became a British Crown colony in 1892 and its people are of British descent. The two countries went to war over the islands in 1982, and although Britain retained possession, Argentina has not relinquished its claim to the territory.

THE ANDES

The Andes mountain range is the longest mountain range in the world and one of the most impressive. From base to summit, the Andes embrace nearly all climatic zones. They are home to a fascinating array of plants and animals including the llama, which is used as a pack animal and as a source of meat. The cloud forest of the lower, eastern side of the Andes is permanently surrounded by mists and dampness caused by condensation formed when the hot, humid tropical air of the river basins meets the cold, arid air of the Andean peaks.

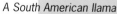

A South American llama

NORTH SEA OIL RIG

North Sea oil and gas are of major importance to the economies of the United Kingdom and Norway.

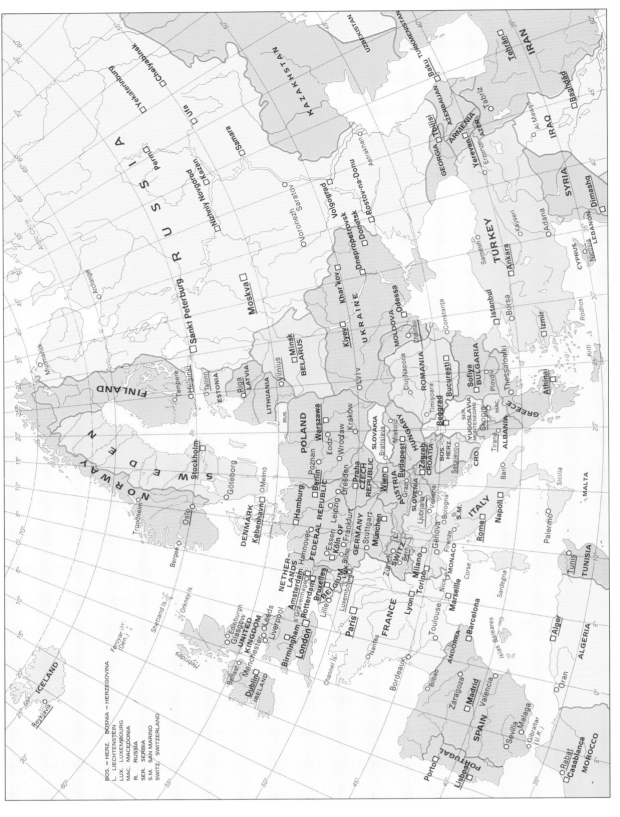

Europe, with its rich and varied history, provides an endless number of historical sites to be visited, such as the beautiful Fountains of Trevi in Rome, which are pictured below.

EUROPE

Europe, the second smallest continent, is densely populated and divided into many different countries which reflect the enormously varied physical, ethnic, cultural and economic nature of the area.

Europe's southern coast fringes the Mediterranean Sea and it is bounded to the west by the Atlantic Ocean. The northern countries of Norway, Sweden and Finland extend inside the Arctic Circle.

The boundaries of Europe owe as much to history and political considerations as they do to geography. Hence Russia, although a part of the European continent, is generally regarded politically as a separate entity, bordering southwards and eastwards with the countries of Asia. However, geographers usually draw the line dividing Europe from Asia down the Ural Mountains and then westwards and southwards to the Caspian and Black Seas. Since the collapse of communism, Russia's former East European allies are now politically, as well as geographically, being regarded as more truly a part of Europe.

Europe has some very fertile land but the continent is too small and densely populated to be self-supporting in food. It does, however, have the greatest concentration of industry of all the continents. The largest cities are Paris and Moscow, both with over eight million inhabitants, followed by London, St Petersburg and Berlin. The western countries of Europe are among the richest countries in the world.

There is a great variety of landscapes within Europe with a lot of climate variation as a result. The highest peaks are in the Alps while north of these the land is flatter until the far north where Norway and Sweden make up the cold, mountainous Scandinavian Peninsula. Areas in the far south, such as the mountains and plateaus of Spain and the many islands that go to make up Greece, are much hotter and drier with limited rainfall.

Europe has so much to offer the traveller, from its many beautiful and varied locations with their own flora and fauna, to its exciting modern cities and many different cultures, to places steeped in history.

The Alps

The Alps stretch from eastern France through northern Italy, southern Germany, Switzerland, Lichtenstein to Austria and northern Slovenia. The highest peak is Mont Blanc (4,785 metres or 15,700 feet), which straddles the border between Italy and France. Other famous peaks include the towering Matterhorn (4,477 metres or 14,688 feet) and the Eiger (3,970 metres or 13,025 feet). The Alps have always been a barrier to communication although important natural passes, such as the Brenner Pass, provide vital road and rail links.

The Pyrenees

The Pyrenees straddle the border and form a natural barrier between France and Spain. They stretch for roughly 400 kilometres or 250 miles from the territory of the Basque people in the west to the Mediterranean coast. Some of the peaks rise to 1,524 metres or 5,000 feet in height, the greatest being Pico de Aneto (3,404 metres or 11,169 feet).

The Pyrenees are physically beautiful, culturally varied and a great deal less developed than the Alps. The whole range is a marvellous country for walkers, especially in the central region around the Parc National des Pyrénées with its 3000-metre peaks, streams and forests, flowers and wildlife, and some 350 kilometres or 217 miles of

marked routes. The hiking season is from mid-June to September.

The European Union

In 1957, the European Community (EC) was formed by six member countries with the aim of improving farming, developing industry and raising living standards. There are now fifteen member countries: Austria, Belgium, Denmark, France, Finland, Germany, Greece, Ireland, Italy, Luxembourg, the Netherlands, Portugal, Spain, Sweden and the United Kingdom. When Austria, Finland and Sweden joined the European Community, it changed its name to become the European Union (EU). The EU has become a political unit where people can travel freely between member countries, live and work where they wish and share a common currency, the euro, if they are members of the European Monetary Union.

Brussels

Brussels is both the capital city of Belgium and home of the government of the EU and of the North Atlantic Treaty Organisation (NATO). It is one of the three federal regions of Belgium, along with Wallonia and Flanders, and is a very ancient city that was founded in 979 with the building of a fortified castle.

At the heart of old Brussels is the beautiful Grand Palace and to the south is the elegant Sablon district, with the Royal Palace and museums and the neo-classical Palais de Justice. Many fine medieval buildings are preserved in the ancient part of the capital but Brussels is also a modern city, as befits its status as the head of some 340 million citizens of the EU. Geographically, Brussels is situated in the northern Flemish, or Dutch-speaking, region of Flanders. Many of the city's residents are French-speaking, however, reflecting the two cultures of Belgium, and about a quarter are foreign nationals whose work is connected either with the EU or with large multinational business interests. Also, some 80 per cent of visitors to Brussels come on business

THE GULF STREAM

The Gulf Stream is a warm ocean current important to north-west Europe. Originating in the Gulf of Mexico and flowing swiftly, as the Florida Current, northwards along the United States coast to about 40°N, it then flows north-eastwards across the Atlantic Ocean. As it nears Britain and Norway it becomes known as the North Atlantic Drift and is responsible for the temperate climate of northwest Europe and for keeping the west coast of Norway ice-free during winter.

The European Union Building, Brussels

British Isles

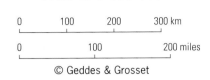

United Kingdom

Language/s spoken: English
Currency: Pound Sterling
Travel requirements: valid
passport usually required but all
potential visitors should contact
relevant authority before
departure for more specific
information
Major cities: London (capital),
Birmingham, Manchester,
Glasgow, Liverpool, Edinburgh,
Cardiff
Climate: temperate climate with
warm wet summers and relatively
mild, wet winters, variable
throughout the year
Crime and safety: take sensible
precautions

Channel Tunnel data

Number of tunnels: 3 (one single
track for trains travelling in each
direction and one service tunnel)
Length of tunnels: 50 kilometres
or 31 miles
Depth beneath seabed: 40 metres
or 130 feet

British Isles

The British Isles are situated off the northwest coast of mainland Europe. They are bounded to the west by the Atlantic Ocean and to the north and east by the North Sea. In the south the English Channel separates the British Isles from northern France. The two main islands of Great Britain and Ireland make up the British Isles. There are also many groups of small islands belonging to the British Isles off the western and northern coasts.

The British Isles consist of two separate nations – the United Kingdom and the Republic of Ireland. The United Kingdom consists of Scotland, England, Wales and the six counties of Northern Ireland in the northeast of the island of Ireland. The Republic of Ireland covers the rest of Ireland.

Because of a shared history over the centuries, Britain and France, and Northern France in particular, have had much in common in terms of their peoples and how they have lived.

The Channel Tunnel

Today, Northern France is linked to the British Isles by the Channel Tunnel, which passes beneath the English Channel to provide a rail link between England and France.

Agreement to build the present tunnel was reached in 1986. Work began in 1987 and the Channel Tunnel opened for business seven years later, in 1994. The terminals are at Folkestone on the English side of the Channel and Sangatte near Calais in France. Two types of services are offered – passenger trains that link with the railway networks of Britain and France and shuttle trains for road vehicles and passengers travelling between the two terminals.

ENGLAND

England is bounded in the north by Scotland and to the west by the Irish Sea. The English Channel and the North Sea separate it from mainland Europe. It is a country of rolling, green hills and rich farmland but with large industrialised cities. The most densely populated parts of England cover the major urban areas of Greater Manchester, Merseyside, South Yorkshire, Birmingham, West Midlands and Greater London.

The Yorkshire Dales

England was once thickly wooded but trees began to be cleared and felled very early on in its human history. As the forests shrank, some of the larger European mammals, including bears, wolves and wild boar, were hunted to extinction. Today there are numerous small areas of woodland but very few extensive tracts of forest. Animals to be found in England include deer, badgers, foxes, squirrels, adders and newts. There are many different species of birds, from birds of prey to smaller songbirds, such as the lark. In parts of England, intensive agricultural and urban developments have posed a threat to wildlife and its habitats and some species, including the lark, are now quite rare.

Principal industries include motor vehicles, electronics and electrical engineering, textiles and clothing, aircraft and consumer goods. Tourism is also an important industry although many visitors look no further than London for their stay.

London

England's capital city, covering an area of about 1,606 square kilometres or 620 square miles and situated on the River Thames, is home to more than 7 million people.

Tower Bridge, London

It was founded and named Londinium by the Romans in AD 43. The Roman wall that enclosed Londinium can still be seen today and it surrounds the City of London, or the Square Mile, which houses England's financial institutions as well as such renowned buildings as the Tower of London and St Paul's Cathedral.

London boasts a long list of famous and historical buildings, such as Buckingham Palace, the Palace of Hampton Court, Westminster Abbey and the Houses of Parliament. There are also museums where visitors can see national collections of paintings and objects relating to the United Kingdom's history.

Sheffield

Sheffield derives its name from the River Sheaf, which is one of the five rivers that traverse the city. Little is known about its early history prior to Norman times, but it is believed that there was once an Anglo-Saxon Viking settlement in the area.

The cutlery industry for which Sheffield is famous began in the medieval period as a small-scale concern using charcoal for smelting and water power to turn the grinding wheels. New technological advances in the 1700s greatly accelerated the expansion of the industry. Between 1750 and 1800, Sheffield became one of the world's major producers of steel, ornamental tableware and cutlery, and its population increased over fourfold.

During the first half of the 19th century, the canal and railway networks were developed and Sheffield's steel makers were able to become the main suppliers of rails. By the 1860s, the steel works had further diversified into the production of heavy armaments while the cutlery manufacturers continued to produce high quality goods that were in great demand. In the 20th century, the two World Wars saw Sheffield once more working to capacity in the production of armaments.

Modern Sheffield has seen the closure and decline of many of the great forge works, although both steel and cutlery are still made in the city. There have been many exciting new developments, such as the construction of new sporting facilities for 1991, when Sheffield hosted the World Student Games, the Meadowhall shopping complex and the return of trams to Sheffield's streets.

Milton Keynes

Milton Keynes is familiar to most people as England's most famous New Town. Far less well known is the fact that the borough of Milton Keynes, comprising the town itself along with surrounding countryside and villages, has a long history of human settlement dating back thousands of years. Stone Age, Bronze Age and Iron Age remains and Roman buildings and settlements have all been uncovered in the immediate area and the Anglo-Saxons established several villages in the 6th and 7th centuries, including that of Milton Keynes itself.

These and other villages that grew up in the Norman and medieval period were all subject to various fluctuations in their growth and patterns of development over the succeeding centuries, so the city planners back in 1967 were, in fact, continuing a very long historical tradition. The designated area of the new town incorporated existing towns and villages including Bletchley, Wolverton, Stony Stratford and Milton Keynes, which gave its name to the new development.

The Milton Keynes Development Corporation undertook to create homes and employment for

HADRIAN'S WALL

Hadrian's Wall was constructed between the years AD 122 and 136 under the orders of the Roman Emperor Hadrian to protect the northern boundary of the Roman Empire in the British Isles. It ran for 118 kilometres or 73 miles from the River Tyne to the Solway Firth and today lies just south of the border between Scotland and England. The wall was built out of stone, about 5 metres or 6 feet high and 3 metres or 10 feet thick, with forts and castles regularly placed along its length. A broad ditch, the vallum, ran along the inside edge of the wall.

Around AD 410, the Romans withdrew from Britain and the wall was abandoned.

HAMPTON COURT, LONDON

Given to Henry VIII by Cardinal Wolsey in 1528, Hampton Court is now one of England's great tourist attractions. From the outside, it is a harmonious blend of Tudor and Baroque architecture while inside there is a much more obvious contrast between the rooms of each period, for example between Wren's Classical royal rooms such as the King's Apartments and the Tudor architecture of the Great Hall. The grounds contain some beautiful gardens including the Pond Garden, a sunken water garden conceived by Henry VIII.

England and Wales
Scale 1: 2 600 000

0   20   40   60   80   100 km

0   15   30   45   60 miles

© Geddes & Grosset

PENZANCE, CORNWALL

Penzance stands on Mount's Bay, with its sandy beaches and the island of St Michael's Mount, where there is an 11th century monastery and a 15th century fort. The town has one of the mildest climates in Britain and is renowned for its beautiful gardens. Some two miles west of Penzance, lies Trengwaiton Gardens, where visitors can see many plants that cannot be grown in the open anywhere else in Britain.

Porthbeor Beach, Cornwall

25,000 people in the following 25 years. It was disbanded in 1992 when the target was well on the way to being achieved. Milton Keynes now boasts several innovative modern buildings, such as the Church of Christ of the Cornerstone, and seeks to combine the most new and up to date with the rich historical heritage of the past.

Cornwall

Cornwall is the most southwesterly county of England and is renowned for its beautiful scenery, rugged coastline and warm climate. Land's End is the most southwesterly point on the British mainland while Lizard Point marks the southernmost extremity. Both consist of headlands of high cliffs rising steeply from the sea. Land's End is a popular tourist destination and also the starting/finish-

ing point for many a long-distance cyclist, hiker, etc, travelling to or from John o'Groats in the north of Scotland, a distance of 1,410 kilometres or 876 miles by road.

Cornwall has a long and colourful history with fishing, smuggling, wrecking and tin mining among its main activities in the past. Smuggling had its heyday in the 18th and 19th centuries. Nearly all the south coast Cornish villages were involved and their inhabitants, calling themselves 'free traders', regarded smuggling as a legitimate way to boost their meagre incomes.

Tin mining, centred upon the area around Redruth, was carried out in Cornwall for many centuries and continued on a small scale until well into the 20th century, with the last mine shutting down only in the 1990s. Today, Cornwall relies to a large extent on tourism to boost its local economy.

The map shows southern England, Wales, the English Channel, and part of France. Labelled cities and features include Norwich, Great Yarmouth, Ipswich, Cambridge, London, Birmingham, Oxford, Bristol, Cardiff, Plymouth, Penzance, Land's End, Isle of Wight, Channel Islands, Dover, Calais, Boulogne, Le Havre, Rouen, Cherbourg, and the regions WALES and FRANCE.

STONEHENGE, WILTSHIRE

The circles of massive stone pillars at Stonehenge and Avebury appear to have undergone several phases of construction and reconstruction, dating from the late Neolithic period through to the early Bronze Age (2500 BC to around 1500 BC).

It is generally thought that Stonehenge was used for religious purposes, possibly involving some form of sun worship, and suggestions have been made that some astronomical aspects were involved. Whatever the function of Stonehenge, its construction was a remarkable feat of engineering, involving a very large number of people and hundreds of thousands of man hours.

Ullswater, the Lake District

The Lake District National Park

The Lake District National Park is situated within the Cumbrian mountain range in northwestern England, and it covers an area of 2,279 square kilometres or 880 square miles. This region has long been recognised as one of the most beautiful and majestic in England and has always been a popular place for visitors.

William Wordsworth, the 19th-century poet, described the Lake District as as a 'sort of national property in which every man has a right and interest who has an eye to perceive and a heart to enjoy'. Wordsworth would no doubt have heartily approved of the creation of the national park in 1951.

There are 16 main lakes in the area, each with its own distinctive setting and individual charm. Among the best known are Windermere, Derwent Water, Buttermere, Coniston Water, Ullswater and Grassmere. England's highest peak, Scafell Pike (978 metres or 3,210 feet), occurs within the Cumbrian mountain range in the national park.

Human occupancy of the Lake District stretches back over the centuries to prehistoric times and it contains a number of important archaeological sites. Today, only 10 per cent of the people living there are employed in agriculture, forestry and fisheries and a much higher proportion are involved, either directly or indirectly, in tourism.

The Lake District attracts more visitors than any other national park in England, providing a welcome boost for the local economy. However, the presence of so many visitors places considerable pressure on the environment, causing problems for the park authorities.

Wales

Rural Wales

This Italianate village on a private peninsula at the top of Cardigan Bay is the creation of the Welsh architect, Sir Clough Williams-Ellis. There are about 50 buildings in the village and visitors can stay at the luxurious hotel or in one of the village cottages. Portmeiron has been used as a location for films and television programmes and is famous for its flowered pottery which can be purchased at the Ship Shop in the village.

WALES

The small kingdom of Wales, which includes the island of Anglesey, is largely a country of mountains, uplands and moorlands. The Cambrian mountains, which extend from north to south, form the backbone of the country but two other ranges are the Snowdon range in the northwest and the Brecon Beacons in the southeast.

The upland region of Blaenau Morganwy in the south is dissected by a series of steep-sided valleys, such as the Rhondda and Taff, where coal was discovered in the 19th century. The largest cities are Cardiff, Swansea and Newport. Several fairly large rivers flow through Wales, including the Dee, Wye and Usk, with woodland areas in the lower valleys. At higher levels, mountain ash or rowan, oak, birch and conifers may be found giving way to moorland vegetation at about 305 metres or 1,000 feet.

Animals and birds are largely the same as those of England with upland and coastal species being particularly well represented. Many animals and birds in Wales are able to thrive fairly free from human interference, thanks to the fact that much of the countryside is relatively sparsely populated and falls under the protection of the national parks. A good example of this is the pine marten, which is still found in Wales, and also the red kite, which has been reintroduced and is thriving.

The Welsh are a Celtic people and the Welsh language is still spoken by about a quarter of the population. Nearly two thirds of the population live in the south, where industry developed around the coalfields. The coalfields of South Wales were once the most important coalfields in the world but coal mining has declined dramatically and light industry is now much more important. Tourism is one of Wales's chief industries with the beautiful scenery of its national parks and some flourishing resorts around the coast.

Cardiff

Cardiff, the capital city of Wales and home of the Welsh Assembly, handled more than 6 million tons of coal in its heyday as the biggest coal-shipping port in the world. Although this role is now over, Cardiff remains important as a civic, industrial and commercial centre and as a seaport and university city.

It was founded by the Romans as a military outpost in AD 75, soon after their conquest of Britain. Its Welsh name is Caerdydd, and it is situated at the mouth of the River Taff on the Severn estuary. The first Norman castle was built at the end of the 11th century but the magnificent shell keep, which still exists today, was erected in the following century by Robert of Caen. Over the succeeding turbulent centuries, the castle passed into various hands and was added to and altered in a number of ways. In 1776, the castle passed to the Earls of Bute who were to prove influential in the subsequent development of Cardiff.

The 3rd Marquis of Bute joined forces with the architect William Burgess and, in 1865, they embarked upon recreating a medieval fantasy in Cardiff Castle. The castle's artwork, embellishments and additions were flamboyant and startling and often produce a strong effect on visitors of either liking or loathing.

An ornate clock in Cardiff Castle

As the coal mining industry grew and accelerated throughout the 19th century, so, too, did the development of Cardiff as an important city and port. The first docks were built in 1839, and, by the end of the 19th century, Cardiff handled and exported more coal than any other city in the world. The beautiful Civic Centre buildings in Cathays Park, including the University, were built from white marble at the height of the city's prosperity.

Swansea

The City of Swansea is the second largest city in Wales after Cardiff. Its name comes from Sweyn's Ea (the island of Sweyn). Sweyn was a Viking pirate whose chose this site as his base for plundering the coast. Swansea featured largely in the writings of the Welsh poet, Dylan Thomas, and there is a memorial to him in Cwmdonkin Park.

Holyhead

Holyhead is situated on Holy Island and is reached from Anglesey by the Stanley Embankment, built by Thomas Telford in 1822. It is the third largest passenger port in Britain and is the main port for the sea route to Dublin. At the entrance to the harbour is Salt Island, where salt was extracted from the sea during the 18th century, while on the southwest slope of Holyhead Mountain are the remains of dwellings believed to date back to 2,000 BC. At the foot of the slopes of Holyhead Mountain is South Stack Island, home to thousands of seabirds, including puffins and fulmars, and to seals, who breed on its beaches.

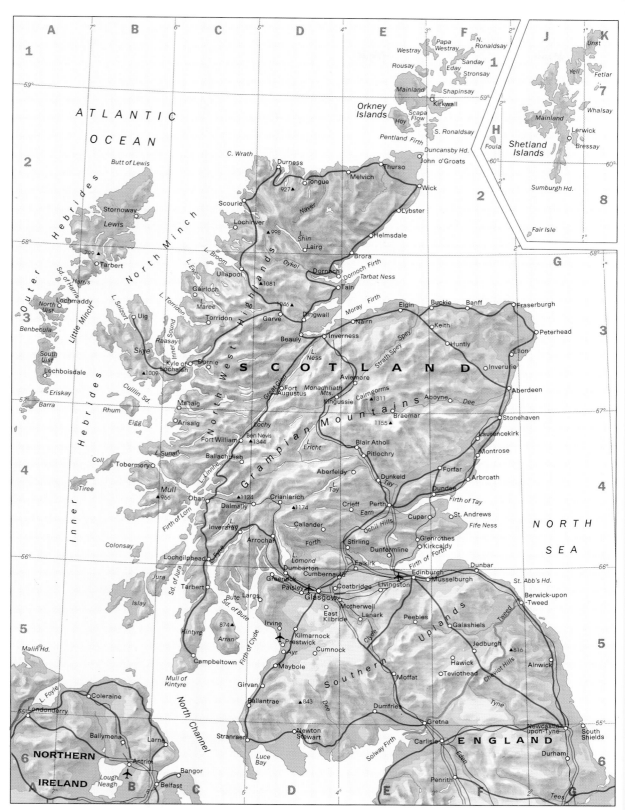

Scotland
Scale 1: 2 600 000

0   20   40   60   80   100 km
0   15   30   45   60 miles

© Geddes & Grosset

Fishing

Fishing has always been a mainstay of the Scottish way of life. Small boats are operated from many of the villages dotted around Scotland's heavily indented coastline, while the main fishing ports are Peterhead, Aberdeen, Fraserburgh and Lerwick in the Shetland Islands.

The imposition of strict regulations and fishing quotas by the European Union has unfortunately caused a decline in the number of fishing boats in Scotland.

Scotland

Scotland is largely a country of mountains, rolling hills and lochs, renowned for the beauty of its scenery. It can be divided into three distinct topographical regions: the Southern Uplands, the Central Lowlands and the Highlands. The Scottish coastline is deeply indented and there are hundreds of offshore islands. The largest island groups are the Western Isles and the Orkney and Shetland Islands in the far north. Another feature of the Scottish landscape is its numerous lochs. Two of the most famous are Loch Lomond and Loch Ness, both of which have attracted tourists for many years.

The Central Valley of Scotland is the industrial heartland of the country and its most densely populated area. It is here that the capital, Edinburgh, and the largest city, Glasgow, are situated.

Scotland's countryside provides a habitat for a variety of flora and fauna. Native trees include oak, beech, birch, rowan, Scots pine and larch, while the hills and moors are covered with heather. Animals and birds include some of the rarer species in the British Isles, such as the pine marten and the osprey.

The Northwest Highlands

The scenery of the Northwest Highlands is among the most wild and beautiful in the whole of the British Isles. This thinly populated region contains rugged mountains, lochs, fast-flowing rivers and waterfalls and miles of empty beaches. Some of the country's rare animals and birds live in this remote area in which the traditional occupations of farming and fishing, along with tourism, are the main economic activities.

The Scottish Highlands

Glasgow is known for its many fine buildings of architectural interest, for its art collections, such as the Burrell Collection in Pollok Park, and for its excellent universities and colleges of higher education. The mock Gothic main building of the University of Glasgow in Hillhead in the city's west end is pictured right.

LOCH NESS

Situated in the Great Glen south-west of the town of Inverness, Loch Ness is one of Scotland's most famous lochs. It is 37 kilometres or 23 miles long and, in places, as deep as 228 metres or 750 feet.

When the mist is swirling over the loch's black and peaty waters, it is hard for even the most sceptical person not to wonder if the loch's most famous and mysterious resident, 'Nessie', is lurking in the deep. Nessie is believed to be some form of aquatic dinosaur and since 1871 there have been numerous sightings of 'something in the loch'.

FINGAL'S CAVE

Fingal's Cave is a cavern on the small island of Staffa, in the Inner Hebridesb. The name Staffa means 'Pillar Island', which describes the many volcanic, black, basalt columns that are strikingly revealed in the surrounding cliffs. There are many caves on the island but Fingal's Cave is the most impressive. In 1829, Felix Mendelssohn visited the island and was so moved by its beauty that he was inspired to compose an overture, The Hebrides, also called Fingal's Cave.

Glasgow

Situated on the River Clyde, Glasgow is Scotland's largest city. It was founded in the 6th century when St Mungo built a church in what was then called *Glasgu* (meaning 'dear green place'). In the 15th century, it was granted the status of a royal burgh. With the discovery of the New World, Glasgow, facing westwards towards the Americas, came into its own. The city's merchants made excellent profits trading in tobacco, sugar, ginger and spices, cotton, coffee and timber.

During the Industrial Revolution, Glasgow expanded at an enormous rate and the industries of cotton milling, shipbuilding and heavy engineering made the city one of the world's largest industrial centres. By the early 1900s, about half the world's ocean-going ships were built on the Clyde.

Since the Second World War, heavy industry has declined and shipbuilding has almost disappeared. In recent years, many areas have been redeveloped and many new businesses now flourish in the city.

St Andrews

St Andrews, on the Fife coast, is one of Scotland's most ancient and beautiful towns. It is named after St Andrew, the disciple of Jesus who is said to have been martyred by crucifixion on an X-shaped cross. His bones were reputed to have been brought to Fife in AD 345 by a Greek monk. St Andrew became Scotland's patron saint and the symbol of his cross, the saltire, became Scotland's flag.

St Andrew's University was founded in 1410 and remains a centre of excellence and the oldest such establishment in Scotland. However, it is because of golf that St Andrews is most famous. Its Royal and Ancient Golf Club and course were established in 1754, the first of their kind in the world. Golf's ruling body is based in St Andrews and the course and its competitions attract top international players.

Edinburgh

Scotland's ancient capital is once again a modern capital city as it has been the home of the Scottish Parliament since 1999. Founded in 626, Edinburgh (the 'fortress of the hill slope') is named after Edwin, a 7th-century Angle king of Northumbria. During the Industrial Revolution, Edinburgh earned the name of 'Auld Reekie' because of the pall of smoke that enveloped the city – smoke generated by the fires and furnaces of its rapidly expanding industries.

Edinburgh is dominated by Arthur's Seat and by the great medieval castle. Arthur's Seat is an ancient volcanic plug forming a hill that rises to a height of 250 metres or 823 feet. Arthur's Seat affords excellent views of the city.

Building of the castle began in the 12th century but it was sacked by the armies of Edward I in 1296. The existing medieval castle stands on top of the granite summit of Castle Hill, at one end of the Royal Mile, the street which forms the heart of the Old Town. A number of fine medieval buildings can be found in this area, jostling together to

Edinburgh

convey a sense of the atmosphere of the past. They include Cannonball House, which has an ancient cannonball lodged in its wall, Boswell's Court, Gladstone's Land, the High Kirk of St Giles and Tron Kirk and Moubray House.

At the far end of the Royal Mile stands the royal Palace of Holyrood House, founded at the close of the 15th century. The palace stands on the site of an even more ancient royal residence and the oldest part of the present building dates from the early 1500s. Among the most famous rooms are those that were used by Mary, Queen of Scots, including the alleged spot where her secretary, David Rizzio, was stabbed to death by assassins in the pay of her husband, Lord Darnley.

The building of the New Town (begun in the late 18th century) produced many fine Georgian buildings. St Giles' Street was the principal road of the New Town. Its name was later changed to Princes' Street by King George III after his two sons. Princes' Street today is famous as Edinburgh's premier shopping area and has attractive gardens overlooked by the castle and the Old Town.

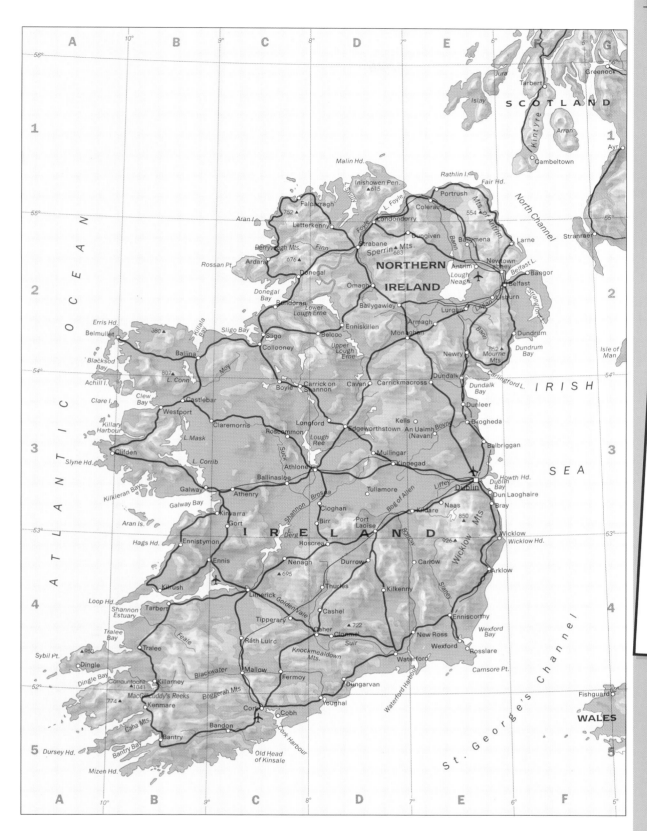

**Ireland
Scale 1 : 2 600 000**

| 0 | 20 | 40 | 60 | 80 | 100 km |

| 0 | 15 | 30 | 45 | 60 miles |

© Geddes & Grosset

THE GIANT'S CAUSEWAY, NORTHERN IRELAND

The Giant's Causeway on the north coast, east of Portrush, is one of Ireland's most famous geological features. A mass of thousands of volcanic, black basalt columns extend into the sea and form a series of giant stepping stones, some as much as 12 metres or 40 feet high. Mainly hexagonal in shape, they were formed from the cooled lava of an ancient volcanic eruption.

Legend, however, has a much more romantic story to tell. It is said that the causeway was formed by the Celtic giant, Fionn Mac Cumhaill or MacCool, so that he could visit his sweetheart on the island of Staffa in Scotland and the basalt columns do indeed reappear at Fingal's Cave on Staffa.

IRELAND

Ireland is a large island located to the west of the British mainland, which is divided politically into two countries. These are Northern Ireland in the northeast and the Republic of Ireland, or Éire, in the south and the west.

The central part of Northern Ireland is low-lying and contains the largest lake in the British Isles, Lough Neagh. A second marshy area in the southwest contains two other sizeable lakes, Lower and Upper Lough Erne. There are three upland areas – the Antrim Mountains in the northeast, the Mourne Mountains in the southeast and the Sperrin Mountains in the northwest.

Much of the Republic of Ireland is low-lying and marshy but interrupted by a number of mountain ranges. These include the Wicklow Mountains in the east, the Caha and Boggeragh Mountains in the southwest and the Derryveagh Mountains in the north. The west coast of Ireland is highly indented, with steep cliffs and numerous bays and small inlets that are exposed to the Atlantic breakers. Inland in the low-lying marshes there are numerous lakes and peat bogs drained by rivers such as the Shannon.

In common with other places in the British Isles, woodlands are now less extensive than they were in the past and animal and bird species are largely similar to those found in other parts of the British Isles.

Ireland, often called the 'Emerald Isle', is famous for its green, rolling farmlands, which support the rearing of cattle, sheep and pigs and some of the finest dairying areas in western Europe. The main areas of population are found around the two capitals, Dublin in the south and Belfast in the north. Both cities function as major commercial

MacGillicuddy's Reeks, County Kerry

KILLARNEY NATIONAL PARK

Killarney National Park in south-west Ireland is famous for its scenic beauty with its three spectacular lakes and the Macgillycuddy's Reeks Mountains in the southwest which contain Ireland's highest peak, Carrantoohill (1,041 metres or 3,414 feet). The park can be explored by coach or car, on foot, by bike or on horseback.

Southwest Ireland enjoys a mild climate that is influenced by the warm waters of the North Atlantic Drift. As a result, many Mediterranean plants grow in favoured spots. One of the most popular tourist attractions in Ireland, the park is often inundated with visitors but it is still possible to enjoy more remote areas away from the main road and the crowds.

and industrial centres. Tourism is an important industry throughout Ireland but especially in Dublin, Killarney and Galway, where the beautiful scenery and beaches are the main attraction.

Dublin

The capital city of the Irish Republic has a beautiful location on the shores of Dublin Bay at the mouth of the River Liffey, nestling beneath the Wicklow Mountains that lie to the south. In ancient times, there was a small settlement called Ath Cliath or the 'Ford of Hurdles' near the river but the history of the city proper begins about AD 841 when the Vikings set up a trading post on the south bank of the Liffey and adopted the Irish name of Dubh Linn ('Dark Pool') for their settlement. The original Dublin Castle was built in 1204 but there have been many additions over the centuries.

Christchurch Cathedral, which was extensively restored in Victorian times, has been a place of worship for many hundreds of years. The church-yard contains the ruins of the Chapter House, which was built in 1230 while beneath the cathedral itself the crypt is of even greater antiquity, dating from about 1172.

The Brazen Head is Dublin's oldest pub, dated 1668, and records show that there has been an inn here since the time of the Vikings. In Georgian times, many fine buildings were erected in the graceful style of that period. Examples include Leinster House, which is the home of the Irish Parliament or Dáil, the City Hall, formerly the Royal Exchange, the Tailor's Hall and the Bank of Ireland, which used to be the House of Parliament. The Book of Kells, a beautiful and delicately illustrated manuscript of the Celts, dating from the year 800, is housed in the library of Dublin's Trinity College.

Modern Dublin is famous for being the home of Guinness, which has been made there since 1759, and also for being the scene of the Easter Rising of 1916, the rebellion that set in motion the events that led to the founding of the Irish Free State in 1921. Dublin's large Phoenix Park contains the official residence of the Irish President as well as a famous racecourse and zoo.

Belfast

Belfast's origins date back to 1177 when the Normans built a castle there, around which a village had developed by the Middle Ages. At the end of the 17th century, Huguenot refugees came to Belfast from France, bringing with them their skills in linen-making for which the city became famous. During the Industrial Revolution, Belfast enjoyed rapid and successful growth. Its position at the head of a large sea lough meant that it was well situated for the import of raw materials. Many industries developed and flourished, including engineering, shipbuilding, rope-making, manufacturing and textiles. At the height of its growth, Belfast doubled in size every ten years, and some of the city's finest buildings date from this period of prosperity and expansion. Belfast became Northern Ireland's capital city in 1920.

Today, although shipbuilding has declined, Belfast has the largest dry dock in the world for the servicing and repair of vessels along with deep-water facilities. Modern Belfast has developed

The Botanic Gardens, Belfast

advanced technologies to replace the traditional industries that have declined. The old dockland areas are being redeveloped and modernised, some for small businesses and others for housing and other projects.

Londonderry

Londonderry is the only walled city in Ireland with its walls still intact. It began life as a monastery founded by St Columba in AD 546. The monastery and the settlement that grew around it were regularly attacked from the sea by the Vikings, Normans and, in the late 16th century, by the English. In the 17th century, the Twelve Companies of the Corporation of London were granted the remains of the town then known as Derry and it became Londonderry for the first time. Settlers from mainland Britain were brought to Londonderry and massive protective walls were built all round the town. Today, visitors can almost make a complete circuit of these walls which have survived repeated attacks over the centuries.

Londonderry flourished during the linen boom of the 19th century which also saw the development of the city as a seaport. A city of music and culture, Londonderry is an ideal base from which to tour the counties of Londonderry, Donegal and Tyrone.

Rathlin Island

Rathlin Island lies some 9 kilometres or 6 miles off the north coast of Ireland. The barrenness of this cliff-ridden island somehow reflects its stormy history. It was the first place in Ireland to be raided by the Vikings and it has been the scene of three bloody massacres. The cliffs are a good place to go birdwatching and it is possible to rent a boat for scuba diving around the many wrecks offshore. Bruce's Cave on the northeast point of the island is supposedly the cave where Robert the Bruce took shelter after being defeated by the English. While there he watched a spider determinedly trying to spin its web and this persuaded him to return to Scotland where he defeated the English at the Battle of Bannockburn.

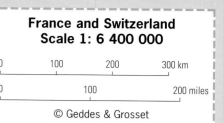

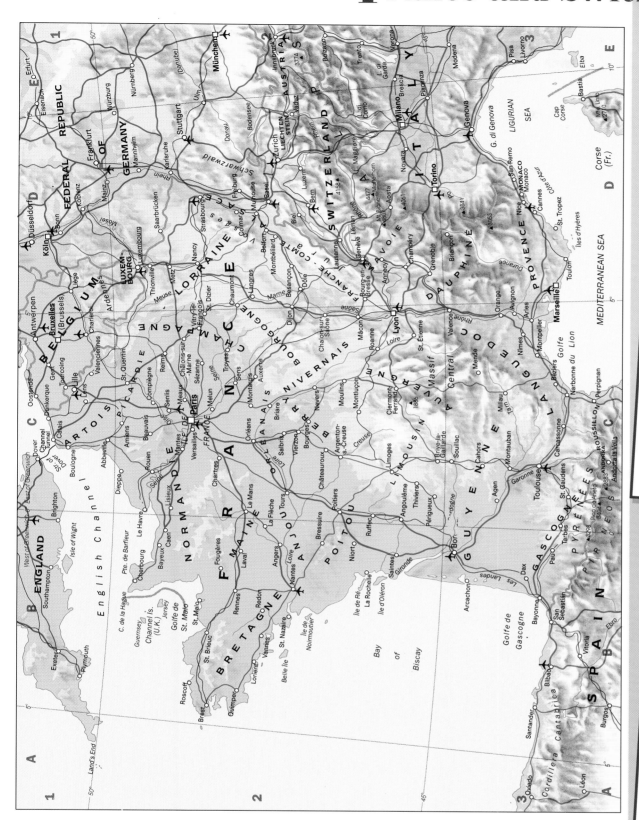

FRANCE

Language/s spoken: French
Currency: French Franc
Travel requirements: return ticket and valid passport usually required but visitors should contact relevant authority before departure for more specific information
Major cities: Paris (capital), Bordeaux, Lyon, Marseille, Nantes, Nice, Toulouse, Strasbourg
Climate: temperate climate in the north and Mediterranean climate in the south
Crime and safety: pickpockets and bag snatchers around stations and tourist areas

THE EIFFEL TOWER

Perhaps more than any other structure, the Eiffel Tower symbolises the unique nature of Paris and its image is instantly recognised throughout the world. Some 321 metres or 1,052 feet high, it was completed in 1889. The tower was the brainchild of the renowned engineer, Gustave Eiffel, who had also been consulted about the design of New York's Statue of Liberty. Visitors can ascend the tower in three stages, being rewarded by spectacular views of Paris at each level.

FRANCE

France, including the island of Corsica, is the largest country in western Europe and a prominent member of the European Union. It is situated in the northwest of the European mainland and has coastlines on the English Channel, the Atlantic Ocean, and the Mediterranean Sea. Its principal topographical features are the mountain ranges of the Massif Central and the higher Alps, Jura and Pyrenees, an upland plateau in the southeast and a large area of rolling plains in the north. Mont Blanc on the France–Italy border is the highest point in the Alps at 4,807 metres or 15,770 feet. The principal rivers of France are the Seine, Rhône, Loire and Garonne along with their many tributaries. Many of these are navigable and are used commercially for the transport of freight.

France was once a largely agricultural country and is famous for its fine wines, champagne and brandy but it has become increasingly industrialised and is now a leading manufacturer of a wide range of goods that are produced both for the home market and for export. It has valuable mineral reserves, including iron ore, petroleum, coal, natural gas, salt, zinc, potash, uranium and lead. A significant proportion of the country is wooded, particularly the marginal areas, which are less suitable for farming, and forestry is an important factor in the economy. Fishing is carried out from many of the towns and villages along the country's extensive coastline.

Paris

France's beautiful capital city is located on the River Seine. It is built on both banks of the river and on the two islands in the middle – the Ile St Louis

THE ARC DE TRIOMPHE, PARIS

The Arc de Triomphe in Paris is a triumphal arch begun by Napoleon I to commemorate his victories of 1805–6 and finally completed in 1836. It is 50 metres or 164 feet high and overlooks the famous Champs-Elysees and the other eleven wide avenues which form the Place-Charles-de-Gaulle – probably the world's first organised roundabout.

SWITZERLAND

Language/s spoken: German, French and some Italian, English is spoken by many
Currency: Swiss Franc
Travel requirements: return ticket and valid passport required, best to contact relevant authority before departure
Major cities: Berne (capital), Zurich, Basle, Geneva, Lausanne
Climate: cool to cold in the Alpine regions, milder elsewhere
Crime and safety: take sensible precautions

The Matterhorn, Switzerland

and the Ile de la Cité. There has been a settlement at the site for at least 2,000 years, and the city itself has been famous for centuries. It has long been a magnet for artists, musicians and writers and was particularly famous for its opera, ballet and street cafés and for being at the centre of the Impressionist movement.

Modern Paris remains one of the most popular cities in the world and visitors come to experience its culture, high fashion, elegant shops and nightlife and to view its many famous historical sights, including the Eiffel Tower, the Arc de Triomphe and the Cathedral of Notre Dame. Notre Dame (Our Lady) is one of the greatest and most beautiful Gothic cathedrals in Europe. It stands on the Ile de la Cité, the island in the middle of the River Seine where Paris began. Construction started in 1163, with Pope Alexander III laying the first stone, and continued for 182 years until it was completed in 1345. Inside, the end walls of the transepts are nearly two thirds glass, including two beautiful rose windows, allowing light to fill the cathedral. Its famous gargoyles were added in the 19th century during extensive renovations. Ravaged by pollution and the weather, restoration is ongoing to this day. South of Paris is the huge Palace of Versailles, which was built by King Louis IV in the 17th century. A more recent attraction is the Euro-Disney theme park located outside the city.

The Camargue

The Camargue is an extensive area of flat land in the delta of the River Rhône near the Mediterranean coast, south of Arles and west of Marseilles. A region of fields, canals, marshes and pools with abundant wildlife, including black bulls and white horses, the Camargue is protected as a nature reserve.

SWITZERLAND

The beautiful mountainous country of Switzerland is dominated by the Alps, which occupy over 60 per cent of the total land area. A second lower mountain range, the Jura, occurs in the west of the country and between them lies a plateau region around 48 kilometres or 30 miles wide at a height of about 396 metres or 1,300 feet above sea level. Switzerland has many spectacular lakes, most of them nestling at the foot of the mountains and some quite large. They include Lake Geneva (Lac Léman), Lake Lugano and Lake Constance.

In all, about a quarter of the total land area is forested and timber is a valuable natural resource although some woodlands have been adversely affected by air pollution. Much of Switzerland is unsuitable for agriculture and most farms are fairly small, family-run enterprises that receive government subsidies. Emmenthal and Gruyère cheese and chocolate are valuable export products.

Switzerland has few mineral resources but its lakes and rivers enable it to generate abundant hydroelectric power. Most raw materials and food have to be imported but Switzerland is an affluent country whose people enjoy a high standard of living. It is renowned for the excellent quality of its

manufacturing, particularly of watches and clocks, precision tools and machines and engineering products. Pharmaceuticals, textiles, hand-crafted products, service industries and tourism are other important areas of the economy. However, it is as a premier centre for international banking that Switzerland is perhaps most respected and renowned, with Zürich being the main city involved in this activity.

Zürich

Zürich is situated beside the Lake of Zürich beneath a backdrop of snow-capped peaks. It is the largest city in Switzerland and an important centre for trading in gold, business and finance and the manufacture of a wide range of goods. Zürich has always played a significant part in the history of Switzerland, becoming an important ecclesiastical centre by AD 800 and seeing the start of the Reformation in the early 16th century. Industry and cultural activities continued to flourish in the 18th and 19th centuries, providing the foundation for the modern city of today. Zürich itself has many fine buildings and numerous attractions for visitors.

Geneva

Geneva is situated picturesquely beside Lake Geneva (Lac Léman) between the Alps and the Jura mountains in southwest Switzerland. People have lived in the area around the lake for many centuries. The growth of the settlement was favoured by its ideal location at the crossroads of ancient trade routes linking northern Europe with the Mediterranean Sea. The name Geneva is first referred to in the writings of Julius Caesar and by the Middle Ages the town had become an important centre for commerce and trade. John Calvin settled in Geneva in the 1540s and commerce, trade and banking prospered during the years of the Reformation.

During the 18th and 19th centuries, watchmaking and the gold industry flourished and Geneva became the home of philosophers, writers and scientists, among whom were Voltaire and Rousseau. In 1863, the organisation that was later to become the International Committee of the Red Cross was founded in Geneva. Many international organisations are associated with Geneva and, in 1919, the city became the home of the League of Nations and later of the European arm of the United Nations Organisation. It continues to be a favoured location for high level international meetings and conferences in the fields of politics, business and worldwide affairs.

MONACO

The minute principality of Monaco is situated on the French Riviera and its coastline stretches for some three kilometres or two miles. Monaco is the haunt of the rich and famous, with sumptuous yachts moored in the harbour of the resort of Monte Carlo, where the renowned casino is located. Monte Carlo is also famous for its car rally and its world championship Grand Prix motor race. The royal palace of the Grimaldi family is situated just outside the town of Monaco.

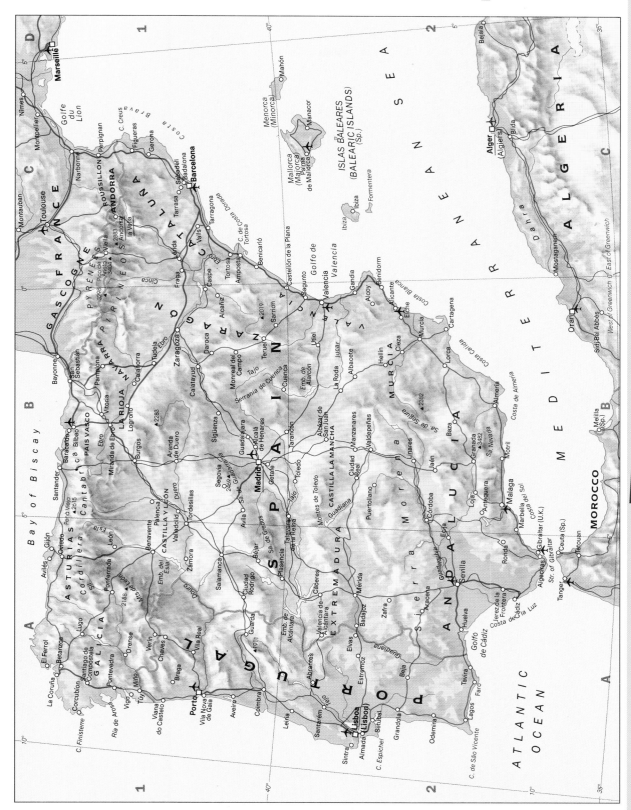

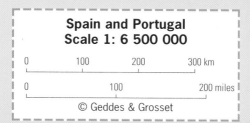

Spain

Language/s spoken: Spanish (Castillan)

Currency: Peseta

Travel requirements: return ticket and valid passport usually required but all potential visitors should contact relevant authority before departure for more specific information

Major cities: Madrid (capital), Barcelona, Valencia, Seville, Malaga, Bilbao, Zaragosa

Climate: varies from dry and hot in the south to temperate in the north

Crime and safety: street crime can be a problem in tourist areas and some cities

Flamenco

Flamenco is the traditional gypsy form of the dance, song and music of Andalucia in southern Spain. An early forerunner of the flamenco guitar was already being played in Andalucia in the 15th century. Gypsy dancing is exciting and passionate, involving colourful costumes, the clicking and stamping of feet, fingers and castanets performed to the intense, unique music of the flamenco guitar.

Spain and Portugal are the two largest countries occupying the Iberian Peninsula, which juts out into the Atlantic Ocean on the western edge of Europe. The small independent principality of Andorra and the self-governing British colony of Gibraltar are also part of the peninsula.

SPAIN

Spain includes the Balearic Islands in the Mediterranean Sea, the Canary Islands in the Atlantic Ocean and the enclaves of Ceuta and Melilla on the coast of Morocco in North Africa.

Spain has a long Mediterranean coast and is a largely mountainous country with a dry, elevated central plateau called the Meseta. The two principal mountain ranges are the Pyrenees, which straddle the border with France, and the Sierra Nevada, which run roughly west to east behind the Mediterranean coast. Considerable areas of Spain are relatively wild and uninhabited and are home to some of Europe's rarer animals, such as the wolf, lynx, wildcat and mountain goat.

Agriculture and fishing still play a significant role in the country's economy and while traditional industries such as shipbuilding, iron and steel and textiles have declined, there has been considerable expansion in new areas such as information technology and electronics. The country has useful reserves of iron ore, copper, lead, zinc, mercury, gypsum and silver but poor fossil fuel reserves. Electricity is generated from hydroelectric schemes and nuclear power and through the burning of mainly imported fossil fuels. Tourism makes a significant contribution to the economy. Each year, numerous visitors come to enjoy Spain's Mediterranean coastal resorts, historical cities and the unspoiled towns and villages of its interior.

Ronda, Spain

Spain and Portugal

THE ALGARVE, PORTUGAL

The Algarve region of southern Portugal enjoys long, hot summers and mild winters and has beautiful sandy beaches washed by the waves of the Atlantic Ocean. In the springtime, the Algarve is at its most beautiful, being adorned with a variety of brightly coloured flowers. The Algarve attracts large numbers of visitors, particularly from other parts of Europe.

CAPE ST VINCENT, PORTUGAL

The peninsula of Cape St Vincent in the southwest of Portugal is the southwestern extremity of Europe. In earlier times, when people believed that the Earth was flat, Cape St Vincent was thought to be the end of the known world. High, rocky cliffs and a lighthouse mark the point on the Cape from where visitors can enjoy a magnificent view of the vast expanse of the Atlantic Ocean.

Madrid

Spain's capital city is located in the centre of the country in the dry, plateau region and there has been a settlement on the site since Roman times. Most of Madrid's grand and beautiful buildings, including the famous Prado museum, were constructed in the mid-to-late 18th century. These form the historic heart of the city which has remained relatively unspoiled by the massive growth and urban sprawl that has developed around it.

The museums and art galleries in the centre of Madrid, particularly the Prado National Museum, the Thyssen-Bornemisza Museum and the Centro de Arte Reina Sofia National Museum, together house one of the world's greatest art collections. Of particular importance is the Prado Museum, which is home to an extensive collection of Spanish art, including works by El Greco, Velásquez, Goya, Murillo, Ribera and Zubaran.

Cordoba

Founded by the Romans, the city of Cordoba is situated in southern Spain on the River Guadalquivir. Roman engineers constructed a great bridge to connect the two banks of the river, which still exists today as El Puente Romano. When the Moors swept through the Iberian Peninsula in the 8th century, Cordoba came to prominence as the capital of their kingdom of El-Andalus.

Today, this phase of the city's history is preserved in its beautiful Moorish architecture, of which the most magnificent example is the church-mosque of Mezquita. When Renaissance and then Baroque ideas of architecture and art spread to Spain, most of the old mosques in the country were knocked down so that new Christian places of worship could be erected. However, the magnificence of Cordoba and its Moorish architecture had long been recognised and a baroque cathedral was simply built in the centre of the Mezquita as it existed then. This created the totally unique blending of styles and forms that exists today in this astonishing building.

PORTUGAL

Portugal, to the west of Spain, includes the island groups of Madeira and the Azores in the Atlantic. Mainland Portugal has a long Atlantic coastline and is mountainous only in the north. To the south, lie the extensive plains of the Alenteja region, which are broken by a range of hills that divide them from the coastal plain of the Algarve. The Iberian Peninsula is traversed by several large rivers that rise in Spain and flow on across Portugal, often through deep gorges cut through the rocks of the mountains, such as the Tejo (Tajo in Spain) with the capital city of Lisbon (Lisboa) at its mouth.

As agricultural methods remain traditional in many areas, wild animals and birds are able to flourish relatively undisturbed. Manufacturing has assumed greater importance as the country slowly moves away from a largely agriculture-based economy but about 25 per cent of people are still engaged in farming and live outside the main cities in small rural villages. About 40 per cent of Portugal is wooded and the country is a leading exporter of cork. It also manufactures other wood products and paper. The country's long coastline has meant that Portuguese fishermen have always enjoyed ready access to the Atlantic fishing grounds.

Portugal has some valuable mineral resources and these include copper ores, wolframite, coal, kaolin, gold, tin and iron ore. A petrochemical plant and oil refinery is located near Lisbon and hydroelectric power has been developed in recent years. Portugal is also renowned for certain high quality craft products, especially lace, pottery and tiles and for its port wine, named after the city of Porto (Oporto).

Porto, Portugal

Lisbon

Lisbon, the capital city of Portugal, is situated in the west of the country and is built on seven hills around the estuary of the River Tejo. The seafaring Phoenicians were the first people to build a settlement on the site, which they called Alis Ubbo (Serene Harbour). The name Lisbon was later derived from the old Phoenician name.

Buildings of note include, first and foremost, the castle of Sao Jorge, which reflects many centuries of human occupation – Roman, Visigoth, Moor and Portuguese. The ruined palace inside its massive outer walls was built in the 13th century and was the home of the Portuguese kings for three centuries. Later, when a new royal palace was built at another site in the city, the castle of Sao Jorge served as a prison.

The white limestone monastery of Jerónimos was built by Emanuel I to honour and express gratitude to his patron saint for the discovery of the ocean route to India and the establishment of the spice trade. The interior is noted for its fine sculptures and stone carvings, which include figures of St Jerónimos and the Virgin and Child, animals, birds, vegetables and fruits.

The pink rococo-style Palace of Queluz was built during the 18th century and was heavily influenced by Versailles. It is lavishly furnished and decorated in the elegant and extravagant style of the period and has fine formal gardens containing statues and fountains. Today, the palace is used to house and entertain visiting foreign dignitaries and for banquets and formal state occasions, as well as being a considerable tourist attraction.

Italy is a long boot-shaped peninsula that sticks out into the Mediterranean Sea in southern Europe. The Balkan States are Slovenia, Croatia, Bosnia-Herzegovina, the Federal Republic of Yugoslavia, Bulgaria, Albania, Macedonia and Greece. From the snow-covered slopes of the Italian Alps to the sunny beaches of the Greek Islands, this region offers a huge variety of landscapes and climates.

ITALY

The huge peaks of the Alps and Dolomites form Italy's northern border with France, Switzerland, Austria and Slovenia. Towards the foothills of the mountains lie a number of large lakes of which the most famous are Maggiore, Como and Garda. These form the spectacular and beautiful region of the Italian Lake District, which attracts many visitors who come to climb in the mountains and to ski and enjoy winter sports.

The fertile Lombardy Plain lies to the south. Numerous rivers rise in the northern mountains and many become tributaries of the great River Po which flows eastwards and drains the Lombardy Plain before emptying into the Adriatic Sea. South of the Lombardy Plain lies the familiar long 'boot' of peninsular Italy, which comprises the majority of the country. The Apennine Mountains extend down the length of the peninsula. The principal rivers of the peninsula are the Arno, which flows through Florence (Firenze) and Pisa, and the Tiber (Tevere), which runs through Rome.

Agriculture remains important to the Italian economy and Italy is one of the leading producers in Europe of wine and olive oil. A variety of cereal crops are grown and the dairy industry produces a number of cheeses, such as Parmesan and Gorgonzola.

The Italians transformed their economy after the Second World War, embarking upon a rapid process of industrialisation and the development of manufacturing from an entirely agricultural base. Tourism is also an important contributor to the economy.

Rome

Rome, Italy's capital city, probably offers visitors the chance to see more than any other city in the world. A modern European capital city, Rome also offers tourists the opportunity to explore the remains of the various eras that are part of its 2,000 years of history. Places to look out for include the Coliseum and the Forum, ancient basilicas, the fountains and churches of the Baroque period and the Vatican City, while a day trip away are Hadrian's Villa at Tivoli and the ancient site of Ostea Antica.

Venice

The ancient and beautiful city of Venice (Venezia) is situated in northeast Italy and throughout its long history has been one of the most important and most visited places in Europe. It is located on the Gulf of Venice and is built on a series of 118 low-lying islands in a natural lagoon that is protected from the sea by sandbars. The islands, on which the different parts of the city are built, are separated by the narrow canals for which Venice is renowned. These are spanned by over 400 bridges, many of which are of great age, beneath which pass the black-painted gondolas – the wooden boats which

Gondolas in Venice

are the traditional form of passenger transport, each propelled by a single oarsman or gondolier.

The heart of Venice and its oldest part is the Rialto with the largest of the canals, the Grand Canal, following a serpentine route of about three kilometres or two miles to divide the city into two halves. Today the most visited part of Venice, in the heart of the old city, is the Piazza San Marco (St Mark's Place). This contains the great Basilica or Cathedral of St Mark and the Doge's Palace, which was the official home of the elected head of state. The famous Bridge of Sighs, across which criminals were led to their fate, spans the canal from the palace to the city's prison. The 16th-century arched and enclosed Rialto Bridge is the most famous of the three canals that cross the Grand Canal and it has a full span of 27.5 metres or 90 feet. Subsidence has long been a problem in Venice and the early architects allowed for movement in their building designs. It is hoped that remedial work to shore up buildings, which continues to be carried out from time to time, will prevent further sinking.

Elba

The Italian island of Elba is situated in the Ligurian Sea between mainland Italy and the island of Corsica. Its strategic position and rich mineral wealth have made Elba a place of importance throughout human history. One of the most significant figures of the 19th century, Napoleon Bonaparte, was imprisoned on Elba for 10 months. Elba has also been famed since Roman times for its fine wines, which continue to be enjoyed today.

Corsica

The island of Corsica (Corse) in the Mediterranean Sea lies about 16 kilometres or 10 miles north of Sardinia. Corsica has belonged to France since 1748 but enjoys a close affinity with Italy, its near neighbour. Because its natural vegetation consists of aromatic plants and shrubs, it is sometimes known as 'the scented isle'. Most of the island consists of rugged mountainous country but the coast has some beautiful sandy bays and deeply indented, rocky coves. The island has been settled since prehistoric times and has many sites of archaeological interest.

ITALY

Language/s spoken: Italian, English in some resorts and cities
Currency: Italian Lira
Travel requirements: valid passport usually required but all potential visitors should contact relevant authority before departure for more specific information
Major cities: Rome (capital), Milan, Naples, Turin, Genoa, Palermo, Florence
Climate: mild in spring and autumn with hot summers, cold winters in the mountains
Crime and safety: some street crime in urban areas

ST PETER'S BASILICA, VATICAN CITY

In AD 324, the Emperor Constantine ordered the building of a basilica over what was believed to have been the tomb of St Peter, the disciple and apostle of Christ. Work on a new and more magnificent building began in 1506. The great Michelangelo, at the age of 71, became chief architect in 1546 and was responsible for the Basilica's beautiful, light-filled dome, which is supported by four great pillars and is 138 metres or 452 feet high. Exquisite statues, art treasures and sculptured monuments are to be found throughout the building, such as Michelangelo's *Pieta* and Bernini's *St Peter's* chair.

POMPEII, HERCULANEUM AND MOUNT VESUVIUS

Vesuvius is an active volcano located near the Italian city of Naples, which has erupted several times throughout its long history. The most famous eruption occurred in August AD 79 when the nearby Roman towns of Pompeii and Herculaneum were devastated and about 3,360 people lost their lives. After hundreds of years, the towns were rediscovered and excavated and, because of their remarkable state of preservation, they have revealed a fascinating insight into the Roman way of life in the 1st century.

Ruins of a Greek temple, Agrigento, Sicily

Sardinia

The Italian island of Sardinia (Sardegna) is the second largest in the Mediterranean region, surpassed in size only by Sicily. Located south of Corsica in the Tyrrhenian Sea, Sardinia is a rugged, mountainous island with a long human history dating back to prehistoric times. It has much to offer the visitor from beautiful beaches to the remains of the various civilisations that have passed through the island.

Sicily

The island of Sicily (Sicilia) lies just beyond the toe of the Italian Peninsula and is separated from Italy by the Strait of Messina. The Aeolian Islands (Isole Eolie), including the island of Stromboli, lie to the north of Sicily.

Sicily is the largest island in the Mediterranean

Sea. There is much to explore, from the foothills and craters of Mount Etna, Europe's highest and most frequently erupting volcano, to the Greek temples at Agrigento and the Baroque churches of Palermo, the island's capital. With its unspoilt coastline, mountainous interior and historical remains, this beautiful island has lots to offer the visitor.

SAN MARINO

The Republic of San Marino is one of two small, independent enclaves, of which the Vatican City is the second, entirely surrounded by the country of Italy, which have survived from the time when almost all of the region consisted of autonomous city states. Since 1862, as the rest of Italy moved towards unification, San Marino has maintained treaties of friendship with its all-embracing neigh-

bour. The country has a population of about 25,000 people. The medieval capital, also called San Marino, is built on a hill and is surrounded by ancient, fortified city walls within which several fine, old buildings are preserved.

THE VATICAN CITY

The Vatican City is the smallest country in the world. It is a fully independent state, surrounded by a city wall, within the Italian capital of Rome and is governed by the Pope and the Roman Catholic Church. It was formally created in 1929 and is the last of the Papal States – the territories that once came under the direct control of the Pope. The old city walls, which are breached by six gates, enclose some of the most famous buildings in the world, notably St Peter's Basilica and the Palace of the Vatican which contains the Sistine Chapel, a number of museums, one of the world's finest libraries and 1,000 rooms and offices.

MALTA

Malta is an archipelago of three large inhabited islands and two small uninhabited ones, which are situated in the Mediterranean Sea between North Africa and Sicily. Malta is the largest of the three inhabited islands, Gozo the second largest and Comino by far the smallest. Comino is an idyllic island paradise with beautiful coves and bays, sparkling clear seas, just one hotel and very few people. Tourism has expanded considerably in recent years, with many visitors attracted by Malta's coastal scenery, pleasant climate and rich archaeological and historical heritage.

Italy and the Balkans

LJUBLJANA, SLOVENIA

Slovenia's capital city, Ljubljana, whose name means 'beloved', is the country's largest city. It began as a Roman town whose remains can be seen throughout the city. Its many pale-coloured churches and buildings date from the Hapsburg period, earning the city the nickname of 'White Ljubljana'. The most beautiful parts of the city can be found in the Old Town below the castle and along the embankment of the Ljubljanica river.

THE ROSE FIELDS OF BULGARIA

Bulgaria is famous for its rose fields in the Kazanlak region. The rose petals are made into oil (attar of roses) which is exported worldwide as a base for the manufacture of perfume. Bulgaria provides about three quarters of the world production of rose oil and the flower petals are picked before sunrise to preserve their beautiful fragrance.

A Byzantine cathedral in Bulgaria

SLOVENIA

Slovenia is a small country that, prior to 1991, was a republic in the former Yugoslavia. It is a mountainous country, bounded by Croatia in the southwest, Hungary in the east, Austria in the north and Italy in the west. Slovenia also has a short stretch of coastline bordering the Adriatic Sea where the port of Koper is located. The Julian Alps are in the densely forested, northwestern part of the country. Slovenia's capital, Ljubljana, is situated fairly centrally within the upland region.

About half of Slovenia's people live in small, rural farming communities where cattle and sheep rearing are particularly important but crops are also grown.

CROATIA

Croatia is folded on two of its sides around neighbouring Bosnia-Herzegovina. The country has a broad northern region and a long strip of land along the Adriatic coast. The region behind the Adriatic coast is mainly mountainous and includes the Dinaric Alps. Dalmatia is a lower-lying region located along the Adriatic coast. Considerable areas are forested and wild animals include bears, wolves, wild cats, and wild boars.

Croatia has various mineral resources including coal, petroleum, iron ore and bauxite. Prior to the outbreak of war in 1991, Croatia was a fairly prosperous republic of the former Yugoslavia, surpassed in productivity only by Slovenia and accounting for one quarter of Yugoslavia's national wealth. However, the fighting in the region has devastated the country's land, economy and infrastructure, and recovery is likely to be a slow process. Croatia's capital, Zagreb, is situated fairly centrally in the northern region.

BOSNIA-HERZEGOVINA

Bosnia-Herzegovina, more commonly known as Bosnia, declared its independence from the former Yugoslavia in 1992 and became the scene of bitter ethnic fighting in the years that followed. Its capital is Sarajevo. Most of the country is mountainous, with ranges of the Dinaric Alps being the principal topographical feature in the west and south. The limestone plateau further to the east and the north is a second prominent feature while the northern strip of the country is lower-lying and densely forested.

The country possesses valuable mineral resources including coal, iron ore, manganese, lead, copper and silver and has vast potential for the development of hydroelectric power. The main industries are agriculture, mining, manufacturing and forestry but the economy has suffered greatly because of the fighting in the country.

FEDERAL REPUBLIC OF YUGOSLAVIA (FRY)

The Federal Republic of Yugoslavia now consists of Serbia and Montenegro, which are the largest and the smallest of the six republics of the former Yugoslavia. The bulk of the country is occupied by Serbia, with Montenegro forming a smaller region in the south and west. In addition, there are two ethnic enclaves within the territory of Yugoslavia – the provinces of Kosovo in the south, which is home to Muslim Albanians who have been in ongoing conflict with Serbia over their status, and of Vojvodina in the north which is home to people of Hungarian descent.

Yugoslavia was recognised as an independent republic by the European Union in 1996 but, because of its role in the wars in the region in the 1990s, the country has been slow to gain further international recognition.

The northern part of Serbia consists of fertile, low-lying plains drained by the River Danube (Dunav) on which the capital, Belgrade (Beograd), is situated. In the east, the land rises to form the ridges and hollows of the limestone plateau while mountains and hills predominate in the southeast. Dense forests cover much of the southern part of upland Serbia. Montenegro is also mountainous and has a 192-kilometre or 120-mile stretch of coastline along the Adriatic Sea providing the republic with its main port of Bar. Here the vegetation is more Mediterranean in type, with citrus fruit trees, palms, olives, figs, grape vines and pomegranates.

About 50 per cent of the people live in rural areas while the rest reside in or near the larger cities or towns, especially in the capital, Belgrade. The economy was severely affected by the war and by the imposition of sanctions by the international community during the early 1990s. Economic sanctions were lifted in 1995 and the situation improved slightly but many ecomomic activities were again affected by NATO's bombing of the country in 1999.

BULGARIA

Bulgaria is bounded in the west by Yugoslavia, in the southwest by Macedonia, in the south by Greece, in the southeast by Turkey and in the north, by Romania. The River Danube (Dunav) flows along Bulgaria's northern boundary and in the east the country borders the Black Sea – a popular area for tourists.

Hills or mountains cover about half the country with a 'finger' of the Balkan Mountains, the Stara Planina, extending eastwards from the northwest of the country. In the south, the Rhodopi Mountains straddle the border with Greece. Sofiya, the country's capital, is situated in the western central region of the country as is the Rila mountain chain.

Farming is responsible for about 16 per cent of the country's national wealth but manufacturing and industrial processes are the largest contributors to the Bulgarian economy. The country has some valuable mineral reserves, including coal, iron ore, lead, zinc, copper and manganese but oil has to be imported. Coal mining, the production of iron ore and other minerals, fishing, forestry and tourism are other significant contributors to the economy.

ALBANIA

Albania is a small, mountainous republic bounded by Montenegro (Yugoslavia) in the northwest, Serbia (Yugoslavia) in the north, Macedonia in the east and Greece in the southeast. The country's western border is formed by the Adriatic Sea and behind the coast the land is low-lying and fertile although rather marshy in places. Away from the coast, the land rises to form a series of wild and rugged hills and mountains. In the north these form the southernmost extension of the Dinaric Alps and are called the Albanian Alps.

Many large rivers, including the Drin and the Vijose, rise in the mountains and flow in a generally westerly direction towards the sea. There are also numerous beautiful freshwater lakes and extensive forests covering the hills and lower mountain slopes. Along the Adriatic coast, where a Mediterranean-type climate prevails, citrus fruit trees, olives, vines, palms, figs, laurel and myrtle are able to grow. The capital, Tirane, is situated in the centre of the country.

Albania is one of the most impoverished and poorly developed countries in Europe, and this is largely because of factors in its recent political history. However, the country possesses valuable mineral resources, especially chromium, nickel, copper, iron ore, coal, petroleum and pyrites, and the mining and processing of these minerals is important to the Albanian economy. Some industries and manufacturing plants have developed and agriculture, fishing and forestry are also important to the country's economy.

MACEDONIA (FYROM)

Macedonia or The Former Yugoslav Republic of Macedonia (FYROM) is a small landlocked country in southeastern Europe. The republic shares a border with Albania in the west, Yugoslavia (Serbia) in the north, Bulgaria in the east and Greece in the south. The characteristic topographical features of the country are steep-sided, rugged hills and mountains dissected by deep valleys. There are numerous rivers and streams, the largest and most important of which is the Vardar.

FYROM's capital, Skopje, is located at the head of the Vardar river in the northwestern territory near the border with Yugoslavia. There are many freshwater lakes throughout the FYROM, including Lake Ohrid (Ohridsko Jezero) and Lake Prespa (Prespansko Jezero). About 35 per cent of the country is forested, providing valuable timber resources.

Agriculture is a very important part of the economy with the other main activity being coal mining. Mineral reserves include zinc, manganese and lead. There are some manufacturing, construction and service industries as well as forestry and freshwater fishing. Tourism is a further contributor to the economy and is now starting to revive, having been badly affected by the fighting in the region in the early 1990s.

GREECE

Greece is a southern European country consisting of a mainland portion and more than 1,400 islands that make up around 20 per cent of the country's total land area. Mainland Greece occupies the southernmost portion of the Balkans Peninsula and shares borders with Albania in the northwest, the FYROM (Macedonia) and Bulgaria in the north and Turkey in the northeast. The Aegean Sea lies to the east, the Mediterranean Sea to the south and the Ionian Sea to the west. The Ionian Islands (Ionioi Nisoi) lie off the coast of the western mainland in the

Ionian Sea, of which the most northerly is Corfu (Kerkira), situated only three kilometres or two miles from the Albanian mainland.

The remaining Greek islands are scattered throughout the Aegean Sea. They include the Cyclades (Kikladhes) group in the southeast, Crete (Kriti) in the south, the Dodecanese group (Dhodhekanisos), including Rhodes (Rodhos), just west of mainland Turkey, the northern Aegean Islands, such as Thasos, Limnos and Lesvos, and the Northern Sporades (Voriai Sporhadhes), situated off the eastern coast of Greece. In general, the islands are quite arid, hilly and stony with thin soils that are difficult to cultivate. The larger ones are visited each year by numerous tourists who are attracted by the beautiful scenery, warm climate and superb archaeological and historical sites.

The northwestern and central regions of mainland Greece are rugged and mountainous, the main chain being the Pindus Mountains (Pindos Oros). Westwards the hills gradually become lower with flatter land towards the coast of the Ionian Sea. A series of extensive plains interrupted by hills and mountains lie in the northeast while to the east of the Pindus Mountains lies the extensive plain of Thessaly, a fertile agricultural region. The southeastern 'finger' of mainland Greece is called Attica and is one of the most important regions historically being the cradle of the city states such as Athens. It consists of a series of hills, valleys and plains, the most famous of which is the Athenian Plain. The Peloponnese Peninsula is largely mountainous, with steep ridges and narrow valleys extending in a northwest–southeast direction, although there is some lower, flatter land in the west.

Greece is not as densely forested as it was in the past but both deciduous and pine forests still occur on the hillsides. At lower levels and around the coasts, citrus fruits, olives, pomegranates, figs, dates and grapes are cultivated. Forestry and fishing are carried out on a small scale. The country is relatively poor in mineral resources although it has significant oil and natural gas reserves in the Aegean Sea.

Greece has traditionally been an agricultural country but it has undergone a rapid process of industrialisation since the Second World War. This received a fresh impetus when the country joined the European Union in 1981. Tourism and service industries are also very important to the economy.

Crete

Crete (Kriti) is the largest and most southerly of the islands belonging to Greece and is situated in the eastern Mediterranean and southern Aegean Sea. It lies about 100 kilometres or 63 miles southeast of mainland Greece and around 320 kilometres or 200 miles north of Africa. The Cyclades Islands are located to the north across the Sea of Crete and the Dodecanese Islands (of which Rhodes is the largest) in the north and east. The long island is divided lengthways by three series of mountain ranges where visitors can hike and enjoy the wild flowers on the lower slopes. Crete also has beautiful sandy beaches and small fishing ports for the tourist to enjoy as well as many rich and varied archaeological sites to explore and this combined with the hot summers and mild winters of its Mediterranean climate make it an ideal holiday destination.

The Parthenon is the most famous of a number of temples and public buildings constructed during the 5th century BC that make up the Acropolis of Athens. An acropolis was a fortified citadel built on top of a nearby hill and overlooking the ordinary houses and buildings of a city.

BELGIUM

Language/s spoken: Flemish and French
Currency: Belgian Franc
Travel requirements: return ticket and valid passport usually required but all potential visitors should contact relevant authority before departure for more specific information
Major cities: Brussels (capital), Antwerp, Charleroi, Ghent, Liege, Bruges
Climate: warm from May to September and cold in the winter months, rain throughout the year
Crime and safety: take sensible precautions

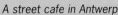
A street cafe in Antwerp

Central Europe extends from the Baltic Sea in the north to the Alps in the south. From the northeastern border of France, it extends through the Low Countries of Belgium, the Netherlands and Luxembourg, Germany, Lichtenstein, Austria, Hungary, Slovakia, the Czech Republic and Poland to Lithuania, Belarus, Ukraine, Romania and Moldova in the east. This is a region that includes some countries in eastern Europe still unfamiliar to many which are opening up more and more to visitors as they become stable and settled.

BELGIUM

Belgium is a small country with three topographical regions: the elevated and forested Ardennes Plateau situated in the southeast near the border with France, Luxembourg and Germany; the rolling, cen-

tral fertile plains; and the coastal plain. The Ardennes Plateau is an area of moorland, woodlands and forests, valued for recreational purposes as well as forestry. The central plains are a fertile agricultural region crossed by Belgium's principal rivers, the Schelde and Meuse. The coastal plain is low-lying, reaching only about 20 metres or 65 feet above sea level at its highest point.

Belgium has a highly developed transport system with one of the highest densities of railway lines in the world. A well-used canal network links the main rivers many of which can be used by large boats. About 97 per cent of Belgians live in cities or urban areas, with the greatest number in the capital, Brussels. The country is poor in mineral reserves and two thirds of its electricity needs are supplied by nuclear power. One of the major industrialised countries of Europe, it produces a great range and quantity of manufactured goods.

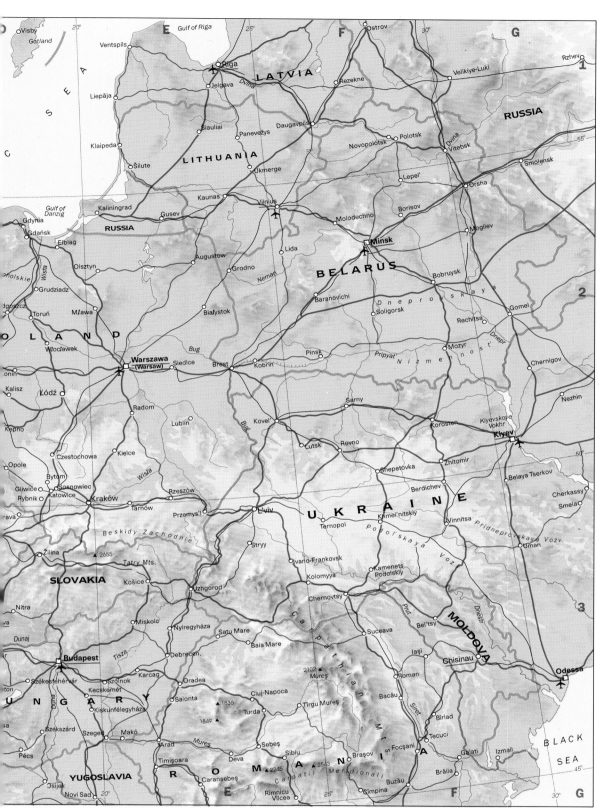

© Geddes & Grosset

Central and Eastern Europe and the Low Countries
Scale 1: 6 500 000

THE NETHERLANDS

Language/s spoken: Dutch, English, French and German
Currency: Guilder
Travel requirements: valid passport required, best to contact relevant authority before departure
Major cities: Amsterdam (capital), Eindhoven, Rotterdam
Climate: warm from May to September and cold in the winter months, rain throughout the year
Crime and safety: take sensible precautions

About 45 per cent of the land area of Belgium is used for agriculture and much of it is farmed intensively but its forestry and fishing industries are fairly small. Belgium is renowned for its lace, damask, fine lawn and chocolates.

THE NETHERLANDS

The Netherlands, also known as Holland, is bounded in the north and west by the North Sea, in the east by Germany and in the south by Belgium. The Netherlands is a very low-lying country with about 16 per cent of its land area having been reclaimed from the sea. About 50 per cent of the country lies below sea level and slightly higher ground is found only in the extreme south where the land rises towards the foothills of the Ardennes.

The Netherlands is crossed by numerous rivers which include the Rhine and its tributaries and there are many navigable canals and lakes. The country also has highly developed road and rail networks. About 90 per cent of its people live in cities or urban areas, such as the capital, Amsterdam. The country has a highly developed industrial and manufacturing base. In addition to natural gas and petroleum from the extensive deposits of natural gas located around Groningen, other important commodities include textiles and a wide range of light industrial and electronic goods.

Fishing has long been carried out from the North Sea coastal villages but there is very little forestry in the Netherlands as any woodland cover that does exist is mainly within national parks or preserved for recreational purposes. Agriculture plays an extremely significant part in the Dutch economy and the land is intensively farmed and cultivated.

The Netherlands is famous for its dairy produce

Dutch tulips

GERMANY

Language/s spoken: German, English and French
Currency: Deutsche Mark
Travel requirements: valid passport usually required but all potential visitors should contact relevant authority before departure for more specific information
Major cities: Berlin (capital), Cologne, Dortmund, Dusseldorf, Essen, Frankfurt, Hamburgh, Leipzig, Munich, Stuttgart
Climate: summers are warm, winters cold, rain throughout the year
Crime and safety: take sensible precautions

THE BLACK FOREST OR SCHWARZWALD

The Black Forest in southwestern Germany is a mountainous region covered with pine forests and dissected by many rivers and streams. Cherry trees grow in some of the valleys of the Black Forest and the fruit is used to make a liqueur called kirsch. The liqueur is used to flavour the rich, dark chocolate gateau, layered with cream and cherries, which bears the name of the Black Forest and for which the region is famous.

Lichtenstein Castle, Germany

and speciality cheeses, such as Edam and Gouda. Some of its land is used for horticulture, with bulbs and other flowers being grown for export. The Dutch bulb fields attract many visitors to the country every spring.

LUXEMBOURG

The small Grand Duchy of Luxembourg is entirely landlocked, bounded by Belgium in the west, Germany in the east and France in the south. The northern part of the country is a continuation of the forested hills of the Ardennes Plateau while the southern two thirds of the country consists of undulating wooded farmland.

Luxembourg is a wealthy and highly industrialised country whose citizens enjoy a very high standard of living. The capital, Luxembourg City, is the seat of the European Court of Justice.

Luxembourg has rich (although declining) deposits of iron ore and the manufacture of iron and steel has traditionally been one of the two mainstays of the economy, the other being banking. Agriculture, insurance services and tourism are all important contributors to the economy.

GERMANY

The Federal Republic of Germany is a large and prosperous country in central Europe which shares its borders with many other European countries and also has a stretch of coastline bordering the North and Baltic Seas. Lying off the coast, the North and East Frisian Islands and Helgoland in the North Sea belong to Germany as do the Fehmarn and Rügen Islands in the Baltic.

There are three main topographical regions in Germany. These are a lowland plain in the north crossed by many rivers and canals, an upland plateau containing several mountain ranges dissected by river valleys in the centre and a region containing still higher peaks in the south.

Germany's most famous river, the mighty Rhine, is a major navigable waterway used for the transportation of considerable amounts of freight. Most of the country's lakes are in the southern Alpine region. Forests and woodlands cover about 30 per cent of the land area. They are home to a number of different species of wild animals and birds, including wild boar, wolf, fox and deer.

Germany is administered as 16 states and one of these is the beautiful and ancient state of Bavaria, which attracts large numbers of tourists each year. Because of the nature of its historical development as a number of nation states, Germany has many fine ancient towns and cities as well as newer industrial centres, including the capital, Berlin. Around 80 per cent of the country's population of 81 million live in cities or urban areas.

Oil and natural gas deposits are found in the north and lignite (brown coal), rock salt, potash, iron, lead, zinc and copper, along with small quantities of some other metallic ores, are also extracted and produced. A huge range of goods and materials are produced in Germany, which has several large industrial areas. The country also has a considerable timber and wood products industry based on its extensive coniferous forests. Most coastal towns have their own fishing fleet.

The most productive farmland is found in the northern plain while fruit growing is important in many areas with vineyards and orchards, for example, along the Rhine and its tributaries. Fine German wines produced from the grapes are famous throughout the world.

Bavaria

Bavaria is the largest state in Germany and certainly one of the most beautiful. Every year it welcomes large numbers of visitors who come to enjoy the beautiful scenery, leisure activities and cultural heritage of the region. Each October, the state capital of Munich hosts its Oktoberfest or October beer festival – an event that attracts beer drinkers from all over the world.

LIECHTENSTEIN

The small, independent state of Liechtenstein is sandwiched between Switzerland in the north, west and south and Austria in the east. Liechtenstein uses the Swiss franc and is generally represented internationally by Switzerland.

The upper reaches of the River Rhine flow along the western boundary of the principality while to the east and south lie the foothills of the Austrian Alps. The capital and principal town is Vaduz, situated overlooking the River Rhine in the centre of the principality.

The mainstays of the highly prosperous economy are international banking and financial services, the sale of postage stamps and tourism. Manufactured goods include precision tools and instruments, foods, pharmaceuticals, metal goods, pottery and furniture. Liechtenstein's small amount of farmland is mainly located within the Rhine valley.

HUNGARY

Hungary is a landlocked country sharing borders with Austria, Slovenia, Croatia, Yugoslavia, Romania and the Ukraine. It is a region of plains ringed by the high mountain ranges of neighbouring countries. The main topographical feature is the Great Plain or Great Alföld.

The Danube and its tributaries, being navigable, form an important part of the country's transportation system and are the source of most of the country's water for domestic and industrial needs. About 18 per cent of the country is covered with forest.

Hungary has traditionally been an agricultural country and around half the land area is suitable for agriculture although irrigation is necessary to ensure productivity. Hungary is relatively poor in mineral resources and heavily reliant upon imports of oil and coal to supply its energy needs although over 40 per cent of electricity is generated by nuclear power. The economy has a sizeable industrial base and tourism also makes a significant contribution to the economy. Hungary's capital, the beautiful ancient city of Budapest, and Lake Balaton are two of Hungary's most popular tourist destinations.

AUSTRIA

Austria is a landlocked Alpine country with most of its territory situated within the eastern Alps. Some lower-lying land does occur, however, in the basin of the River Danube and along the country's eastern border south of Vienna, the country's capital. About 61 per cent of Austrians live in cities or urban areas.

Over a third of Austria is forested, providing the country with valuable timber resources. Hydroelectric power schemes supply about two thirds of the country's electricity needs, with some being exported. Austria has modest reserves of iron ore, lignite, oil, natural gas, lead, zinc, copper, magnesium, salt, gypsum, talc and kaolin and although there is only a limited amount of land available for agriculture, the country is able to produce enough food to meet most of its own domestic needs.

Austria is a prosperous country with a fairly wide manufacturing base. The Alpine scenery, picturesque and historical villages and towns, music festivals and sporting opportunities make Austria a popular holiday destination and tourism makes a significant contribution to the economy.

SLOVAKIA

Slovakia or the Slovak Republic is a small, landlocked republic that came into being in 1993. It shares borders with Hungary, Austria, the Czech Republic, Poland and the Ukraine. A mountainous country, its main topographical feature is the Carpathian Mountains which occupy most of the northern and central part of the republic. Flatter land is mainly confined to the Danubian lowland basin in the southwest, a strip along the southern border and between the mountains in the east. The main river is the Danube (Dunaj) which forms the border with Hungary for about 120 kilometres or 75 miles. There are many other rivers and numerous freshwater lakes in the mountains and over a third of Slovakia is forested. Nearly 60 per cent of the people live in urban areas, particularly in and around Bratislava, Slovakia's capital and largest city.

Cultivatable land is located mainly in the Danubian lowlands, in the south and west and in the river valleys. Slovakia has reserves of iron ore, lead, copper, manganese, zinc and lignite (brown coal). Although hydroelectric power schemes supply some of the country's energy needs, Slovakia is still heavily dependent upon imports of oil and gas. Manufactured goods include military equipment and weapons and processed foods. Tourism is a growing contributor to the economy, with visitors coming to Slovakia for skiing and mountain pursuits as well as to enjoy the historical and cultural attractions of its towns and cities.

THE CZECH REPUBLIC

The Czech Republic was created in 1993 when it separated from Slovakia, the two having formerly been united as Czechoslovakia. It is a landlocked country that shares borders with Austria, Germany, Poland and Slovakia. The country is almost ringed by mountains that stretch over the borders with neighbouring countries. Lying east of the centre of the country, the Moravian Highlands give way to lower-lying, rolling plains. There are numerous rivers in the country and a number of freshwater lakes. Forests, including the Bohemian Forest, cover about a third of the Czech Republic. The republic's capital is the beautiful, ancient city of

Prague (Praha) located on the bank of the Vltava river. More than two thirds of Czechs live in cities or towns.

The lower-lying areas and river valleys provide suitable farming land and the country has valuable timber resources, particularly in the Bohemian Forest. Lignite is the most abundant mineral resource but there are also some reserves of hard coal, uranium, tin, antimony and mercury, iron ore, lead and zinc. The country relies heavily on imported oil and gas and coal-fired power stations to generate electricity. Mining and heavy industries have declined in recent years although iron and steel, machinery and vehicle production are still significant. Traditional craft products include beautiful crystal from Bohemia, decorated glass and painted eggs.

KALININGRAD

The Kaliningrad region is an isolated western outpost of Russia alongside the Baltic Sea that is cut off from the rest of its homeland by Lithuania, Latvia and Belarus. Kaliningrad is sandwiched between Poland in the south and west and Lithuania in the north and east with about 140 kilometres or 87 miles of Baltic coastline in the west. It has a population in the order of one million people. The world's largest amber mine is located here and the region is also known for being the original breeding area of Trakehener horses. The city of Kaliningrad itself was founded in the 13th century and became Königsberg, the grand capital city of eastern Prussia.

POLAND

The republic of Poland shares borders with Russia (Kaliningrad), Lithuania, Belarus, the Ukraine, Slovakia, the Czech Republic and Germany. In the north, a low-lying narrow coastal plain of sandy beaches and dunes forms most of the Baltic Sea coastline. Further inland, lies the Baltic Heights region, consisting of low-lying wooded hills and valleys. The extensive central lowlands are crossed by numerous rivers and streams in a series of shallow valleys. In the south, lies a region of uplands and valleys. The land then rises more steeply to form the Sudeten Mountains and ranges of the Carpathians. The Plain of Silesia lies in the southwest beyond the Sudeten Mountains. Poland's capital and largest city is Warsaw (Warszawa), situated on the River Vistula (Wista) in the central part of the country. About 62 per cent of Poles live in cities or towns.

Agriculture plays a very important part in the country's economy with almost two thirds of the land area suitable for farming. Poland's forests cover over a quarter of the land area and provide valuable timber resources. There are both marine and freshwater fishing industries. The country has valuable reserves of both hard coal and lignite, sulphur, copper, iron ore, lead, zinc, magnesium, gypsum and rock salt but it has very little oil or natural gas so is heavily dependent upon imports to supply its domestic needs. The main industrial activities are in shipbuilding, iron and steel, chemicals, cement, vehicles, processed foods and textiles. Tourism is a growing industry, with visitors coming to enjoy Poland's Baltic sea resorts, mountainous regions and historic cities.

The House of Parliament, Budapest, Hungary

TRANSYLVANIA AND COUNT DRACULA

Beautiful Transylvania, in Romania, with its dramatic mountains, dark, mysterious forests and ruins of medieval castles, is the setting for Bram Stoker's famous novel about the vampire, Count Dracula. The historical Dracula was Vlad the Impaler (1430–77), who earned his bloodthirsty title of 'the Impaler' because of his unpleasant habit of skewering his enemies on stakes. Stoker, writing in 1897, drew on the legends and the historical record about the cruel Vlad Dracul to create the archetypal vampire.

LITHUANIA

Lithuania is bounded by Latvia, Belarus, Poland and Russia (Kaliningrad) with a Baltic Sea coastline to the west. Lithuania is a country of plains, broken by low hills with numerous rivers and lakes and many marshes and wetlands, some of which have been drained. The upland areas are generally to be found in the west while the majority of the lakes are in the southern and northeastern parts of the republic. The Neman river, with its tributaries, forms part of the border with Russia and supplies the country with hydroelectric power. Vilnius is the country's capital and largest city. Over two thirds of the people live in cities, towns or urban areas.

Agriculture is very important to the economy and Lithuania's forests, which cover about a quarter of the country, provide valuable timber resources. There is also a small but important fishing industry. Lithuania lacks exploitable mineral reserves and the country is completely dependent upon imports of oil. Nuclear power accounts for about half the country's energy needs with some additional power from hydroelectric schemes. Industries and manufacturing include shipbuilding, engineering, food processing, production of cement, machinery and electronic equipment.

BELARUS

Belarus is a landlocked republic that shares boundaries with the Ukraine, Poland, Lithuania, Latvia and Russia. Most of Belarus is fairly level and low-lying but it is interrupted by forested hills in the north where there are also a number of lakes. The west is mainly an area of farmland and forest while the south is a region of marshes drained by many rivers and streams. In the east, there is a slightly higher plain that continues until it meets the low hills of the northeast. Major rivers include the Pripyat and Dnepr and their tributaries. Minsk, the country's capital and largest city, is located in the centre of the country.

Agriculture is one of the country's most important economic activities while its timber industry operates on a fairly small scale. Fishing is mainly carried out to supply local needs.

The only abundant natural resource is peat. There are additional small scale deposits of lignite, hard coal and petroleum but Belarus has to import oil for its domestic needs. Manufactured products include fertilisers, textiles and vehicles.

UKRAINE

Surpassed in size within Europe only by Russia, the Ukraine shares borders with Romania, Moldova, Hungary, Slovakia, Poland, Belarus and Russia. The Crimean Peninsula in the south (Crimea), which borders the Black Sea and the Sea of Azov, has been an autonomous region within the Ukraine since 1996.

Most of the country is an elevated continuation of the Russian plain with a swathe of higher ground in the west and a smaller area in the southeast around Donetsk. The Carpathian Mountains cut across the extreme western portion of Ukraine while the Crimean Mountains occupy the extreme south of the peninsula. The plains are generally lower-lying in the east and south, and in the northwest there is a region of marshes. The Ukraine is drained by numerous rivers, of which the most important is the River Dnieper (Dnipro) and its tributaries. As well as being Europe's third longest river, it is an important source of hydroelectric power.

The main farming region is in the west. The Ukraine has valuable reserves of timber and a small-scale fishing industry. The country is rich in natural mineral resources, especially coal, iron ore and manganese. Industries and manufacturing include iron and metals, heavy machinery, chemicals, refining of oil and gas and food processing.

ROMANIA

Romania is a fairly large republic that shares borders with the Ukraine, Moldova, Bulgaria, Yugoslavia (Serbia) and Hungary. In the southeast, the republic's coastline stretches for approximately 200 kilometres or 125 miles along the shores of the Black Sea. The main topographic feature is the broad swathe of the Carpathian Mountains that dominates most of the country. In the centre of the country, almost enclosed by the mountains, is Transylvania, a high and extensive plateau of uplands and forests. There is a continuation of the Hungarian Plain or Great Alföld in the west while further plains lie to the east, southeast and south of the mountains. The Danube (Dunav, Dunarea), with its tributaries, is Romania's most important river. Bucharest (Bucuresti), Romania's capital and largest city, is situated in the southeast of the country.

Farmland takes up about 43 per cent of the total land area. The cultivated areas are mainly on the plains, particularly in the Danubian basin. Vineyards for Romania's wine industry flourish on the more sheltered lower hill slopes. Valuable timber resources are provided by Romania's extensive forests. The country has both marine and freshwater fishing industries.

Mineral reserves include petroleum and natural gas, coal, lignite, iron ore, lead, copper, aluminium (bauxite) and zinc. Electricity is generated from oil, coal, gas, hydroelectric and nuclear facilities and a small amount is exported. Manufactured products include cement, construction materials, iron and steel. Tourism is a growing industry in Romania and an important contributor to the economy. Visitors come to enjoy the Black Sea resorts, the bird life of the Danube delta and the spectacular mountains and forests of the Carpathians and Transylvania.

MOLDOVA

Moldova is a landlocked republic that was formerly called the Moldavian Soviet Socialist Republic and was part of the USSR. It is bordered by Romania in the west and bounded on all other sides by the Ukraine. The River Prut forms the whole of the western boundary with Romania while the River Dnister (Nistru) flows close to the eastern border and coincides with it in the northeast and southeast. Moldova is a predominantly hilly plain with an average height of around 150 metres or 500 feet.

Moldova's capital and largest city is Chisinau (Kishinev). The majority of people live in rural areas and are engaged in agriculture. Moldova lacks natural mineral resources and has to import most of its energy supplies. Its most important industries are in the area of food processing.

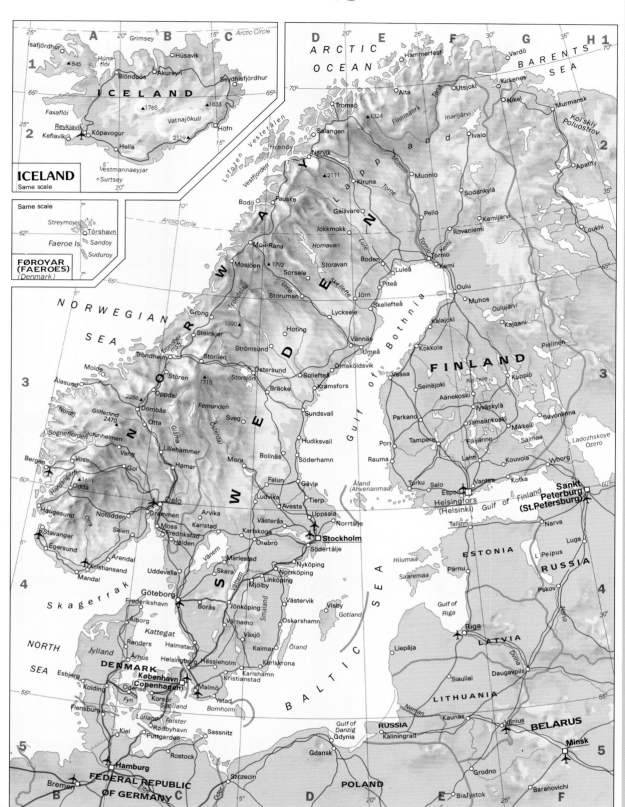

**Scandinavia and the Baltic
Scale 1: 9 600 000**

| 0 | 100 | 200 | 300 km |
| 0 | | 100 | 200 miles |

SCANDINAVIAN COUNTRIES

Language/s spoken: Although each of the Scandinavian countries have their own language, English is also widely spoken

Currency: Danish Krone, Norwegian Krone, Swedish Krone, Finnish Markla

Travel requirements: valid passport required, best to contact relevant authority before departure

Capital cities: Copenhagen (Denmark), Oslo (Norway), Stockholm (Sweden), Helsinki (Finland)

Climate: summers are warm to hot, spring and autumn mild and winters cold with snow, rain throughout the year

Crime and safety: take sensible precautions

TROLLS

Although familiar to Western children as ugly, plastic figures with brightly coloured hair, trolls are, in fact, creatures of Norse folklore. Sometimes they are represented as dwarves with a tendency for mischief – mining, working and stealing precious metals – but not actively malignant. In other tales, they take on a more sinister form as flesh-eating ogres who live in caves or wild mountain places. The wild mountain scenery and dense forests of Scandinavia lend themselves to the idea of the existence of mysterious, non-human inhabitants able to meddle in and thwart the plans of the people in the valleys below.

A typical Scandinavian fjord

SCANDINAVIA AND THE BALTIC

Scandinavia is a region in northern Europe made up of the countries of Norway, Sweden, Denmark, Finland and Iceland while the Baltic includes the countries of Latvia and Estonia on the eastern coast of the Baltic Sea. This region contains some of the wealthiest, some of coldest and some of the least visited countries in the world. It also boasts some spectacular scenery and wildlife and offers the visitor many opportunities for outdoor pursuits.

LATVIA

A former constituent republic of the USSR, Latvia is a republic in northeastern Europe that shares borders with Estonia, Russia, Belarus and Lithuania. It is bounded in the west by the Baltic Sea and the Gulf of Riga, a large inlet of the sea. Most of the country consists of a wooded lowland plain with numerous marshy areas and lakes. Inland and eastwards, there is some more hilly, forested country and towards the eastern border, there are more marshes, woodlands and lakes. Latvia is crossed by numerous rivers and streams. Woodlands, which cover about a quarter of Latvia, consist of both coniferous and deciduous trees and the republic is home to a variety of wild animals and birds.

Riga, a large and important Baltic port, is Latvia's capital city and home to a third of its people. About 70 per cent of people live in cities, towns or urban areas, and there are numerous villages spread throughout the country. Agriculture is an important part of the Latvian economy and employs about 20 per cent of the workforce. The

country also has a large marine fishing industry operating out of its Baltic Sea ports while its forests provide a valuable timber resource.

Latvia has abundant deposits of peat and gypsum but lacks other fossil fuels and minerals and although hydroelectric plants are able to supply over half the country's electricity, it is still dependent upon imports of oil, gas and electricity. Latvia has a well-developed industrial base.

ESTONIA

Estonia is a low-lying republic in northeastern Europe bounded by the Gulf of Finland and the Baltic Sea in the north and west, Russia in the east and Latvia in the south. Estonia is also a former constituent republic of the USSR and consists largely of a marshy, undulating plain with numerous forests, lakes and wetlands and offshore islands. Numerous rivers and streams drain the country and almost one quarter of the land is forested. Estonia's capital and largest city and port is Tallinn. Over 70 per cent of the population live in cities, towns or urban areas.

Agriculture is very important in Estonia, with the raising of livestock being the prime activity. The forests provide valuable sawn timber and raw materials for paper, pulp and furniture making and there is a modest marine and freshwater fishing industry. Most industries are based in the north. Tourism is a small but growing contributor to the economy.

DENMARK

The most southerly and smallest of the countries of Scandinavia, the Kingdom of Denmark is a constitutional monarchy in northern Europe. It comprises most of the Jutland Peninsula, which protrudes northwards from the North German Plain, and more than 500 islands, 100 of which are inhabited. The North Sea lies to the west of the Jutland Peninsula. The Faroe Islands in the Atlantic Ocean and Greenland off the coast of Canada are self-governing, dependent territories of Denmark.

Most of Denmark, including the islands, is low-lying with small hills found only in the central part of Jutland. Several fjords penetrate eastern Jutland from the Kattegat, and the most extensive of these, the Limfjorden, cuts right across the northernmost part of the peninsula, broadening in the west to form an extensive series of waterways. The western seaboard of Jutland is low with many sand dunes and sandbars cutting off lagoons and sandy beaches. The country is intensively cultivated, so very little natural vegetation or wild areas remain.

Well-developed road, causeway and ferry systems link the Danish islands to one another and to the mainland and connect with the railway network. The Danish capital and largest city is Copenhagen, situated mainly on the island of Sjælland but extending onto the nearby island of Amager. Denmark is a wealthy country and the standard of living is high. About 85 per cent of people live in the cities, towns or urban areas.

Agriculture has always been important to the Danish economy. The country produces a range of produce for export, particularly bacon, butter, cheese and pork. Danish beer and lager are famous throughout the world and are significant export products and important contributors to the economy. Denmark also has a large fishing fleet operating in international waters, catching mainly cod, herring and salmon. There are offshore reserves of oil and natural gas and land deposits of kaolin, lignite and some other minerals. Most of the country's electricity is generated from coal or oil-fired power stations. In addition to its food processing and brewing industries, Denmark also produces a wide range of products from iron and steel to porcelain. Denmark attracts many foreign tourists each year who visit not only the capital, Copenhagen, but also the islands and the Jutland Peninsula.

NORWAY

The Kingdom of Norway is a constitutional monarchy occupying the western part of the Scandinavian Peninsula. It is a sparsely populated and very mountainous country with hundreds of fjords along the whole length of its western coast. Most of Norway's eastern border is shared with Sweden but in the northeast, the border is with Finland and Russia. Its northwestern, western and southern boundary is formed by its long coastline. Scattered close to the mainland throughout most of the length of the coastline are hundreds of islands known as the Skerryguard. The Jan Mayen and Svalbard Islands in the Arctic Ocean, northeast of Iceland, and Bouvet Island in the South Atlantic, are also Norwegian territories.

Mainland Norway consists of a series of high plateaux, called vidder, from which rise mountain peaks permanently covered in snow and ice, including, in the far north, the most extensive glaciers in Europe. Extending into the Arctic Circle, the far north of Norway is also home to the Saami or Lapp people. The country has many lakes and is drained by numerous rivers and streams. About half the population lives in the southeast, a quarter live in Oslo, the capital, and the rest live in other towns, villages or urban areas.

Agriculture is a small-scale enterprise in Norway since only 3 per cent of the land can be cultivated. However, about a quarter of Norway is forested and the country has an important wood pulp and paper industry. Fishing has always been an important part of the Norwegian economy and Norway's fishing fleet operates as far afield as the waters off Newfoundland. Norway has also established many fish farms.

Norway has modest reserves of lead, iron, coal, copper and zinc and oil and natural gas were discovered in Norwegian waters during the 1970s. The country has exploited its abundant potential for hydroelectric power to the full and the availability of cheap electricity has enabled it to develop a major metallurgical industry. Other manufactured goods include wood products and processed foods. Norway is a popular tourist destination, with visitors coming to enjoy the country's spectacular and beautiful scenery, outdoor sports and rich historical and cultural heritage.

SWEDEN

The Kingdom of Sweden occupies the larger and longer eastern section of the Scandinavian Peninsula and is a constitutional monarchy. It is bordered by Norway in the west and northwest and Finland in the northeast and its eastern and southern boundary is formed by its long coastline. Apart from the larger inhabited islands of Oland and Gotland, many thousands of small islets line Sweden's western coast, particularly in the region of Stockholm, the country's capital.

Sweden is less mountainous than neighbouring Norway although the great mountain ranges of the Scandinavian Peninsula extend across much of Sweden's western boundary and glaciers occur at higher levels. East of the mountains there is a plateau region with the land sloping gradually eastwards towards the sea. The southern part of Sweden consists mainly of lowland plains interrupted only by an isolated upland region, called the Smaland Highlands. The far north of Sweden lies within the Arctic Circle and contains the Swedish part of Lapland.

Among the most striking features of the Swedish landscape are the 96,000 lakes which are a relic of the last Ice Age. Lake Vänern is the most extensive and covers an area of 5,543 square kilometres or 2,140 square miles. The country is also crossed by numerous rivers and streams, some of which provide hydroelectric power. About 60 per cent of the country is covered by natural forest. A large proportion of Sweden's forests and lakes have been affected by acid rain and environmental concerns are high on the agenda of the Swedish government. Most people live in southern Sweden with the great majority in cities, towns or urban areas.

Most agricultural production is for the home market and the important marine fishing industry also supplies mainly the domestic market. The country makes full use of its extensive forests to produce large quantities of cut timber for export and as a basis for wood pulp and paper industries. Iron ore, uranium silver, lead, copper, gold and zinc are among the minerals that are extracted but Sweden lacks oil or coal reserves and is particularly dependent upon imported petroleum. It has, however, fully exploited its potential for hydroelectric power, which supplies about 47 per cent of the country's electricity needs. A wide variety of manufactured goods is produced from paper to stainless steel.

Sweden attracts many visitors each year who come to enjoy its beautiful scenery, opportunities for outdoor pursuits, such as sailing, fishing, cycling and walking, and many sites of historical and cultural interest. A wealthy country, Sweden has excellent road, rail, canal and ferry networks which make it easy for visitors to travel to even the more remote parts of the country.

FINLAND

Finland is a Scandinavian, north European republic with about a third of its territory lying within the Arctic Circle. It is a country of forests, lakes and islands that shares borders with Sweden in the northwest, Norway in the north and Russia in the east. In the west and southwest, its coastline is along the Gulf of Bothnia and in the south lies the Gulf of Finland, both of which are arms of the Baltic Sea. Some 30,000 islands and islets line Finland's coast, the densest concentration being in the southwest and south. Most of Finland is a low-lying, rolling plain or plateau which becomes more hilly towards the north. Mountains are found only in the extreme

northwest where a 'finger' of Finland projects into the mountainous spine of Norway and Sweden. Northern Finland consists of Finnish Lapland. Home to the country's population of Lapps or Saami people, it lies within the Arctic Circle.

There are some 187,888 lakes in Finland, many of them containing thousands of islands, and numerous rivers and streams. The country's large tracts of forest and wilderness areas with few human inhabitants are home to a wide variety of north European wildlife. The capital and largest city is Helsinki. Most people live in southern Finland, particularly in the cities and towns.

Only about 8 per cent of the land is suitable for cultivation and farming is mainly carried out in the south. Forestry and its spin-off industries are important factors in the country's economy as is the fishing industry. The country has valuable deposits of copper, zinc, silver, iron, lead, nickel and gold. Its only natural fuels are peat and wood but it has plenty of hydroelectric power. Finland has many diverse industries including a productive manufacturing industry. Finland's beautiful countryside and architectural, cultural and historical sites attract numbers of visitors each year and tourism's contribution to the economy is of growing significance.

ICELAND

The island republic of Iceland is located in the North Atlantic Ocean about 298 kilometres or 186 miles east of Greenland. It is composed of volcanic rock and lies in an active earthquake zone. It has a deeply indented coastline and numerous fjords and bays. The centre of the island is a barren, uninhabited, high, rocky plateau composed of solidified lava from which rise volcanic mountains. A large, broad peninsula projects from the northwestern corner of the island. The inhabited lowlands of Iceland, comprising about a sixth of the total land area, occur in the coastal regions, especially in the southwest and southeast. Several small islands lie off Iceland's coast. Iceland has numerous lakes, fast-flowing rivers and waterfalls that are harnessed to generate the hydroelectric power that supplies the electricity needs of the island.

With its numerous volcanoes and extensive glaciers and snowfields, Iceland is truly a 'land of ice and fire'. Other signs of the volcanic activity lying just beneath the surface are provided by numerous geysers, bubbling mud pools, hot springs and heated geothermal pools. Hot springs are used to heat most of the homes and businesses in Reykjavik, the country's capital.

Very little of the land in Iceland can be cultivated, and the main crops are root vegetables such as turnips and potatoes. Fishing and fish processing are the mainstay of the Icelandic economy, with much of the catch being exported. Iceland lacks exploitable minerals, apart from diatomite, and must import raw materials for its industries which do, however, benefit from the availability of cheap electricity. Aluminium and ferrosilicon, nitrates for fertilisers, cement and chemicals are produced for export. Other manufactured goods include paints, textiles, clothing and footwear.

Tourism is of growing importance to the island. Visitors are attracted by Iceland's spectacular scenery and volcanic features, cultural and historical sites and opportunities for outdoor activities.

A thermal steam vent, Iceland

THE SIBERIAN TIGER

The Amur forests in southeast Russia are home to a unique collection of plants and animals including the Amur leopard, the Himalayan black bear and the magnificent Siberian tiger. Reduced by poaching to less than 200 tigers, the Siberian tiger is facing extinction in the wild. The tigers are killed by poachers who make huge profits by selling tiger bones and body parts for use in Eastern medicine. Vigorous efforts are being made to protect the world's remaining wild tigers through education and the deployment of anti-poaching patrols.

MOUNT EVEREST

The highest mountain in the world, Mount Everest is located in the Himalayas of central Asia on the Tibet-Nepal border. It was named after Sir George Everest (1790–1866), the surveyor-general of India. The peak was first reached in 1953 by Sir Edmund Hillary and Sherpa Tenzing Norkay of Nepal. There are now many attempts made each year to conquer this great peak by groups of climbers from all over the world.

Mount Everest

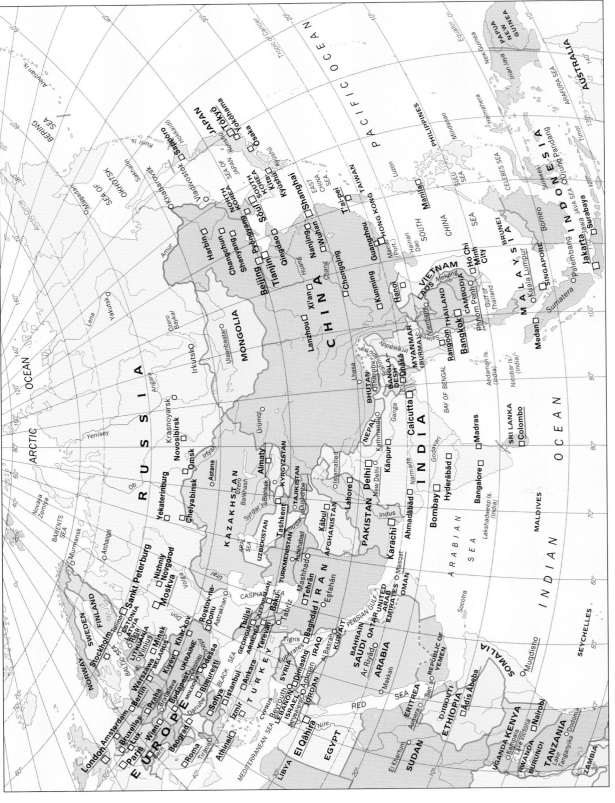

ASIA

Asia is the largest of the world's continents. A third of the total land area of the Earth, it extends from far north of the Arctic Circle to just below the equator and all except the most southerly parts lie within the northern hemisphere.

The great landmass of Asia is extremely diverse, both geographically, climatically and with regard to its plants, animals and human inhabitants. It has a great variety of environments from the frozen wastes of the Arctic to the lush, hot, humid, tropical jungles of Malaysia. It contains the world's highest place, Mount Everest (8,848 metres or 29,028 feet), and its lowest point, the Dead Sea (408 metres or 1,338 feet below sea level). It is home to three out of every five of the world's people and has followers of all the world's main religious faiths among its many diverse peoples.

Asia is divided into five geopolitical regions or subcontinents: North Asia, comprising Siberia and most of Russia east of the Ural Mountains; the Middle East, consisting of western parts of Asia including Turkey, Syria, Iraq, Israel, Arabia, Iran and Afghanistan; Middle South Asia including the Indian subcontinent, Pakistan and Sri Lanka; the Far East or East Asia including Mongolia, China, Korea and Japan; and Southeast Asia including Burma, Thailand, Laos, Cambodia, Vietnam, Malaysia, Indonesia and the Philippines.

With such a wealth of diversity, this huge continent has something to offer every traveller: climbing in the massive Himalayas, trekking and rafting in Nepal, exploring the history and architectural delights of Russia, enjoying the beautiful beaches of Sri Lanka, the deserts of Saudi Arabia, or trying to come to terms with the contradictions that are India – the list is endless.

RUSSIA

Russia (or the Russian Federation) is the largest single country in the world, extending into two continents and around almost half of the globe. Mainland Russia stretches from the Gulf of Finland in the west to the shores of the Pacific Ocean in the east and from the Arctic Ocean in the north to the Caucasus Mountains in the south. Russian territory also includes several large islands and the enclave of Kaliningrad.

The Russian coastline is the longest in the world, bordering extensions of the Arctic Ocean in the north and the Pacific Ocean in the east. Russia also has a coastline along the Sea of Azov, the Black Sea and the Caspian Sea. The Black Sea is a tideless sea with its sole outlet to the Mediterranean through the narrow Bosporus Strait while the Caspian Sea is, in fact, a saline lake and the largest of its kind in the world. It is made salty by evaporation and the slow accumulation of minerals and is the habitat of the sturgeon, whose roe is the source of Russian caviar. The Ural Mountains (Uralskiy Khrebet) divide the country into two unequal parts, the smaller European Russia in the west and Asian Russia in the east, most of which consists of Siberia.

Much of European Russia is an eroded, undulating plateau, and apart from the Urals and the Caucasus (Kavkaz), the only other mountains in this region are to be found in the far northwest in the Kola Peninsula (Kol'skiy Poluostrov). The Urals form an ancient, eroded mountain chain which extends from the Arctic coast to the border with Kazakhstan. The Caucasus Mountains contain Mount Elbrus, the highest mountain in Europe, and are situated in an active earthquake zone. There are several broad, marshy areas in European Russia, occurring mainly in the north, and an extensive region of lakes in the northwest called the Great Lakes. The principal river system of European Russia is the Volga and its tributaries. The river, which is navigable for almost its entire length, has been used as a means of trade and communication for many centuries and today is also a source of hydroelectric power.

Asian Russia is essentially a vast plain with a large central plateau and is fringed by mountains in the south, east and northeast. The huge, low-lying West Siberian Plain is a marshy, poorly-drained area of swamps situated east of the Ural Mountains. It continues southwards to the border with Kazakhstan and also southeastwards, until the land begins to rise towards the southern mountains. In the east, the plain is interrupted by the great mass of the Central Siberian Plateau, an area of rolling uplands with deeply dissected river valleys and, in places, spectacular gorges. The plain continues to the north of the plateau as the North Siberian Lowland and also to the east although here the land is slightly higher and less marshy.

High mountain ranges which occur in the northeastern corner of Kazakhstan and occupy most of Mongolia continue across the southern border of Asian Russia and occupy most of Eastern Siberia. Asian Russia contains several rivers, which flow for hundreds, if not thousands of miles, and numerous lakes in the marshy, low-lying plains. Lake Baikal in the mountains of the south is Russia's largest and deepest lake and is now at the centre of a national park.

The vast area occupied by Russia encompasses several natural vegetational zones which reflect prevailing climatic conditions. In the far north, lie the cold tundra lands extending in a band between the frozen Arctic Ocean southwards to the fringes of the treeline. South of the tundra lies the taiga or boreal forest of the northern hemisphere which, in Russia, is very extensive and in which coniferous trees predominate. The coniferous forests give way to a zone of mixed forests in much of western European Russia and also in the extreme southeast of Asian Russia. The mixed forest zone gradually becomes an area of forest-steppe in which the natural vegetation is clumps of trees and grassland. In the extreme south, north of the Caucasus and extending in a narrow strip across the lower Volga valley, Southern Urals and into southwest Siberia, there is a belt of true steppe where the natural vegetation is grassland. Wildlife in Russia is extremely diverse and while some species are abundant and thriving others have now become rare, either due to direct pressure by man or through loss of habitat.

The Russian people comprise over 100 different ethnic groups or nationalities and this makes Russia one of the most culturally diverse countries in the world. Most people live in European Russia and three quarters of the population inhabit the cities or urban areas. Moscow (Moskva) is the capital and Russia's largest city.

Agriculture experienced a considerable decline in the early 1990s due to the economic uncertainties which accompanied the collapse of communism. Recovery is slow but agriculture remains a very important part of the economy with most of the output being produced for the home market.

Forestry is also of great importance to Russia which has about 50 per cent of the world's coniferous forests. The cut timber is exported in addition to being used in other industries such as pulp and paper. As with agriculture, the forestry industry was severely affected by the economic upheaval which accompanied the collapse of communism. However, forestry remains an important sustainable natural resource.

Fishing is of great importance to Russia, not only for economic reasons but also because fish are a mainstay of the national diet. The greatest proportion of the marine catch is harvested from the Pacific Ocean, the Sea of Okhotsk and the Bering Sea. Vladivostok in the far southeast is the major fishing port.

Russia has valuable and abundant reserves of many precious mineral resources and these include both fossil fuels and metallic and precious ores. Russia has a wide range of industries and manufacturing output but these have suffered greatly as a result of the break-up of the old USSR and the change over to a more Western-style economy. However, one of the factors in the country's favour is its abundance of energy supplies, which include renewable sources, particularly of hydroelectric power.

Russia, with its spectacular and varied scenery and rich cultural, historical and architectural heritage, has always been a magnet for tourists. The number of Western visitors has increased considerably since the collapse of communism and tourism provides a welcome boost for the economy.

RUSSIA

Language/s spoken: Russian, English, French and German spoken by some
Currency: Rouble
Travel requirements: return ticket and valid passport required, best to contact relevant authority before departure
Major cities: Moscow (capital), St Petersburg, Nizhniy Novgorod, Novosibirsk, Samara
Climate: considerable variations, but mainly very cold winters, mild, warm or hot summers depending on location
Crime and safety: muggings, theft and pickpocketing occur in all cities, take sensible precautions

'Kremlin' means citadel or fortified city in Russian. In Moscow's case, it represents the ancient heart of the capital, containing its most venerable and beautiful buildings, such as the Cathedral of the Assumption, the Cathedral of the Annunciation, and one of Moscow's most famous landmarks, St Basil's Cathedral. Almost every building bears testimony to the greatness and grandeur of the past and yet as the home of the government, the Kremlin continues to dominate the events of the present and future.

ALMATY, KAZAKHSTAN

Surrounded by snow-capped mountains, the city of Almaty is located near Kazakhstan's southern border with Kyrgyzstan. It is the country's largest city and an important industrial and cultural centre, having a long history dating back to its emergence as a stopping-off point on the 'Silk Road' used by merchants trading between China and the West. Almaty (Alma-Ata) means 'apple place' and the name is derived from the apple orchards which cover the neighbouring river valleys.

THE ARAL SEA, KAZAKHSTAN

The once huge Aral Sea, which used to straddle the border with Uzbekistan, is now reduced to two lakes, one in each country. The shrinkage has been caused by the siphoning-off of water from the rivers that feed the sea for irrigation purposes. The policy has been a disaster for the fishing communities which once relied upon the Aral Sea and has had severe environmental and health consequences for all the people in the region. If this process is not reversed, the sea could dry up altogether in the next 10 to 15 years.

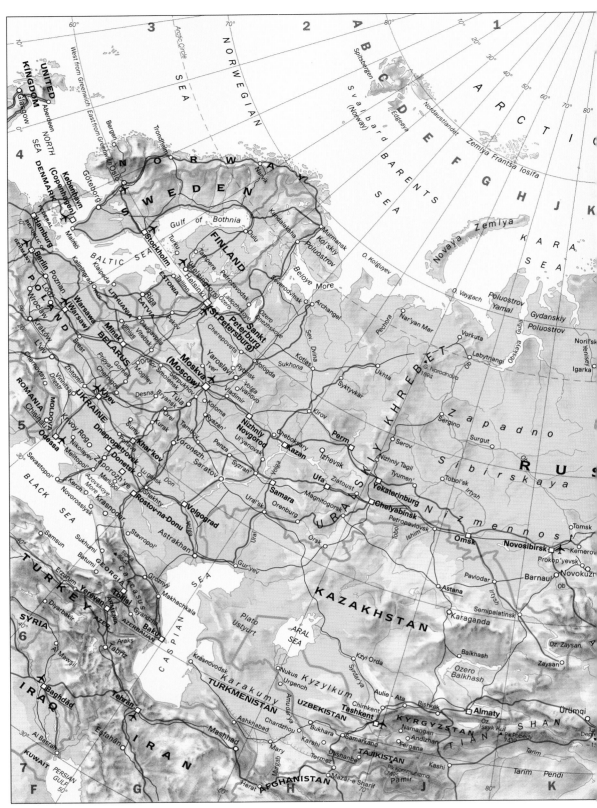

An Orthodox church, Almaty, Kazakhstan

KAZAKHASTAN

The huge, central Asian republic of Kazakhstan is similar in size to India. It is bordered by Russia in the northwest and north, Mongolia (at one point) and China in the east, Kyrgyzstan in the southeast, Uzbekistan in the southwest, the Caspian Sea in the west and Turkmenistan in the south-southwest.

Most of Kazakhstan consists of vast, arid plains or steppes with semidesert or desert characteristics. In the west, the land dips below sea level in the marshes beside the Caspian Sea and, in the east and southeast in Kazakhstan's border regions, the plains are interrupted by hills and high mountains. The Kazakh Highlands, containing several high mountain ranges, occupy the eastern, central part of the country and it is here that the large, mineral-rich Lake Balkhash is located. Kazakhstan has several major rivers. Parts of Kazakhstan are subject to earthquakes and the former capital, Almaty, has been largely rebuilt on two occasions following extensive damage. In 1997, the country's capital was moved to Akmola (Astana), located in a more stable geological region north of the Kazakh Highlands.

Kazakhstan is a major producer of grain, particularly wheat, but fishing is a small-scale activity and timber is cut for local construction purposes only. The republic has valuable reserves of copper, tin, titanium, phosphorus, magnesium, chromium, lead, tungsten, zinc, coal, oil and natural gas. Mining of these minerals is the main economic activity but oil and gas reserves have yet to be developed to any great extent. Tourism is a small but growing industry in Kazakhstan with most visitors coming from Russia or other neighbouring countries.

Russia, Transcaucasia and Central Asia
Scale 1: 27 000 000

| 0 | 200 | 400 | 600 | 800 | 1000 km |

| 0 | 150 | 300 | 450 | 600 miles |

KYRGYZSTAN

Language/s spoken: Kyrghz, Russian

Currency: Som

Travel requirements: valid passport required, best to contact relevant authority before departure

Major cities: Bishkek (capital), Osh

Climate: warm to hot in summer, cold in winter with heavy snowfalls

Crime and safety: mugging becoming more common in cities and rural areas, take sensible precautions at all times

LAKE SARY CHELEK, KYRGYZSTAN

The vast mountain wilderness of Kyrgyzstan has much to offer the visitor who likes the outdoors and unspoilt scenery. Hiking and trekking are still not formally organised but detailed maps are available and local trekking agents will help organise lodging and a guide. The nature reserve and alpine lake of Sary Chelek in the west of the country are typical of the attractions on offer to the outdoors tourist with wonderful forest hikes and beautiful scenery.

KYRGYSTAN

Kyrgyzstan is a small republic in central Asia bounded in the southwest by Tajikistan, in the west by Uzbekistan, in the north by Kazakhstan, and in the east and southeast by China. The land consists almost entirely of the high, rugged mountain range of the Tien Shan, an area of outstanding natural beauty containing some of the largest glaciers in the world. Forests cover about 4 per cent of the land area of Kyrgyzstan. The River Naryn is the main river system in the country while the country's largest lake, Issyk Kul, is located in the northeast. The capital and largest city is Bishek (formerly Frunze).

Agriculture is the second most important economic activity after mining and it employs a large number of Kyrgystan's 4 million people. Forests cover a relatively small area of the country and are harvested for local use. Fish are caught for local consumption from rivers and lakes. Kyrgyzstan has valuable resources of oil, natural gas, coal, uranium and other mineral ores and mining is the principal contributor to the economy. Oil and gas have not, as yet, been developed and the country is dependent upon imports of fuel. Hydroelectric power supplies most of the country's electricity. The government is actively encouraging foreign visitors, especially climbers wanting to scale the country's many mountains.

UZBEKISTAN

The Republic of Uzbekistan in central Asia shares borders with Kyrgyzstan and Tajikistan in the east, Afghanistan in the south and Turkmenistan in the west. The area covered by the country also includes an autonomous state, the Karakalpakstan

The Tien Shan Mountains, Kyrgyzstan

Some Mongolian herdsmen still live in the traditional, circular, felt tent or 'ger' ('yurt' in Russian) which can withstand the Mongolian weather and is easy to pack up and transport when it is time to move on to find new grazing for their animals.

Republic, in the far west around the Aral Sea. Most of the territory of Uzbekistan lies between the Amudarya and Syrdarya rivers and consists of low-lying plains with a huge desert region, the Kyzylkum, in the central and northern part of the country. In the east and northeast, the land rises to form the foothills and peaks of mountain ranges that merge with the Pamirs and Tien Shan Mountains of Tajikistan and Kyrgyzstan. The whole region is seismically active and subject to quite frequent earthquakes.

The Aral Sea, which is a large inland sea, used to straddle the border with Kazakhstan but its area has shrunk to less than half its original size. Water is scarce in Uzbekistan and there is very little rainfall. As a result, many reservoirs and artificial lakes have been created, particularly in the east where most of the population is concentrated. The capital and largest city is Tashkent which is located in the northeast of the country. Tashkent had to be substantially rebuilt following an earthquake in 1966.

Agriculture is the most important economic activity, even though the land is so dry that it can only be practised in the east and northeast with the aid of irrigation. Cotton is the most abundant crop and much of it is exported. Another more unusual activity is the raising of silkworms for the production of silk. Forestry and fishing are small-scale economic activities and Uzbekistan has to import many of its basic foodstuffs.

Uzbekistan has valuable reserves of gold, oil and natural gas and produces farm machinery and equipment for the textile industry, aircraft, textiles, cotton, natural gas and gold. The oil industry is, as yet, underdeveloped so imports of fuel are needed for domestic and industrial use. Hydroelectric schemes supply much of the Republic's electricity needs.

TURKMENISTAN

Turkmenistan is a republic in central Asia bounded in the west by the Caspian Sea, in the northwest by Kazakhstan, in the north and northeast by Uzbekistan, in the southeast by Afghanistan and in the southwest by Iran. All but about 20 per cent of the land consists of the arid 'black sands' of the Karakum Desert. In the central and northern part of the country, lies the Adzhakya Basin where the land descends to 80 metres or 265 feet below sea level. The Kopet Dag Mountains in the south and east extend for over 1,449 kilometres or 900 miles and straddle the border with Iran and Afghanistan.

Turkmenistan is an extremely dry country where surface water of any kind is scarce. The only major rivers are the Amudarya, which crosses the east and northeastern part of the country, and the Murgab which arises in Afghanistan. The Amudarya has been diverted to form the important Kara Kum Canal which is one of the longest in the world and provides irrigation and drinking water for southeastern parts of the country. The republic is sparsely populated with about 4 million inhabitants, the majority of whom favour a rural, nomadic way of life. The capital and largest city is Ashgabat ('city of love').

Agriculture remains one of the most important activities in Turkmenistan and employs about 45 per cent of the workforce. Under Russian rule, irrigation schemes were put in place for the growing of cotton and this remains the most important crop. Silkworms are raised for silk which is used in the traditional clothing still commonly worn by the Turkmen.

Turkmenistan has valuable and extensive reserves of oil, natural gas, sulphur, copper and coal and the mining and processing of fossil fuels are the principal industrial activities. Other industries include food processing, cotton and textiles, especially silk but also wool for the manufacture of traditionally patterned red carpets and rugs for which the Turkmen are renowned.

TAJIKISTAN

The central Asian Republic of Tajikistan is bounded by China in the east, Afghanistan to the south, Uzbekistan to the west and Kyrgyzstan to the north. It also includes the autonomous region of Gorno-Badakh Shan. Some 93 per cent of Tajikistan is mountainous with almost all of eastern Tajikistan above 3,000 metres or 9,840 feet. Mountain glaciers are the source of its rivers and agriculture is conducted mainly on irrigated land. Cotton, grain, vegetable oil and fruits are the main exports along with aluminium and textiles.

MONGOLIA

Mongolia is a large, central Asian republic which shares a long northern border with Russia and is surrounded on all other sides by China. Mongolia consists largely of a high plateau from which mountains rise, mainly in the west. The principal ranges are the Altai which extend southeastwards and the Hangayn Mountains in the central western area. In the east and southeast the elevation of the plateau is generally lower and here the arid, semidesert scrubland gives way to the true desert of the Gobi. A number of large lakes are to be found in Mongolia's mountainous regions. Also, there are salt lakes and salt pans in the arid, desert regions. Several extensive rivers cross the country, arising mainly in the mountains. Four vegetational zones can be recognised in Mongolia which merge into one another: coniferous forest in the mountains, forest-steppe, steppe and semidesert/desert. The capital and largest city in Mongolia is Ulaanbatar.

Although 58 per cent of Mongolians are classed as urban dwellers, many continue to follow a traditional, pastoral way of life based on the herding of grazing animals. Living close to the land as they do, the Mongolian people have a great sense of respect for the natural flora and fauna of their country. Hence Mongolia preserves a wide range of species which have become rare in other parts of central Asia and the importance of conservation is well recognised by the government.

Agriculture, and more particularly the rearing and herding of livestock, is the main economic activity and source of employment in Mongolia. The country has valuable reserves of iron ore, coal, copper, molybdenum, fluorspar, tungsten, uranium gold and silver but only some of these minerals are extracted. Manufacturing industries are generally on a small scale and include the processing of wool, hides, leather, furs and meat and dairy produce, textiles, wooden goods, agricultural equipment and building products.

China

The People's Republic of China dominates the region of East Asia, not only in terms of size, since it is the third largest country in the world, but also because of its huge population – one fifth of the world's people live in China. The area occupied by China includes about 3,400 islands but excludes the disputed territory of Taiwan. Recently the territories of British Hong Kong and Portuguese Macao have reverted to China. The People's Republic shares borders with many other countries: Vietnam, Laos, Myanmar (Burma), India, Bhutan, Nepal, Pakistan, Afghanistan, Tajikistan, Kyrgyzstan, Kazakhstan, Mongolia, Russia and North Korea. In the east, it has a long coastline with extensions of the Pacific Ocean.

The dominant topographical features are huge mountain ranges and high plateaux, particularly in the west and north, interspersed with lower-lying basins and plains, particularly in the east. The principal mountain ranges are the Himalayas which extend along the southwestern border, the Altai in the northwest border region with Mongolia, the Tian Shan which push in northeastwards from Kyrgyzstan and the Kunlun Shan, Altun Shan and Qilian Shan in northwestern, central regions.

The northwestern region of China consists mainly of two large basins, the Junggar Pendi in the north and the Tarim Pendi in the south. The Tarim Pendi contains the extensive Taklamakan Shano or Taklamakan Desert, a dry, stony inhospitable landscape with enormous sand dunes. To the south and southwest lies the world's highest plateau – Tibet or Xizang Zizhiqu, also known as 'the roof of the world'. Ringed by huge mountain ranges, most of the Tibetan Plateau is uninhabited. Many great southern Asian rivers have their origins in Tibet including the Huang He and Yangtze of China.

Northern China is a region of immensely varied landscapes. It comprises the steppes of Inner Mongolia and the loess plateaux lands of the Huang He river which extend into Shanxi and Henan provinces. The loess is a fine silt which was blown and deposited by the wind after the last glaciation to blanket the underlying rocks. Although it is easily eroded, it is a fertile soil and terrace cultivation on steep slopes is a common feature in this region.

To the south and east lies the flat North China Plain which is the largest level, low-lying area in China. It has highly fertile loess soils and is an area of dense settlement and intense cultivation. The monotony of the plain is relieved by the Shandong Plateau which guards the entrance to the Shandong Peninsula jutting out into the Yellow Sea. Northeastern China is the region east of the Da Hinggan Ling Mountains comprising all of old Manchuria which includes the modern provinces of Heilongjian, Jilin and Liaoning.

Southern and southeastern China comprises the large Yangtze river system and all the lands to the south, lying east of the highlands of Tibet. It is a varied region of rugged hills and mountains, valleys and plains presenting many contrasting landscapes. It has rich, alluvial soils which are extensively cultivated. China is crossed by many rivers and streams but the most important are the Yangtze, which is the longest in the country, and the Huang He, the great river of the north. The most important and largest freshwater lakes in China are found along the Yangtze river valley and salt lakes occur on the Tibetan plateau and in Inner Mongolia.

China's diversity of landscapes, plants and habitats provide a home for a vast array of widely differing animals and birds, some of which are not found elsewhere. China has also added to the list of common domesticated animals by making use of the water buffalo in the south and the yak in Tibet. The versatile yak is used as a source of meat and milk, its dung is collected and dried for fuel and its hide is turned into clothing, tents and bedding.

Although encompassing a huge land area, much of China consists of difficult and inhospitable terrain and this is reflected in the pattern of human settlement. Most people live in eastern China, the historical heartland of the country, but in recent years the Chinese government has promoted settlement in the west and in the five autonomous regions. In spite of the fact that China has several vast cities and large towns, three quarters of the people are classed as rural dwellers. The capital city and historical and cultural heart of China is Beijing although it is surpassed in terms of population size by Shanghai.

In spite of its great size, only about 10 per cent of China's land is suitable for cultivation and, in many areas, cultivation is only possible because of irrigation schemes. The presence of a large population and a limited amount of land means that most cultivation is devoted to the raising of food crops, notably rice, with most production concentrated in the east.

China is traditionally associated with the production of fine silk and silkworm raising or sericulture remains important in many parts of eastern and southern China. Tea is another crop traditionally linked with China and Chinese plantations produce about a fifth of the world's output, providing a valuable commodity for export as well as for domestic consumption. Fishing also provides a valuable food resource for the people.

China has abundant reserves of many valuable minerals especially coal, graphite, tungsten and antimony ores, of which it is the world's largest producer. Energy generation is generally by means of coal-fired power stations and hydroelectric schemes. China has a large and varied industrial sector mainly devoted to heavy industry. However, since the 1980s, greater emphasis has been placed on the development of light industries and new technologies.

Now is an exciting time to visit China as the practical aspects are easier than they have been for years and the Chinese suspicion of foreign travellers has abated considerably.

Beijing

There has been settlement in or near Beijing since the dawn of human history, including the remains of 'Peking Man' who has been classified as belonging to an early human species called Homo Erectus. The immensely powerful Mongol Emperor, Kublai Khan (grandson of Ghengis), chose Beijing to be his capital, not only of China but of the whole of his huge empire, and from that time onwards, the city was destined to play a central role in Chinese affairs. The city did not receive its present name of Beijing until the early 15th century during the period of the Ming Dynasty.

Clearly visible from space, the Great Wall of China was built during the Zhou Dynasty as a defensive barrier against the warring Xiongnu tribes in the north. It was repaired many times over the succeeding centuries, particularly during the Ming Dynasty (1368–1644) when it was largely rebuilt. The wall as it is today largely dates from this period.

East Asia
Scale 1: 19 500 000

0   200   400   600   800 km

0 100 200 300 400 500 miles

© Geddes & Grosset

GIANT PANDAS OF CHINA

Giant pandas are one of the most popular and endearing animals on Earth but also one of the most endangered. Very few now exist in the wild and their distribution has shrunk to six remote pockets of southwestern China. Loss of habitat and disturbance due to human activity, hunting and poaching, decline in the quantity and availability of bamboo shoots upon which the animals depend for their food and the lifestyle of the pandas themselves have all contributed to their decline.

The Chinese government is committed to conserving the panda and has put into place a number of measures to boost their numbers in the wild such as the creation of new reserves and the establishment of 'corridors' of forest to connect panda areas.

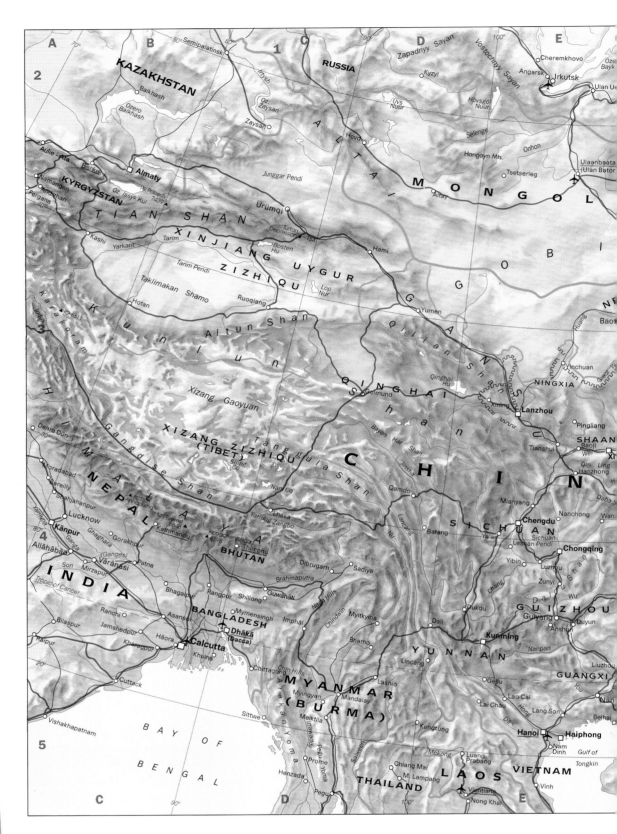

Hong Kong

As travel in the country becomes easier and less restricted, increasing numbers of visitors come to see Beijing's many important historical sites such as the Forbidden City, the Summer Palace, part of the Great Wall and Tiananmen Square, the largest public square in the world housing the mausoleum of Chairman Mao Zedong and a place of great significance to the Chinese people.

HONG KONG

The former British Crown Colony of Hong Kong in South China comprises Hong Kong Island (Xianggang) and about 235 nearby islets, Kowloon Peninsula and a region on the mainland called the New Territories or New Kowloon. About six million people are packed into this one small area of 1,075 square kilometres or 415 square miles and the only way that they can all be accommodated has been to build numerous skyscrapers and expand upwards instead of outwards.

The colony became a brash, noisy, colourful and vibrant place which stood in stark contrast to the rest of mainland China. In 1984, an accord was reached between Britain and China agreeing that Hong Kong would be handed back to the Chinese in 1997 but with many safeguards in place to protect its way of life. The handover duly took place and Hong Kong is now a Special Administrative Region with the ability to continue as a business, financial and commercial centre and to operate as a free port.

Hong Kong has much more to offer the visitor than sky scrapers and neon lights, including the Bird Market, walled villages (such as Kam Tin), and traffic-free Cheung Island.

THE YETI OR 'ABOMINABLE SNOWMAN'

A powerful belief among the Nepalese and Tibetans who live surrounded by the high Himalayas, is that they share their mountain homeland with yeti – elusive and mysterious manlike creatures which are covered with shaggy hair. The yeti is variously described as having dark or sometimes white hair and is also called the 'Abominable Snowman' by Westerners. There have been several reported sightings of yeti, along with other encounters, stretching back over many years. More usually, however, the creature's footprints are found.

Similar stories about the existence of 'wildmen' also occur in other continents – notably the Bigfoot of North America and the Yowie of Australia. These creatures, like the yeti, remain a mystery which will no doubt continue to fascinate people for many years to come.

NEPAL

The Kingdom of Nepal is a constitutional monarchy which shares its northern border with the autonomous region of Tibet (China) and its other borders with India. The kingdom can be divided into three topographical bands running in a northwesterly–southeasterly direction: the high Himalayas which extend along the northern border with Tibet, the more modest ranges of the Himalayas and a narrow band of lower-lying land called the Tarai.

The Tarai region extends across Nepal's southern border into India to form the upper reaches of the plain of the Ganges river system. A second area of lower ground is the basin, formed by a river valley in the lower Himalayas, where Kathmandu, the kingdom's capital and largest city, is situated. Most rivers in Nepal flow southwards to join the Ganges river system. Most of the population of about 21 million people live in the Tarai region or in the area around Kathmandu.

Most Nepalese are employed in agriculture which is the mainstay of the economy. Cultivatable land, amounting to about 17 per cent of the total area, is found only in the Tarai region and the Kathmandu basin. Forestry is an important but overexploited industry in Nepal providing raw materials for the pulp and paper industry and for export. Tourism is Nepal's top foreign currency earner. Thousands of visitors come each year to enjoy long distance trekking, exhilarating white water rafting and climbing in the country's majestic mountains.

BHUTAN

The small country of Bhutan is an absolute hereditary monarchy sharing a boundary in the north with

Kathesimbhu Stupa, Nepal

CHEJU ISLAND, SOUTH KOREA

Cheju Island to the south of the country is regarded as South Korea's main beach resort. It is also thought of as 'Honeymoon Island' by the many newly married couples who queue to have their photo taken at the Chongbang Waterfall at Sogwipo in the south of the island. Travellers can see some unique thatched traditional Cheju houses and some large stone heads similar to those found on Easter Island at Songup in the north of the island.

SONGNISAN NATIONAL PARK, SOUTH KOREA

South Korea has some beautiful national parks, including the Songnisan Park in the centre of the country, where visitors can enjoy hiking and other outdoor activities. Close by Songni-dong, at the entrance to the Songnisan Park, is Popju where visitors can see the oldest wooden pagoda in Korea and a huge bronze statue of Buddha.

The ruined city of Mahastanagar, Bangladesh

Tibet (China) but surrounded elsewhere by India. It is situated within the broad swathe of the Himalayan mountain chain and can be divided into three topographical regions: the high Himalayas in the north, the central middle Himalayan region to the south, and further south the foothills and plains of a region called the Duars.

Bhutan has been isolated historically for centuries, only opening its doors to the outside world in the 1970s. Its small population continues to follow a traditional way of life that is kind to the environment and as a result, the country has a wealth of habitats and flora and fauna. Over 70 per cent of Bhutan is covered with forest and the laws of the land ensure that 60 per cent of the natural woodland must remain forever. The capital and largest city is Thimphu but most of Bhutan's people live in villages.

Agriculture is the most important economic activity in Bhutan and sustains most of its people. A strictly controlled, state logging company extracts timber in Bhutan and some timber and wood products are exported. Bhutan's mineral resources include coal, limestone, gypsum and dolomite. Small-scale industrial activities are strictly controlled to minimise negative effects on the environment. Tourism is the country's main source of foreign income but the number of visitors is strictly limited and visas are only granted to members of government tours. Nonetheless, the country's pristine and protected environment and its vibrant culture make it well worth a visit.

BANGLADESH

The People's Republic of Bangladesh is an extremely low-lying country with a stretch of coastline along the Bay of Bengal in the south and bordered in the west, north and east by India and in the extreme southeast by Myanmar (Burma). The only appreciable higher ground is a series of forested ridges in the southeast called the Chittagong Hill Tracts district. The country's highest peak, Mowdok Mual, is situated here. Most of Bangladesh consists of the wide alluvial delta of the Ganges and Brahmaputra river systems and their numerous tributaries.

Rivers and water are the dominant natural features in Bangladesh and regular and extensive flooding plays a major role in the life of its people, particularly in the lower delta region. However, the flooding rivers also deposit considerable quantities of fertile alluvial silt across their flood plains, supporting the cash crops upon which the country's economy depends. A wide variety of mammals, reptiles, amphibians and birds inhabit Bangladesh with the Bengal tiger among the most spectacular and the most endangered species. The capital and largest city is Dacca (Dhaka). Some 80 per cent of Bangladesh's 120 million people live in rural villages.

Agriculture is the most important economic activity in Bangladesh but returns for most families are poor and at subsistence level. The most important non-food cash crop is jute and Bangladesh is the world's main exporter of this fibre.

Bangladesh has both a marine and freshwater fishing industry but forestry is a small-scale enterprise and the amount of remaining forest cover is fairly small. The country has few mineral resources apart from good reserves of natural gas which are exploited on a fairly small scale. Manufacturing is likewise generally run as small, local enterprises lacking in modern technology.

THE DEMOCRATIC PEOPLE'S REPUBLIC OF KOREA

The Democratic People's Republic of Korea, formerly North Korea, occupies the northern half of the Korean Peninsula. It is bounded by China in the north and Russia in the extreme northeast. The Korean Bay coastline lies to the west while the coastline in the east is with the Sea of Japan. The Republic of Korea, formerly South Korea, occupies the southern part of the peninsula and is separated from the north by a buffer, demilitarised zone.

Mountains are the dominant topographical feature of North Korea occupying the whole of the northern part of the country and extending southwards in a broad band beside the coast of the Sea of Japan. The mountains in the north are rugged and forested and dissected by steep river gorges while those along the eastern seaboard consist mainly of bare, weather-beaten rock. Some flatter ground and lower-lying plains occur in the west and in the river valleys but this amounts to only about 20 per cent of the total land area. The largest and most important river is the Yalu which, for a considerable part of its course, forms the border with China. A variety of wildlife is found in the country, particularly in the sparsely populated mountains and forests. Increasingly rare, large carnivores include tiger, leopard, wolf and bear. The capital is Pyongyang.

Flat land suitable for cultivation is at a premium in North Korea and soil improvement schemes, water conservation and irrigation, land reclamation and mechanisation are all very highly developed. Except in periods of drought or flooding, this has resulted in improved food yields. A marine fishing fleet catches mainly tuna, anchovy and mackerel. Seaweeds are also harvested. Wood is extracted from the forests mainly for domestic use.

North Korea is richly endowed with a wide variety of minerals and mining is an important contributor to the economy. Of particular importance are coal and iron ore but there are also good reserves of copper, tungsten, lead, zinc, graphite, magnesite, gold, silver and phosphates. North Korea fully exploits its fast-flowing rivers for the production of hydroelectric power which supplies about 60 per cent of its energy needs. Industry is centred on heavy industrial developments including iron and steel, large machinery and engines, locomotives, rolling stock, trucks, construction equipment and vehicles.

Tourists can visit North Korea but only as members of government tours and this tends to give visitors a very one-sided impression of the country.

THE REPUBLIC OF KOREA

The Republic of Korea, formerly South Korea, occupies the southern half of the Korean Peninsula. The country is bordered in the north by a demilitarised zone which acts as a buffer between South and North Korea. It has a long coastline bordering the Yellow Sea in the west, the Korea Strait in the south and the Sea of Japan in the east. Many islands lie off the western and southern coastline.

Most of the country is hilly or mountainous. The most extensive range, the Taebaek-sanmaek, runs down most of the length of the eastern coast but other hilly regions occur centrally and in the south. Flatter land and plains constitute about 25 per cent of the total area and occur mainly in the west and south and in the river valleys. Several major rivers, notably the Han and Naktong, arise in the Taebaek-sanmaek Mountains and flow generally westwards or southwards to empty into the Yellow Sea or the Korea Strait. Wildlife species are similar to those in the north. The country's capital and largest city is Seoul (Soul).

About 23 per cent of the land is available for agriculture and most of this is under cultivation on small plots. Rice, wheat and barley and a wide variety of vegetables and fruit are grown. Other crops include soya beans, hemp and cotton. Pigs, cattle, goats and poultry are the principal livestock and silkworms are raised in some areas. Forests have been extensively cut and cleared except in the more remote areas but the country has one of the largest deep-sea fisheries in the world. Fish processing is an important subsidiary industry resulting from the large annual catch.

South Korea is poor in mineral resources compared to the north but has small reserves of coal, zinc, tungsten, iron ore, graphite, lead, kaolin, silver and gold which are exploited. The republic has concentrated mainly on the development of light industries but during the 1990s it turned to heavy industrial development. A wide variety of goods are produced including ships, vehicles, machinery, iron and steel, electronic equipment and electrical goods, textiles, footwear, processed foods, toys, chemicals and fertilisers.

Tourists can enjoy South Korea's beautiful national parks, mountain walks and, in winter, some of the most accessible skiing in Asia.

TAIWAN

Taiwan or the Republic of China was formerly known to the West by its Portuguese name of Formosa ('beautiful island'). It is the largest of a group of islands located in the Pacific Ocean about 100 miles from southeast China, across the Taiwan Strait. An additional 78 islands make up the province of Taiwan, including those called the Pescadores by the Portuguese but known as Penghu to the Chinese. Other islands, such as Quemoy and Maju, lie closer to the coast of the mainland China.

Mountains dominate the island, covering three quarters of the land area and absent only from western, coastal regions. The mountain slopes are mostly covered with coniferous forests. A variety of wildlife is indigenous to Taiwan, such as the Formosan black bear and the Formosan rock monkey, but many species are now confined to remote mountain regions where they are less disturbed by humans. The capital and largest city is T'aipei.

Low-lying land in the west of Taiwan is fertile and heavily cultivated for a variety of crops including rice, sugar cane, tea, coffee, cashew nuts, sweet potatoes, bananas, pineapples, tobacco, cotton, sisal and cloves. Forestry is carried out in Taiwan to supply a plywood industry and numerous fish species are harvested from the surrounding seas, providing an important food source. Taiwan has relatively few mineral resources but is the leading 'tiger' economy of the Pacific rim countries based on its broad range of manufactured goods and 'high tech' goods. Products include steel, electrical and electronic goods, textiles, clothing, footwear,

foodstuffs, plastics, toys and chemicals.

Visitors can enjoy mountain hikes, beautiful scenery around the Taroko Gorge and the many temples of T'ainan, the country's cultural capital.

JAPAN

The Constitutional Monarchy of Japan consists of a series of over 1,000 islands which cover a broad range of latitude in a roughly crescent-shaped arc from 26° N to 45°N. There are four principal, large islands running from north to south: Hokkaido, Honshu (the largest and known as the mainland), Shikoku and Kyushu. These four islands, all in close proximity to one another, make up 98 per cent of the total area of Japan. The country has a very long coastline which is highly indented in places.

The dominant topographic feature is a series of high mountains, hills and ridges interrupted by deeply cut valleys which occupy about 80 per cent of the total land area. Lower land is found only in some of the larger river valleys and coastal plains and is mostly intensely cultivated. The Japanese Alps run from north to south through central Honshu. There are numerous lakes, particularly in the mountainous regions giving additional beauty to already spectacular mountain scenery. Most valleys on the islands have fast-flowing rivers or streams which ensure an abundant supply of water and potential for the development of hydroelectric power.

The islands of Japan occur in a seismically active area of the Earth's crust. There are frequent earthquakes and many of the country's mountains are extinct or still active volcanoes, including Japan's highest mountain, the beautiful, snow-covered Mount Fuji-san in eastern Honshu. Wildlife species include a wide variety of mammals, reptiles, amphibians, fish and birds. The islands support a dense population of about 125 million people, the great majority of whom live in crowded cities or towns. Japan's capital and largest city is Tokyo in central eastern Honshu.

About 15 per cent of land in Japan is cultivated intensively with extensive use of fertilisers and technology. Cultivation is mainly of rice but also important are wheat, barley, sugar beet, potatoes and other vegetables, soya beans and sweet potatoes. Fruits are grown and tea and tobacco cultivation are also important. Mulberry bushes are cultivated for the raising of silkworms. Much of Japan is covered with coniferous woodland but this is insufficient for domestic needs and the country has to import timber from elsewhere.

The country's fishing industry is highly important and well developed with fish being caught both for domestic consumption and for export. Japan is lacking in mineral resources and many raw materials have to be imported. Leading manufacturing industries at present include cars and electronic equipment but heavy industries, such as iron and steel and shipbuilding, continue to play an important role in Japan's economy.

Japan can boast more forest cover than most Asian countries and tourists can enjoy its many attractive forest hikes and some good shorter hikes in the Japanese Alps. The country has much to offer visitors from the beautiful scenery in cherry blossom season to the hustle and bustle of modern Tokyo.

JAPAN

Language/s spoken: Japanese, some English spoken in main cities
Currency: Japanese Yen
Travel requirements: return ticket and valid passport required, best to contact relevant authority before departure
Major cities: Tokyo (capital), Osaka, Nagoya, Sapporo, Kobe, Kyoto, Yokohama
Climate: summers warm to hot, winters cold to very cold
Crime and safety: take sensible precautions

TOKYO, JAPAN

Located in the centre and east of Honshu close to Tokyo Bay, the bustling, modern city of Tokyo is one of the largest and most densely populated cities in the world, being home to over 11 million people. It has large commercial, industrial, financial and residential areas with many skyscrapers, built using anti-earthquake technology. The city forms the heart of modern Japan, attracting many foreign visitors each year particularly in the business sector.

Mount Fuji, Japan

Myanmar (Burma)

Language/s spoken: Burmese, some English

Currency: Kyat

Travel requirements: return ticket and valid passport required, best to contact relevant authority before departure

Major cities: Rangoon/Yangon (capital), Mandalay, Moulmein, Pegu

Climate: February to May hot with little or no rain, May to October rainy season, October to February cooler

Crime and safety: avoid political discussions, keep to officially designated tourist areas

The Swedagon Pagoda, Rangoon

This beautiful pagoda was established around 500 BC and enlarged to its present size in the 13th century. The base of the pagoda has a perimeter of 426 metres or 1,420 feet and the tip of its stupa (dome) is decorated with thousands of diamonds and rubies. When visiting a pagoda, visitors should remove their shoes and walk around the pagoda in a clockwise direction. Appropriate dress consists of long trousers or skirts (not shorts).

Hysinbyume Pagoda, Myanmar

Southeast Asia comprises both mainland and islands and extends from southern India and China southwards to Malaysia and Indonesia and eastwards to Papua New Guinea and the northern tip of Australia. Also included are the Andaman Islands and Matera (Sumatra) in the west and Taiwan and the Philippines, along with many small islands lying farther east in the Pacific Ocean.

Myanmar

Myanmar, formerly called Burma, is a large country in southeast Asia, ringed by high mountains which surround a central plain containing the valley of the great Irrawaddy river system. Myanmar retains large tracts of tropical forest containing commercially valuable species such as teak and rubber. Wildlife is abundant and includes some of the rarer Asian mammals.

Although Rangoon (Yangon) is now the country's capital, it is Mandalay, its ancient royal seat, which is its cultural and spiritual heart. Mandalay has many treasures including the complete Buddhist holy writings inscribed on 729 huge marble slabs commissioned by King Mindon.

Agriculture employs about 64 per cent of the population and rice, maize, pulses and sugar cane are the main crops. Forestry is also important and teak is one of the country's top exports along with rice and precious stones, notably rubies. Manufacturing is on a small scale.

Laos

Landlocked Laos is a mountainous, forested country which is economically poor and underdeveloped but, like neighbouring Myanmar, has a wealth of plant and animal life.

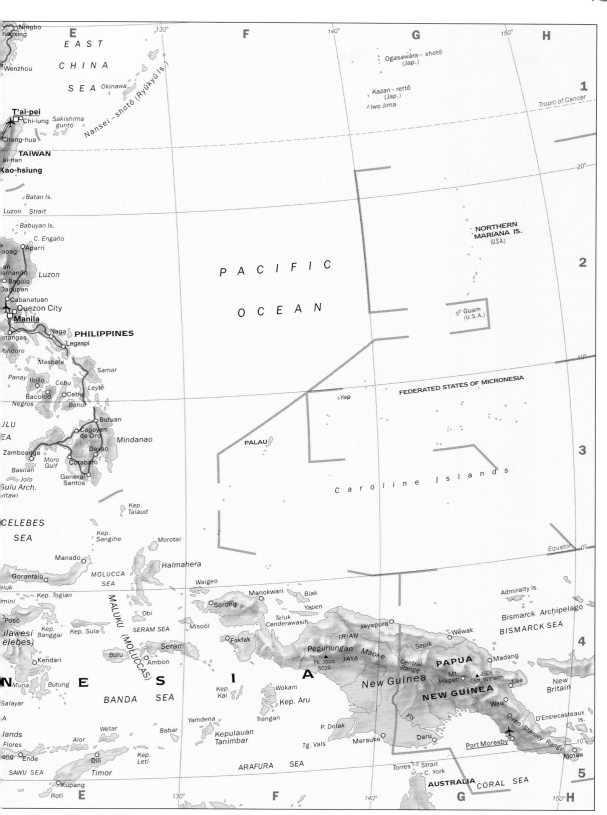

THAILAND

Language/s spoken: Thai with English, Chinese and Malay also spoken
Currency: Baht
Travel requirements: return ticket and valid passport required, best to contact relevant authority before departure
Major cities: Bangkok/Krung Thep (capital), Chiang Mai, Nakhon Si Thammarat, Ratchasima, Songkhla
Climate: heavy monsoon rains from June to October, cool from November to February and hot from March to May
Crime and safety: very strict laws on the use and transportation of narcotic drugs

BANGKOK (KRUNG THEP)

Bangkok, known as Krung Thep to the Thai people, is the capital and historical and cultural heart of Thailand and one of the most important cities in southeast Asia. It is a centre of industry and commerce famed for the intertwining canals (klongs) of the old city, the royal palace, many ornate Buddhist temples and an internationally famous jewellery market.

Unfortunately, Bangkok has a much less happy reputation as a city which trades in sex. There are allegedly many very young prostitutes who have been forced into this way of life and Bangkok has been dubbed the 'sex capital of the world'. Nonetheless, Bangkok attracts very many foreign visitors each year who come to view its historical buildings and to experience the sights and sounds of a bustling southern Asian city.

An elephant at work in Thailand

The mighty Mekong river flows through Laos and provides the main means of transport and communication as well as irrigation for the rice paddies upon which the people's subsistence depends. The great majority of the people live in small rural villages and are engaged in agriculture. Electricity is exported from power stations along the Mekong river. Timber and coffee are also exported and Laos is the world's third biggest source of opium.

THAILAND

The royal kingdom of Thailand was formerly known as Siam. A 'horseshoe' of mountains ring western and central Thailand, surrounding the fertile plain and valley of the country's principal river, the Chao Phraya. This region is the country's 'rice bowl'.

A thin 'finger' of Thailand extends southwards into the Malay Peninsula and the country has an extensive coastline surrounding the Gulf of Thailand (South China Sea). The natural vegetation of the coastal region is tropical forest which is home to a variety of animals including tiger, leopard and Asian rhinoceros. Some 66 per cent of the population are employed in agriculture and rice is the country's main crop. Tin and other minerals are mined and tourism contributes to the country's economy.

CAMBODIA

Formerly called Kampuchea, Cambodia is largely a low-lying country fringed by modest mountain ranges or upland plateaux in the southwest, north and east. The most prominent topographical

ANGKOR, CAMBODIA

The splendours of the Khymer Empire, which flourished in Cambodia from AD 802–1432, are vividly represented in the ruined capital city of Angkor in the jungles of northwest Cambodia. The city of Angkor is considered to be one of the most important archaeological sites in Asia. It covers an area of 190 square kilometres or 75 square miles and contains numerous Buddhist and Hindu temples, the most important of which is the funeral temple of Angkor Way – a huge, stepped pyramid surrounded by a broad moat with five richly carved towers. Its walls are covered with carved reliefs and decoration depicting the mythology and beliefs of the Hindu religion. Lost in the Cambodian jungle for centuries, the city of Angkor was unknown to Europeans until 1860, when a French naturalist was shown the site by local people.

BALI, INDONESIA

Although many parts of Indonesia attract foreign visitors, the island of Bali seems particularly to typify the European ideal of a tropical island paradise. This beautiful island is unique in Indonesia in preserving a Hindu culture and lifestyle which is expressed in arts, crafts and dance and enjoys some of the most spectacular scenery in the world.

Singapore skyscrapers

feature is the broad, central, alluvial basin of the Mekong river.

The western part of the basin is occupied by a large lake, the Tônlé Sap. Three quarters of Cambodia is forested but overexploitation of the forests has led to the imposition of a government ban on exports of timber. Wildlife species include tiger, panther and elephant. Most people live in rural villages and are largely engaged in subsistence agriculture. Rice is the mainstay of the economy.

VIETNAM

The Socialist Republic of Vietnam was formerly divided into a Communist north and a republican, Western-backed south but the two parts were reunited in 1976, at the close of the Vietnam War. Vietnam has a varied topography which includes mountains, coastal plains and the broad plains of river deltas. High mountains occur in the north and northwest and continue southwards along most of Vietnam's western border.

One of the most extensive areas of flat land is formed by the valley and delta plain of the Red River (Hong river) in the north. A second large delta plain in the far south is formed by the Mekong river. Vietnam has a wide range of wildlife including rare Asian mammals such as the tiger, leopard and elephant. Most people live in rural villages in the plains and are engaged in agriculture, forestry or fishing. Rice is the most important food crop. The country also produces tin, phosphates, chromium and oil.

MALAYSIA

The kingdom of Malaysia is a federation of 13 states, 11 of which are located in the southernmost part of the Malay Peninsula and comprise West Malaysia. The remaining two states of Sarawak and Sabah in northern Borneo comprise East Malaysia. They are separated from the western part of the kingdom by 650 kilometres or 400 miles of the South China Sea.

Peninsular West Malaysia has rugged mountains in the north and centre with broad plains in the south and along each coast. Sarawak has a mainly low-lying and marshy broad coastal plain but with high mountain ranges in the east and along the border with Borneo. Mountains are also the predominant feature of Sabah and Malaysia's highest peak, Kinabalu (4,094 metres or 13,455 feet), is located here.

The natural vegetation of Malaysia is dense, tropical rainforest and coastal mangrove swamps The tropical jungles contain a wealth of plant and animal species but they are threatened by logging and clearance for agriculture. Palm oil, rubber and tin are produced by Malaysia and its manufacturing industry has an increasingly important role in the economy with rubber and wood products, electrical goods, plastics, chemicals and textiles among the goods produced.

SINGAPORE

Singapore, a small island republic and a former British Crown colony, is located just off the southern tip of peninsular Malaysia to which it is linked by a causeway. It comprises the larger Singapore island and about 58 small islets. Singapore island is mainly low-lying and flat but with small central hills. With the exception of one small, hilly region, the nat-

ural tropical jungle and swamp vegetation have all been cleared and a considerable area of marshland has been drained and reclaimed. Singapore is a modern, vibrant and wealthy kingdom whose economy is based on trade and finance.

BRUNEI

Formerly a British Protected State until independence was declared in 1984, the Islamic Sultanate of Brunei is a small, independent oil-rich state in two parts located in north Borneo. It is surrounded on all landward sides by Malaysia. Brunei has a marshy, low-lying coastal plain but the land rises to form small hills inland and most of the country is covered with tropical rainforest. Brunei is a prosperous country thanks to its oil revenues and its Sultan is one of the world's richest men.

INDONESIA

The Republic of Indonesia comprises 13,677 islands, less than half of which are inhabited, stretching over a huge area of the southern seas, from the Indian Ocean in the west to the Arafura Sea and Pacific Ocean in the east. Five main islands take up three quarters of Indonesia's total area and are home to 80 per cent of its people: Sumatra, Java, Kalimantan (southern Borneo), Sulawesi (Celebes) and Irian Jaya (western New Guinea).

The Indonesian islands have an extremely varied topography, ranging from high mountains, including a volcanic belt containing 130 active volcanoes, to coastal plains. Natural vegetation varies according to the exact location and topography of each island but ranges from lowland tropical jungle to coastal mangrove swamps and upland mountain forest. An enormous variety of wildlife can be found throughout Indonesia. Its resources include oil, natural gas, tin and other minerals and rice is the main food crop.

In 1976, East (formerly Portuguese) Timor was invaded and annexed by Indonesia. The international community has never recognised Indonesia's controversial claim to East Timor and it further condemned Indonesia's brutal suppression of the Timorese nationalists who had voted for independence in August 1999. The country's developing economy has been adversely affected as a result.

PHILIPPINES

The Republic of the Philippines comprises 7,107 islands and islets, which extend in a north–south direction for a distance of some 1,127 kilometres or 700 miles, forming the northernmost group of the Malay Archipelago. The bulk of the population live on 11 of the islands, namely Luzon in the north and Mindano in the south (the two largest islands), Mindoro, Samar, Masbate, Leyte, Cebu, Bohol, Negros, Panay and Palawan. Most of the islands consist of volcanic mountains with larger plains occurring only in Luzon and Mindano.

Over a third of the islands are wooded with a range of different species and there are many varieties of wild flowers and plants. Beautiful pearls, highly prized on the world market, are harvested from oysters found around the Sulu Archipelago. Agriculture employs about 45 per cent of the workforce, with rice and maize being the main crops, and there is a developing manufacturing industry.

The vast region of South Asia and the Middle East stretches from the Mediterranean and Red Seas in the west to the eastern coasts of the Bay of Bengal. It has a wide variety of topographical features from parched, sandy deserts to snow-capped mountains. The archaeological remains of ancient human civilisations together with the many different traditions and faiths of its modern peoples make this a culturally rich and fascinating part of the world for visitors.

TURKEY

The Republic of Turkey spans the continents of Europe and Asia. European Turkey (Thrace) is a fairly small, fertile area comprising some 3 per cent of the total area of the country. It is separated from the much larger region of Asiatic Turkey (Anatolia) by the Bosporus Straits (Istanbul Bogazi), the Dardanelles Mountains and the Sea of Marmara (Marmara Denizi). Anatolia is largely a region of plateaux, highlands and rugged mountains dominated by a central plateau. The country's two great rivers, the Tigris and Euphrates, both rise in eastern Turkey. Turkey regularly experiences devastating earthquakes.

Agriculture employs some 47 per cent of the population and the country is self-sufficient in most foodstuffs. Turkey is a major producer of chromium and chrome, cotton, nuts, fruit and tobacco are exported. The growing manufacturing industry produces mainly processed foods and textiles and tourism plays an increasingly important role in the economy.

SYRIA

Much of the Syrian Arab Republic, as it is officially called, consists of arid plateau lands and plains which grade into desert in the southeast. There is a narrow, fertile coastal plain along the Mediterranean shore but this soon gives way to a belt of hills running north to south which rise to form the higher Anti-Lebanon Mountains extending across the border with Lebanon. The River Euphrates (Al Furat) enters the country from Turkey in the northwest and flows southeastwards into Iraq. Syria's resources include oil, hydroelectric power and fertile land. Agriculture employs some 20 per cent of the workforce and the country exports farm products as well as oil and textiles.

JORDAN

The Hashemite Kingdom of Jordan is a predominantly arid country whose main topographical feature is a high, rugged plateau which rises up on the east side of the River Jordan and is dissected by steep-sided gorges. The plateau loses height on its eastern side into a large area of semidesert and desert. Jordan lost most of its agricultural land when Israel occupied the West Bank in 1967 and fertile, watered land is found only in the extreme west. As a result, Jordan has to import some of its food. The manufacturing industry produces cement, pharmaceuticals, processed food, fertilisers and textiles but the country's economy relies to a large extent on foreign aid.

IRAQ

The Republic of Iraq is dominated by the Rivers Tigris and Euphrates. These two rivers flow through Iraq before finally uniting to form the Shatt al Arab, a tidal river which empties into The Gulf. The lower part of this river courses through marshland while west of the Euphrates, the land rises and grades into the semidesert and desert of Syria. The northeast of Iraq is mountainous. Farmland takes up about 20 per cent of the land and products include barley, wheat, cotton, dates, fruit, livestock and wool but Iraq has to import most of its food.

Iraq has many archaeological sites and the ancient region of Mesopotamia was the birthplace of several early civilisations. Internal and external conflict and economic sanctions imposed by the international community continue to have a severe effect upon Iraq's economy.

KUWAIT

The Emirate of Kuwait is a small desert kingdom whose economy is entirely dependent upon oil. Most of the land is barren and consists of a gently undulating plain with no natural water courses. Desalination plants use seawater from the Persian Gulf to supply Kuwait's freshwater needs. Kuwait was invaded by Iraq in 1990 which led to international involvement and the Gulf War. Before being driven out of Kuwait, the Iraqi forces set fire to the country's oil wells with devastating environmental and economic consequences.

SAUDI ARABIA

Saudi Arabia is a monarchy whose government and laws are based on the sacred teachings of Islam. This arid land occupies 80 per cent of the land area of the Arabian Peninsula and over half of its territory is desert. One of the most extensive areas of desert is the Empty Quarter (Rub al Khali), a harsh, uninhabited region hardly ever visited by man. A series of plateaux and mountains (Asir) rise behind the narrow coastal plain of the Red Sea while along the Persian Gulf there is a second fertile coastal plain where Saudi Arabia's great reserves of oil are to be found. Saudi Arabia has more oil than any other country in the world but it has little else in the way of natural resources.

Saudi Arabia has no permanent lakes, rivers or streams and, in recent years, modern irrigation and desalination schemes have greatly increased crop production. Saudi Arabia has 25 per cent of the world's oil reserves and the country makes use of its oil revenues to help diversify its own economy and support poorer Arab nations.

BAHRAIN

Bahrain, a small, oil-rich state in the Persian Gulf, is a hereditary monarchy which became fully independent from Britain in 1971. It comprises three larger islands and 30 very small ones which lie about 25 kilometres or 15 miles from the mainland of Saudi Arabia. Fresh water is supplied by artesian wells which have so far proved more than adequate for the needs of the islands.

Istanbul has a history stretching back over many centuries. The city's most famous building, the church of Hagia Sofia, was constructed as a Christian church between AD 532 and 537. It became a mosque when the city fell to the forces of Islam but it is now a museum which attracts many thousands of visitors each year. Equally famous is the beautiful Blue Mosque, named after the colour of the tiles which decorate the inside of the building.

THE RUINED CITY OF PETRA, JORDAN

The 2000-year-old city of Petra is located in southern Jordan. Carved out of and into sheer cliffs of rose-coloured sandstone, Petra was the capital city of an Arab tribe, known as the Nabateans. It appears to have been finally abandoned after AD 551, when the region experienced a strong earthquake, but this was long after the decline of the Nabateans, who had been overwhelmed and absorbed by the might of Rome. Modern visitors still come to marvel at the 'rose-red city half as old as time' which suddenly rises out of the desert cliffs.

MECCA AND THE BIRTH OF ISLAM

The prophet Mohammed was born in the city of Mecca in AD 570. Mohammed died in AD 632 but within a few years Islam had spread throughout the surrounding nations and beyond. Mecca is revered as the sacred city of the Islamic faith and the Koran, the Holy Book of Islam, states that every Muslim, who is in good health and who possesses the means to do so, should make a pilgrimage to Mecca (the hajj) at least once in his life. In modern times, the large number of pilgrims has forced Syria to introduce a quota system on Islamic countries whose citizens wish to undertake the hajj.

Mutrah Fort, Oman

QATAR

Qatar is another small, oil-rich peninsula state in the Persian Gulf. An absolute monarchy, it became fully independent in 1971.

Apart from low hills in the northwest, it consists of low-lying, arid, stony desert and salt flats. Oil is the mainstay of this properous little country's economy.

UNITED ARAB EMIRATES

The United Arab Emirates (UAE) is an oil-rich federation of seven, independent sheikdoms or states, each ruled by its own hereditary emir. The Emirates have loosely defined boundaries and occupy a region known as the Trucial States. The largest is Abu Dhabi (Abu Zaby) while the others are Dubai (Dubayy), Sharjah, Ras al Khaymah, Al Fujayrah, Ajman and Umm al Qawayn. Most of the region is hot and dry consisting of largely flat, sandy or stony desert. The UAE's economy depends on oil production and its oil revenues have made it a very prosperous country.

OMAN

The Sultanate of Oman is an oil-rich state in the southern Arabian Peninsula with an additional enclave at the northern tip of the Musandam Peninsula. A fertile coastal plain (Al Batinah) extends along the Gulf of Oman but the land soon rises to the rugged peaks of the Jebel Akhdar Highlands and Hajar Mountains. West of the mountains, there is an extensive desert and plateau region.

In the far southwest, in the region of Dhofar (Zufar), there are further mountain ranges between the coastal plain and inner desert region. Half the

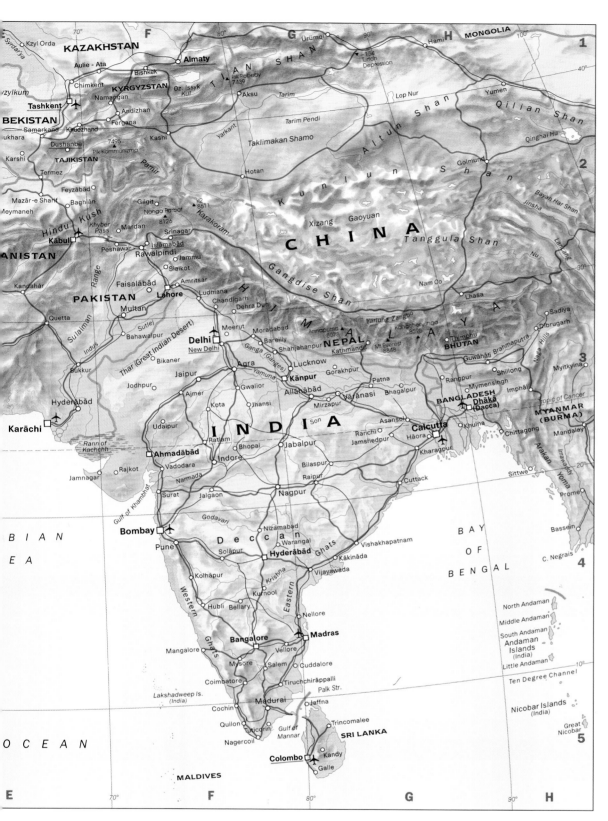

THE CITY OF BABYLON

One of the most famous cities of the ancient world, Babylon is located on the eastern side of the River Euphrates, 801 kilometres or 497 miles south of Baghdad. During the dynasty of King Nechuchadnezzar II and his successors (604–539 BC), which is described so vividly in the Old Testament book of Daniel, Babylon became one of the Seven Wonders of the World for the strangeness and magnificence of its buildings and the grandeur of its king. Only traces remain of its most famous structures, the Tower of Babel and the Hanging Gardens, along with the foundations of temples dedicated to the god, Marduk. The best preserved remains are those of the main Procession Street, the entrance to which is guarded by the fine Ishtar Gate, standing at a height of 11 metres or 36 feet.

SABA (SHEBA), YEMEN

The kingdom of Saba or Sheba, which was founded in the 10th century BC, was famous for its highly developed irrigated agricultural system. Its capital city was Marib in Western Yemen. The state visit by Queen Bilqis of Sheba to King Solomon of Israel is vividly recorded in the Bible and has been the inspiration for many artistic and musical works.

country's people are involved in agriculture but some foodstuffs have to be imported. Oman's economy is mainly based on its oil production.

YEMEN

Yemen is a republic in the southwestern part of the Arabian Peninsula. Several large islands belong to Yemen. Most of the country consists of a high plateau which becomes gradually lower eastwards and northwards until it merges with the desert lands of the Empty Quarter (Rub al Khali). In the west, high mountains extend in a north–south direction and west and south of these lies an arid, coastal plain called the Tihama. The mountains are dissected by steep-sided waddies through which water is channelled during the summer monsoon rains. This water allows some cultivation to be

carried out and agriculture employs some 60 per cent of the population. Cash crops include cotton and coffee. Manufactured goods include textiles and leather goods.

IRAN

The Islamic Republic of Iran extends from the southern shores of the Caspian Sea in the north to the eastern coast of the Persian Gulf in the south. It is a country of high mountains, plateaux and desert, notably the Zagros Mountains in the west, the Elburz (Reshteh ye Kuhha ye Alborz) range in the north and the sandy Dasht-e Lut and salty Dasht-e Kavir Deserts of central and eastern Iran.

Agriculture plays an important role in Iran's economy with wheat and barley being the main crops grown. Oil accounts for some 95 per cent of

Desert dunes

INDIA

Language/s spoken: English, Hindi and Urdu
Currency: Rupee
Travel requirements: valid passport required, best to contact relevant authority before departure
Major cities: New Delhi (capital), Ahmadabad, Bangalore, Bombay, Calcutta, Delhi, Madras, Hyderabad, Kampur
Climate: hot tropical weather with variations from region to region
Crime and safety: usual precautions should be taken, avoid Jammu and Kashmir because of civil unrest

TAJ MAHAL

The beautiful Taj Mahal is situated on a bend of the River Jumna in Agra. It was built in the 17th century by order of Emperor Shah-Jahan, as a monument and mausoleum for his beloved wife who died in childbirth in 1631. Shah Jahan employed the finest architects, craftsmen and artisans to build the Taj Mahal which occupied the labour of 20,000 workmen for over 12 years. The mausoleum itself consists of a central, large onion-shaped dome flanked by four lower domes and four identical arched facades. The tombs of the emperor and his wife lie inside, guarded by an intricately carved and decorated marble screen inlaid with jewels.

the country's exports but the economy was badly damaged by the Iran–Iraq war in the 1980s.

AFGHANISTAN

The Republic of Afghanistan is a landlocked country which is dominated by a central mass of huge mountain ranges, the highest of which are the Hindu Kush. Lower-lying areas are found only in the northwest, west and south of Afghanistan but much of this is arid or desert land. Cultivation is possible only in river valleys or where other sources of water are available. Despite the production of some natural gas, coal, gold, precious stones and salt, Afghanistan remains one of the poorest countries in the world and ongoing civil strife has further devastated the country and its people.

ARMENIA

The mountainous Republic of Armenia is dominated by the rugged peaks of the Southern Caucasus whose high plateaux and steep-sided valleys are interspersed with numerous lakes. Lowland areas occur mainly in the river valleys and the Ararat Plain in the west. Irrigation schemes allow for cultivation in lower-lying areas. Many of the trees in the once extensive areas of forest were cut down during the Soviet-led drive towards the development of a highly industrialised economy. Even more have been felled in recent years for fuel because of the economic blockade imposed by neighbouring Azerbaijan.

AZERBAIJAN

A mountainous, oil-rich republic, Azerbaijan is bounded by the southeastern ranges of the Great Caucasus in the north and the Lesser Caucasus in the west, with the Talish Mountains in the extreme south. Rivers descend from the mountains and flow through lower-lying valleys to empty into the Caspian Sea. The Lankaran region is an important agricultural area but in recent years, the country's economy has revolved around the development of its huge reserves of oil and natural gas. Azerbaijan includes the autonomous republic of Naxcivan, cut off from the rest of the country by southern Armenia, and the disputed Armenian enclave of Nagorno-Karabakh.

GEORGIA

Georgia became an independent republic in 1991 following the break-up of the Soviet Union. Stretching eastwards from the shores of the Black Sea, it consists of a coastal plain and lower-lying river valleys sandwiched between two high mountain ranges – the Great Caucasus in the north and the Lesser Caucasus in the south.

Although the land is small it has 5,000 metre or 16,000 feet peaks, lush sub-tropical forests, and rolling semidesert. The country also includes the breakaway Republic of Abkhazia and the semi-autonomous regions of Adzharia and South Ossetia. The country has been devastated by internal strife during the last decade and its economy and the life of its people have been severely disrupted.

PAKISTAN

The Islamic Republic of Pakistan is a country of varied topography whose principal feature is the Indus river system. The Indus enters the country in the northeast and is joined by four other major rivers (the Jelum, Cheenab, Ravi and Sutlej) which dominate the north central area before flowing south-westwards to the Arabian Sea. The alluvial plain of the Indus river valley provides useful agricultural land. West of the Indus valley, lies the Baluchistan Plateau – an arid, rugged plateau interrupted by many mountain ranges which push southwards from the high Hindu Kush in the north.

The north of Pakistan is dominated by the huge mountains of the Hindu Kush and the Karakorum range, containing K2 which, at 8,607 metres or 28,238 feet, is second in height only to Everest. The far north of Pakistan covers the disputed territory of Jammu and Kashmir which has been the cause of a serious conflict with India. In southeast Pakistan, the Thar Desert extends across the border into India. The country's economy depends on agriculture which employs almost half its people.

INDIA

The diverse and fascinating Republic of India is the second most densely populated country in the world and many of its people live in conditions of extreme poverty.The country has three main geographical divisions: the high peaks of the Himalayas which dominate the northern border, the northern plains and the Deccan Plateau region which occupies most of peninsular India.

The Himalayas form a massive mountain barrier which extends across the entire length of India's northern boundary. The northern plains region, which lies south of the Himalayas and extends into the northeastern states, is drained by the great River Ganges and its tributaries and by the River Brahmaputra in the east. It is a low-lying, well-watered region of fertile alluvial soils and contains the greatest proportion of India's people. The Deccan Plateau is bounded on either side by the Western and Eastern Ghats Mountains.

For the visitor, India is more like a continent than a country with everything from the high Himalayas to the deserts of Rajasthan, and Asia's best dive sites (the Andaman islands).

SRI LANKA

The island Republic of Sri Lanka (previously Ceylon) is situated just off the southeastern tip of India. It is separated from the Indian mainland by the shallow Palk Strait, which contains a chain of reefs and islands known as Adam's Bridge. The island is dominated by a central, southern mass of hills and mountains surrounded by lower, coastal plains. Sri Lanka's economy is based on agriculture and it has long been famous for its tea plantations.

MALDIVE ISLANDS

The Maldives is a republic consisting of 1,200 low-lying coral islands grouped into 12 atolls, lying 640 kilometres or 398 miles southwest of Sri Lanka in the Indian Ocean. Tourism has overtaken fishing as the major foreign currency earner.

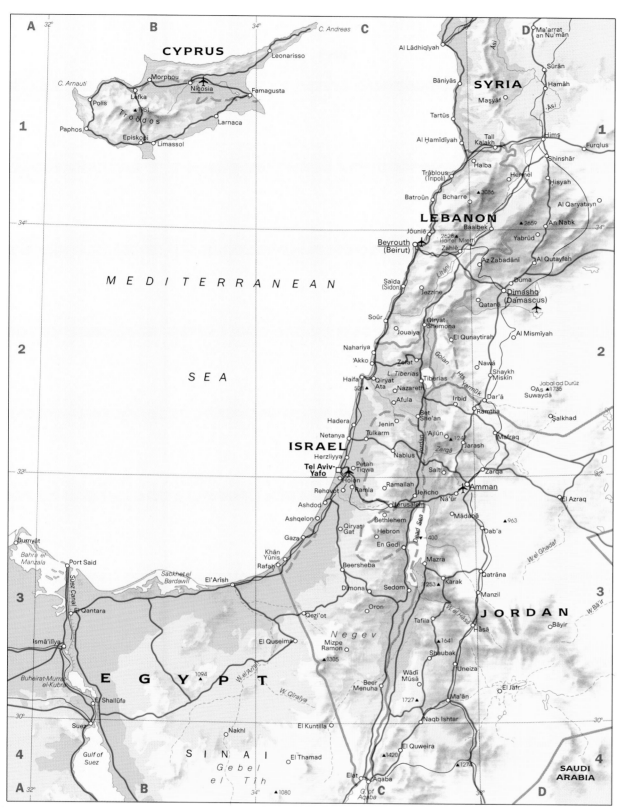

Israel, Lebanon and Cyprus
Scale 1: 3 250 000

| 0 | 25 | 50 | 75 | 100 km |

| 0 | 15 | 30 | 45 | 60 miles |

© Geddes & Grosset

Israel

Language/s spoken: Hebrew, Arabic, some English
Currency: New Israeli Shekel
Travel requirements: return ticket and valid passport required, best to contact relevant authority before departure
Major cities: Tel Aviv-Yafo (capital), Jerusalem, Haifa
Climate: hot summers, mild winters with rain, colder in the north
Crime and safety: terrorist attacks mean that visitors should be very careful to avoid any risks to their safety

Tel Aviv, Israel

In contrast to Jerusalem, Tel Aviv is a relatively young city at the heart of the country's most densely populated region. It was founded in 1909 north of the ancient city of Jaffa. The commerial capital of Israel, it also attracts many visitors thanks to the beautiful beaches along its Mediterranean seafront and its vibrant night life.

Israel

The Republic of Israel was created in 1948 after the British withdrawal from Palestine, when the region was partitioned in accordance with a recommendation made by the United Nations. The new country was born into conflict, for the declaration of its existence by Jewish leaders led to immediate warfare with Arab neighbours – the first of five such Arab–Israeli wars.

Although it is a small country, Israel has quite a varied topography of plains, hills, mountains and desert. Narrow coastal plains extend from north to south along the Mediterranean shores and are densely populated. The Plain of Esdraelon extends across the northern part of Israel from Haifa to the valley of the River Jordan and is reclaimed marshland which is intensively cultivated and settled. The Hills of Galilee, which rise to nearly 1,216 metres or 4,000 feet, occupy the northern part of Israel from the Sea of Galilee to the coast. The Judean and Samarian Hills extend in a north–south direction behind the coastal plains throughout most of Israel and beyond them, in the south of the country, lies the Negev Desert.

Israel's only major river, the Jordan, arises in Mount Hermon on the Jordanian-Syrian border and flows southwards through the Sea of Galilee (Lake Tiberias) and into the Dead Sea, which lies 408 metres or 1,338 feet below sea level and is the lowest point on the Earth's land surface. The River Jordan, the Sea of Galilee and the Dead Sea occupy the Great Rift Valley which extends from beyond the source of the Jordan through the Gulf of Aqaba and the Red Sea and on into East Africa.

Israel has a Mediterranean-type climate with hot, dry summers and mild to cool winters when rainfall is experienced. The north of Israel receives con-

The Wailing Wall and Dome of the Rock, Jerusalem

Israel, Lebanon and Cyprus

THE DEAD SEA SCROLLS

Discovered accidentally by a shepherd boy in 1947 in caves in the cliffs above the Dead Sea in Qumran, Palestine, the Dead Sea scrolls are the oldest known Hebrew books. They represent the religious writings of the Essenes, an aesthetic, monastic Jewish sect who lived at Qumran some 2000 years ago. Some of the scrolls represent books of the Old Testament such as Isaiah and Deuteronomy but they predate other versions by many hundreds of years. The scrolls have thrown light on complex passages of scriptures and have helped to reveal the origins of early Christianity and Judaism. They are housed in a museum in Jerusalem.

CYPRUS

Language/s spoken: mostly Greek, some Turkish, English
Currency: Cyprus Pound
Travel requirements: return ticket and valid passport required, best to contact relevant authority before departure
Major cities: Nicosia (capital), Famagusta, Limassol, Larnaca
Climate: hot, dry summers, mild winters, most rainfall in winter
Crime and safety: take sensible precautions

Kyrenia Harbour, Cyprus

siderably more rainfall than the south which is very dry. Natural vegetation varies according to location and amount of rainfall but most plants are adapted to withstand drought. Wooded areas cover about 6 per cent of Israel and there has been an extensive programme of replanting of native species such as dwarf oak. Wildlife species include wolf, jackal, hyena, mongoose, porcupine and gazelle.

Fruits and vegetables, which are grown intensively and with the help of modern technology, are two of the country's leading exports. There is a large manufacturing industry and products include jewellery, military equipment, fertilisers, chemicals, processed food, electronic equipment and plastics. Tourism also makes an important contribution to the economy.

The Dead Sea

The toxic waters of the Dead Sea are so saturated with minerals that they sustain no life and in the summer pillars of salt can be seen protruding from the surface. The water of the Dead Sea is believed to have healing properties (although it is dangerous if swallowed or inhaled) and many people flock to it each year to bathe and to have mud baths. The high mineral content makes it impossible to sink and although the climate is hot, very little damaging UV radiation penetrates down to the low altitude of the Dead Sea so that sunburn is seldom a problem. The Dead Sea has no natural outflow and is fed only by the Jordan itself. Water is being taken from the Jordan for irrigation purposes and there is a net loss of moisture through evaporation, hence the area of the Dead Sea is shrinking.

Jerusalem

The city of Jerusalem is not only the historic heartland of ancient and modern Israel but also a holy place for three of the world's great religions, namely Judaism, Christianity and Islam. For Israel's Jewish population, Jerusalem is the royal capital of King David and its most sacred site is the Wailing Wall, the only remaining part of the Holy Temple sacked by the Romans in AD 70. For Christians, it is intimately associated with the last days of Christ before His crucifixion and contains many holy sites including the Mount of Olives, Calvary and the Church of the Holy Sepulchre, built in the 4th century AD over the tomb where Jesus' body had been laid prior to His resurrection. The Dome of the Rock is a mosque built in the 7th century on the site where the prophet Mohammed ascended into heaven and is one of the places in the city most revered by Muslims.

LEBANON

The small, troubled republic of Lebanon has, throughout its long human history, seen the rise and fall of many civilisations and empires and its capital, Beirut (Beyrouth), has come to symbolise all the complex troubles of the Middle East. Apart from a narrow, fertile, coastal strip which hardly exceeds 6 kilometres or 3 miles in width, the country's topography is dominated by two high, parallel ranges of mountains, the Lebanon and Anti-Lebanon, running roughly northeast–southwest. Between these two ranges lies the fertile Bekaa Valley through which flows Lebanon's only large river, the Litani.

The mountains not only dominate the geography but have played a significant role in the country's history. They have provided a refuge for various religious groups and tribes fleeing from persecution elsewhere and enabled these peoples to preserve their cultural identities because of the physical barriers that have separated them. This situation was aided by the fact that Lebanon is relatively well-watered with fairly plentiful rainfall which falls mainly during the winter months. The mountains also provide a home for Lebanon's remaining wildlife which includes wolves, jackals, gazelles and wild donkeys. Summers are hot and dry although temperatures are lower at high altitude and winters generally mild and wet but colder, with snow, in the mountains.

Since earliest times, Lebanon has been famous for its cedar trees – the 'cedars of Lebanon' – which were used, according to the biblical account, in the construction of Solomon's temple. Hence deforestation has been taking place for thousands of years and today very little natural forest remains other than isolated strands of trees in the mountains.

Lebanon is an agricultural country and main products include olives, grapes, bananas, citrus fruits, apples, cotton, tobacco and sugar beet. Industry is small scale and manufactured goods include cement, fertilisers and jewellery. There are oil refineries at Tripoli (Trablous) and Sidon (Saida). Lebanon's main economy is based on commercial services such as banking but, as a result of the civil war in the 1970s and 1980s, invasion by Israel and factional fighting, the economy has suffered greatly causing high inflation and unemployment.

CYPRUS

Cyprus is an island republic in the eastern Mediterranean which has been unofficially partitioned since 1974 – the northeastern portion forming the Turkish Republic of Northern Cyprus. The island's shape somewhat resembles a saucepan with the 'handle' formed by the long, narrow Karpas Peninsula pointing northeastwards towards Turkey. A range of mountains extends along much of the northern coast with a still higher range, the Troodos Mountains, in the centre and southwest. Between the mountains lies an extensive plain used for agriculture called the Messoria Plain.

The island has a Mediterranean climate with dry, hot summers and mild, moist winters during which most of the annual rainfall is experienced. Forests, mainly confined to the mountain slopes, cover about 13 per cent of Cyprus and include cedar, cypress, pine and juniper. Native wildlife is poorly represented except for birds, many species of which use the island as a stopover point during migration.

The economy of Cyprus is mainly agricultural and this accounts for about 17 per cent of the land. A great variety of crops is grown including grapes, which are used for the strong wines and sherries for which Cyprus is famous. Cyprus has been an important centre for copper mining since ancient times, when the island was the main known source. Fishing is a significant industry but, above all, the island depends on visitors and it is the tourist industry which has led to a recovery in the economy since 1974.

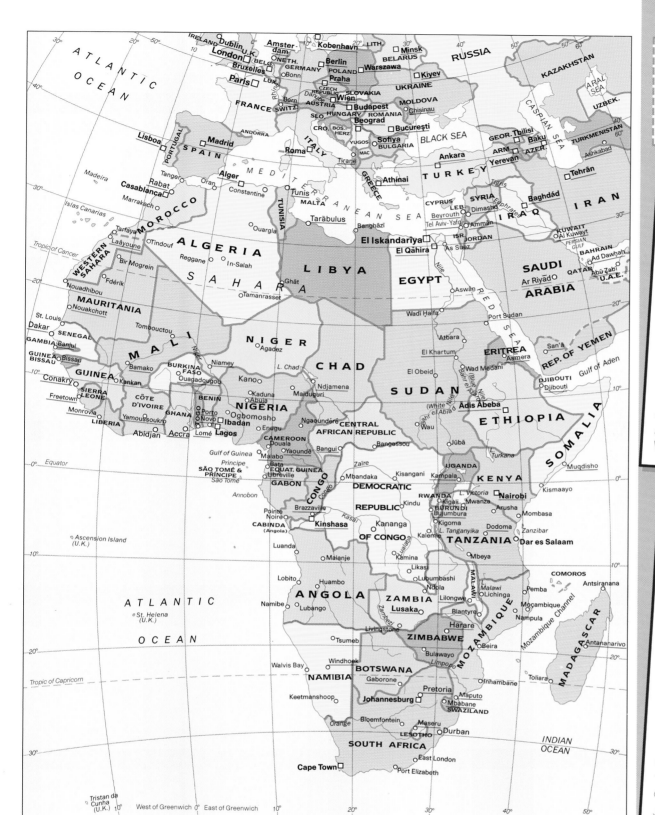

Africa, Political
Scale 1: 48 000 000

0   400   800   1200   1600 km

0   250   500   750   1000 miles

© Geddes & Grosset

WATAMU MARINE NATIONAL PARK, KENYA

This beautiful park can be found north of Mombasa on the east coast of Kenya and a visit there is a must for anyone who enjoys exploring the underwater world. Watamu is a protected area of white coral sand beaches and clear blue lagoons full of brilliantly coloured tropical fish. It is forbidden to fish or collect shells or coral within its waters. Trips in glass-bottomed boats over the coral reefs can be arranged from hotels in Malindi or Watamu.

EGYPTIAN ANTIQUITIES MUSEUM, CAIRO

This museum contains treasures of the pharaohs going back 5,000 years and is the richest museum of Egyptian antiquities in the world. Visitors come from all over the world to see the gold and alabaster artefacts from Tutankhamun's tomb. All the trappings of the pharaoh's life are here – golden chariots, golden furniture, alabaster perfume jars to name but a few. One of the few artefacts that has never been seen outside of Egypt is the famous statue of Anubis, god of the dead – a lifesize ebony jackal with gold-lined ears and golden collar.

The Mask of Tutankhamun

Africa's peoples are as varied as her contrasting landscapes with many hundreds of different ethnic groups encompassing diverse cultures, religions, languages and lifestyles.

Shaped roughly like a triangle, Africa is the second largest of the world's continents and comprises 53 separate countries. Most of northern and north-western Africa consists of low plateaux and plains, interrupted by isolated mountain ranges and dominated by the Sahara, the world's greatest desert. In the east, south and southeast lie higher plateaux and mountains and the complex Great African Rift Valley system. This extends from the Dead Sea through the Red Sea continuing southwards to cut through a large part of East Africa and containing many of the continent's great lakes. Some of the world's great river systems flow through Africa, notably the Nile, Niger, Zaire (Congo), Zambezi, Limpopo and Orange. Island states off the coast of Africa include Madagascar, Seychelles and São Tomé and Príncipe.

The continent is home to some of the world's most spectacular and endangered wildlife such as the shy, forest-dwelling okapi of the Congo and the mountain gorilla of Rwanda. Among the best known animals are those of the savannah grasslands of east Africa including the vast, migratory herds of wildebeest and zebra, tall, graceful giraffe, elephant and the largest of all land-dwelling mammals and their attendant predators and scavengers – lion, leopard, cheetah, hyena and vulture.

Africa offers so much to the traveller from the pyramids of Egypt to South Africa's beautiful beaches, from snorkelling off the coast of east Africa to being able to watch the fabled gorillas in the mist of Rwanda. Perhaps nowhere else in the world will the traveller find such a variety of cultures and vistas, such a combination of old and new.

Morocco

Language/s spoken: Arabic, some French and English

Currency: Moroccan Dirham

Travel requirements: return ticket and valid passport required, best to contact relevant authority before departure

Major cities: Rabat (capital), Casablanca, Fez, Marrakech, Tangier

Climate: high temperatures, mostly dry, cooler in the mountains

Crime and safety: take sensible precautions

Fes el Bali, Morocco

Fes el Bali (old Fes) is a living example of a medieval town and a World Heritage Site. Many of its inhabitants lead a way of life that has changed little from the 14th century. Licensed guides can be hired from tourist offices as it is all too easy to get lost in the maze of streets and alleyways.

Marrakech, Morocco

The pink walls of the ancient former capital of Marrakech set against the snow-capped peaks of the Atlas Mountains, appear almost like a mirage as the traveller approaches the city on the route south from Casablanca. There is much for the traveller to see and enjoy in the city from its colourful souks (street markets), where all manner of goods and crafts are for sale, to its beautiful minarets, notably the Jemaa el Fna.

Kasbah Ait-Benhaddou, Morocco

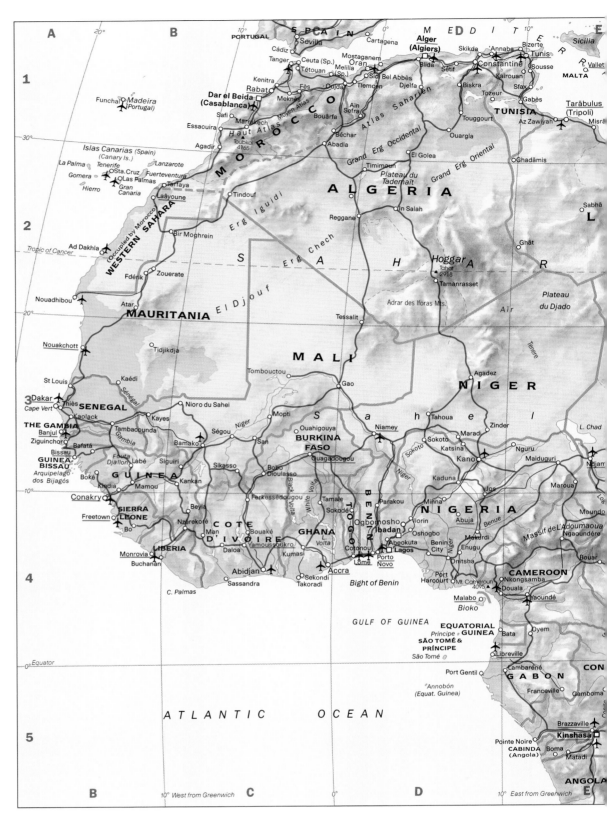

Morocco

Morocco is a northern African country of diverse topography, climate and human history whose cities, including Tanger, Fes, Marrakech and Casablanca, have long held a fascination for Europeans. The Atlas Mountains dominate the landscape but give way to fertile coastal plains along the Atlantic coast. The Er Rif Mountains command the Mediterranean coast while southeast of the Atlas, the land falls away to join the Sahara Desert. The ports of Melilla and Ceuta are administered by Spain while Morocco lays claim to the territory of Western Sahara. Mainly a farming country, the country's main wealth comes from phosphates, reserves of which are the largest in the world.

Tourism is also a major source of revenue. Despite being only 20 kilometres or 12 miles from the Spanish coast, the moment visitors set foot in Morocco, they know and feel that they are very far from Europe. Some come to enjoy the holiday resorts of Tanger and Agadir but there is much to explore further afield in this colourful and vibrant country.

Western Sahara

Formerly Spanish Sahara, Western Sahara is a thinly populated desert country of rocky plains and plateaux with low hills in the extreme northeast of Africa, administered by Morocco. Moroccan sovereignty is not universally recognised. It is a poor country with many following a nomadic existence. Phosphates comprise two thirds of the meagre exports.

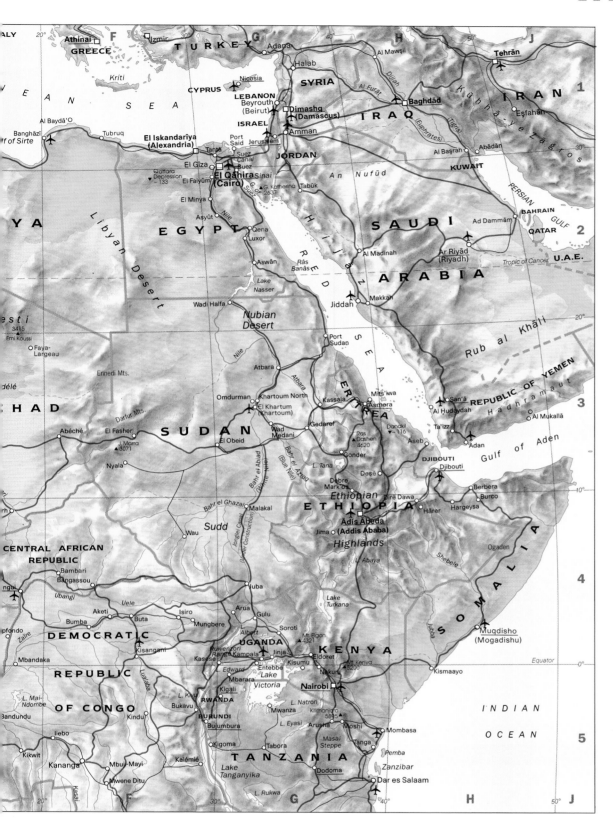

**Northern Africa
Scale 1: 23 500 000**

0   200   400   600   800 km

0   100   200   300   400   500 miles

© Geddes & Grosset

TUNISIA

Language/s spoken: Arabic, some French and English
Currency: Tunisian Dinar
Travel requirements: return ticket and valid passport required, best to contact relevant authority before departure
Major cities: Tunis (capital), Sfax, Bizerte, Djerba, Sousse
Climate: warm temperatures all year, hotter inland
Crime and safety: take sensible precautions

CARTHAGE, TUNISIA

The ruins of Carthage lie 18 kilometres or 12 miles northeast of Tunis city centre. Carthage was founded in 814 BC by the Phoenicians and the success of her inhabitants in trade led to conflicts with Greece and later with Rome. Although little of the Phoenician city survived, some of its treasures have been recovered from the Roman foundations and these are preserved in the Bardo Museum in Tunis. The National Museum of Carthage also contains antiquities from the Phoenician, Greek and Roman periods as well as from other stages in Tunisia's long human history.

ALGERIA

The Democratic and Popular Republic of Algeria is the second largest country in Africa although most of its territory is desert. The most fertile area is a narrow coastal strip, the Tell, containing most of the country's cultivatable land and the greatest concentration of people. Behind the plain lie the hills and mountains of the High Plateaux, the Atlas Mountains (Tell Atlas) and the Saharan Atlas Mountains. Beyond these, and comprising more than 85 per cent of the total land area, lies the vast expanse of the Sahara Desert interrupted in the southeast by the dramatic massif of the Hoggar and Tassil-n-Ajer Mountains.

Algeria has some of the largest reserves of natural gas and oil in the world. Its main exports are oil-based products, fruit, vegetables, tobacco, phosphates and cork. In recent years, the country has been wracked by civil strife and terrorist attacks with the opposing forces unable to agree on peace proposals.

TUNISIA

The small Republic of Tunisia has a fairly long, indented Mediterranean coastline with several islands, notably Djerba and Kerkennah, lying near the shore. The foothills of the Atlas Mountains project into the northwestern part of the country. To the south and southeast, the land descends to a region of salt lakes and salt pans (called shotts), some of which lie below sea level. Beyond the salt lakes lie the fringes of the Sahara Desert which occupies two fifths of Tunisia's total land area.

Agriculture produces wheat, barley, olives, grapes, tomatoes, dates, vegetables and citrus fruits and the fishing industry is of growing impor-

A Roman amphitheatre, Tunisia

A camel resting near the Pyramids of Giza, Egypt

tance but the mainstay of Tunisia's modern economy is oil from the Sahara, phosphates, natural gas and tourism on the Mediterranean coast. Tourists come to enjoy Tunisia's rich and varied culture and its beautiful beaches. There are many ruined temples, forbidding fortresses, magnificent mosaics and ornate architecture for the history-loving tourist and the resorts of Hammamet, Monastir and Djerba for those looking for a beach holiday.

LIBYA

The Socialist People's Libyan Arab Jamahiriyah is a large, oil-rich country but most of its territory is uninhabited and consists of rocky or sandy desert with extensive 'sand seas'. In general, Libya's terrain consists of undulating rocky plains with two areas of hills in the northwest and northeast and an outcrop of the Tibesti Massif across the border with Chad. Almost all Libyans live in the cities and urban areas along the north coast. The main agricultural region is in the northwest near Tripoli but this is dependent on rainfall. Libya is one of the world's largest producers of oil and natural gas and also produces potash and marine salt.

EGYPT

Although over 90 cent of the Arab Republic of Egypt consists of desert, most of which is uninhabited, the country was the birthplace of one of the most astonishing, ancient civilisations in the world, with a written record dating back to about 3 200 years BC. The development of this civilisation was made possible by the presence of the River Nile which flows southwards through Egypt from Sudan.

The deserts of Egypt are far from uniform, varying from the huge Great Sand Sea in the Libyan or Western Desert to rocky, mountainous regions in the Eastern Desert along the shores of the Red Sea and in the southern Sinai Peninsula. Sinai is separated from the rest of Egypt by the Suez Canal. In the Western or Libyan Desert, there are several areas which lie well below sea level.

Around 99 per cent of the population lives in the Nile valley and delta where the main crops are rice, cotton, sugar cane, maize, tomatoes and wheat. The main industries are food processing and textiles. The economy has been boosted by the discovery of oil while the Suez Canal, shipping and tourism are all important revenue earners. Militant Muslim fundamentalists who wish to see Egypt become a strict Islamic state, have posed a threat during the 1990s by attacking foreign visitors and damaging the country's important tourist trade.

Tourists come to see the art and architecture of the pharaohs, to enjoy deep-sea fishing and skin diving off the Red Sea coast or to cruise the waters of the River Nile in the comfort of a floating hotel in cruisers which allows them to explore many of Egypt's greatest antiquities without having to pack and unpack every few days.

SUDAN

The Republic of the Sudan finally gained its independence in 1956 but it has been beset by problems of civil war, drought and famine. It is the largest country in Africa and divides naturally into three main regions – desert in the north, dry grasslands and steppe in the centre and marshland, giving way to tropical forest and mountains in the south. Cutting through the country is the great river system of the Nile. Its two main headwaters, the White Nile and the Blue Nile, unite at Sudan's capital, Khartoum. An upland mountainous plateau, the Darfur, rises in the west near the border with Chad and the Red Sea Hills lie behind the coast in the northeast. North of the mountains which straddle the border with Uganda and traversed by the many tributaries of the White Nile, lies a huge area of marshland called the Sudd.

Cotton is farmed commercially and accounts for about two thirds of the country's exports. Sudan is the world's greatest source of gum arabic which is used in medicines, perfumes, processed foods and inks.

ERITREA

The independent state of Eritrea was created in 1993 following a long, armed struggle against Ethiopia. Eritrea has a coastal plain rising to plateaux and mountains in the centre and north. West of the mountains, the ground descends to form a region of undulating plains.

Most people have traditionally followed an agricultural or pastoral way of life. Warfare, with its consequent loss of life and displacement of people, coupled with drought and famine, has had a disastrous effect upon Eritrea in recent years and the country faces a long struggle to rebuild its economy and improve the lot of its people.

DJIBOUTI

The small Republic of Djibouti achieved independence from France in 1977. It is a hot, dry, land of plateaux, mountains and a coastal plain with a salt lake, Lac Assal, which is the second lowest point on land in Africa. About half of the country's small population are engaged in agriculture which is limited to oases or areas where water is available. However, the economy is largely dependent on trade through the capital, also Djibouti, which serves as a major port for landlocked Ethiopia.

ETHIOPIA

The large Republic of Ethiopia, formerly known as Abyssinia, is dominated by a high, central plateau of volcanic rock from which rise rugged mountains. The Great African Rift Valley divides the plateau into the higher, more rugged and extensive Western Highlands and the smaller area of the Eastern Highlands. The plateau is deeply dissected by river valleys forming towering cliffs and escarpments, especially in the northeast. Lake Tana, the source of the Blue Nile, is found in this region. To the east of the plateau lie two sun-scorched desert regions – the Denakil Depression in the northeast and the Ogaden Plain in the southeast. The western and southern border regions also consist of lower-lying plains. Around 80 per cent of the population are involved in subsistence farming. Coffee is the main source of rural income and teff is the main food grain.

SOMALIA

The Somali Democratic Republic or Somalia has a long coastline bordering the Gulf of Aden in the north and the Indian Ocean in the east. Hills and mountains dominate the north behind the coastal plain while most of the southern interior comprises a dry and rugged plateau. Two rivers, the Jubba and the Shebele, enter southern Somalia from Ethiopia and their valleys provide useful agricultural land. The country has little in the way of natural resources. Civil war broke out in the 1980s and early 1990s resulting in a huge loss of life and widespread famine. The situation remains unresolved although there has been some recovery in agriculture and food production.

CHAD

Chad is a landlocked republic whose principal feature is the large, shallow Lake Chad in the west with its surrounding basin and river systems. The basin is ringed by plateaux, the Ennedi Mountains in the east and the Tibesti Mountains in the far north. The volcanic Tibesti Massif rises impressively from the parched, sun-baked sand dunes of the Sahara Desert. Most people live in rural areas. Cotton is the main cash crop and the principal industries are cotton ginning and the manufacture of peanut oil.

NIGER

The landlocked Republic of Niger has three principal regions: desert in the north, occupying about half of the total area; semiarid grasslands called the Sahel in the centre and east; and a greener, forested region in the south and west. The Ténéré Desert, part of the Sahara, is alternately stony and sandy and interrupted by plateaux and mountains. In the far west, the River Niger flows southeastwards for 483 kilometres or 300 miles, cutting off Niger's far western territory. In the extreme southeast, a part of Lake Chad extends into Niger's territory. Most people are employed in subsistence agriculture. Uranium is the country's main export.

MALI

The landlocked Republic of Mali consists mainly of level plains interrupted by isolated groups of hills and mountains. The northern third lies within the Sahara Desert. Southwest of the true desert, there is a region of dry Sahel grassland and this gives way to the land surrounding the Rivers Niger and Senegal and their tributaries. The Niger is especially valuable as it is navigable throughout its entire length for most of the year. Most people live in the south and follow an agricultural way of life. Mali has limited natural resources. The country's main exports include cotton, gold, foodstuffs, livestock and mangoes.

MAURITANIA

Almost all of the Islamic Republic of Mauritania lies within the sandy, stony wastes of the Sahara Desert and is mainly a vast plain, rising in places to plateaux of 500–600 metres or 1,640–1,968 feet.

In the south, there is a belt of dry Sahel grassland but the only fertile region is a belt of land along the northern side of the valley of the River Senegal. The river itself forms part of the southern border. Most of the people follow a nomadic way of life centred around the herding of grazing animals but there are some settled farmers. Mauritania has rich deposits of iron ore and valuable Atlantic fish stocks.

SENEGAL

Senegal consists mainly of a low-lying plain with higher ground only in the extreme southeast. The River Senegal forms the northern boundary and other rivers further south include the Gambia. The independent Cape Verde Islands lie 560 kilometres or 350 miles west of Senegal in the Atlantic Ocean. Almost 80 per cent of the labour force work in agriculture. The country's economy is largely dependent on peanuts but there is a growing manufacturing sector, which produces cement, chemicals and tinned tuna, and tourism is also expanding.

THE GAMBIA

The Republic of the Gambia comprises a small finger of land, pushing in eastwards from the Atlantic coast in a narrow band along either side of the Gambia river. On the coast, there are pristine beaches and sand cliffs backed by mangrove swamps, with tropical jungle clothing much of the river banks away from the coast. Beyond the river valley, lies some more thinly wooded savannah grassland containing commercially valuable trees. Groundnuts are the main and only export crop of any significance. The white sandy beaches on the coast attract an increasing number of tourists each year.

GUINEA-BISSAU

Guinea-Bissau is a small republic whose territory includes over 60 coastal islands including the Bissagos (Bijagós) Archipelago. The land consists mainly of a low, marshy plain, rising slightly to a plateau and hills on the border with neighbouring Guinea. Mangrove swamps and tropical jungle cover the land near the coast giving way to savannah-type grassland on the plateau. The forests contain commercially valuable trees but the majority of the people are engaged in subsistence farming. Fishing is an important export industry although cashew nuts are the principal export.

GUINEA

The Republic of Guinea is a country of varied topography crossed by many rivers, including the upper reaches of the Senegal, Gambia and Niger. The land rises inland from the coastal plain to form the central massif of the Fouta Djallon Highlands, a sandstone plateau dissected by deep valleys. The south of the country is occupied by the Guinea Highlands and between the two upland areas lies a region of savannah grassland extending northeastwards into Mali. The majority of Gambia's people are engaged in subsistence farming. The country is rich in mineral reserves and has the potential for hydroelectric power.

TIMBUKTU (TIMBOUCTOU), MALI

Timbuktu is located in southern central Mali near the river Niger and was founded in the 11th century. It developed as a leading trading centre, being located on the trans-Saharan camel train route and connected by a canal network to the Niger river. The city became a leading cultural and religious centre of the Islamic faith but fell into decline after it was ravaged by warfare at the end of the 16th century. Timbuktu was known to the Europeans of the Middle Ages and, in Britain, it came to symbolise a remote and far away place at the 'end of the Earth'.

THE GAMBIA

Language/s spoken: English
Currency: Gambian Dalasi
Travel requirements: return ticket and valid passport required, best to contact relevant authority before departure
Major towns: Banjul (capital), Bakau, Serekunda
Climate: mid-November to mid-May dry on the coast, June to October rainy season
Crime and safety: watch out for pickpockets and bag snatchers

Mountain homes in Mali

Northern Africa

ACCRA, GHANA

Ghana's capital city is a sprawling, friendly city with colourful markets such as the Makola Market to visit, nearby beaches and the Aburi Botanical Gardens to relax in and a wide selection of arts to explore at the Arts Centre, including samples of the kente cloth for which Ghana is renowned. Accra also has three forts, James Fort, Ussher Fort and Christiansborg Castle built in the 17th century by the British, Dutch and Danish respectively although these can only be looked at from a distance as they are off-limits to tourists.

NIGERIA

Language/s spoken: English and local African languages
Currency: Naira
Travel requirements: return ticket and valid passport required, best to contact relevant authority before departure
Major cities: Abuja (new federal capital), Lagos, Aba, Ede, Enugu, Ibadan, Kano, Ogbomosho
Climate: humid and hot most of the year, rainy season March to November at the coast, April to September in the north
Crime and safety: do not travel after dark, take sensible precautions

Waterfall at Ikom, southeast Nigeria

SIERRA LEONE

The Republic of Sierra Leone possesses a fine natural harbour where the capital and major port of Freetown is situated. The Sierra Lyoa Mountains rise directly behind the capital on the Freetown Peninsula but elsewhere the coastal plain is up to 110 kilometres or 70 miles wide rising to a plateau and then mountains which are part of the Guinea Highlands Massif. Eight rivers and many streams descend from the higher ground. Most people are engaged in either agriculture or mining.

LIBERIA

Liberia was founded in 1847 as a homeland for freed slaves from North America. The country has a low-lying, well-watered coastal plain in which there are many mangrove swamps. The land rises inland to a jungle-covered, slightly elevated plateau. North of this, lies a belt of hills and mountains which are also forested. Iron ore accounts for 70 per cent of export earnings and wood, rubber, diamonds and coffee are also exported. Liberia has a very large tanker fleet, most of which have foreign owners. A devastating civil war in the 1990s resulted in many deaths and produced thousands of refugees.

CÔTE D'IVOIRE

Côte d'Ivoire comprises an undulating plain in the south and west rising to mountainous territory in the northwestern border regions. The interior and northern areas consist of savannah grasslands with thinly scattered trees. Coastal lagoons are a notable feature attracting many species of birds. Agriculture employs about 55 per cent of the workforce. Côte d'Ivoire is the world's largest producer of cocoa and the fourth largest producer of coffee.

BURKINA FASO

The landlocked People's Democratic Republic of Burkina Faso was formerly called Upper Volta and is one of the poorest countries in the world. It comprises a plateau region in the north which gives way southwards to an area of plains. The northern part of the country is an arid extension of the Sahara Desert. The south is less dry and has savannah type vegetation and scattered trees, although desertification threatens part of this land. Three main rivers, the Black Volta (Mouhoun), Red Volta (Nazinon) and White Volta (Nakanbe), descend from the plateau across the plains. About 85 per cent of the people live by subsistence farming. The manufacturing industry produces textiles, metal products, consumer items such as footwear and soap, and agricultural products.

GHANA

Ghana is mainly low lying but has a range of mountains along its eastern border with Togo and forested hills and plateaux in the interior and north. A coastal, grassy plain gives way to dense jungle in the southwest and savannah country and woodland in the interior and north. The country's two main rivers, the Black Volta and the White Volta, unite in central eastern Ghana to form the River Volta which flows southwards to the sea. Construction of the Akosombo Dam on the lower reaches of the river led to the creation of the world's largest manmade lake, Lake Volta. Agriculture and mining are the principal economic activities. Ghana's most important crop is cocoa. Tourism is increasing and there is lots for tourists to see and enjoy, from colourful local markets to Kumasi, the capital of the Ashanti kingdom.

TOGO

The Republic of Togo is a narrow country, pushing inland and northwards from the Gulf of Guinea and sandwiched on either side between Ghana and Benin. Its main feature is a central range of low mountains which extend northeast–southwest. Northeast of these, lie the plateau and plain of the River Oti covered by savannah grassland. In the south, there is a region of coastal marshes and lagoons with thick mangrove forest while there is an area of tropical jungle in the southwest. Over 80 per cent of the population is involved in subsistence farming. Minerals, particularly phosphates, are now the main exports along with raw cotton, coffee, cocoa, cement and palm kernels.

BENIN

Benin was formerly called Dahomey. The coastal region on the Gulf of Guinea is sandy with many lagoons but inland the ground rises to a fertile plain and then a plateau. In the far northwest, the Atakora Mountains rise from the plateau in the region of the Niger/Nigeria border. The majority of the population live in the south of the country. Farming is predominantly subsistence and accounts for around 60 per cent of the workforce. The main exports are palm oil, palm kernels, and cotton and tourism is slowly being developed.

NIGERIA

The Federal Republic of Nigeria is not only the most densely populated country in Africa but also one of the most powerful and important. Nigeria's topography, climate and natural vegetation vary considerably. The coastal belt is a region of sandy beaches, lagoons and swampy mangrove forests. Beyond this, lies a region of tropical rainforest with the land gradually rising towards extensive central and northern plateaux. Surrounding the plateaux are savannah plains which grade into semidesert and desert in the extreme north of the country. Crossing the eastern border with Cameroon is the high Adamawa Plateau (Massif de L'Adoumaoua) where Nigeria's highest peak, Vogel (2,042 metres or 6,699 feet), is located.

The Niger river system with its many tributaries drains the country and Lake Chad stretches across the far northeastern border. The main agricultural products are cocoa, rubber, groundnuts and cotton with only cocoa being of any export significance. The economy is heavily dependent upon the exploitation of large reserves of oil and natural gas but other minerals include extensive deposits of coal, iron ore and salt.

CAMEROON

The Republic of Cameroon is a country of varied topography and natural vegetation. The far north is a region of savannah plain with marshland near the shores of Lake Chad. Eastwards, the land becomes drier as it grades towards the Sahel grasslands of Chad. The Mandara Mountains spill over the border with Nigeria in the west while the savannah plains further south rise gradually to form the extensive Adamawa Plateau. The coastal plain is covered with tropical rainforests. Mount Cameroon is one of a group of still active volcanic mountains that rise up in the west behind the coastal plain. Most people are engaged in agricultural activities and cocoa is produced for export. Oil also makes a significant contribution to the economy.

EQUATORIAL GUINEA

The Republic of Equatorial Guinea comprises a small, square mainland section (Rio Muni), the large island of Bioko and smaller island of Annobon in the Bight of Biafra and the coastal islets of Corisco, Elobey Grande and Elobey Chico. The mainland is mainly densely forested, rolling landscape broken by some hills but Bioko is volcanic with two high mountains, steep slopes and tropical jungle. Most people are engaged in agriculture and some crops are produced for export along with tropical hardwoods harvested from the forests.

GABON

The Gabonese Republic comprises the land which surrounds the basin of the River Ogooué and its tributaries, most of which is covered with lush tropical rainforests. Beyond the coastal plain and the flatter land of the valley bottoms, Gabon is ringed by upland plateaux and mountains. Agriculture, forestry, mining (of oil, manganese, iron ore and uranium) and fishing are the principal economic activities.

CENTRAL AFRICAN REPUBLIC

The landlocked Central African Republic consists mainly of plateaux. Mountains in the northwest extend across the Cameroon border. The plateaux support dry, open woodland and savannah grassland but grade into arid scrub and semidesert in the far northeast. In the far southwest, thick tropical rainforest is the predominant vegetation. Over 86 per cent of the working population are subsistence farmers. Mining is an important contributor to the economy. The country's main exports are coffee, diamonds, cotton, tobacco and timber.

UGANDA

The Republic of Uganda is a country of plateaux, mountains, lakes and plains, presenting a great variety of landscapes and vegetation. Almost half of Lake Victoria lies within Uganda's territory while the country's western border extends along the Great Rift Valley, in which lie Lake Albert and Lake Edward. The White Nile river flows from Lake Victoria across the northern part of the country. High mountains arise on or near the eastern border while the southwest is occupied by the massif of the Ruwenzori Mountains. Tropical forests and tea plantations clothe the lower slopes of the Ruwenzori Mountains.

Most people are engaged in agriculture with some crops being produced for export. Copper mining used to be important but has now declined and other mineral reserves have not yet been exploited.

Since the 1980s and following years of civil turmoil and unrest, Uganda has slowly been rebuilding its shattered economy. Attempts are being made to expand the tea plantations in the west and to introduce new industries to Kampala.

KENYA

Kenya is a country of moderate size in east Africa. It has an Indian Ocean coastline in the southeast and borders on Tanzania to the south, Uganda to the west, Sudan to the northwest, Ethiopia to the north and Somalia to the east. The coastal plains rise to high plains and highlands in the interior. Tea, coffee and petroleum are exported but other mineral resources are few or undeveloped. The tourism industry is very important to the country's economy.

RWANDA

Rwanda is a small, hilly, landlocked republic in which the predominant feature is a central high plateau. High mountains dominate the north and west of the country sloping downwards to the basin of Lake Kivu on the western border. East of the plateau, the land drops downwards to a region of marshes and lakes surrounding the Kagera river.

Most people depend upon farming for their livelihood and the main cash crops are arabic coffee, tea and pyrethrum. There are major reserves of natural gas but these are largely unexploited. Rwandans comprise three ethnic tribes: the Hutu (90 per cent), Tutsi (9 per cent – the ruling, élite class) and the Twa (1 per cent – believed to be the original people of the country). Throughout much of the 20th century, there have been serious ethnic divisions between the Hutu and Tutsi and many acts of violence. The country's economy has been faced with massive disruption following the tribal genocide wars of 1994 and ongoing ethnic rivalry.

BURUNDI

Burundi is a small, landlocked republic consisting mainly of an upland plateau. It is a poor country and most of its people are involved in subsistence farming. The main cash crop is coffee, which accounts for 90 per cent of Burundi's export earnings. Cotton and tea are also cultivated for export. The population characteristics are similar to those of Rwanda with a majority of Hutus, a minority of Tutsis and a small number of Twa pygmy people. Unfortunately, the same pattern of ethnic violence and political instability that has plagued Rwanda has also afflicted Burundi.

ALBERT SCHWEITZER

In 1913, after some years at medical school, Albert Schweitzer (1875-1965) left German Alsace for Lambarene in Gabon, where he established a hospital. Interred during the First World War, Schweitzer later returned to the hospital which he rebuilt and extended, adding a wing for the care of those with leprosy. His humanitarian work was recognised internationally when he was awarded the Nobel Peace Prize in 1952. The hospital he founded still exists in Lambarene, Gabon.

KENYA

Language/s spoken: English and Kiswahili

Currency: Kenyan Shilling

Travel requirements: return ticket and valid passport required, best to contact relevant authority before departure

Major cities: Nairobi (capital), Mombasa, Eldoret, Kisumu, Nakuru

Climate: humid and hot at the coast, hot and dry inland, rainy seasons March to May and October to November

Crime and safety: do not travel after dark, muggings take place in Nairobi and Mombasa, take sensible precautions

The Parc National des Volcans in the volcanic mountains of Rwanda is one of the last remaining strongholds of the endangered and beautiful mountain gorillas. These animals were studied and their plight brought to international attention by the American zoologist, Dian Fossey. The importance of conserving the gorillas has generated worldwide interest and support.

Southern Africa

THE RIVER CONGO

The River Congo is one of the world's longest rivers and, at a little over 4,300 kilometres or 2,670 miles, is the second longest in Africa after the Nile. It flows from the southeast of the DRC through a northerly and westerly arc into Congo and thence on to the Atlantic Ocean. With over 1,600 kilometres or 994 miles of navigable river, the Congo provides a major means of access to much of central Africa.

NGORONGORO CRATER AND THE SERENGETI, TANZANIA

Tanzania has much to offer the tourist and two places well worth a visit are the Ngorongoro Crater and the Serengeti National Park. Descending into the Ngorongoro Crater from its misty rim, the volcanic basin comes into view with its near circular crater floor containing open grassland, forest, a lake and some 20,000 large and small African animals – truly one of the world's greatest wildlife sanctuaries. The Serengeti National Park is most famous for the Serengeti wildebeest migration – an annual event involving two million or more animals moving in search of food.

Mount Kilimanjaro, Tanzania

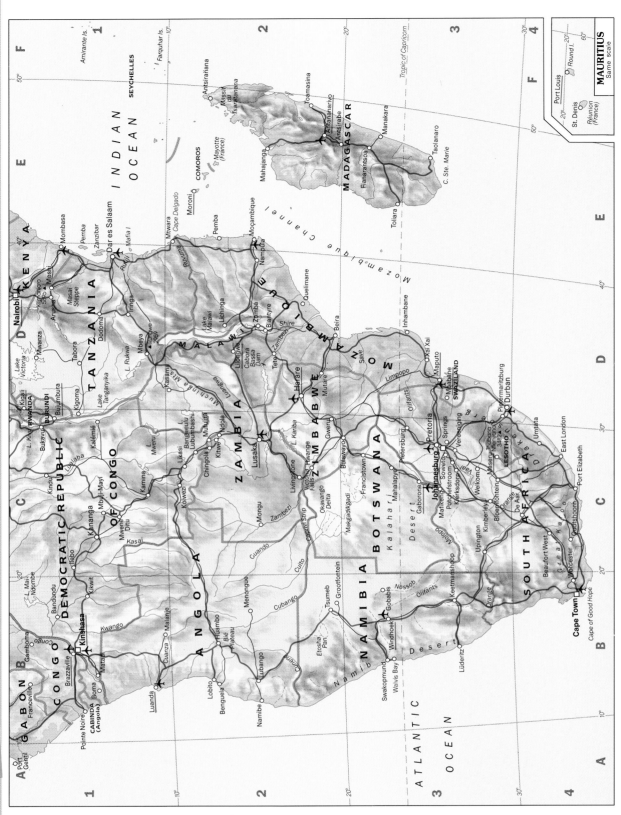

DEMOCRATIC REPUBLIC OF THE CONGO (DRC)

Formerly Zaire, the DRC is a large almost landlocked state in central Africa with a narrow coastal strip. The Congo river basin dominates the land while there are rainforests on the western border, a huge central plain and mountains in the north and west. Offshore oil and the mining of uranium, cobalt and copper are all important to the country's economy.

REPUBLIC OF THE CONGO

The Congo is situated on the west coast of southern Africa between Gabon to the west and the DRC to the east. The Congo river basin is in the north-east of the country. Much of the country is swamp and over half the land is covered with thick rainforests. Most people are involved in subsistence farming. Offshore oil is the country's principal source of wealth, although timber is also important.

TANZANIA

Tanzania lies east of the DRC and Zambia, south of Kenya and north of Mozambique with a coastline on the Indian Ocean in the east. Behind the narrow coastal strip, most of the country consists of inland plateaux and mountains. Lake Tanganyika lies in the west of the country, Lake Victoria in the north and Lake Malawi further to the south. Tanzania is essentially an agricultural country and cotton, tobacco and coffee are important exports. Tourism is vital to the country's economy.

ANGOLA

Angola lies on the west coast of southern Africa with the DRC to the north, Zambia to the east and Namibia to the south. The enclave of Cabinda is separated from Angola by a small strip of the DRC. An inland plateau makes up most of the country and the land in the south merges into the Namib Desert. Coffee is the only crop that is exported but Angola is rich in natural resources.

ZAMBIA

Located in central southern Africa, Zambia is essentially a massive plateau surrounded by Mozambique, Zimbabwe, Botswana, Namibia, Angola, the DRC and Tanzania. Maize is the chief crop and copper, cobalt, zinc and diamonds are of prime importance to the economy.

MALAWI

Malawi is a small, narrow country in east southern Africa. It is bounded by Tanzania to the north, Zambia to the northwest and Mozambique to the south and east. Moving from south to north the landscape changes from plateau to mountains but Malawi is dominated by Lake Malawi. Malawi produces tobacco, tea and sugar for export. The country is a popular tourist destination.

NAMIBIA

Situated on the southwestern coast of southern Africa, Namibia shares borders with Angola and Zambia to the north, Botswana to the east and South Africa to the east and south. The whole of the coastal strip comprises the Namib Desert while inland is a central plateau and the massive basin of the Kalahari Desert. Namibia possesses some of the world's largest and richest diamond fields. Tourism is an increasingly important industry.

BOTSWANA

Botswana is surrounded by South Africa on the south and east, Namibia to the west, Zimbabwe to the northeast and Zambia just west of the Victoria Falls. The country is dominated by a plateau and towards the southwest by the Kalahari Desert. Many tourists come see the wildlife in the Okavango Delta in the northwest, often travelling silently through the swamps in canoes.

ZIMBABWE

Bounded to the west by Zambia and Botswana, to the north and east by Mozambique and to the south by South Africa, Zimbabwe comprises a wide ridge running across the country with mountains to the east. The Zambezi and the Limpopo rivers flow on the north and south sides of the ridge respectively. Tourism is also important to the economy but the country gets a lot more export revenue from its mineral resources.

MOZAMBIQUE

Mozambique lies on the east coast of Africa and faces Madagascar across the Mozambique Channel. The coastline is fringed by lagoons, islands and reefs and moving inland the coastal plain gives way to a plateau and then to hills. The country is crossed by numerous rivers, the largest being the Zambezi. Forestry, the mining of minerals and tourism are potential sources of revenue which are largely untapped.

MADAGASCAR

Madagascar is a large island country in the Indian Ocean to the east of Mozambique. There is a chain of mountains in the centre of the island, rainforest on the narrow coastal strip to the east and savannah to the west. Coffee, vanilla and sugar cane are grown for export. The fishing industry is expanding and there are unexploited mineral deposits. Many tourists come to explore the island's unique wildlife.

SWAZILAND

Swaziland is a small country surrounded by South Africa and Mozambique and a short distance from the Indian Ocean. Mountains in the west of the country rise to almost 2,000 metres or 6,562 feet then descend in steps of savannah toward hilly country in the east. Most people are involved in subsistence farming. Mineral resources include diamonds, gold, coal and asbestos, the last two being major exports.

LESOTHO

Lesotho is a small, mountainous country cut by rivers and completely enclosed by South Africa. It consists of mountains in the east while to the west the land forms rolling foothills before descending to the more populated lowland areas. Wool and mohair are exported, mainly to South Africa. Tourism is beginning to flourish with mountain pony trails on hardy Lesotho ponies one of the main attractions.

SOUTH AFRICA

At the tip of the continent, South Africa is bounded by the Indian Ocean to the east, the Atlantic Ocean to the west and by Namibia, Botswana, Zimbabwe, Mozambique and Swaziland to the north. The country consists of a vast, high central plateau, mountains and a coastal belt. The highest mountains are the Drakensberg Mountains and the major rivers are the Limpopo, Vaal and the Orange.

South Africa has a strong economy with a good agricultural base. The country is known for its rich mineral resources, including gold, coal and diamonds, and manufacturing is the country's largest industry. Tourism plays an increasingly important role in the country's economy.

SEYCHELLES, MAURITIUS, COMOROS, RÉUNION

These four island-countries are situated in the Indian Ocean off the east coast of Africa. Tourism is vital to their economy and visitors come to enjoy their beautiful coral beaches and clear blue seas.

SOUTH AFRICA

Language/s spoken: English, Afrikaans and African languages
Currency: Rand
Travel requirements: return ticket and valid passport required, best to contact relevant authority before departure
Major cities: Pretoria (administrative), Cape Town (legislative), Johannesburg, Durban, Port Elizabeth, Soweto
Climate: sunny and hot with summer rain in the north and winter rain in the south
Crime and safety: risk of car hijack and muggings, particulary in Johannesburg, take sensible precautions

THE KRUGER NATIONAL PARK, SOUTH AFRICA

Arguably South Africa's most famous park, the Kruger National Park stretches over 500 kilometres or 311 miles north to south and has more species of wildlife than any similar park in Africa. It contains large populations of big game and other African wildlife and there are also numerous species of birds making this an ideal destination for nature and wildlife lovers.

Cape Town, South Africa

Australasia

AUSTRALIA

Language/s spoken: English
Currency: Australian Dollar
Travel requirements: return ticket and valid passport required, best to contact relevant authority before departure
Major cities: Canberra (capital), Sydney, Adelaide, Brisbane, Melbourne, Perth
Climate: tropical to temperate, from November to March warm or hot everywhere
Crime and safety: take sensible precautions, be cautious when using automatic teller machines (ATMs)

THE GREAT BARRIER REEF, AUSTRALIA

The Great Barrier Reef stretches along the northeast coast of Australia in the Coral Sea for about 2,000 kilometres or 1,250 miles and extends for up to 300 kilometres or 186 miles from land in the south. The Reef is made up of more than 2,500 separate coral reefs which provide a home for over 2,000 species of fish. There are some 500 islands strung along the Reef which have become tourist resorts and bases for scuba divers who have come to explore the Reef.

Sydney Harbour, Australia

The name Australasia is not a rigid term and although it covers Australia and New Zealand, it can also include Micronesia, Polynesia, Melanesia and New Guinea. It commonly refers to the two larger countries and their former or current dependencies.

Australasia is situated on the western fringe of the Pacific Ocean and is bordered to the west by the Indian Ocean. The Tasman Sea lies between Australia and New Zealand. The nearest landfall is to the north where the tips of Queensland and the Northern Territory reach towards the island of New Guinea.

AUSTRALIA

Australia, the world's sixth largest country, is also a continent. This huge, sparsely populated country is divided up into the seven self-governing states of New South Wales, Northern Territory, Queensland, South Australia, Tasmania, Victoria and Western Australia. The capital, Canberra, is situated in the Australian Capital Territory (ACT). The country can be divided into three main topographical regions: the high ground and plateau in the west, the interior lowlands in the central part of the country and the mountain ranges in the east.

Within its total area of almost 7.7 million square kilometres or 2.9 million square miles can be found vast tracts of inhospitable desert, great swathes of fertile agricultural land, coastal plains separated from the rest of the country by mountain ranges and at the coast itself, mile upon mile of wonderful beaches. Australia also has a tremendous diversity in its flora and fauna and has a monopoly on many species. Most of the population live in or near the coast, mainly in the cities of Sydney, Melbourne and Brisbane.

Dry pasture land takes up 58 per cent of the land while crops can only be grown on 6 per cent but the country is a major exporter of farm products such as wheat and wool. Sugar cane is grown in Queensland while Tasmania produces apples and timber and all the states produce wine. Australia's wealth of resources has led to it becoming an important world economic player and it now occupies an important position in the region.

In such a vast land, it is not surprising that there are many attractions, both natural and man-made – from the Great Barrier Reef which fringes the coast of Queensland to the sails of the Sydney Opera House. There are also many places to visit away from the major tourist centres. Alice Springs, a town at the centre of the country, formed a staging point for the overland telegraph line (in 1870) although it took more than 100 years for the road to Adelaide to be completed. The Flinders Range is a mountain range in South Australia ideal for viewing wildlife and walking although the Great Dividing Range is much longer at over 3,500 kilometres or 2,173 miles. The Snowy Mountains form the highest part of this range and this area has many popular winter sports resorts. Melbourne and Brisbane are Australia's second and third cities respectively.

Sydney

Sydney is the oldest settlement in Australia but it has some of the most striking modern architecture, including the Sydney Opera House and the Harbour Bridge. With nearly four million people living there, Sydney is Australia's largest city and it has much to offer the visitor, including the Australian Museum which features the natural history and human history of the country, plenty of beautiful parks and a lots of excellent restaurants.

Canberra

About a three-hour drive from Sydney is the Australian Capital Territory. Surrounded by New South Wales, this tiny territory is synonymous with its city of Canberra, which has developed in the twentieth century as the political and administrative centre of Australia and is now its capital. There is much to see in Canberra, which also has a vibrant nightlife with cinemas, clubs and dance venues as well as theatres and lots of restaurants.

NEW ZEALAND

Comprising two major islands, North and South Islands, New Zealand is a land of green countryside, mountains and interesting natural geological features. It lies in the southern Pacific Ocean over 2,000 kilometres or 1,242 miles southeast of Australia and is the closest country in the region to the Antarctic Circle. It has many smaller islands, including Stewart Island and the Chatham Islands. The countryside varies from extensive grassland and alpine meadows to mountains, fjords and subtropical rainforests.

Most of the population live on North Island, which has many active volcanoes and in some places the underground pressure is so great that tall geysers of water and steam are forced out of the ground. North Island also has lots of fertile grazing land highly favourable for raising dairy cattle and sheep. Wellington, the country's capital city, is on North Island.

South Island is fringed on the east coast by extensive plains while the west has mountains and fjords. The snow-capped peaks of the Southern Alps run the whole length of the island and in the higher regions there are ice fields and glaciers.

New Zealand's wildlife is perhaps unusual in that many species have been introduced by man. Land mammals including chamois, rabbit and hare, possum and deer were brought in by Europeans for their fur. There are flightless birds, notably the kiwi and kakapo, and many endemic bird species such as warbler, flycatcher and parrot. In the waters around New Zealand, there are a number of marine mammals, including varieties of whale and dolphin, and the fur seal. Although the latter, along with the whale, were the focus of an entire industry in days gone by, numbers have now stabilised.

Farming and farming-related industries are the basis for New Zealand's wealth and a high proportion of the country's farm products, notably lamb and dairy products, are exported. However, the manufacturing industry now employs twice as many people as agriculture. The timber industry is also important. New Zealand's splendid scenery means that it is a popular venue for tourists with diverse attractions to suit all tastes.

Auckland

Auckland is the largest city in New Zealand and its chief port and industrial centre. It is situated on North Island and is spread over many extinct volcanoes. It lies within easy reach of beaches, forests, harbours, and parks. Its coastal islands and bays provide a perfect habitat for many birds and a perfect venue for bird-watchers.

Christchurch

Christchurch is situated on South Island. Known as the Garden City, it is a popular venue for various types of festivals and is often referred to as the most English city outside England. A nearby national park, beaches and imposing mountains provide lots of opportunities for outdoor activities.

VANUATU

Vanuatu, formerly the New Hebrides, became independent in 1980 and it consists of 12 islands and some 60 islets in the southwest Pacific Ocean. The islands are volcanic and densely forested, with raised coral beaches and fringed by coral reefs. Its economy is based on agriculture.

SOLOMON ISLANDS

The Solomon Islands, formerly known as the New Hebrides, is an archipelago of several hundred islands in the southwest Pacific Ocean. The main islands have rainforest-covered volcanic mountains, deep narrow valleys and coastal belts lined with coconut palms and ringed by reefs. Agriculture, including forestry and fisheries, is the mainstay of the economy.

An evening view of the Sky Tower, Auckland

CHRISTMAS ISLAND (KIRITIMATI)

Although it is over 2,500 kilometres or 1,553 miles away, Christmas Island belongs to Australia who bought it in 1957 from Singapore for £2.9 million. It is the largest coral atoll in the world. Its name was chosen by Captain Mynors of the East India Company who arrived there without landing on Christmas Day, 1643. The island is now known as Kiritimati. To offset the decline of its phosphate industry, an expensive casino development opened in 1993 and this has made a significant contribution to the growing numbers of tourists. The island may also become a launching station for satellites.

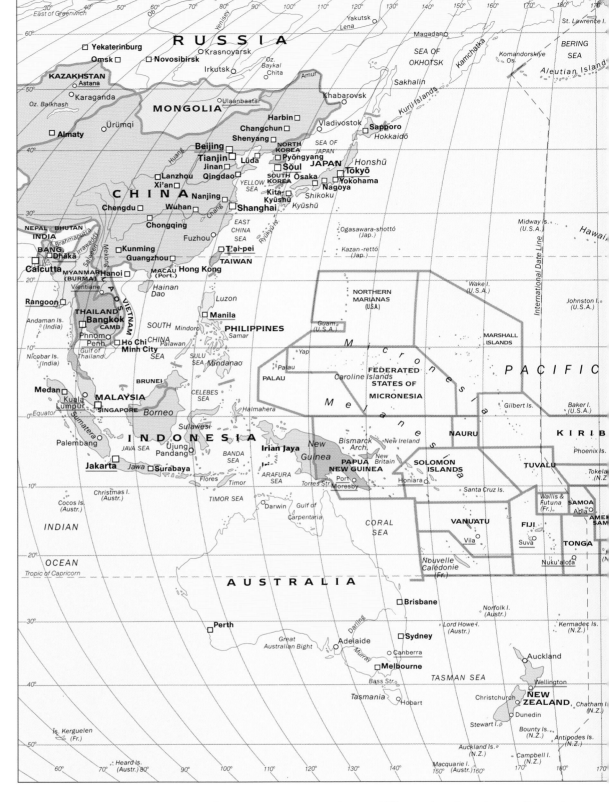

The Fiji Islands

Oceania comprises a collection of islands scattered across the Pacific Ocean including Australia and New Zealand, Fiji, Vanuatu, the Marshall Islands, the Solomon Islands, the Mariana Islands, the Pitcairn Islands, Guam, Western Samoa, American Samoa, Tonga, Palau, Tuvalu, New Caledonia, Papua New Guinea and others. The islands are either volcanic in origin or coral atolls. In addition to specific island groups, there are three major but rather informal associations, namely Micronesia, Melanesia and French Polynesia.

FIJI

Fiji, like New Caledonia, is a part of Melanesia and comprises more than 800 islands with a population of some 800,000. The main cash crop is sugar cane but tropical fruits, cotton and copra are important. Tourists are attracted in ever-growing numbers to Fiji's coral reefs and unspoilt beaches.

MICRONESIA

Officially referred to as the Federated States of Micronesia, this large group of island states lie scattered across the western Pacific Ocean. Independence from the USA was formerly gained in 1990. Tourism is a growing trade but Micronesia is still heavily dependent on US aid.

MARSHALL ISLANDS

The Marshall Islands Archipelago is a republic consisting of over 1,000 atolls and islets in eastern Micronesia in the western Pacific Ocean, which achieved full independence from the USA in 1991. The USA retains a military base and payment of rent contributes to the Islands' economy which oth-

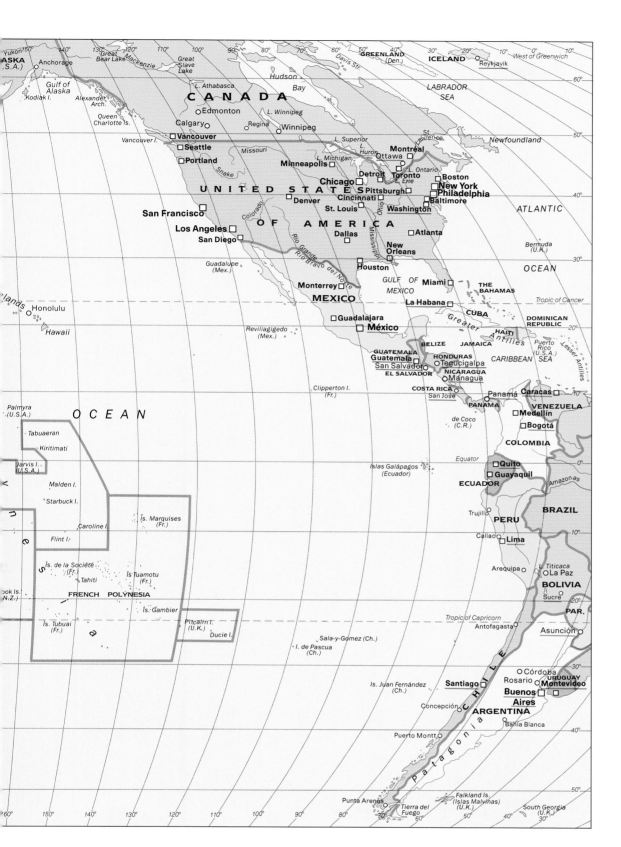

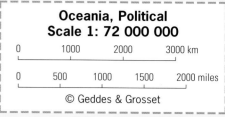

PAPUA NEW GUINEA

Language/s spoken: English, local dialects

Currency: Kina

Travel requirements: return ticket and valid passport required, best to contact relevant authority before departure

Major cities: Port Moresby (capital), Lae, Madang

Climate: tropical climate with a rainy season from December to March

Crime and safety: violent crime on the increase, occasional rioting and looting, extra care to be taken

ORCHIDS

The beautiful, waxlike orchid is the passion of many a collector, botanist and grower. The whole island of New Guinea contains over ten per cent of all known species of orchid.

Tribal dancers, Papua New Guinea

erwise depends upon agriculture and fishing, with copra as the main export.

NAURU

A coral island with a population of around 11,000, Nauru is the smallest of the states in Oceania. High-quality phosphate is the island's single export and upon its exhaustion the administration will face the twin problems of environmental destruction and financial downturn.

KIRIBATI

The few islands comprising Kiribati have a population of approximately 80,000. This republic includes the former Gilbert Islands, the Phoenix Islands (now Rawaki), the southern Line Islands and, until independence from Great Britain in 1979, was named the Gilbert and Ellice Islands. The largest island is Kiritimati, formerly known as Christmas Island. Coconuts and copra form the major commercial crops. Tourism is becoming increasingly important but overseas aid remains a vital part of the economy.

PAPUA NEW GUINEA

The eastern half of the Melanesian tropical island of New Guinea forms the majority and 'mainland' of Papua New Guinea. A number of islands and archipelagoes are included in the state, namely New Ireland, New Britain and the Bismarck Archipelago. Many of the smaller islands are volcanic in origin, with dramatic mountains, and some volcanoes on the north coast and smaller islands are still active.

THE NORTHERN LIGHTS

South Greenland and Disko Bay (mid-west coast) are centres for a growing tourism industry. Among the many attractions are the Northern Lights which are best seen during the autumn, winter and early spring. These multicoloured flames undulate and sweep across the sky, producing a magnificent natural display.

ICEBERGS

Icebergs in the northern hemisphere come from glaciers in Greenland while those in the south come from the ice shelves of Antarctica. It is calculated that icebergs can weigh up to 400 million tons, rising hundreds of feet above the surface. Such an iceberg would provide sufficient water for a large city for about a year.

Icebergs in Antarctica

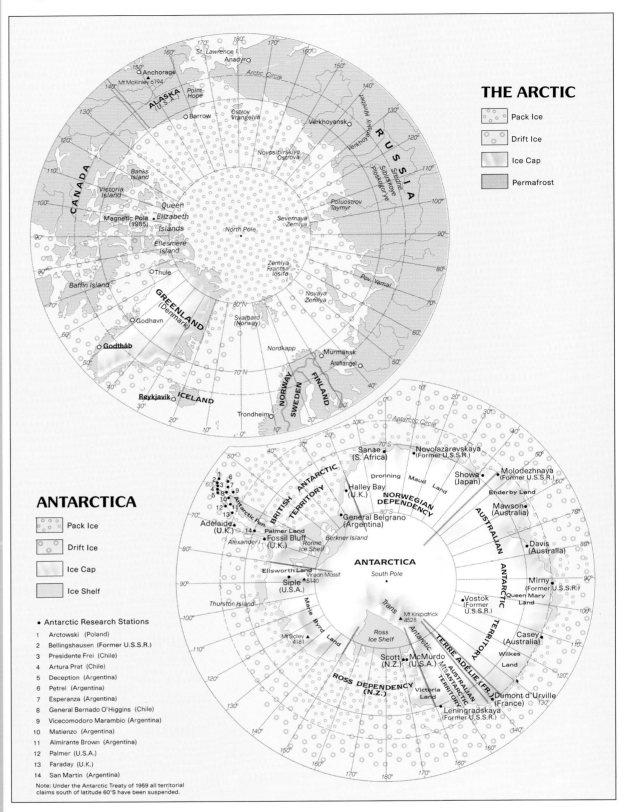

THE ARCTIC

⬜	Pack Ice
⬜	Drift Ice
⬜	Ice Cap
⬛	Permafrost

ANTARCTICA

⬜	Pack Ice
⬜	Drift Ice
⬜	Ice Cap
⬛	Ice Shelf

• Antarctic Research Stations

1   Arctowski   (Poland)
2   Bellingshausen (Former U.S.S.R.)
3   Presidente Frei (Chile)
4   Artura Prat (Chile)
5   Deception (Argentina)
6   Petrel (Argentina)
7   Esperanza (Argentina)
8   General Bernado O'Higgins (Chile)
9   Vicecomodoro Marambio (Argentina)
10   Matienzo (Argentina)
11   Almirante Brown (Argentina)
12   Palmer (U.S.A.)
13   Faraday (U.K.)
14   San Martin (Argentina)

Note: Under the Antarctic Treaty of 1959 all territorial claims south of latitude 60°S have been suspended.

The polar regions of the world are the cold areas inside the Arctic and Antarctic Circles and there are three main regions: the Arctic, Greenland and the Antarctic.

The Arctic stretches from the North Pole to the tree line. It is not limited by a specific boundary but includes Greenland, northern Iceland, the Arctic Ocean, numerous small islands and the northern shores of Canada, Europe and Russia. In winter, when the sun does not rise above the horizon and only the stars, moon and Northern Lights provide light, temperatures fall to between -20°C or -4°F and -30°C or -22°F. However, during spring and summer, the temperature rises to as high as 10°C or 50°F. During the short summer, when the sun shines even at midnight, the region north of the Arctic Circle becomes the 'Land of the Midnight Sun'.

Greenland, the largest island in the world, is situated with over three quarters of its land north of the Arctic Circle. Ice covers 85 per cent of its area inland. Around the coasts, the land that remains ice-free is roughly eight times the size of Denmark and yet the population is only 53,000. Greenland is an overseas territory of Denmark in association with the European Union.

The massive continent of Antarctica is situated over the South Pole. The ice sheet covering Antarctica consists of 90 per cent of the world's ice and is equivalent to 70 per cent of the world's fresh water. The continent is surrounded in part by the Southern Ocean, over half of which freezes in winter, and its climate is one of the coldest and the harshest in the world. There are no permanent inhabitants in Antarctica but there are a number of manned research camps and weather stations.

WORLD DATA

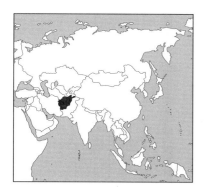

AFGHANISTAN is a landlocked republic in southern Asia. The greater part of the country is mountainous with a central mass of huge mountain ranges, the highest of which are the Hindu Kush. Many of the peaks rise to enormous heights, the greatest being Nowshak (7,845 metres or 24,557 feet) on the border with Pakistan. Glaciers and permanent snow-fields cover the highest peaks. Routes through the mountains depend upon lower-lying passes such as the famous Khyber Pass in the east. Lower-lying areas are found only in the northwest, west and south of Afghanistan but much of this is arid or desert land as in the Registan Desert in the south.

The high mountains of Afghanistan experience an Arctic climate with precipitation falling as snow for much of the year. At lower levels, a continental type of climate prevails with extremely hot, dry summers and cold winters but temperatures can vary greatly, even during the course of one day. Rainfall occurs mainly in the spring.

Natural vegetation varies from evergreen forests and woodlands with oak, hazelnut, almond and pistachio trees to dry grasslands and desert plants. Severe deforestation has taken place resulting in damage to the environment which has been worsened by overgrazing. The trees have been cut down mainly for use as fuel as most of the Afghan people live at subsistence level. Wildlife, both animals and birds, is extremely diverse but many species are hunted and are consequently rare.

Cultivation is possible only in river valleys or where other sources of water are available and, overall, very little land is available for agriculture, most being used for grazing. Agriculture, however, is the main economic activity, with some 60 per cent of the people living by farming. Natural gas is produced in northern Afghanistan and over 90 per cent of this is piped across the border to the former USSR. Large oil reserves have been discovered in the north of the country but these have not been exploited, due mainly to ongoing civil conflict. Other mineral resources are scattered and so far underdeveloped. The main exports are Karakul lambskins, raw cotton and foodstuffs such as dried fruit.

Since 1994, the Taliban, an extreme, fundamentalist, Islamic group, have battled for control of parts of Afghanistan, including the capital, Kabul. Due to the difficult nature of much of Afghanistan's terrain, its people have generally led a hard and precarious existence. War with Russia (1979–1989) and ongoing civil strife have further devastated the country and its people, leading to a mass exodus of refugees and severe hardship for those who remain. Since the Russian withdrawal from Afghanistan in 1989, the country has still been troubled by, mainly ethnic, conflict. Afghanistan has one of the highest rates of infant mortality in the world, life expectancy is low and malnourishment and disease are widespread.

QUICK FACTS

Area: 652,090 square kilometres or 251,773 square miles
Population: 20,883,000
Capital: Kabul
Other major cities: Herat, Kandahar, Mazar-e-Sharif
Form of government: Republic
Religions: Sunni Islam, Shia Islam
Currency: Afghani

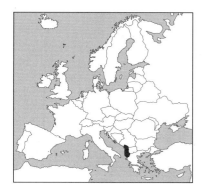

ALBANIA is a small mountainous republic in the Balkan region of south-eastern Europe. Its immediate neighbours are Greece, Serbia (Montenegro) and the former Yugoslav Republic of Macedonia and it is bounded to the west by the Adriatic Sea. Away from the coast, the land rises to form a series of wild and rugged hills and mountains that attain heights of 2,134–2,438 metres or 7,000–8,000 feet. In the north, these form the southernmost extension of the Dinaric Alps and are called the Albanian Alps.

Many large rivers rise in the mountains and flow in a generally westerly direction towards the sea, including the Drin and the Vijose. There are also numerous freshwater lakes and Albania's border runs through the three largest of these, Lake Skadarsko in the northwest and Lakes Ohridsko and Prespansko in the east. Extensive forests cover the hills and lower mountain slopes, with both deciduous and coniferous trees being well represented and providing important timber resources. The rail and road networks are fairly poorly developed and Albania has only one airport at Tirane.

The climate inland and in the mountains is continental in character, with hot, dry summers and bitterly cold winters. Along the Adriatic coast, a Mediterranean climate prevails with hot summers and mild, moist winters. Severe thunderstorms frequently occur on the coastal plains in summer.

All land is state owned, with the main agricultural areas lying along the Adriatic coast and in the Korce Basin. About half Albania's population is engaged in agriculture, and drainage and reclamation schemes have increased the amount of land available for farming. Much of the farming is carried out at a fairly basic level, however, and grain and other foodstuffs have to be imported. The forests provide timber for fuel, construction and wood products. Fish, both from the sea and from the numerous rivers and lakes, are another valuable natural resource.

Industry is also nationalised and output is small. The principal industries are agricultural product processing, textiles, oil products, cement, iron and steel. Most trade is with neighbouring Serbia and the former Yugoslav Republic of Macedonia and major imports are consumables, grains and machinery. Many Albanians live and work abroad, both in neighbouring countries and farther afield, and the money that they send home is a further mainstay of the economy.

Albania remains one of the most impoverished and poorly developed countries in Europe, and this is largely because of factors in its recent political history. However, the country possesses valuable mineral resources, especially chromium, nickel, copper, iron ore, coal, petroleum and pyrites, and the mining and processing of these minerals is important to the Albanian economy. The country also has the potential to produce its own hydroelectricity thanks to its many mountain streams.

QUICK FACTS

Area: 28,748 square kilometres or 11,009 square miles
Population: 3,670,000
Capital: Tirane
Other major cities: Durrès, Shkodèr, Vlorë
Form of government: Socialist Republic
Religion: Constitutionally atheist but mainly Sunni Islam
Currency: Lek

QUICK FACTS:

Area: 2,381,741 square kilometres or
    919,595 square miles
Population: 29,168,000
Capital: Algiers (Alger)
Other major cities: Oran, Constantine,
    Annaba
Form of government: Republic
Religion: Sunni Islam
Currency: Algerian Dinar

QUICK FACTS

Area: 199 square kilometres or
    77 square miles
Population: 56,000
Capital: Pago Pago
Form of government: Unincorporated
    Territory of the USA
Religion: Christianity
Currency: US Dollar

QUICK FACTS

Area: 453 square kilometres or
    175 square miles
Population: 65,877
Capital: Andorra la Vella
Form of government: Republic
Religion: Roman Catholicism
Currency: Franc, Peseta

QUICK FACTS

Area: 1,246,700 square kilometres or
    481,354 square miles
Population: 11,185,000
Capital: Luanda
Other major cities: Huambo, Lobito,
    Benguela, Lubango
Form of government: People's Republic
Religions: Roman Catholicism, Animism
Currency: Kwanza

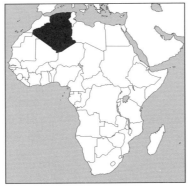

ALGERIA is a large country in northern Africa with a Mediterranean Sea coastline in the north. The Democratic and Popular Republic of Algeria is the second largest country in Africa although over four fifths of its total area is covered by the vast expanse of the Sahara Desert.

The most fertile area is a narrow coastal plain, the Tell, containing most of the country's cultivable land and the greatest concentration of its people. Behind the plain, lie the hills and mountains of the High Plateaux, Atlas Mountains (Tell Atlas) and the Saharan Atlas Mountains. Beyond these, lies the vast expanse of the Sahara Desert, interrupted in the southeast by the dramatic massif of the Hoggar and Tassil-n-Ajer Mountains which reach a height of 3,003 metres or 9,852 feet. The Chelif, at 724 kilometres or 450 miles long, is the country's main river, rising in the Tell Atlas and flowing to the Mediterranean.

Due to the arid nature of the country and generally poor soils, natural vegetation is limited to areas along the coast and most of this has been removed through intensive land use. There are a few remnants of woodland and scrub vegetation but plant life in the desert is mainly limited to oases. Wildlife species are relatively few but include snakes, lizards, gazelles, antelope, hyenas, jackals and vultures.

The climate in the coastal areas is warm and temperate with most of the rain falling in winter. The summers are dry and hot with temperatures rising to over 32°C or 89°F. Inland beyond the Atlas Mountains conditions become more arid and temperatures range from 49°C or 120°F during the day to 10°C or 50°F at night. A hot, dry wind, the Sirocco, blows northwards from the Sahara during the summer, generating sand and dust storms.

Most of Algeria is unproductive agriculturally but it does possess one of the largest reserves of natural gas and oil in the world. Algeria's main exports are oil-based products, fruit, vegetables, tobacco, phosphates and cork. Its imports include textiles, foodstuffs, machinery, iron and steel. In recent years, the country has been wracked by civil strife and terrorist attacks with the various opposing forces unable to agree peace proposals.

AMERICAN SAMOA is an 'unincorporated' territory of the USA. It lies close to Western Samoa in the Pacific Ocean and comprises 5 main volcanic islands and 2 coral atolls. The bulk of the population live on the islands of Tutaila and Ta'u. The 5 main islands are hilly and for the most part covered in thick forest or bush and the climate is tropical with lots of rain. The chief exports are canned tuna, pet foods, watches and handicrafts.

ANDORRA is a tiny state, situated high in the eastern Pyrenees between France and Spain. The state consists of deep valleys and high mountain peaks which reach heights of 3,000 metres or 9,843 feet. Although only 20 kilometres or 12 miles wide and 30 kilometres or 19 miles long, the country's spectacular scenery and climate attract many tourists.

About 10 million visitors arrive each year, during the cold weather when heavy snowfalls make for ideal skiing or in summer when the weather is mild and sunny and the mountains can be used for walking. Tourism and the duty-free trade are now Andorra's chief sources of income. Andorrans who are not involved in the tourist industry may raise sheep and cattle on the high pastures.

Although Andorra has no airport or railroad, there is a good road system. The average life expectancy from birth is 95 for women, 86 for men and 91 years overall. In 1993, an Andorran government was elected and has its own Parliament after 715 years of being ruled by France's leader and the Spanish Bishop of Urgel.

ANGOLA is situated on the Atlantic coast of southern Africa, with the Democratic Republic of the Congo to the north, Zambia to the east and Namibia to the south. Cabinda, a small enclave of Angola, is enclosed by the two Congos a few kilometres north. The enclave of Cabinda has an importance disproportionate to its size due to the discovery of offshore oil.

An inland plateau makes up most of the country. This averages 1,000–1,500 metres or 3,280–4,920 feet in height with Mount Moco the highest point at 2,620 metres or 8,595 feet. The plateau is separated from the coastal plain by a strip of hills and scarps which varies from 30–150 kilometres or 18–93 miles in width. The country becomes more arid to the south where it merges into the Namib Desert. There are tropical rainforests in the north while in the south are grasslands and poor desert vegetation. In between, is a mix of trees and grasslands. This provides a good habitat for a typical mix of African wildlife, including elephant, rhinoceros, zebra, hippopotamus and lion. The climate is tropical and the rainfall is heaviest in inland areas where there are vast equatorial forests.

Around 70 per cent of the workforce are engaged in agriculture. The country is rich in minerals although deposits of manganese, copper and phosphate are as yet unexploited. Diamonds are mined in the northeast and oil is produced near Luanda. Oil production is the most important aspect of the economy, making up about 90 per cent of exports which have traditionally included diamonds, fish, coffee and palm oil. The Angolan economy has been severely damaged by the civil war of the 1980s and 1990s.

ANGUILLA is a British Overseas Territory. It was formerly part of St Kitts and Nevis and became a British dependency in 1980. The country's main source of revenue is tourism and lobsters account for half of the island's exports.

ANTIGUA AND BARBUDA is a tiny state comprising three islands – Antigua, Barbuda and Redonda, an uninhabited rocky islet, located on the eastern side of the Leeward Islands. Formerly under British rule, they became independent in 1981. Antigua's strategic position was recognised by the British in the 18th century when it was an important naval base and later by the USA who built the island's airport during World War II to defend the Caribbean and the Panama Canal.

Mainly low-lying, the country's highest point is Boggy Peak at 405 metres or 1,329 feet. The climate is tropical although its average rainfall of 100 millimetres or 4 inches makes it drier than most of the other West Indian islands. Tourism is the main industry as its numerous sandy beaches make it an ideal holiday destination. Barbuda is surrounded by coral reefs and the island is home to a wide range of wildlife. Cotton, sugar cane and fruits are cultivated and fishing is an important industry in Barbuda. Great damage was inflicted on Antigua and Barbuda in 1995 by Hurricane Luis when over 75 per cent of property was destroyed or damaged.

ARGENTINA, the world's eighth largest country, stretches from the Tropic of Capricorn to Cape Horn on the southern tip of the South American continent. It is 3,331 kilometres or 2,070 miles long and nowhere exceeds 1,384 kilometres or 860 miles in width and it also includes the eastern part of Tierra del Fuego. To the west the massive mountain chain of the Andes forms the border with Chile. The country's highest peak is Aconagua in the northern Andes (6,960 metres or 22,834 feet) which lies just north and east of the Chilean capital, Santiago. Several other peaks also reach elevations in excess of 6,705 metres or 22,000 feet but, farther south, the Patagonian Andes are lower and do not usually exceed 3,658 metres or 12,000 feet in height.

In the north, the plains form part of the subtropical region known as the Gran Chaco. South of the Chaco and extending for about 1,609 kilometres or 1,000 miles are the grassy plains known as the Pampas. The soils of the Pampas are alluvial clays, silts and sands washed from the Andes by rivers and streams and deposited on the flatter land in a fertile layer. The climate ranges from warm temperate over the Pampas in the central region, to a more arid climate in the north and west, while in the extreme south, conditions although also dry are much cooler.

The vast fertile plains of the Pampas are the main agricultural area and produce cereals and wheat, while in other irrigated areas sugar cane, fruit and grapes for wine are raised. Meat processing, animal products and livestock production are major industries and also feature prominently in the country's export trade. A series of military regimes has resulted in an unstable economy which fails to provide reasonable living standards for the population, although more recently a trade agreement with other South American countries has aided economic recovery.

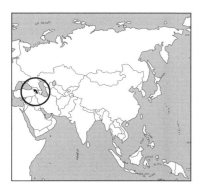

ARMENIA is the smallest republic of the former USSR and part of the former kingdom of Armenia which was divided between Turkey, Iran and the former USSR. It declared independence from the USSR in 1991. It is a mountainous country dominated by the rugged peaks of the Southern Caucasus Mountains, with high plateaux and steep-sided valleys interspersed with numerous lakes. Many of the peaks are over 3,000 metres or 9,900 feet and Lake Sevan is the largest lake. Lowland areas occur mainly in the river valleys and on the Ararat Plain in the west. Mount Ararat, now in eastern Turkey, has traditionally been very important to the people of Armenia. The climate varies according to location, with the lowlands having hot, dry summers and cold winters and even lower temperatures in the upland regions.

Natural vegetation once included extensive areas of forest. Many of the trees were cut down during the Soviet-led drive towards the development of a highly industrialised economy. In recent years, even more have been felled to provide fuel, made necessary by the economic blockade imposed by neighbouring Azerbaijan. Hydroelectricity is produced from stations on the River Razdan as it falls 1,000 metres or 3,281 feet from Lake Sevan to its confluence with the River Araks.

Irrigation schemes allow for cultivation in lower-lying areas where agriculture is mixed. The main crops grown are grain, sugar beet and potatoes, and livestock reared include cattle, pigs and sheep. Mining of copper, zinc and lead is important and, to a lesser extent, gold, aluminium and molybdenum, and industrial development is increasing. Territorial conflict with Azerbaijan over Nagorny Karabakh put a brake on economic development for many years.

ARUBA is one of the islands in the Netherlands Antilles in the Caribbean Sea and it has been a self-governing Dutch territory since 1986. The island rises to 189 metres or 620 feet at Jamanota in the southeast of the island. The climate is tropical with a short rainy season from October to January. Tourism is the main earner of foreign revenue but other industries include some oil refining, rum distilling and the production of cigarettes and beverages.

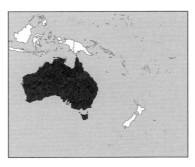

AUSTRALIA, the world's smallest continental landmass, is a vast and sparsely populated country in the southern hemisphere, whose head of state is the British Sovereign. It consists of seven self-governing states: New South Wales, Northern Territory, Queensland, South Australia, Tasmania, Victoria and Western Australia. The capital, Canberra, is situated in the Australian Capital Territory (ACT).

The country can be divided into three main topographical regions: the high ground and plateau in the west, the interior lowlands in the central part of the country and the mountain ranges in the east. The most mountainous region is the Great Dividing Range which runs down the entire east coast. The majority of the country's natural inland lakes are salt water and are the remnants of a huge inland sea. The longest rivers, the Murray and the Darling, drain the southeastern part of the central lowlands. The Great Barrier Reef off the northeast coast is approximately 2,000 kilometres or 1,250 miles long and is the largest coral formation known to the world. Because of its great size, Australia's climates range from tropical monsoon to cool temperate with large areas of desert.

Australia has a tremendous diversity in its flora and fauna and has a monopoly on many species. Most of the native mammals are marsupials, such as the kangaroo, koala and the Tasmanian Devil (a burrowing carnivorous species). The monotremes are a very primitive form of egg-laying mammals, represented by the platypus and spiny anteater. Reptiles are also found, with crocodiles in the northern coastal swamps, lizards and numerous species of snakes, many of which are venomous. Other animals include the dingo, possum and wombat and there are many exotic birds – cockatoos, parrots, kookaburras and the emu. The plant life is equally varied and the predominant tree is the eucalyptus of which there are several hundred species.

Australia's wealth of resources led to it becoming an important world economic player and it now occupies an important role in the region. Much of Australia's wealth comes from agriculture, with huge sheep and cattle stations extending over large parts of the interior known as the Outback. Australia is the world's leading producer of wool, particularly Merino wool. Cereal growing is dominated by wheat. Mining continues to be an important industry which produces coal, natural gas, oil, gold and iron ore and Australia is the world's largest producer of diamonds. The country's manufacturing industry produces mainly consumer goods, such as foods and household articles.

AUSTRIA is a landlocked country in central Europe which is surrounded by seven nations: Italy, Germany, Switzerland, the Czech Republic, the Slovak Republic, Hungary and Slovenia. The wall of mountains which runs across the centre of the country dominates the scenery. The mountain chains, with their intervening valleys, run in a generally west–east direction and the highest peak, Grossglockner (3,798 metres or 12,457 feet), is located centrally in the Tauern range. The presence of the mountains means that the average height of land in Austria is 914 metres or 3,000 feet above sea level.

Some lower-lying land does occur, however, in the basin of the River Danube (Donau) and along the country's eastern border south of Vienna. The Danube, with its tributaries, is the main river system in Austria and its valley provides the country with its most important west–east communications link. There are many other rivers, however, such as the Mur in the south, and numerous lakes, principally Lake Constance (Bodensee) and Lake Neusiedler. In the warm summers, tourists come to walk in the forests and mountains and, in the cold winters, skiers come to the mountains which now boast over 50 ski resorts.

Austria has modest reserves of iron ore, lignite, oil, natural gas, lead, zinc, copper, magnesium, salt, gypsum, talc and kaolin but fossil fuel reserves are not enough to supply the country's needs and the shortfall has to be imported. Although there is only a limited amount of land available for agriculture, the country is able to produce enough food to meet most of its own domestic needs. More than 37 per cent of Austria is covered in forest, resulting in the paper-making industry near Graz.

Formerly, many of the larger industries were under state control but in recent years private investors have been able to buy shares in many of these enterprises. In modern Austria, there are both private and public industries producing iron and steel and metal goods, electrical and other machinery, chemicals, foods, paper and wood products. Unemployment in Austria is very low and its low strike record has attracted multinational companies. Attachment to local customs, however, is still strong and in rural areas men still wear lederhosen and women the traditional dirndl skirt on feast days and holidays. For historical reasons, the country has close links with Eastern Europe which continue to be maintained.

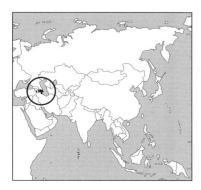

AZERBAIJAN, a republic of the former USSR, declared itself independent in 1991. The country has been plagued by political uncertainty and conflict with Armenia. It is situated on the southwest coast of the Caspian Sea and shares borders with Iran, Armenia, Georgia and the Russian Federation. The River Araks separates Azerbaijan from the region known as Azerbaijan in northern Iran. Azerbaijan's territory also includes the autonomous republic of Naxcivan, cut off from the rest of the country by southern Armenia, and the disputed Armenian enclave of Nagorno-Karabakh.

A mountainous, oil-rich country, it is bounded by the southeastern ranges of the Great Caucasus Mountains in the north and the Lesser Caucasus Mountains in the west, with the Talish Mountains in the extreme south. Rivers descend from the mountains and flow through lower-lying valleys to empty into the Caspian Sea.

The country has a generally arid climate with hot summers and cold winters although this is less extreme in the Lankaran region which is an important agricultural area. About 70 per cent of the land is irrigated for the production of cotton, wheat, maize, potatoes, tobacco, tea and citrus fruits.

In recent years, the country's economy has revolved around the development of its huge reserves of oil and natural gas which are found in the Baku area from where it is piped to Batumi on the Black Sea. It also has rich mineral deposits of iron and aluminium. There are steel, synthetic rubber and aluminium works at Sumqayit just north of the capital, Baku. However, further industrial development is being hindered by the country's dispute with Armenia over the Nagorno-Karabakh region.

BAHAMAS consist of an archipelago of 700 islands located in the Atlantic Ocean off the southeast coast of Florida. The largest island is Andros (4,144 square kilometres or 1,600 square miles) but most islanders live on Grand Bahama or New Providence where the capital, Nassau, lies. Winters in the Bahamas are mild and summers warm. Most rain falls in May, June, September and October and thunderstorms are frequent in summer. The islands are also subject to hurricanes and other tropical storms.

The Bahamas have few natural resources and for many years fishing and small-scale farming (citrus fruits and vegetables) were the only ways to make a living. Now, however, tourism, which employs almost half of the workforce, is the most important industry. It continues to be developed on a vast scale and about three million tourists, mainly from North America, visit the Bahamas each year. Offshore banking is also a growing source of income for the country.

BAHRAIN, a small, oil-rich Emirate comprising 33 low-lying islands situated between the Qatar Peninsula and the mainland of Saudi Arabia, is a hereditary monarchy. The largest island is Bahrain Island on which the capital, Manama (Al Manamah), is located. The King Fahd Causeway, opened in 1986, links Bahrain Island to the mainland of Saudi Arabia. The highest point in the state is only 122 metres or 402 feet above sea level.

The islands have hot, dry summers and mild winters during which the slight amount of annual rainfall (less than 100 millimetres or 4 inches) is experienced. However, fresh water for the islands is supplied by artesian wells which have so far proved more than adequate for the needs of the islands. The natural vegetation consists of desert plants but irrigated areas are able to support date palms, fruits and vegetables. Wildlife includes a variety of birds, reptiles and desert rats.

Most of Bahrain is sandy and too saline to support crops but drainage schemes are now used to reduce salinity and fertile soil is imported from other islands. Agricultural products include vegetables, dates and fruits with artesian wells providing irrigation, mainly on the north coast. Oil was discovered in 1931 and revenues from oil now account for about 80 per cent of the country's total revenue. Bahrain is being developed as a major manufacturing state, the main enterprises being aluminum smelting and the manufacture of clothing, paper products and consumer goods. Traditional industries include pearl fishing, boat building, weaving and pottery.

QUICK FACTS

Area: 143,998 square kilometres or
 55,598 square miles
Population: 120,073,000
Capital: Dhaka
Other cities: Chittagong, Khulna,
 Narayanganj, Saidpur
Form of government: Republic
Religion: Sunni Islam
Currency: Taka

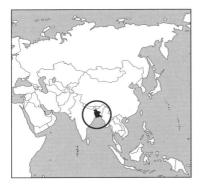

BANGLADESH, the People's Republic of Bangladesh, was formerly the Eastern Province of Pakistan and is the world's eighth most populated country. It is an extremely low-lying country in southeast Asia which is surrounded in the west, north and east by India. It has a border with Myanmar (Burma) in the extreme southeast, and it has a stretch of coastline along the Bay of Bengal in the south. Only about 20 per cent of its people inhabit the cities and urban areas with the vast majority living in rural villages.

Most of Bangladesh consists of the wide alluvial delta of the Ganges and Brahmaputra river systems and their numerous tributaries. This is the world's most extensive estuarine delta. The only appreciable higher ground is a series of forested ridges in the southeast border region with Myanmar, called the Chittagong Hill Tracts District. The country's highest peak, Mowdok Mual (1,003 metres or 3,292 feet), is situated here, straddling the border with Myanmar. Other small hills arise occasionally in the eastern and northern border regions, standing slightly above the surrounding plains. Most of Bangladesh's natural forest cover has been removed with only about 15 per cent remaining in the Chittagong Hill Tracts District and on the low hills in the north and northeast.

The whole of Bangladesh has a tropical, hot, moist climate with monsoon rainfall from April to October. Most rainfall occurs during the monsoon and amounts vary according to location, but the average rainfall exceeds 2,564 millimetres or 100 inches per annum. Temperatures are cooler between November and March but generally remain mild at all times. The country is subject to devastating floods and most villages are built on mud platforms to keep them above water. Cyclones, which arise out in the Bay of Bengal, occur most frequently during spring and autumn and have caused severe devastation and loss of life. In addition, tornadoes may occur in the monsoon season and these too are sometimes responsible for death and destruction.

However, the flooding rivers deposit considerable quantities of fertile alluvial silt across their flood plains, supporting the cash crops upon which the country's economy depends. The combination of rainfall, sun and silt from the rivers makes the land productive, and it is often possible to grow three crops a year. Tea and jute are important cash crops. Bangladesh produces about 70 per cent of the world's jute and the production of jute-related products is a principal industry. There are few mineral resources although natural gas, coal and peat are found.

QUICK FACTS

Area: 430 square kilometres or
 166 square miles
Population: 265,000
Capital: Bridgetown
Form of government: Constitutional
 Monarchy
Religions: Anglicanism, Methodism
Currency: Barbados Dollar

BARBADOS is the most easterly island of the West Indies and lies well outside the group of islands which makes up the Lesser Antilles. Mainly surrounded by coral reefs, most of the island is low-lying and only in the north does it rise to 336 metres or 1,104 feet at Mount Hillaby. The climate is tropical, but the cooling effect of the northeast trade winds prevents the temperatures rising above 30°C or 86°F. There are only two seasons, the dry and the wet, when rainfall is very heavy. At one time, the economy depended almost exclusively on the production of sugar and its by-products molasses and rum and, although the industry is now declining, sugar is still the principal export. More recently, deposits of natural gas and petroleum have been discovered and fishing is an important activity. There are industries manufacturing furniture, clothing, electrical and electronic equipment.The island is surrounded by pink and white sandy beaches and coral reefs which are visited by around 400,000 tourists each year. Tourism has now taken over as the main industry and employs approximately 40 per cent of the island's labour force.

QUICK FACTS

Area: 207,600 square kilometres or
 80,155 square miles
Population: 10,203,000
Capital: Minsk
Other major cities: Homyel (Gomel),
 Vitsyebsk, Mahilyov
Form of government: Republic
Religions: Russian Orthodox, Roman
 Catholicism
Currency: Rouble

BELARUS (Belorussia, Byelorussia), a republic of the former USSR, declared itself independent in 1991. It borders Poland to the west, Ukraine to the south, Latvia and Lithuania to the north, and the Russian Federation to the east. The country consists mainly of a low-lying plain, and forests cover approximately one third of the country. Belarus has a moist, continental climate with warm summers and long, cold winters with abundant rain and snowfall.

Although the economy is overwhelmingly based on industry, including oil refining, food processing, woodworking, chemicals, textiles and machinery, output has gradually declined since 1991 and problems persist in the supply of raw materials from other republics that previously formed parts of the USSR.

In 1986, large areas of Belarus were contaminated by radioactive fallout following the accident at the Chernobyl nuclear power plant in neighbouring Ukraine. Agriculture, although seriously affected by contamination from this accident, still accounts for approximately 20 per cent of the workforce, the main crops being flax, potatoes and hemp. The main livestock raised are cattle and pigs. The country's extensive forest areas also contribute to its economy by supplying raw material for the woodwork and paper-making industries. Peat is the fuel used to provide power for industry and the country's power plants. Belarus has a good transport system of road, rail, navigable rivers and canals.

BELGIUM is a highly industrialised, relatively small country in northwest Europe with a short coastline on the North Sea. It has three topographical regions: the elevated and forested Ardennes plateau, which is situated in the southeast near the border with France, Luxembourg and Germany; the rolling, central fertile plains; and the North Sea coastal plain. The Ardennes plateau is an area of moorland, woodlands and forests, valued for recreational purposes as well as forestry. The central plains are a fertile agricultural region crossed by Belgium's principal rivers, the Schelde and Meuse. The coastal plain is low-lying, reaching only about 20 metres or 65 feet above sea level at its highest point.

The Ardennes plateau is rocky with poor soils and has an average height of about 457 metres or 1,500 feet. The highest peak in Belgium, Mount Botrange (694 metres or 2,277 feet), is located in this area near the eastern border with Germany. Most of the North Sea coastline is marked by a narrow belt of huge sand dunes that are among the largest in Europe. These are carefully managed to preserve marram grass and encourage the growth of other vegetation, including trees, wherever possible. These stabilise the dunes, which are important in providing protection for the low-lying farmland behind the coast, including a small area of polders – low-lying fields drained by canals on land that has been reclaimed from the sea. The amount of polder land is small compared to that in the Netherlands but the reclaimed fields have highly fertile soils.

The climate is generally warm to hot in summer and cool or cold in winter, with the greatest extremes of temperature being experienced in the Ardennes where there is snow on higher ground in the winter. The coastal regions have a more moderate climate and rainfall may occur at any time during the year.

A well-used canal network links the main rivers, and altogether Belgium has nearly 1,600 kilometres or 1,000 miles of navigable waterways, many of which can be used by large boats. Antwerp is situated 80 kilometres or 50 miles from the open sea on the River Schelde and yet it is one of Europe's busiest ports and the second largest city in the country.

Belgium is a densely populated country with few natural resources. Agriculture, which uses about 45 per cent of the land for cultivation or rearing of livestock, employs only 3 per cent of the workforce. About one fifth of the country is covered with forests but these wooded areas are mainly used for recreation. The metal-working industry, originally based on the small mineral deposits in the Ardennes, is the most important industry, and in the northern cities new textile industries are producing carpets and clothing. Nearly all raw materials are now imported through the main port of Antwerp. Two thirds of Belgium's electricity needs are supplied by nuclear power although alternative, renewable energy sources are being explored. The country is at present reliant on imports of petroleum, gas and coal.

Politically, Belgium is divided into three federal regions: Flanders, in the north, the capital city, Brussels, and Wallonia in the south. The people are divided into two linguistic groups – Flemish or Dutch-speaking Flemings and French-speaking Walloons. The Flemings live mainly in Flanders and the Walloons in Wallonia although Brussels has a mixed population. There are three officially recognised languages in Belgium – Dutch, French and German.

QUICK FACTS

Area: 30,519 square kilometres or 11,783 square miles
Population: 10,159,000
Capital: Brussels
Other major cities: Antwerp, Charleroi, Ghent, Liège, Oostende
Form of government: Constitutional Monarchy
Religion: Roman Catholicism
Currency: Belgian Franc

BELIZE is a small Central American country on the southeast of the Yucatan Peninsula in the Caribbean Sea. Its coastline on the Gulf of Honduras is approached through some 550 kilometres or 342 miles of coral reefs and keys (cayo). The coastal area and north of the country are low-lying and swampy with dense forests inland. In the south, the Maya Mountains rise to 1,100 metres or 3,609 feet. The subtropical climate is warm and humid and the trade winds bring cooling sea breezes. Rainfall is heavy, particularly in the south, and hurricanes may occur in summer.

The dense forests which cover most of the country provide valuable hardwoods such as mahogany. Most of the population make a living from forestry, fishing or agriculture although only 5 per cent of the land is cultivated. The main crops grown for export are sugar cane, citrus fruits (mainly grapefruit), bananas and coconuts. Industry is very underdeveloped, causing many people to emigrate to find work. Belize is becoming increasingly popular as a tourist resort and has a rich archaeological heritage of Maya sites. The official language is English although many others are spoken including Mayan, Carib and Spanish.

QUICK FACTS

Area: 22,696 square kilometres or 8,763 square miles
Population: 222,000
Capital: Belmopan
Other major city: Belize City
Form of government: Constitutional Monarchy
Religions: Roman Catholicism, Protestantism
Currency: Belize Dollar

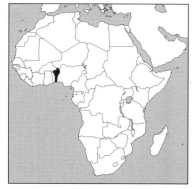

BENIN, a republic on the southern coast of west Africa, was formerly called Dahomey after the African kingdom which dominated the region between the 17th and 19th centuries. In the south, it has a very short coastline on the Bight of Benin and the coastal region is sandy with many lagoons. Inland, the ground rises to a fertile plain and then to a plateau. In the far northwest, the Atakora Mountains rise from the plateau in the region of the Niger/Nigeria border. The main rivers of Benin are the Donga, Couffo and Niger with its tributaries. The natural vegetation of tropical jungle in the coastal regions of the south, has largely been cleared. Woodlands cover parts of the plateau, giving way to savannah-type grassland in the north. Wildlife species are varied although some animals have declined due to forest clearance.

The south of the country has an equatorial climate with four seasons including two periods of rainfall. Temperatures are more extreme in the north where conditions are generally drier and there is one main rainy season. Farming is predominantly subsistence and accounts for around 60 per cent of the workforce with yams,

QUICK FACTS

Area: 112,622 square kilometres or 43,484 square miles
Population: 5,563,000
Capital: Porto Novo
Other major city: Cotonou
Form of government: Republic
Religions: Animism, Roman Catholicism, Sunni Islam, Christianity
Currency: CFA Franc

cassava, maize, rice, groundnuts and vegetables forming most of the produce. The country is very poor, although since the late 1980s economic reforms have been towards a market economy and Western financial aid has been sought. The main exports are palm oil, palm kernels, and cotton. Tourism is now being developed but as yet facilities for this are few except in some coastal towns.

BERMUDA consists of a group of 150 small islands in the western Atlantic Ocean. It lies about 920 kilometres or 572 miles east of Cape Hatteras on the coast of the USA. The hilly limestone islands are the caps of ancient volcanoes rising from the sea bed. The main island, Great Bermuda, is linked to the other islands by bridges and causeways. The climate is warm and humid with rain spread evenly throughout the year but with the risk of hurricanes from June to November. Bermuda's chief agricultural products are fresh vegetables, bananas and citrus fruit but 80 per cent of food requirements are imported. Many foreign banks and financial institutions operate from the island, taking advantage of the lenient tax laws. Other industries include ship repair and pharmaceuticals. Bermuda's proximity to the USA and its pleasant climate have led to a flourishing tourist industry.

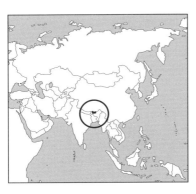

BHUTAN is surrounded by India to the south and China to the north. It rises from foothills overlooking the Brahmaputra river to the southern slopes of the Himalayas. The Himalayas, which rise to over 7,500 metres or 24,608 feet in Bhutan, make up most of the country. Bhutan can be divided into three topographical regions: the high Himalayas; the middle Himalayas, where the mountains are lower and are dissected by fertile valleys occupied by rivers which are mainly tributaries of India's Brahmaputra river; and the foothills and plains of a region called the Duars, the southern part of which is used for agriculture. The climate is hot and wet on the plains but temperatures drop progressively with altitude, resulting in glaciers and permanent snow cover in the north. There are no railways but roads join many parts of the country.

Bhutan has been isolated historically for centuries, only opening its doors to the outside world in the 1970s and its small population continues to follow a traditional way of life which is kind to the environment. As a result, the country has a wealth of habitats and flora and fauna, many of which are endangered. At least 5,000 species of plants have been identified, many of them valuable in traditional and Western medicine along with 165 species of mammals and 675 species of birds. Rare wildlife includes tigers, snow leopards, red pandas, golden langur monkeys and black-necked cranes.

Some 95 per cent of the workforce are farmers growing wheat, rice, potatoes and corn. Fruit such as plums, pears, apples and also cardamom are grown for export. Yaks reared on the high pasture land provide milk, cheese and meat. As there is little demand for new farmland, vast areas of the country still remain forested and the laws of the land ensure that 60 per cent of the natural woodland must remain forever. Bhutan's mineral resources include coal, limestone, gypsum and dolomite. Industries are all small-scale activities and are strictly controlled to minimise negative effects on the environment. They include mining, manufacture of wood products, food processing, cement, production of hydroelectric power for home use and export to India and craft goods. Tourism is the country's main source of foreign income but the number of visitors is strictly limited as too great an influx is regarded as a threat to Bhutan's culture and environment.

The political system is an absolute hereditary monarchy. The monarch has the title of 'druk gyalpo' or 'dragon king' and the country was once known as Druk Yul (Land of the Dragon). There is a council of ministers or National Assembly, under the king, who are now required to stand for election.

BOLIVIA is one of only two South American countries to be surrounded by land on all sides, having lost its Pacific coastline to Peru and Chile in the late 1800s. The dominant topographical feature is the Andes mountain chain. This forms two main ranges, the Cordillera Occidental and the Cordillera Oriental running from north to south in the southwestern third of the country. Lying in between them is a high, fairly barren, treeless plateau called the Altiplano, which is where most Bolivians live. Lake Titicaca, which straddles the border with Peru, is in the northern part of the Altiplano. The country's administrative capital and largest city, La Paz, lies just to the south and the east of Lake Titicaca and is the highest capital city in the world, built 3,612 metres or 11,850 feet above sea level.

The lower, eastern slopes of the mountains form a region of forested, fertile valleys called the Yungas. In the southeastern corner, separated from the rest of the region by the Chiquitos Highlands, are the arid plains known as the Chaco. Farther north, there are hot savannah lands and dense tropical jungles blanketing the river valleys that traverse the region. The northeast experiences heavy rainfall while the southwest of the country has very little rain. Temperatures vary with altitude from extremely cold on the mountain summits to cool on the Altiplano and hot in the tropical areas.

Although rich in natural resources, Bolivia remains a poor country. A lack of investment in the country and political instability mean that there are not enough funds available to pay for the extraction of its natural resources of lead, silver, copper, zinc, oil and tin. However, Bolivia is self-sufficient in petroleum and exports natural gas. Agriculture produces soya beans, sugar cane and cotton for export. Coca is also grown on a large scale to supply the illegal trade in cocaine, although the government is endeavouring to bring this to an end.

BOSNIA-HERZEGOVINA, more commonly known as Bosnia, declared its independence from the former Yugoslavia in 1992 and became the scene of bitter ethnic fighting in the years that followed.

Densely forested and deeply cut by rivers flowing northwards to join the River Sava, the Dinaric Alps are the principal topographical feature in the west and south. The limestone plateau further to the east and the north is a second prominent feature while the northern strip of the country is lower-lying and densely forested and includes part of the Dinaric Alps. Half the country is forested and timber is an important product of the northern areas. One quarter of the land is cultivated, and corn, wheat and flax are the principal products of the north. In the south, tobacco, cotton, fruits and grapes are the main products.

Prior to the break-up of the former Yugoslavia, Bosnia was the second poorest country in economic terms, despite having valuable mineral resources, including coal, iron ore, manganese, lead, copper and silver, and vast potential for the development of hydroelectric power. The economy has been devastated by civil war which began in 1991 following the secession of Croatia and Slovenia from the former Yugoslavia. Dispute over who should control Bosnia continued, leading to UN intervention in an attempt to devise a territorial plan acceptable to all factions. A peace agreement signed in late 1995 resulted in the division of the country into two self-governing provinces, one Bosnian Serb and the other Muslim Croat, under a central, unified, multi-ethnic government. The population of the state was significantly diminished when refugees from the civil war fled between 1992 and 1993.

QUICK FACTS

Area: 51,129 square kilometres or
   19,735 square miles
Population: 4,510,000
Capital: Sarajevo
Other major cities: Banja Luka, Mostar,
   Tuzla
Form of government: Republic
Religions: Eastern Orthodox, Sunni Islam,
   Roman Catholicism
Currency: Dinar

BOTSWANA is a landlocked republic in southern Africa which straddles the Tropic of Capricorn. The country is surrounded by South Africa to the south and east, Namibia to the west, Zimbabwe to the northeast and just meets in a point with Zambia west of the Victoria Falls. Much of the west and southwest of the country forms part of the Kalahari Desert. In the north, there is a huge area of marshland around the Okavango Delta, which is home to a wide variety of wildlife. East and south of the delta are the Makgadikgadi Salt Pans.

The bulk of the population live in the south and east of the country. With the exception of the desert area, most of the country has a subtropical climate but it is subject to drought. In winter, days are warm and nights cold while summer is hot with sporadic rainfall. The climate also has a stranglehold on agriculture with recent droughts making the already difficult nomadic mode of agriculture virtually impossible. Cattle were previously a mainstay of the country's export earnings but in common with many other African countries, mining has come to the fore with the extraction of diamonds, copper, coal, platinum, oil and gold among the country's growing mineral wealth. Botswana is the largest supplier of diamonds in the world. Exploitation of these mineral resources has facilitated a high rate of economic growth within the country. Coal is also mined but the majority is for domestic use. About 17 per cent of Botswana is set aside for wildlife preservation in national parks, game reserves, game sanctuaries and controlled hunting areas but much is dependent upon good seasonal rains.

QUICK FACTS

Area: 581,730 square kilometres or
   224,607 square miles
Population: 1,490,000
Capital: Gaborone
Other cities: Francistown, Molepolole,
   Mahalapye
Form of government: Republic
Religions: Animism, Christianity
Currency: Pula

BRAZIL is a huge South American country bounded to the north, south and east by the Atlantic Ocean. It is the fifth largest country in the world and covers nearly half of South America.

There are two dominant topographical features – the great Amazon river basin and the ancient plateau region of crystalline rocks called the Brazilian Highlands. The Amazon river basin occupies a huge area of land, over one third of the country's area, and much of this is covered with tropical rainforests. The Amazon system is navigable by large ocean-going vessels for about 3,700 kilometres or 2,300 miles, a factor that has been of immense importance to the development of Brazil. In the central interior, the Brazilian Highlands form a raised tableland called the Mato Grosso and throughout their extent they are cut by deep river valleys and ridged by mountain ranges. The mountains are, however, modest by South American standards and do not exceed 2,896 metres or 9,500 feet in height with an average elevation of about 1,219 metres or 4,000 feet.

In the far north, beyond the Amazon basin, lies the southern upland extremity of the Guiana Highlands, another region of very ancient rocks. Brazil's highest mountain, Pico de Neblina (3,014 metres or 9,888 feet), is situated

QUICK FACTS

Area: 8,547,403 square kilometres or
   3,300,171square miles
Population: 157,872,000
Capital: Brasília
Other major cities: Belem, Belo Horizonte,
   Curitiba, Porto Alegre, Recife, Rio de
   Janeiro, Salvador, São Paulo
Form of government: Federal Republic
Religion: Roman Catholicism
Currency: Cruzeiro

in an offshoot of these on the border with Venezuela. Other important rivers cut through Brazil, including those of the Rio de la Plata system, the Parana, Uruguay and Paraguay and the São Francisco and Parnaiba.

The climate is mainly tropical but altitude, distance from the sea and prevailing winds cause many variations. In the tropical areas, winters are dry and summers wet and droughts may occur in the northeast, where it is hot and arid.

About 14 per cent of the population is employed in agriculture, which occupies only about 7 per cent of the land area, and the main products exported are coffee, soya beans, orange juice and cocoa. Brazil is rich in minerals and is the only source of high grade quartz crystal in commercial quantities. It is also a major producer of chrome ore and it is now developing what is thought to be the richest iron ore deposits in the world. Fishing, mainly of lobsters, shrimp and sardines, is also an important industry. Brazil has valuable timber reserves but there has been worldwide concern over the ruthless and unregulated felling and clearing of vast sections of rainforest.

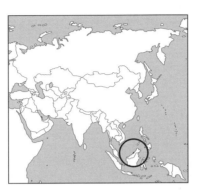

BRUNEI is a sultanate located on the northwest coast of the island of Borneo in southeast Asia. It is bounded on all sides by the Malaysian state of Sarawak which splits the country into two separate parts. Broad tidal swamplands cover the coastal plains and inland Brunei is hilly and covered with tropical rainforests. The climate is hot and moist with plenty of rainfall all year but especially during the monsoon months of October to March. Political power in the sultanate (formerly a British Protected State until independence was declared in 1984) resides in the person of the Sultan of Brunei who is believed to be one of the top three most wealthy men in the world.

The main crops grown are rice, vegetables and fruit but economically the country depends on its oil industry, which employs 7 per cent of the working population. Oil production began in the 1920s and now oil and natural gas account for almost all exports. Cloth weaving and metalwork are also small local industries. Other minor products are rubber, pepper, gravel and animal hides.

BULGARIA is a southeast European republic located on the east of the Balkan Peninsula with a coast on the Black Sea to the east. It is bounded to the north by Romania, to the west by Serbia and the Former Yugoslav Republic of Macedonia and to the south by Greece and Turkey. Hills or mountains cover about half of Bulgaria's land area. The centre of Bulgaria is crossed from west to east by the Balkan Mountains. In the south, the Rhodopi Mountains straddle the border with Greece and, in the western central region of the country, the Rila mountain chain contains the country's highest peak, Musala (2,925 metres or 9,597 feet). The main river in Bulgaria is the Danube (Dunav) which flows along the Bulgaria/Romania border and about a third of the country is covered with forests which provide commercially valuable timber. The south of the country has a Mediterranean climate with hot dry summers and mild winters. Further north, the temperatures become more extreme and rainfall is higher in summer.

Bulgaria was almost entirely an agricultural country until the end of the 1940s. However, during the 1950s, the collectivisation of farms and the use of more machinery, fertilisers and irrigation led to great increases in output. Farming remains highly important and is responsible for about 16 per cent of the country's national wealth. Wheat, barley, rice, maize, cotton, grapes (for wine), tobacco, sugar beet, vegetables and fruits are among the crops grown and cattle, sheep, pigs and poultry are reared.

Increased mechanisation led to more of the workforce being available to work in mines and industry with the result that manufacturing and industrial processes are now the largest contributors to the Bulgarian economy. Chemicals, petrochemicals, textiles, leather goods, footwear and clothing, glass, cement, machine building (especially forklift trucks and bulk carriers), tobacco processing and glass-making are among the industrial activities. Coal mining and production of iron ore and other minerals are also important. Fishing, forestry and tourism are other significant contributors to the economy.

However, the country suffered very high rates of inflation and unemployment in the early 1990s after the break-up of the former Soviet Union, with whom Bulgaria had very close trade links, and industrial pollution affects its rivers, soils and the Black Sea coastline, an area that is extremely important for tourism with over 10,000,000 people visiting the Black Sea resorts annually.

BURKINA FASO is a landlocked country in west Africa. The People's Democratic Republic of Burkina Faso was formerly called Upper Volta and is one of the poorest countries in the world. It comprises a plateau region in the north on the fringe of the Sahara which gives way southwards to an area of plains. The northern part of the country is arid and is more or less an extension of the Sahara Desert. The south is less dry and has savannah-type vegetation and scattered trees, although desertification threatens part of this land. Three main rivers, the Black Volta (Mouhoun), Red Volta (Nazinon) and White Volta (Nakanbe), which are the headwaters of the great Volta river system to the south, descend from the plateau across the plains. Although the river valleys contain the most fertile land, people avoid these areas due to the prevalence of disease.

Precipitation is generally low, the heaviest rain falling in the southwest, while the rest of the country is semidesert. The dusty grey plains in the north and west have infertile soils which have been further impoverished by overgrazing and overcultivation. Subsistence agriculture supports the majority of the largely rural population and food crops include sorghum, millet, pulses, corn and rice. The country is known to possess some valuable mineral reserves, notably manganese and gold. Cotton is the main export along with animal products and minerals such as gold. Manufacturing industries include food processing, textiles and metal products and the production of consumer items such as footwear and soap. There is great poverty and shortage of work in the country and many of the younger population go to Ghana and Côte d'Ivoire for employment. Full independence was gained in 1960 but drought severely affected the country during the 1970s along with political instability during the 1980s. The situation has improved since 1992.

BURUNDI is a small, densely populated republic in central east Africa bounded by Rwanda to the north, Tanzania to the east and south and the Democratic Republic of Congo to the west. One of the poorest nations in the world, Burundi consists mainly of an upland plateau at an elevation of around 1,400–1,800 metres or 4,600–5,900 feet. In the west, the land falls away to the valley of the River Rusizi and Lake Tanganyika, lying within the African Rift Valley. The plateau also drops away eastwards and southeastwards towards the valleys of the Ruyuvu and Malagarasi rivers. The predominant natural vegetation is savannah grassland and open woodland supporting a diversity of wildlife species. As in Rwanda, the tropical climate is tempered by altitude in most areas and there are two rainy seasons.

The soils are not rich but there is enough rain in most areas for subsistence farming. The main food crops are bananas, sweet potatoes, peas, lentils and beans. Cassava is grown near the shores of Lake Tanganyika. The main cash crop is coffee, which accounts for 90 per cent of Burundi's export earnings. Cotton and tea are also cultivated for export. There is a little commercial fishing on Lake Tanganyika, otherwise the industry is very basic. Since 1994, Burundi has been afflicted by ethnic conflict between the majority Hutu and minority Tutsi. Between 1994 and 1995, it is estimated that 150,000 were killed as a result of ethnic violence and the political situation remains highly volatile.

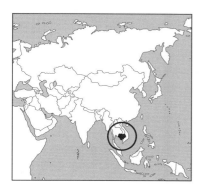

CAMBODIA, formerly called Kampuchea, is a southeast Asian state bounded by Thailand, Laos and Vietnam and its southern coast lies on the Gulf of Thailand. The country was devastated by its involvement in the Vietnam War (1960–75) followed by the brutal regime of the Khymer Rouge under Pol Pot (1975–79) when it is thought that as many as two million people were killed. Since that time, extreme political instability along with sporadic fighting has hampered development within the country.

Cambodia is largely a low-lying country fringed by modest-sized mountain ranges and upland plateaux in the southwest, north and east. The Dangrek Mountains form the frontier with Thailand in the northwest. The heart of the country is a saucer-shaped basin whose gently rolling alluvial plains are drained by the Mekong river. The western part of the basin is occupied by a large lake, the Tônlé Sap (Great Lake). About three quarters of Cambodia is covered in tropical forest and overexploitation of the forests has led to the imposition of a government ban on exports of timber. Wildlife species include some of the rare large mammals of southeast Asia such as the tiger, panther and elephant.

In general, Cambodia has a tropical monsoon climate and during the rainy season the Mekong river swells and backs into the Tônlé Sap, increasing its size threefold to about 10,400 square kilometres or 4,015 square miles. This seasonal flooding means the area is left with rich silt when the floodwaters recede. Crop production depends entirely on this flooding but production was badly disrupted during the civil war and yields still remain low. The cultivation of rice accounts for about 80 per cent of agricultural land and the other main crop is rubber which grows on the eastern plateau. Despite the gradual rebuilding of its infrastructure in the early 1990s, Cambodia remains one of the world's poorest nations.

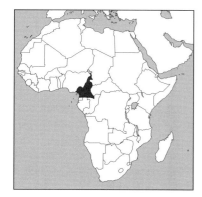

CAMEROON is a triangular-shaped republic of diverse landscapes in west central Africa. It stretches from Lake Chad at its apex to the northern borders of Equatorial Guinea, Gabon and the Congo in the south. Cameroon is a country of varied topography and natural vegetation. The far north is a region of savannah plain with marshland near the shores of Lake Chad. Eastwards, the land becomes drier, grading towards the Sahel grasslands in Chad. In the west, a belt of volcanic mountains and bamboo forests spill over the border with Nigeria. Further south, the savannah plains rise gradually to form the extensive Adamawa Plateau (Massif de l'Adoumaoua), which is partly covered in woodland. In the south, the coastal plain is covered with tropical rainforests and out of this, in the west, rises a group of high volcanic mountains, including the sporadically active Mount Cameroon (4,100 metres or 1,250 feet).

Cameroon's jungles contain not only commercially valuable trees but also an immense diversity of other plants, many of which have been identified as useful for their medicinal properties. Wildlife is equally varied and includes apes (gorillas and chimpanzees), various monkeys, many bird species and numerous snakes and amphibians. The climate is tropical but both temperature and amounts of rainfall vary according to locality. The south is humid but conditions become drier towards the north with the timing of the rainy season varying between the different regions of the country.

The majority of the population are farmers who live in south and central Cameroon, where they grow maize, millet, cassava and vegetables. In the drier north, where drought and hunger are well known, life is harder and this area is populated by seminomadic herders. Bananas, coffee and cocoa are the major exports although oil, gas and aluminum are becoming increasingly important.

QUICK FACTS

Area: 9,970,610 square kilometres or
3,849,674 square miles
Population: 29,964,000
Capital: Ottawa
Other major cities: Calgary, Toronto,
Montréal, Vancouver, Québec City,
Winnipeg
Form of government: Federal Parliamentary
State
Religions: Roman Catholicism, United
Church of Canada, Anglicanism
Currency: Canadian Dollar

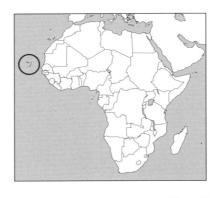

CANADA is the second largest country in the world, and the largest in North America. Canada is a land of great climatic and geographical extremes. It lies to the north of the USA and has Pacific, Atlantic and Arctic coasts. The country has the highest number of inland waters and lakes in the world, including the Great Lakes on the border with the USA. The Rocky Mountains and Coast Mountains run down the west side, and the highest point, Mount Logan (6,050 metres or 19,524 feet); is in the Yukon. Climates range from polar conditions in the north to cool temperate in the south with considerable differences from west to east.

More than 80 per cent of its farmland is in the prairies that stretch from Alberta to Manitoba. Wheat and grain crops cover three quarters of the arable land. Canada is rich in forest reserves which cover more than half the total land area. The most valuable mineral deposits (oil, gas, coal and iron ore) are found in Alberta. Most industry in Canada is associated with processing its natural resources and it is one of the world's main exporters of food products.

QUICK FACTS

Area: 4,033 square kilometres or
1,557 square miles
Population: 396,000
Capital: Praia
Form of government: Republic
Religion: Roman Catholicism
Currency: Cape Verde Escudo

CAPE VERDE, one of the world's smallest nations, is situated in the Atlantic Ocean, about 640 kilometres or 400 miles northwest of Senegal. It consists of ten islands and five islets and there is an active volcano on Fogo, one of the islands. The islands are divided into the Windward group and the Leeward group. Over 50 per cent of the population live on the island of São Tiago on which is Praia, the capital. The climate is arid with a cool dry season from December to June and warm dry conditions for the rest of the year. Rainfall is sparse and the islands suffer from periods of severe drought. Agriculture is mostly confined to irrigated inland valleys and the chief crops are coconuts, sugar cane, potatoes, cassava and dates. Bananas and some coffee are grown for export. Fishing for tuna and lobsters is an important industry but in general the economy is shaky and Cape Verde relies heavily on foreign aid. Due to its lack of natural resources and droughts, large numbers of its people have emigrated for many years. Tourism is being encouraged although the number of visitors is at present relatively low.

QUICK FACTS

Area: 264 square kilometres or
102 square miles
Population: 38,000
Capital: George Town
Other main town: West Bay
Form of government: British Overseas
Territory
Religion: Christianity
Currency: Cayman Islands Dollar

CAYMAN ISLANDS consist of three low-lying islands situated in the Caribbean Sea some 240 kilometres or 149 miles south of Cuba. They are a British overseas territory. The islands are fringed by coral reefs and are visited every year by thousands of tourists from the USA. The climate is tropical with a hurricane season from July to November. The economy of the country depends for the most part on tourism, international finance, real estate transactions and property development.

QUICK FACTS

Area: 622,984 square kilometres or
240,535 square miles
Population: 3,344,000
Capital: Bangui
Other major cities: Bambari, Bangassou
Form of government: Republic
Religions: Animism, Roman Catholicism
Currency: CFA Franc

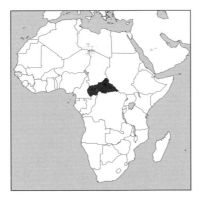

CENTRAL AFRICAN REPUBLIC is a landlocked country in central Africa bordered by Chad in the north, Cameroon in the west, Sudan in the east and the Congo and the Democratic Republic of Congo in the south. The terrain consists mainly of undulating plateaux (610–915 metres or 2,000–3,000 feet high) but with dense tropical forests in the south and southwest. The plateaux support dry, open woodland and savannah grassland and grade into arid scrub and semidesert in the far northeast. In the northwest and extending across the Cameroon border, are mountains which reach about 1,410 metres or 4,600 feet in height.

The tropical forests contain some commercially valuable trees, such as mahogany, and the country's varied landscape and vegetation are home to a wide variety of African wildlife. The climate is tropical with little variation in temperature throughout the year. The wet months are May, June, October and November. Floods and tornadoes can occur at the beginning of the rainy season. Most of the population live in the west and in the hot, humid south and southwest.

Over 86 per cent of the working population are subsistence farmers and the main crops grown are cassava, groundnuts, bananas, plantains, millet and maize. Livestock rearing is minimal because of the prevalence of the tsetse fly. Gems and industrial diamonds are mined and deposits of uranium, iron ore, lime, zinc and gold have been discovered although they remain relatively undeveloped. The country's main exports are coffee, diamonds, cotton, tobacco and timber although this is hampered by distance from a port. The Central African Republic achieved independence in 1960 but its political and economic fortunes have been very mixed since that time with widespread corruption and violence.

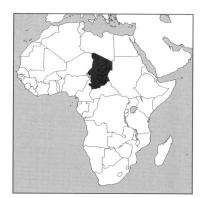

CHAD, a landlocked republic in the centre of northern Africa, extends from the edge of the equatorial forests in the south to the middle of the Sahara Desert in the north. It lies more than 1,600 kilometres or 944 miles from the sea. The principal feature is the large, shallow Lake Chad in the west with its surrounding basin and river systems.

Lake Chad has a minimum area of about 10,000 square kilometres or 3,861 square miles but swells enormously in the rainy season to about 25,000 square kilometres or 9,652 square miles. The basin is ringed by plateaux and the Enneddi Mountains in the extreme southeast and the Tibesti Mountains, rising to 3,415 metres or 11,204 feet, in the far north. The volcanic Tibesti Massif rises impressively from the parched, sunbaked sand dunes of the Sahara Desert.

Chad has a hot climate and is very dry in the north. Central and southern regions receive progressively more rain during a summer rainy season. Southern Chad is the most densely populated part of the country and its relatively well-watered savannah has always been the country's main source of arable land. Unless there is drought, this area is farmed for cotton (the main cash crop along with livestock exports), millet, sorghum, groundnuts, rice and vegetables. Fishing is carried out in the rivers and in Lake Chad. Cotton ginning and the manufacture of peanut oil are the principal industries.

As a result of ongoing drought and civil war, Chad remains one of the poorest countries in the world. The country has been torn by civil strife for much of the latter part of the 20th century but a ceasefire has been in place since 1994 and a territorial dispute with Libya has also been resolved.

QUICK FACTS
Area: 1,284,000 square kilometres or 495,755 square miles
Population: 6,515,000
Capital: N'Djamena
Other major cities: Sarh, Moundou, Abéché
Form of government: Republic
Religions: Sunni Islam, Animism
Currency: CFA Franc

CHILE lies like a backbone down the Pacific coast of the South American continent. It extends from Peru in the north right down to Cape Horn on the southern tip of Tierra del Fuego, a total length from north to south of about 4,184 kilometres or 2,600 miles. At its widest point, Chile does not exceed 185 kilometres or 115 miles. The country experiences volcanic explosions and earthquakes.

The dominant topographical feature is the Andes mountain chain in the east, which runs the whole length of the country. The highest peaks are in the northern half of the country and many are active volcanoes. A second, lower range of coastal mountains extends from north to south along the coast. In the southern region, these coastal mountains are submerged and their peaks form numerous archipelagos.

The two ranges are linked in the north by mountains running transversely from west to east to form a region of peaks and plateaux. This extremely arid land is occupied by the Atacama Desert, one of the world's driest places. South of the Atacama Desert lies a fertile, central region and farther south forests gives way to steppe-like grasslands. About 86 per cent of Chile's people live in urban areas with a third of them in the capital, Santiago, which lies in the central region between the Andes and the coastal mountains. There is tremendous climatic variation in Chile with changes attributable both to latitude and altitude.

Grapes, tomatoes, apples, maize, sugar beet, wheat, potatoes and other vegetables are grown in the central region where there is also a significant wine-making industry. Sheep are reared in the steppe-like grasslands along with cattle, pigs and horses.

The Atacama Desert is rich in mineral deposits, notably copper and nitrates, which are extensively mined. Other mineral resources include natural gas, petroleum, coal, iron ore, manganese, zinc, molybdenum, lithium, iodine, silver and gold. The vast copper mine of El Teniente, located in the central region, is one of the largest copper mines in the world and accounts for Chile's most important source of foreign exchange.

QUICK FACTS
Area: 756,626 square kilometres or 292,135 square miles
Population: 14,419,000
Capital: Santiago
Other major cities: Arica, Concepcion, Valparaiso, Viña del Mar
Form of government: Republic
Religion: Roman Catholicism
Currency: Chilean Peso

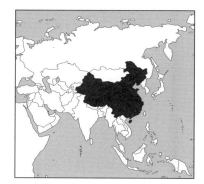

CHINA or **THE PEOPLE'S REPUBLIC OF CHINA** dominates the region of East Asia, not only in terms of size since it is the third largest country in the world, but also because of its huge population. One fifth of the world's people (numbering approximately 1,246,871,951) live in China and it has a larger population than any other individual country. The area occupied by China includes about 3,400 islands but excludes the disputed territory of Taiwan. The People's Republic shares borders with many other countries: Vietnam, Laos, Myanmar (Burma), India, Bhutan, Nepal, Pakistan, Afghanistan, Tajikistan, Kyrgyzstan, Kazakhstan, Mongolia, Russia and North Korea. In the east, China has an extensive coastline with the Yellow Sea, East China Sea and South China Sea which all open into the Pacific Ocean.

QUICK FACTS
Area: 9,596,961 square kilometres or 3,705,408 square miles
Population: 1,246,871,951
Capital: Beijing (Peking)
Other major cities: Chengdu, Guangzhou, Harbin, Shanghai, Tianjin, Wuhan
Form of government: People's Republic
Religions: Buddhism, Confucianism, Taoism
Currency: Yuan

The dominant topographical features are huge mountain ranges and high plateaux, particularly in the west and north, interspersed with lower-lying basins and plains, particularly in the east. Mountains and plateaux cover about two thirds of China's terrain and true plains account for only 12 per cent of the land area. The principal mountain ranges are the Himalayas which extend along the southwestern border, the Altai in the northwest border region with Mongolia, the Tian Shan Mountains which push in northeastwards from Kyrgyzstan and the Kunlun Shan, Altun Shan and Qilian Shan in northwestern, central regions.

The northwestern region of China consists mainly of two large basins, the Junggar Pendi in the north and the Tarim Pendi in the south, separated by the enormous heights of the Tian Shan Mountains. The Tarim Pendi contains the extensive Taklamakan Shano or Takla Makan Desert – a dry, stony, inhospitable landscape with enormous dunes reaching over 91 metres or 300 feet in height.

To the south and southwest lies the world's highest plateau of Tibet (Xizang Zizhiqu). Most of the Tibetan plateau is an uninhabited region of salt lakes, marshes and frozen wastes with a bitterly cold climate and thin, oxygen-starved air. The majority of Tibet's human inhabitants live in the lower southeastern regions beyond the plateau, where a milder climate allows vegetation to grow for grazing animals and cultivation is possible. Many great southern Asian rivers have their origins in Tibet including the Huang He and Chang Jiang (Yangtze) of China itself but also the Ganges, Mekong, Indus and Brahmaputra.

Northern China, which stretches from the Mongolian border to the Yangtze river but lies west of Manchuria, is a region of immensely varied landscapes. It comprises the steppes of Inner Mongolia and the loess (a fine silt) plateaux lands of the Huang He river which extend into the provinces of Shanxi and Henan. Although it is easily eroded, loess is a fertile soil and terrace cultivation on steep slopes is a common feature in this region.

Northeastern China is the region east of the Da Hinggan Ling hills comprising all of old Manchuria which includes the modern provinces of Heilongjian, Jilin and Liaoning. It consists mainly of the Manchurian plain which is ringed and interrupted by uplands and hills such as Xao Hinggan Ling and is a region of generally fertile soils which can be cultivated.

Southern and southeastern China comprises the large Yangtze river system and all the lands to the south, east of the highlands of Tibet. It is a varied region of rugged hills and mountains, valleys and plains, presenting many contrasting landscapes. The middle and lower Yangtze valley consists of a number of broad basins in which there are many lakes, both natural and manmade, and tributary streams. It has rich, alluvial soils which are extensively cultivated. In the upper reaches of the Yangtze, lies another basin, the Sichuan Pendi. This elevated basin is ringed by high mountains and is another fertile, intensively cultivated and densely populated area in which terraced rice fields predominate. Rugged, rocky hills guard the coast of southeastern China where there is an archipelago of numerous small islands providing sheltered natural harbours.

In the northeast of Guizhou Province in the south of the country, the underlying limestone rocks have been fashioned by erosion to form natural pinnacles and spires to form one of the most beautiful and unusual landscapes in China. Southernmost parts of China lie within the subtropics and tropics and, in places, areas of rainforest remain but much of the natural vegetation has been cleared during many centuries of human occupation.

Most of China has a temperate climate but, in such a large country, wide ranges of latitude and altitude produce local variations, from the Tibetan plateau's extremely cold Arctic climate with cool summers and very little rainfall to the far south's tropical climate with warm winters and typhoons affecting coastal regions.

China is an agricultural country but only 10 per cent of its land is suitable for cultivation. Intensive farming methods have had to be employed to feed the country's population of over one billion, including the widespread use of fertilisers, irrigation and the use of terracing to exploit all available land. China has a greater percentage of land supported by irrigation schemes than any other country in the world.

About 85 per cent of cultivation is devoted to the growth of food crops, with most production concentrated in the east of the country. The type of crop grown varies according to location and climate but the most important by far is rice. China produces more rice than any other country in the world, with the greatest areas of cultivation being the Yangtze river basin, Sichuan basin and the Canton (Guangzhou) delta. The country is also the world's leading producer of cotton and China is traditionally associated with the production of fine silk which has been highly prized for centuries. Raising silkworm or sericulture remains important in many parts of eastern and southern China. Another crop which is traditionally linked with China is tea and Chinese plantations produce about a fifth of the world's output, providing a valuable commodity for export as well as for domestic consumption.

The raising of livestock, sometimes involving traditional nomadic herding, is the other principal area of agriculture in China involving a wide variety of animals. The most important are pigs, with the country rearing almost half of the world's total number of animals. The versatile yak is used in Tibet as a source of meat and milk, its dung is collected and dried for fuel and its hide is turned into clothing, tents and bedding.

The rearing of freshwater fish, particularly carp, has been important for centuries and continues to be significant in the present day. Marine fishing was of lesser significance until comparatively recently but China now harvests a greater total tonnage of fish than any other country in the world providing a valuable food resource for its people. China's forest reserves have been severely depleted over many hundreds of years of human depredation. An extensive tree-planting programme has been undertaken but it will take some time before these can be utilised.

China has abundant reserves of many valuable minerals especially coal, graphite, tungsten and antimony ores, of which it is the world's largest producer. It also has a large and varied industrial sector which, in the early years of the Communist government, was mainly devoted to heavy industry. However, since the 1980s, readjustment has taken place with greater emphasis being placed on the development of light industries and new technologies.

More recently, the country has been opened up to tourists and to a degree has adopted the philosophy of free enterprise, resulting in a dramatic improvement in living standards for a significant proportion of its population. However, the change towards a market economy has created internal political problems and the 1989 Tianmen Square massacre raised questions regarding China's approach to human rights.

COLOMBIA is situated in the north of South America and most of the country lies between the equator and 10°N. The Andes Mountains are split into three ranges in Colombia: the Cordillera Occidental, the Cordillera Central and the Cordillera Oriental. The most westerly range is the Cordillera Occidental, which consists of fairly low but rugged foothills that rise behind the Pacific coast. On the east side of these, the River Cauca flows from south to north, joining with Colombia's main river, the Magdalena, 322 kilometres or 200 miles south of the Caribbean coast. Rising on the eastern side of the Cauca valley, the high peaks of the Cordillera Central attain heights of more than 5,029 metres or 16,500 feet and many are active volcanoes. On the far side of these lies the great Magdalena river, running northwards for a distance of over 15,289 kilometres or 9,500 miles, which is nearly the entire length of the country. To the east again are found the Andean range of the Cordillera Oriental, which is a region of plateaux, plains, peaks and lakes. On one of the plateaux is situated the capital city, Bogotá, which is built at an altitude of 2,590 metres or 8,500 feet. However, Colombia's highest mountain is not to be found in the Andes but is located in a separate group called the Sierra Nevada de Santa Marta, which are situated just behind the Caribbean coast. The peak is named Pico Cristobel Colon and is a massive 5,800 metres or 18,500 feet in height. Half of Colombia lies east of the Andes and much of this region is covered in tropical grassland. Towards the Amazon Basin in the south, the vegetation changes to tropical forest.

Because of its varied topography, Colombia has a wealth of habitats that provide a home for many different types of plants and animals. Many of these are thriving in areas that are relatively untouched by any human activity. The animals of the forest include jaguars, monkeys, snakes, pumas, alligators, peccaries, sloths, tapirs, anteaters and armadillos. The climates in Colombia include equatorial and tropical according to altitude.

Very little of the country is under cultivation, although much of the soil is fertile and the range of climates results in an extraordinary variety of crops. Colombia's most important crop is coffee but bananas, sugar cane, rice, cocoa beans, flowers, cotton, tobacco and potatoes are also cultivated. Cattle, sheep, pigs and horses are the most important farm animals. The country has large natural reserves of minerals and precious stones, particularly emeralds, silver, gold, petroleum, coal, natural gas, platinum, nickel and copper. It is South America's leading producer of coal while petroleum is the country's most important foreign revenue earner.

QUICK FACTS
Area: 1,138,914 square kilometres or 439,737 square miles
Population: 35,626,000
Capital: Bogotá
Other major cities: Barranquilla, Cali, Cartagena, Medellin
Form of government: Republic
Religion: Roman Catholicism
Currency: Colombian Peso

COMOROS, consists of three volcanic islands in the Indian Ocean situated between mainland Africa and Madagascar. Physically, four islands make up the group but the island of Mayotte remained a French dependency when the three western islands became a federal Islamic republic in 1975. The islands are mostly forested and the tropical climate is affected by Indian monsoon winds from the north. There is a wet season from November to April which is accompanied by cyclones. Only small areas of the islands are cultivated and most of this land belongs to foreign plantation owners. The chief product was formerly sugar cane but now vanilla, copra, maize, cloves and essential oils are the most important products. The forests provide timber for building and there is a small fishing industry. The coelacanth, a primitive bony fish, previously thought to have been extinct for millions of years, was discovered living in the seas off the Comoros.

QUICK FACTS
Area: 1,865 square kilometres or 720 square miles (excluding Mayotte)
Population: 538,000
Capital: Moroni
Other towns: Dornoni, Fomboni, Mutsamudu, Mitsamiouli
Form of government: Federal Islamic Republic
Religion: Sunni Islam
Currency: Comorian Franc

CONGO, formerly a French colony and now a republic, is situated between Gabon to the west and the Democratic Republic of the Congo (previously Zaire) to the east on the west coast of southern Africa. The Congo river basin is in the northeast of the country and the enormous River Congo forms most of the country's border with the Democratic Republic of Congo. Much of the country is swamp, crisscrossed by river tributaries and a little over half the land is covered with thick rainforests. The flatter coastal plain is essentially treeless with lagoons and moving inland there are highlands. Congo's capital, Brazzaville, lies very near to the border with the DRC (and its capital, Kinshasa). The majority of the population lives in the south with roughly one quarter in Brazzaville. The Congo has an equatorial climate with rains from October to December and January to May.

Cash crops, such as coffee and cacao, are mainly grown on large plantations but food crops are grown on small farms usually worked by women. The natural resource of timber is an important part of the economy (about half the forests are regarded as exploitable) and valuable hardwoods, such as mahogany, are exported. However, the principal source of wealth is offshore oil, accounting for about 90 per cent of the Congo's revenues and exports. There are other smaller mineral resources, including gold and copper, and a growing manufacturing industry.

QUICK FACTS
Area: 342,000 square kilometres or 132,047 square miles
Population: 2,668,000
Capital: Brazzaville
Other major city: Pointe-Noire
Form of government: Republic
Religions: Christianity, Animism
Currency: CFA Franc

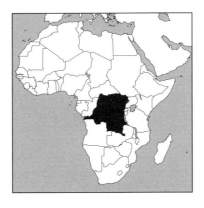

CONGO, THE DEMOCRATIC REPUBLIC OF (DRC), formerly Zaire, is situated in west central Africa. It is a vast country with a short coastline of only 40 kilometres or 25 miles on the Atlantic Ocean. There is a considerable variety in the geography of the country, from the rainforests on the western border to the huge central plain and mountains in the northeast, east and south. However, the Congo (Zaire) river basin dominates the land and reaches from the centre of the country to mountains or plateaux on all sides. In the east, the Ruwenzori Mountains overlook the lakes in the Great Rift Valley. The country has an enormously rich fauna and flora with many varieties of trees (oil palms, rubber, teak, ebony, cedar, mahogany and redwood) and diverse wildlife (lions, elephants, gorillas, giraffes, leopards and birds, reptiles and insects). In the central region, the climate is hot and wet all year but elsewhere there are well-marked wet and dry seasons.

The capital, Kinshasa, on the southern bank of the Congo river, was founded as a trading depot in the late 19th century. In addition to being the country's cultural and administrative centre, it has a strong manufacturing base, producing food, paper, chemicals and plastics, textiles, wood and construction products.

Much of the population is still occupied in subsistence farming. Cassava is the main subsistence crop and coffee, tea, cocoa beans, rubber and palms are grown for export. The country has huge mineral resources, particularly cobalt (around 65 per cent of the world's deposits), with copper, uranium, gold and diamonds being exported. Other natural resources include silver, iron ore and coal while offshore oil is an important asset. There is great potential for hydroelectricity but, as yet, this has not been exploited.

COSTA RICA is a small country bounded by Nicaragua to the north, Panama to the south, the Pacific Ocean to the south and west and the Caribbean Sea to the east. Three mountain ranges, including some active volcanoes, form the backbone of the land. About half the population is concentrated on the Meseta Central, a fertile plateau on the western side of the country which was first settled by the Spanish in the 16th century.

The climate is tropical with a small temperature range and abundant rain. The dry season is from December to April. The upland areas have rich volcanic soils which are good for coffee growing and the slopes provide lush pastures for cattle. Coffee and bananas are grown commercially and are the country's major agricultural exports. Costa Rica's mountainous terrain provides attractive scenery for its growing tourist industry and enough hydroelectric power to makes it almost self-sufficient in electricity. The country has a high literacy rate (around 92 per cent) and a culture which reflects its Spanish heritage.

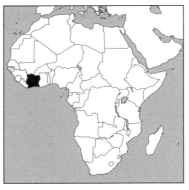

CÔTE D'IVOIRE, a former French colony in west Africa, is located on the Gulf of Guinea with Ghana to the east and Liberia and Guinea to the west. A roughly square-shaped country, the Republic of Côte d'Ivoire comprises a once thickly forested, undulating plain in the south and west, rising to mountainous territory in the northwestern border regions. Much of the forest has now been cleared and the interior and northern areas consist of savannah grasslands with thinly scattered trees. Coastal lagoons are a notable feature, attracting many species of birds, but wildlife is varied and well represented throughout the country.

A tropical climate prevails in the south where it is hot and humid with four distinct seasons – a long and a short rainy season interspersed with a long and a short dry season. In the northern savannah regions, temperatures are more extreme with a longer dry and rainy season.

Côte d'Ivoire is basically an agricultural country with about 55 per cent of the workforce involved in producing cocoa beans, coffee, rubber, bananas and pineapples. It is the world's largest producer of cocoa beans and the fourth largest producer of coffee. These two crops bring in half the country's export revenue although timber production is also of economic importance. Oil was discovered offshore in the late 1970s and there is some mining for gold and diamonds. Since independence, industrialisation has developed rapidly, particularly food processing, textiles and sawmills. Independence was achieved in 1960 and the country has been one of the most politically stable of the African states.

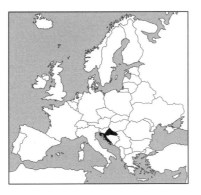

CROATIA, a republic of former Yugoslavia, made a unilateral declaration of independence on 25 June 1991. Sovereignty was not formally recognised by the international community until early in 1992. Located in southeast Europe, it is bounded to the west by the Adriatic Sea, to the north by Slovenia and Hungary, to the east by Yugoslavia and to the south by Bosnia-Herzegovina.

The country has a broad northern region and a long strip of land along the Adriatic coast The region behind the Adriatic coast is mainly mountainous and includes the Dinaric Alps. Dalmatia is a lower-lying region located to the southwest along the Adriatic coast. The country's chief farming region is part of the Pannonian Plain which lies to the east of the country. This low-lying, agricultural region is drained by the Rivers Sava and Drava which both flow into the Danube. Over one third of the country is forested with beech and oak trees being predominant, and timber is a major export. Deposits of coal, bauxite, copper, petroleum, oil and iron ore are substantial, and most of the republic's industry is based on their processing.

Prior to the outbreak of war in 1991, Croatia was a fairly prosperous republic of the former Yugoslavia, surpassed in productivity only by Slovenia and accounting for one quarter of Yugoslavia's national wealth. However, the fighting in the region has devastated the country's land, economy and infrastructure, and recovery is likely to be a slow process. In Istria in the northwest and on the Dalmatian coast, tourism was a major industry and, although tourists are beginning to return, the tourism industry continues to suffer from the effects of the ongoing hostilities in other parts of the former Yugoslavia.

CUBA is the largest and most westerly of the Greater Antilles group of islands in the West Indies. It is strategically positioned at the entrance to the Gulf of Mexico and lies about 140 kilometres or 87 miles south of the tip of Florida. Cuba is as big as all the other Caribbean islands put together and is home to a third of the whole West Indian population. It possesses unusual natural subsurface limestone caverns and its rivers tend to be short and unnavigable. The island consists mainly of extensive plains with fertile soil. The climate is warm and generally rainy and hurricanes are liable to occur between June and November.

The most important agricultural product is sugar and its by-products and the processing of these is the country's most important industry. Tobacco is also of commercial significance, with Havana cigars being well known internationally.

Most of Cuba's trade has been with other communist countries and the loss of Russian aid in 1991, when the former Russia broke up, has greatly damaged the country's economy. As a result, Cuba has been trying to increase its trade with China and Latin American countries.

QUICK FACTS

Area: 110,861 square kilometres or 42,804
  square miles
Population: 11,019,000
Capital: Havana
Other major cities: Camaguey, Holguin,
  Santa Clara, Santiago de Cuba
Form of government: Socialist Republic
Religion: Roman Catholicism
Currency: Cuban Peso

CYPRUS is an island republic which lies in the eastern Mediterranean about 85 kilometres or 53 miles south of Turkey. It has been unofficially partitioned since 1974 – the northeastern portion forming the Turkish Republic of Northern Cyprus.

The island's shape somewhat resembles a saucepan with the 'handle' formed by the long, narrow Karpas Peninsula pointing northeastwards towards Turkey. A range of mountains extends along much of the northern coast with a still higher range, the Troodos Mountains, in the centre and southwest. Between the mountains lies the extensive Messoria Plain. The highest point is Mount Olympus (1,951 metres or 6,401 feet) in the southwest.

Forests, mainly confined to the mountain slopes, cover about 13 per cent of Cyprus and include cedar, cypress, pine and juniper trees. Native wildlife is poorly represented except for birds, many species of which use the island as a stopover point during migration. The island has a Mediterranean climate with dry, hot summers and mild, moist winters during which most of the annual rainfall is experienced.

Agriculture accounts for about 17 per cent of the land and the Mediterranean climate contributes towards the great variety of crops grown, such as early potatoes, vegetables, cereals, tobacco, olives, bananas and grapes. The grapes are used for the strong wines and sherries for which Cyprus is famous. The main mineral found is copper while asbestos, gypsum and iron pyrites are also important. Fishing is a significant industry but, above all, the island depends on visitors and it is the tourist industry which has led to a recovery in the economy since 1974.

QUICK FACTS

Area: 9,251 square kilometres or
  3,572 square miles
Population: 756,000
Capital: Nicosia
Other major cities: Famagusta, Limassol,
  Larnaca
Form of government: Republic
Religions: Greek Orthodox, Sunni Islam
Currency: Cyprus Pound

CZECH REPUBLIC was newly constituted on 1 January 1993 with the dissolution of the 74-year-old federal republic of Czechoslovakia. The Czech Republic consists of two ancient former kingdoms and part of a third: Bohemia in the centre and west, Moravia in the east and a part of Silesia in the northeast of the republic. It is a landlocked country at the heart of central Europe, bounded by Slovakia (the Slovak Republic), Germany, Poland and Austria. Natural boundaries are formed by the Sudeten Mountains in the north, the Erzgebirge or Ore Mountains to the northwest and the Bohemian Forest in the southwest. Lying east of the centre of the country, the Moravian Highlands give way to lower-lying, rolling plains. There are numerous rivers in the country and a number of freshwater lakes.

The Czech Republic has a continental climate with warm, moist summers and cold winters with considerable snowfall in the mountains. The republic's capital is the beautiful, ancient city of Prague (Praha) located on the bank of the Vltava river. More than two thirds of the Czech Republic's population live in cities or towns.

The country has valuable timber resources, particularly in the Bohemian Forest, although, in some areas, trees have been severely affected by atmospheric pollution. The lower-lying areas and river valleys provide suitable farming land and agriculture is highly developed and efficient but it accounts for only a small percentage of the national income. The most important crops are cereals (notably wheat, corn, barley and rye), sugar beet, vegetables (especially potatoes), and hops for beer and flax. The main farm animals are pigs, poultry, cattle and sheep.

Lignite is the country's most abundant mineral resource but there are also some reserves of hard coal,

QUICK FACTS

Area: 78,864 square kilometres or
  30,450 square miles
Population: 10,315,000
Capital: Prague (Praha)
Other major cities: Brno, Olomouc,
  Ostrava, Plzen
Form of government: Republic
Religions: Roman Catholicism,
  Protestantism
Currency: Koruna

uranium, tin, antimony and mercury, iron ore, lead and zinc. Many of the lignite mines have closed in recent years as they were found to be uneconomic and inefficient and could not comply with tighter environmental controls.

Over a third of the labour force is employed in industry which has to import its raw materials and energy. The most important industries are iron and steel, coal, machinery, cement, paper and vehicle production. There has been a slow change from state to private ownership of the old industries and modern, privately owned service and technical companies have been formed. Traditional craft products include beautiful crystal from Bohemia, decorated glass and painted eggs. Tourism has increased and the country's many resorts, historic cities and winter sports facilities are attracting more and more visitors.

Environmental pollution of the country's air and water has caused serious damage to its flora and fauna and exposed its people to possible health hazards. The Czech Republic was considered to be the most polluted country in eastern Europe in the early 1990s, mainly because of industrial developments during the communist years that failed to include environmental safeguards. The problems have begun to be addressed during the last decade with the closure of lignite mines and endeavours to clean up the emissions from coal-fired power stations. The Czech government also plans to increase its production of nuclear power as a means of reducing the environmental pollution caused by the burning of coal.

DENMARK, the most southerly and smallest of the countries of Scandinavia, is a constitutional monarchy in northern Europe. It comprises most of the Jutland or Jylland Peninsula, which protrudes northwards from the North German Plain, and more than 500 islands, 100 of which are inhabited. The main islands, sandwiched between the east coast of Jutland and the southwest of Sweden, are Fyn, Langeland, Olland, Falster, Mon and Sjælland. Bornholm, which lies about 128 kilometres or 80 miles east of Sjælland off the southeastern tip of Sweden, also belongs to Denmark. The Faeroe (Føroyar) Islands in the Atlantic Ocean and Greenland off the coast of Canada are self-governing, dependent territories of Denmark.

The North Sea lies to the west of the Jutland Peninsula. The arm of the North Sea between northwest Jutland and Norway is called the Skagerrak, while that between northeast Jutland and Sweden is named the Kattegat. The Baltic Sea lies to the east of the Danish islands and the southernmost portion of the Jutland Peninsula is within Germany. Most of Denmark, including the islands, is low-lying, with small hills found only in the central part of Jutland. Several fjords penetrate eastern Jutland from the Kattegat, and the most extensive of these, the Limfjorden, cuts right across the northernmost part of the peninsula, broadening in the west to form an extensive series of waterways. The western seaboard of Jutland is low with many sand dunes and sandbars cutting off lagoons and sandy beaches. The country is intensively cultivated, so very little natural vegetation or wild areas remain. The proximity of the sea combined with the effects of the Gulf Stream result in warm sunny summers and cold, cloudy winters, with precipitation at its greatest in summer and autumn.

Well-developed road, causeway and ferry systems link the Danish islands to one another and to the mainland and connect with the country's railway network. The Danish capital and largest city is Copenhagen (København), situated mainly on Sjælland but extending onto the nearby island of Amager. A high proportion of the people (about 85 per cent) live in the cities, towns or urban areas. Denmark is a wealthy country and the standard of living is high.

Agriculture has always been important to the Danish economy and the land is intensively farmed with extensive use of fertilisers since the soils are acidic with low mineral content. Jutland is the main agricultural area and most farms are quite modest in size. A cooperative system of marketing and involvement in all aspects of agriculture is very much a part of farming in Denmark.

The rearing of dairy cattle, pigs and beef cattle is particularly important and Denmark produces a range of produce for export, particularly bacon, butter, cheese and pork. The most important crops grown are cereals (barley, wheat, oats and rye) but also hops, flax, hemp, tobacco and grass for grazing and hay. Danish beer and lager are famous throughout the world and make a significant contribution to the country's economy. The country also has a large fishing fleet operating in international waters and catching mainly cod, herring and salmon, much of which is exported.

Denmark has offshore reserves of oil and natural gas and land deposits of kaolin, lignite and some other minerals. Most electricity generation is from coal or oilfired power stations but Denmark has been active in developing renewable energy technology, including 'wind farms' and solar power. In addition to the food processing and brewing industries, manufacturing includes iron and steel, metal goods, heavy machinery, engines, shipbuilding, vehicle components, electronic and electrical equipment, chemicals, cement, biotechnology, clothing, textiles, furniture, ceramics, paper and printing and crafts (porcelain, ceramics, silver and fine textiles). The country has many business interests abroad that contribute to the overall wealth of the country. Denmark attracts many foreign tourists each year who not only visit the capital, Copenhagen, but also the islands and the Jutland Peninsula.

DJIBOUTI is a republic situated in northeast Africa bounded almost entirely by Ethiopia except in the southeast where it shares a border with Somalia and in the northwest where it shares a border with Eritrea. Its coastline is on the Gulf of Aden. The small republic of Djibouti achieved independence in 1977 having formerly been a French overseas territory.

It is a hot, dry, land with a coastal plain, plateaux, mountains and a salt lake, Lac Assal, which, at 144 metres or 471 feet below sea level, is the second lowest point on the Earth's surface. Some of the mountains rise to over 1,500 metres or 4,922 feet.

The country has a desert-type climate with very little rainfall. About half of the country's small population are engaged in agriculture although this is limited to oases or areas where water is available. Crops raised include fruits, vegetables and dates. Less than a tenth of the land can be farmed even for grazing so Eritrea has great difficulty supporting its modest population.

The economy is largely dependent on trade through the capital of Djibouti which serves as a major port for landlocked Ethiopia. The capital is linked to Addis Ababa by a railway. Cattle, hides and skins are the main exports. There are small deposits of copper, iron ore and gypsum but these are not mined.

DOMINICA, discovered by Columbus, is the most northerly of the Windward Islands in the West Indies. It is situated between the islands of Martinique and Guadeloupe. The island is very rugged and, with the exception of 225 square kilometres or 87 square miles of flat land, it consists of three inactive volcanoes, the highest of which is 1,447 metres or 4,747 feet. There are many unnavigable rivers and Boiling Lake in the south often gives off sulphurous gases. The climate is tropical and even on the leeward coast it rains two days out of three. The wettest season is from June to October when hurricanes often occur. The steep slopes are difficult to farm but agriculture provides almost all Dominica's exports. Bananas are the main agricultural export but copra, citrus fruits, cocoa beans, coconuts, bay leaves, cinnamon and vanilla are also revenue earners. Industry is mostly based on the processing of the agricultural products.

DOMINICAN REPUBLIC forms the eastern portion of the island of Hispaniola in the West Indies. It covers two thirds of the island, the smaller portion consisting of Haiti. The climate is semitropical and occasional hurricanes cause great destruction. The west of the country is made up of four almost parallel mountain ranges and between the two most northerly is the fertile Cibao Valley. The southeast is made up of fertile plains. Although well endowed with fertile land, only about 30 per cent is cultivated. Sugar is the main crop and mainstay of the country's economy and is grown on plantations in the southeast plains. Other crops grown are rice, coffee, bananas, cocoa beans and tobacco. Mining of gold, silver, platinum, nickel and aluminium is carried out but the main industries are food processing and making consumer goods. Fishing is also carried out but not to any great extent due to lack of equipment and refrigeration facilities. The island has fine beaches and the tourism industry is now very important to its economy.

ECUADOR is an Andean country situated in the northwest of the South American continent. It is bounded to the north by Colombia, to the east and south by Peru and to the west by the Pacific Ocean. It also includes the Galapagos Islands which are located about 965 kilometres or 600 miles west of the mainland.

The country contains over 30 active volcanoes. Running down the middle of Ecuador from north to south and rising inland from the coastal plain are the Sierra or Central Highlands, consisting of the Western and Eastern Cordillera ranges of the Andes. These are separated by a long, narrow valley forming a high plateau and they contain vast, towering peaks, several of which exceed 4,876 metres or 16,000 feet in height and a number of which are active volcanoes. They include Mount Cotopaxi, which at 5,895 metres or 19,340 feet is the highest active volcano on Earth, and Mount Chimborazo, which is an even more massive 6,310 metres or 20,556 feet high.

The coastal area or the Costa consists of plains and is up to 160 kilometres or 100 miles wide. Lying to the east of the Andes and comprising about one third of the total land area is the region known as the Oriente. Drained by rivers, which form some of the headwaters of the mighty Amazon, this region is covered by dense tropical rainforest and is well known for its biodiversity. The climate varies according to altitude from equatorial through warm temperate to mountain conditions.

Much of Ecuador's coastal area has been cleared of forests to make way for the cultivation of bananas, sugar cane, coffee, cocoa beans, rice, manioc and maize. In contrast to this, the highland areas are adapted to grazing, dairying and cereal growing. The fishing industry is important on the Pacific Coast and processed fish, such as tuna and shrimp, is one of the country's main exports. Ecuador is one of the world's leading producers of balsa wood. Oil is produced in the eastern region and crude oil is Ecuador's most important export.

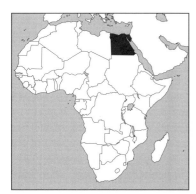

EGYPT is a republic in northeast Africa situated between Africa and Asia. The country's outstanding physical feature is the River Nile, the valley and delta of which cover about 35,580 square kilometres or 13,737 square miles. Although over 90 per cent of the Arab Republic of Egypt consists of desert, most of which is uninhabited, the country was the birthplace of one of the most astonishing, ancient civilisations in the world, with a written record dating back to about 3,200 years BC. The development of this civilisation was made possible by the presence of the River Nile.

Then, as now, human settlement was concentrated along the banks of the Nile, whose annual flooding deposited rich alluvial sediments which could be cultivated. At its lower end, the Nile divides to form a fan-shaped delta where the greatest amount of alluvial silt is deposited, making this the most fertile area. However, construction of the Aswân High Dam at the head of Lake Nasser has greatly reduced the silt deposits and led to a consequent loss of fertility. In addition, coastal erosion along the country's Mediterranean shores has resulted in increased salinisation of its water supplies.

The deserts of Egypt are far from uniform, varying from the huge Great Sand Sea in the Libyan or Western Desert to rocky, mountainous regions in the Eastern Desert along the shores of the Red Sea and in the southern Sinai Peninsula. Mount Sinai or Jebel Musa (2,285 metres or 7,500 feet) is located in Sinai which is separated from the rest of Egypt by the Suez Canal. In the Western or Libyan Desert, there are several areas which lie well below sea level, the greatest being the Qattara Depression. Descending to 133 metres or 436 feet below sea level and covering an area of 18,000 square kilometres or 7,000 square miles, it is the lowest place in Africa. Also in this region are several oases which provide small areas for human settlement. Archaeological evidence has revealed that the climate and environment of Egypt was once more hospitable and widely settled and the oases are the remnants of this period.

Natural vegetation is limited to the Nile Valley and oases and includes the date palm, tamarisk and acacia. Papyrus, a type of reed which was used to make 'paper' by the ancient Egyptians and was once widespread along the Nile, is now found only near the southern border. Mammal species are relatively few but other wildlife, especially reptiles, birds and invertebrates, are well represented.

All of Egypt experiences hot summers and mild winters. There is some rainfall in winter on the Mediterranean coast where temperatures are moderated by sea breezes. Conditions become drier and more extreme southwards, particularly in the desert where great fluctuations in daily temperature occur from very hot during the day to freezing at night.

Around 99 per cent of the population lives in the Nile river valley and delta and this concentration makes it one of the most densely populated areas in the world. The rich soils deposited by floodwaters along the banks of the Nile can support a large population and the delta is one of the world's most fertile agricultural regions where the main crops are rice, cotton, sugar cane, maize, tomatoes and wheat. The main industries are food processing and textiles. The economy has been boosted by the discovery of oil and there is enough to supply the country's needs and leave surplus for export. Natural gas production is increasing for domestic use and Egypt has a significant fishing industry, mainly in the shallow lakes and Red Sea. The Suez Canal, shipping and tourism (connected with the ancient sites) are also important revenue earners.

QUICK FACTS

Area: 21,041 square kilometres or
   8,124 square miles
Population: 5,796,000
Capital: San Salvador
Other major cities: Santa Ana, San Miguel,
Form of government: Republic
Religion: Roman Catholicism
Currency: Colón

EL SALVADOR is the smallest and most densely populated state in Central America. It is bounded to the north and west by Guatemala, to the north and east by Honduras and to the south by the Pacific Ocean. Behind the narrow coastal plain, there is a range of volcanic peaks which overlook a densely populated inland plateau. Further inland the land rises to the interior highlands. The Lempa river cuts through the centre of the country and opens to the south as a large sandy delta to the Pacific Ocean. Although fairly near to the equator, the climate tends to be warm rather than hot and the highlands have a cooler temperate climate. The capital is San Salvador and two thirds of the people live here or in the towns of Santa Ana, San Miguel and San Vicente.

The country is predominantly agricultural with about 32 per cent of the land used for crops and a slightly smaller area for grazing cattle, pigs, sheep and goats. Past volcanic eruptions have deposited a fertile layer of material on the high, central plateau, providing excellent conditions for coffee plantations. Coffee is El Salvador's main crop but tobacco, maize, beans, rice, cotton, sorghum and sugar cane are also grown. Fishing is carried out, with shrimp being the most important catch, followed by tuna, mackerel and swordfish. A few industries such as food processing, textiles and chemicals are found in the major towns. El Salvador suffers from a high rate of inflation and unemployment and is one of the poorest countries in the west.

QUICK FACTS

Area: 28,051 square kilometres or
   10,831 square miles
Population: 410,000
Capital: Malabo
Other major town: Bata
Form of government: Republic
Religion: Roman Catholicism
Currency: CFA Franc

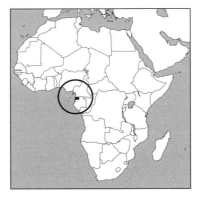

EQUATORIAL GUINEA lies about 200 kilometres or 124 miles north of the Equator on the hot, humid coast of west Africa. The country consists of a square-shaped mainland area (Mbini) with its few small off-shore islets and the islands of Bioko and Pagalu (Annobon).

The mainland has a densely forested, rolling landscape broken by some hills. Bioko is a very fertile volcanic island with two high mountains, steep slopes and tropical jungle and it is here that the capital, Malabo, is sited beside a volcanic crater flooded by the sea. The climate is tropical with plentiful rainfall all year and hot, humid conditions. Wildlife species are varied and abundant in the forests.

Most people are engaged in agriculture. Coffee and timber are produced for export on the mainland, while Bioko is the centre of the country's cocoa production. There is potential for a successful tourist industry. The country achieved independence in 1968 but ongoing politcal unrest and internal strife have hampered the country's economy and further development.

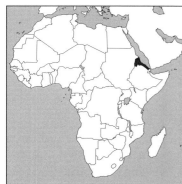

ERITREA, formerly an autonomous province of Ethiopia, gained independence in May 1993 following a long, armed struggle against Ethiopia which had been in control since 1945. Bounded by Djibouti, Sudan and Ethiopia, Eritrea has acquired Ethiopia's entire coastline along the Red Sea. The small Eritrean port of Aseb, in the southeast corner of the country has, however, been designated a 'free port' guaranteeing the right of access to the now landlocked Ethiopia. Eritrea has a coastal plain rising to a belt of plateaux and mountains in the centre and north. West of the mountains, the ground descends to form a region of undulating plains. Eritrea's climate is hot and dry along its desert coast but colder and wetter in the central highland regions.

People have traditionally followed an agricultural or pastoral way of life. Eritrea's natural resources include gold, potash, zinc, copper, salt, fish and probably oil. Deforestation and the consequent erosion are partly responsible for the frequent droughts and resultant famines that have blighted this area in recent years. Future revenues may come from developing fishing, tourism and oil industries. Warfare, with its consequent loss of life and displacement of people, coupled with drought and famine, has had a disastrous effect upon Eritrea in the second half of the 20th century. The threat of starvation continues to hang over the country which faces a long struggle to rebuild its economy and improve the lot of its people.

QUICK FACTS

Area: 28,051 square kilometres or
   10,831 square miles
Population: 410,000
Capital: Malabo
Other major town: Bata
Form of government: Republic
Religion: Roman Catholicism
Currency: CFA Franc

ESTONIA is a low-lying republic in northeastern Europe bounded by the Gulf of Finland and the Baltic Sea in the north and west, Russia in the east and Latvia in the south. Estonia is a former constituent republic of the USSR and consists largely of a marshy, undulating plain with numerous forests, lakes, wetlands and offshore islands. The largest of the islands, Saaremaa and Hiiumaa, lie across the mouth of the Gulf of Riga. The largest lakes are Peipus, which straddles the Russian border, and Vorts-Jarv in the southern central part of the country.

Numerous rivers and streams drain the country, including the Narva, which runs along the border with Russia, and the Pärnu. Almost one quarter of Estonia is forested, mainly with coniferous species such as firs and pine but also some birch, aspen and oak. There is a good variety of wild animals, including beaver, elk and wild boar and birds, especially wetland species. The republic has a temperate climate but inland it becomes more continental. The summers are generally warm to hot and the winters can be very cold with plenty of snow. Precipitation falls all year but is most plentiful in late summer and autumn.

About 62 per cent of the people of the republic are Estonians, who are closely related to the Finns, and the second largest group are Russians, making up about 30 per cent of the population. Over 70 per cent of the population live in cities, towns or urban areas and this is particularly true of the Russians who are mainly employed in industrial centres.

Agriculture is very important in Estonia, with the raising of livestock, particularly dairy cattle and pigs, being the prime activity. Crops grown include oats and rye, vegetables, especially potatoes, and flax. The forests provide valuable sawn timber and raw materials for paper, pulp and furniture-making. The country has a modest marine and freshwater fishing industry.

Estonia has significant reserves of high quality oil shale and some deposits of phosphorus. The oil shale is mined and processed to provide fuel, gas, electricity and petrochemicals. Peat deposits are substantial and supply some of the electric power stations. Most industries are based in the north and the manufacturing industry includes the production of light machinery, electronic equipment, electrical goods, vehicle parts, textiles (flax, wool), leather and wooden goods, furniture and foods. The economy is currently undergoing a major transformation to a free market system. Tourism and investment from the West have greatly contributed to the country's economy.

QUICK FACTS

Area: 45,227 square kilometres or
   17,413 square miles.
Population: 1,453,844
Capital: Tallinn
Other major cities: Narva, Pärnu
Form of government: Republic
Religions: Eastern Orthodox, Lutheranism
Currency: Kroon

ETHIOPIA is a landlocked, east African republic which borders on Sudan, Kenya, Somalia, Djibouti and Eritrea. Formerly known as Abyssinia, the country is dominated by a high, central plateau of volcanic rock from which rise rugged mountains ascending to heights of 4,572 metres or 15,000 feet. The Great African Rift Valley divides the plateau into the higher, more rugged and extensive Western Highlands and the smaller area of the Eastern Highlands. The plateau is deeply dissected by river valleys forming towering cliffs and escarpments, especially in the northeast. Lake Tana, the source of the Blue Nile (Abay), is found in this region. To the east of the plateau lie two sun-scorched desert regions – the Denakil Depression in the northeast which descends to 116 metres or 381 feet below sea level and the Ogaden Plain in the southeast. The western and southern border regions also consist of lower-lying plains.

The highest parts of the plateau experience temperate conditions with plentiful rainfall. At lower levels, there is a subtropical and a tropical zone with less rainfall and higher temperatures. The main rainy season is from June to September. The desert regions experience high temperatures and limited rainfall. There is a great range and diversity of natural vegetation, reflecting the different climatic zones, and an equally wide variety of wildlife. However, the forests of the highlands have been extensively cleared leading to soil erosion and a decline in biodiversity.

QUICK FACTS

Area: 1,104,300 square kilometres or
   426,373 square miles
Population: 58,506,000
Capital: Addis Ababa (Adis Abeba)
Other major towns: Dire Dawa, Gonder,
   Jima
Form of government: Federation
Religions: Ethiopian Orthodox, Sunni Islam
Currency: Ethiopian Birr

Around 80 per cent of the population is involved in subsistence farming. Teff is the main food grain and coffee is the main source of rural income. Employment outside agriculture is confined to a small manufacturing sector in the capital, Addis Ababa. There are mineral deposits of copper, iron, petroleum, platinum and gold which have been exploited. Ethiopia was involved in a costly war with breakaway Eritrea and the effects of this civil war were compounded by periods of severe drought and famine in the 1970s and 1980s. The situation remains precarious, particularly in some of the more marginal areas of the country.

QUICK FACTS

Area: 12,173 square kilometres or
    4,700 square miles
Population: 2,221
Capital: Stanley
Form of government: British Crown Colony
Religion: Christianity
Currency: Falkland Islands Pound

FALKLAND ISLANDS (Islas Malvinas) are situated in the South Atlantic about 650 kilometres or 410 miles east of southern Argentina. They are a British Crown Colony consisting of two large islands (West and East Falkland), separated by the 16-kilometre or 10-mile-wide Falkland Sound and surrounded by some 200 smaller islands. In 1982, the islands were invaded by Argentina, who had long laid claim to these 'Islas Malvinas', only to be recaptured by a British marine task force a few months later. The main economic activity is sheep farming with open grazing on the windswept, treeless, rugged moorland that rises to over 700 metres or 2,295 feet on both main islands. The highest point is Mount Usborne at 705 metres. Substantial income has been gained over recent years from the sales of licences to permit foreign trawlers to fish in the Falklands exclusion zone. There are also considerable offshore oil reserves available.

QUICK FACTS

Area: 1,399 square kilometres or
    540 square miles
Population: 47,000
Capital: Tørshavn
Form of government: Self-governing
    Region of Denmark
Religion: Lutheranism
Currency: Danish Krone

FAEROE (FAROE) ISLANDS (Føroyar) have been a self-governing region of Denmark since 1948. They consist of a group of 18 basaltic islands and are situated in the North Atlantic, approximately halfway between the Shetland Islands and Iceland. The landscape of these islands is characterised by steep, stepped peaks rising out of the sea to nearly 900 metres or 3,000 feet and glaciated, trough-shaped valleys. Although the islands are inhabited, poor agricultural conditions compel the population to seek their living at sea. Fishing, including some whaling, is the main occupation and exports comprise fish and associated products.

QUICK FACTS

Area: 18,274 square kilometres or
    7,056 square miles
Population: 797,000
Capital: Suva
Form of government: Republic
Religions: Christianity, Hinduism
Currency: Fijian Dollar

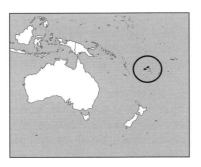

FIJI is a part of Melanesia and comprises more than 800 islands, only about 100 of which are inhabited. It is one of the largest nations in the western Pacific and is situated around the 180° International Date Line and about 17° south of the Equator. The two main islands, Viti Levu and Vanua Levu, are extinct volcanoes and most of the islands in the group are fringed with coral reefs.

Fiji has high rainfall, high temperatures and plenty of sunshine all year round. The southeast of the islands have tropical rainforests but a lot of timber has been felled and soil erosion is a growing problem. The main cash crop is sugar cane although copra, ginger and fish are also exported. With tourists attracted in ever-growing numbers to Fiji's coral reefs and unspoilt beaches, tourism is now a major industry and source of revenue although it was adversely affected by political coups in the late 1980s and ongoing unrest.

QUICK FACTS

Area: 338,145 square kilometres or
    130,559 square miles
Population: 5,125,000
Capital: Helsinki (Helsingfors)
Other major cities: Turku, Tampere
Form of government: Republic
Religion: Lutheranism
Currency: Markka

FINLAND is a north European republic with about a third of its territory lying within the Arctic Circle. A Scandinavian country of forests, lakes and islands, it shares borders with Sweden in the northwest, Norway in the north and the Russian Federation in the east. Its coastline lies along the Gulf of Bothnia in the west and southwest and the Gulf of Finland in the south, both of which are arms of the Baltic Sea. Some 30,000 islands and islets line Finland's coast with the densest concentration in the southwest and south. Of these, the most important are the 6,500 Ahvenanmaa or Aland Islands which lie in the Gulf of Bothnia between the mainlands of Finland and Sweden.

Most of mainland Finland consists of a low-lying, rolling plain or plateau which becomes more hilly towards the north. Mountains are found only in the extreme northwest where a 'finger' of Finland projects into the mountainous spine of Norway and Sweden. There are thousands of lakes in Finland – 187,888 have been counted – and many rivers and streams. Lake Saimaa in the southwest of Finland is the most extensive lake system in Europe. Finland has an efficient transport system which makes use of canals, road, rail and air services.

Finnish Lapland in the north of Finland lies within the Arctic Circle and is home to the country's population of Lapps or Saami people. This is a region of peat bogs with tundra-type vegetation, including mosses, lichens and scrub birch. Much of the rest of Finland is covered by the forests that occupy about 70 per cent of the land area. Coniferous species, such as fir, pine and spruce, predominate but birch and some other deciduous trees can also be found. Finland's large tracts of forest and wilderness areas with few human inhabitants are home to a good variety of north European wildlife such as wolves, lynx, bears, Arctic foxes, Arctic hares, elk, deer and the more familiar (although now mainly domesticated) reindeer.

Finland is known as 'the land of the midnight sun' because in the far north there is continual darkness for two months in the long cold winter and the same period of continual daylight in the short Arctic summer. During winter, snow cover lasts for seven months in the north and for three to five months in the south but summer temperatures can be warm to hot. Precipitation falls all year but is generally greater from July to December.

Finland is largely self-sufficient in food and produces a surplus of dairy produce. Most crops are grown in the southwest of the country. In the north, reindeer are herded and forests yield great quantities of timber for export. Just under 20 per cent of the country's electricity was supplied by hydroelectric power stations in the early 1990s. Major industries are involved in the production of timber products, wood pulp and paper and machinery. Shipbuilding has developed due to the country's great need for an efficient fleet of ice breakers.

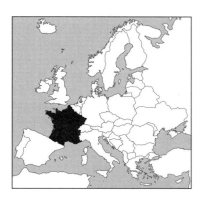

FRANCE is the largest country in Western Europe with coastlines on the English Channel, Mediterranean Sea and Atlantic Ocean. It shares borders with Belgium, Luxembourg, Germany, Switzerland, Italy and Spain. The lowest parts of the country are the great basins and low-lying plains of the north and southwest, which rise to meet the Massif Central, an extensive upland area, and the mountains of the higher Alps, Jura and Pyrenees. Mont Blanc on the France–Italy border is the highest point in the Alps at 4,807 metres or 15,770 feet. The principal rivers of France are the Seine, Rhône, Loire and Garonne along with their many tributaries. Many of these are navigable and are used commercially for the transport of freight. Climate ranges from moderate maritime in the northwest to Mediterranean in the south. France has a long cultural history of art, literature, sculpture and music and is famous for its immense Gothic churches.

Farming is possible in all parts of France with forestry and fishing also providing some employment. The western shores are ideal for rearing livestock while the Paris Basin provides good arable land. In the southwest around Bordeaux, vineyards produce some of the world's best wines. Wines and spirits are a valuable export for France although they are also produced for the home market. France has valuable mineral reserves, including iron ore, petroleum, coal, natural gas, salt, zinc, potash, uranium and lead. The main industrial area of France is in the north and east and the main industries are in iron and steel, engineering, chemicals, textiles and electrical goods.

FRENCH GUIANA, or **GUYANE**, as the name suggests, remains an overseas department of France and its economy is heavily subsidised by the mother country. It is bounded to the south and east by Brazil and to the west by Suriname. The coastal belt is a narrow strip of marshy mangrove swamps but the land gradually rises inland towards the Tumac-Humac Mountains. These straddle the Brazilian border but are of modest height by South American standards. Behind the coast there is some savannah but 90 per cent of French Guiana is covered with hot, humid, tropical forests that are thinly populated by people but inhabited by South American jungle animals such as tapirs, monkeys, anteaters, jaguars, ocelots, caimans and exotic birds. Off the coast, lie the Iles de Salut (Salvation Islands) and Devil's Island, the latter having a particularly notorious place in the country's history as a prison settlement. The climate is tropical with heavy rainfall.

French Guiana was originally inhabited by Arawak and Carib Indian peoples but Europeans – French, Dutch and British – arrived from the mid-17th century onwards and struggled to establish colonies. Their efforts to survive were severely limited by the natural forces of tropical diseases, difficult terrain and climate. The country came under French control in 1817 and, from 1852 to 1949, France decided that this was an ideal place to send its convicts. Penal settlements were established, both on the coast and on Devil's Island. The prisons were finally closed after the Second World War and, since that time, the country's inhabitants have enjoyed a relatively high standard of living thanks to support from France.

Most of the population live either in the capital, Cayenne, or in the coastal belt and are engaged in limited agriculture, fishing, forestry or mining. Recently the French have tried to develop the tourist industry and exploit the extensive reserves of hardwood in the jungle interior. This has led to a growing sawmill industry and the export of logs. Natural resources, in addition to timber, include bauxite, cinnabar (mercury ore) and some gold. French Guiana has one extremely modern development – the satellite launch base at Kourou, jointly run by the European Space Agency, the French Space Agency and Arianespace, the company responsible for the Ariane rocket.

QUICK FACTS

Area: 4,000 square kilometres or
 1,544 square miles
Population: 223,000
Capital: Papeete
Form of government: Overseas Territory of
 France
Religions: Protestantism, Roman
 Catholicism
Currency: Franc

QUICK FACTS

Area: 267,668 square kilometres or
 103,347 square miles
Population: 1,106,000
Capital: Libreville
Other major city: Port Gentil
Form of government: Republic
Religions: Roman Catholicism, Animism
Currency: CFA Franc

QUICK FACTS

Area: 11,295 square kilometres or
 4,361 square miles
Population: 1,141,000
Capital: Banjul
Form of government: Republic
Religions: Sunni Islam, Christianity
Currency: Dalasi

QUICK FACTS

Area: 69,700 square kilometres or
 26,911 square miles
Population: 5,411,000
Capital: T'bilisi
Other major cities: Sukhumi, Batumi
Form of government: Republic
Religions: Georgian and Russian Orthodox,
 Islam
Currency: Lari

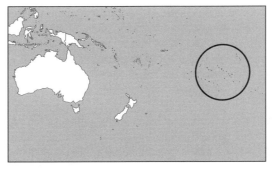

FRENCH POLYNESIA is an island territory whose links with France mean a relatively high standard of living for its citizens. It consists of 5 separate archipelagoes whose islands are scattered between the Cook Islands to the west and the Pitcairn Islands to the east over 4 million square kilometres or 1.5 million square miles of the southeast Pacific Ocean. Most of the islands are mountainous and volcanic but some are low-lying coral atolls. French Polynesia is hot and humid but cooler and drier from May to October. The economy is based on agriculture which produces coconut oil, vanilla and citrus fruits for export. Tourism also makes a significant contribution to the economy with visitors coming to enjoy the coral reefs that ring most of the islands.

GABON is a small republic in west central Africa which straddles the Equator. It comprises the land which surrounds the Ogooué river basin and its tributaries and most of the country is covered with lush tropical rainforests. Beyond the coastal plain and the flatter land of the valley bottoms, Gabon is ringed by upland plateaux and mountains ranging in height from 900–1,575 metres or 3,000–5,167 feet. The forests contain a huge diversity of plants and animals, including commercially valuable trees which are harvested for export. It was at Lambarene in east Gabon that Albert Schweitzer, the medical missionary, had his hospital.

The climate is hot, humid and typically equatorial with little seasonal variation. Until the 1960s, timber was virtually Gabon's only resource and then oil was discovered. By the mid-1980s, Gabon was Africa's sixth largest oil producer and other minerals such as manganese, uranium and iron ore were being exploited. Deposits of lead and silver have also been discovered. Much of the earnings from these resources has been squandered and around two thirds of the Gabonese people remain subsistence farmers growing cassava, sugar cane, plantains and yams. The country has great tourist potential but, because of the dense hardwood forests, transport links with the uninhabited interior are very difficult.

GAMBIA is the smallest country in Africa. The Republic of the Gambia comprises a small finger of land, pushing eastwards into Senegal from the Atlantic coast in a narrow band along either side of the Gambia river. The republic is enclosed on all its landward sides by the territory of Senegal and mostly does not exceed 24 kilometres or 15 miles in width only broadening to 48 kilometres or 30 miles in the east. The country is divided along its entire length by the River Gambia which can only be crossed at two main ferry crossings. The country consists of the river and the low plateau through which it flows interspersed with a few small, flattened hills.

On the coast, there are pristine beaches and sand cliffs backed by mangrove swamps, with tropical jungle clothing much of the river banks away from the coast. Beyond the river valley, lies some more thinly wooded savannah grassland containing commercially valuable trees such as rosewood, mahogany, rubber and oil palm. Gambia has two very different seasons. In the dry season, there is little rainfall but then the southwest monsoon sets in with spectacular storms producing heavy rain for four months.

Most Gambians live in villages with a few animals and grow enough millet and sorghum to feed themselves. Groundnuts and palm oil are valuable export commodities. The river provides a thriving local fishing industry and the white sandy beaches on the coast are becoming increasingly popular with foreign tourists. The country has enjoyed greater stability than almost every other west African state (in spite of a failed coup attempt in 1981) and attracts an increasing number of tourists each year which is helping to boost its economy.

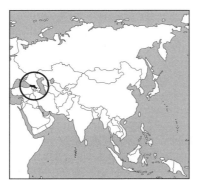

GEORGIA, a republic in the southwest of the former USSR, gained full independence from Russia in 1991. It shares borders with Turkey, Armenia, Azerbaijan and the Russian Federation and is bounded to the west by the Black Sea. The country incorporates the breakaway republic of Abkhazia, as well as the semi-autonomous regions of Adzharia and South Ossetia. It consists of a coastal plain and low-lying river valleys sandwiched between two high mountain ranges – the Great Caucasus in the north and the Lesser Caucasus in the south.

The climate on the coast is moist and warm, while inland it is dry, with hot summers and cold winters. Glaciers and snowfields occur on the highest peaks of the Caucasus Mountains and about one third of the country is forested, with conifers on the mountain slopes and deciduous species lower down. Wildlife includes deer, lynx, wolf, wild boar and eagle.

Agriculture, which is the main occupation of the population, includes tea cultivation and fruit growing, especially citrus fruits and viticulture. The republic is rich in minerals, especially manganese, but imports the majority of its energy needs. Industries include coal, timber, machinery, chemicals, silk, food processing and furniture. In the past, the Black Sea tourist trade exploited the country's wealth of thermal and mineral springs very successfully and tourism should again become an economic mainstay. However, the country has been devastated, and the economy and the life of its people have been severely disrupted, by internal strife during the last decade as ethnic minorities have struggled for regional autonomy.

GERMANY is a large populous country in northern central Europe which comprises the former East and West German Republics, reunified in 1990. In the north, lies the North German Plain which merges with the North Rhinelands in the west. Further south, a plateau which stretches across the country from east to west, is divided by the River Rhine. In the southwest, the Black Forest Mountains, or Schwarzwald, separate the Rhine Valley from the fertile valleys and scarplands of Swabia. The Bavarian Forest is in the southeast, approaching the border with the Czech Republic. The Bohemian Uplands and Erz Mountains mark the border with the Czech Republic. The beautiful River Danube, the second longest river in Europe, rises in the Bavarian Alps and crosses most of southern Germany. Germany's most famous river, however, is the mighty Rhine, which flows along the border with Switzerland and France before heading northwards towards the Netherlands and the North Sea.

The Rhine has several large and important tributaries, including the Neckar, Main, Lahn, Mosel, Ruhr and Lippe, and is a major navigable waterway used for the transportation of considerable amounts of freight. Because of heavy industrial development along much of the length of the Rhine valley, there are considerable problems with water pollution. Efforts continue to be made, however, to address this situation and to improve water quality. Most of Germany's lakes are in the southern Alpine region, the largest being Lake Constance (Bodensee) which straddles the border with Switzerland and Austria. Forests and woodlands are well represented in Germany, covering about 30 per cent of the land area but mainly in the southern mountainous regions. Germany is administered as 16 states or Länder, one of which is Berlin, with ten of the remaining 15 states being in the former West Germany and five in the former East Germany.

Generally the country has warm summers and cold winters. Agricultural products include wheat, rye, barley, oats, potatoes and sugar beet but agriculture accounts for only a small percentage of employment and a third of the country's food has to be imported. The fishing fleet is based in the coastal towns of the North and Baltic Seas, such as Bremerhaven, Cuxhaven, Kiel and Rostock, and the species caught include herring, cod, haddock, whiting and flat fish. Germany has a considerable timber and wood products industry based on its extensive coniferous forests but there have been problems in recent years caused by acid rain.

Formerly, the most important mineral resource in Germany was coal from the Ruhr valley and Sauerland which fuelled massive industrial developments in these regions. High grade coal is now much depleted and mining has consequently declined although Germany remains a major producer of lignite (brown coal) found in the east. Oil and natural gas deposits are found in the north and are exploited although they are insufficient to supply the country's domestic needs. Rock salt, potash, iron, lead, zinc and copper, along with small quantities of some other metallic ores, are also extracted and produced.

Products of the principal manufacturing industries include iron and steel, motor vehicles, mechanical and electrical equipment, aircraft, ships, computers, electronic and technical goods, chemicals and petrochemicals, pharmaceuticals, textiles, clothing and footwear, foods, beer, optical and high precision instruments. Many German products are exported and enjoy a good reputation for high quality and reliability.

QUICK FACTS

Area: 356,733 square kilometres or 137,735 square miles
Population: 81,912,000
Capital: Berlin, Bonn (seat of government)
Other major cities: Cologne (Köln), Dortmund, Düsseldorf, Essen, Frankfurt, Hamburg, Leipzig, Munich (München), Stuttgart
Form of government: Republic
Religions: Lutheranism, Roman Catholicism
Currency: Deutsche Mark

GHANA is located on the southern coast of west Africa between Côte d'Ivoire and Togo. In 1957, as the former British Gold Coast, it became the first black African state to achieve independence from European colonial rule.

The country has palm-fringed beaches of white sand along the Gulf of Guinea and where the great River Volta meets the sea there are peaceful blue lagoons. A coastal, grassy plain gives way to dense jungle in the southwest and savannah country and woodland in the interior and north. There is a range of modest-sized mountains (up to 900 metres or 2,950 feet) along the eastern border with Togo. The landscape becomes harsh and barren near the border with Burkina Faso in the far north. Forested areas have been greatly reduced and cleared during the 20th century although some efforts are now being made to halt this process.

The country's two main rivers, the Black Volta and White Volta, unite in central, eastern Ghana to form the River Volta which then flows southwards to the sea. Construction of the Akosombo Dam on the lower reaches of the river led to the creation of the world's largest manmade lake, Lake Volta. A tropical climate prevails but the north is drier than the south. There is one main rainy season from April to July and a minor one from September to November. Natural vegetation is varied but severely depleted and there has been a consequent decline in the numbers of some wild animals. Species include monkeys, warthog, buffalo, leopard, elephant, snakes and tropical birds. Most of Ghana's towns are in the south but rapid growth has turned many of them into unplanned, sprawling shanty towns.

Agriculture and mining are the country's principal economic activities. Ghana's most important crop is cocoa

QUICK FACTS

Area: 238,537 square kilometres or 92,100 square miles
Population: 17,459,350
Capital: Accra
Other major cities: Sekondi-Takoradi, Kumasi, Tamale
Form of government: Republic
Religions: Protestantism, Animism, Roman Catholicism
Currency: Cedi

beans and others include coffee, palm kernels, coconut oil, copra, shea nuts and bananas, all of which are exported. Fishing is also of major importance and has increased in recent years. Ghana has important mineral resources, notably gold, diamonds, manganese and bauxite. Independence was gained in 1957 and the country has, at times, been troubled by periods of political instability but it appears to have become more settled during the 1990s.

QUICK FACTS

Area: 6.5 square kilometres or
   2.5 square miles
Population: 27,192
Capital: Gibraltar
Form of government: Self-governing British
   Colony
Religion: Christianity
Currency: Gibraltar Pound

QUICK FACTS

Area: 131,957 square kilometres or
   50,949 square miles
Population: 10,475,000
Capital: Athens (Athínai)
Other major cities: Iráklion, Lárisa, Patras
   (Patrai), Piraeus (Piraiévs), Thessaloníki
Form of government: Republic
Religion: Greek Orthodox
Currency: Drachma

GIBRALTAR, or 'The Rock', is a limestone promontory situated at the end of a peninsula that forms the southernmost tip of Spain. Its strategic importance, guarding as it does the western approaches to the Mediterranean and separated from Morocco by the narrow Straits of Gibraltar, has meant that it has had a fascinating human history stretching back over thousands of years to Neolithic times. It has variously been occupied by Phoenicians, Carthaginians, Romans, Visigoths, Moors, Spaniards and the British. In 1713, the Treaty of Utrecht awarded Gibraltar to Britain and its present status is that of a self-governing British colony. Spain has never relinquished its claim to the Rock and relations have sometimes been tricky but at the present time there is easy access across the border in both directions.

There are over 100 natural caves in the limestone, in addition to man-made tunnels, and the steep, rocky slopes are home to a famous and much photographed colony of Barbary Apes. The British armed forces, tourism, banking and construction are the main sources of employment and most imports are from Britain. The Mediterranean climate and many sites of natural and historical interest ensure that Gibraltar attracts numerous visitors each year and there is easy access to Tangier in Morocco for those wanting to travel further afield.

GREECE or the Hellenic Republic consists of a mainland portion and more than 1,400 islands. Mainland Greece occupies the southernmost portion of the Balkans Peninsula and shares borders with Albania in the northwest, with Macedonia (FYROM) and Bulgaria in the north and with Turkey in the northeast. The Aegean Sea lies to the east, the Mediterranean Sea to the south and the Ionian Sea to the west.

The Ionian Islands (Ionioi Nisoi), including Corfu (Kerkira), lie off the coast of the western mainland in the Ionian Sea. The remaining Greek islands are scattered throughout the Aegean Sea. They include the Cyclades (Kikladhes) group in the southeast, Crete (Kriti) in the south, the Dodecanese group (Dhodhekanisos), including Rhodes (Rodhos), just west of mainland Turkey, the northern Aegean Islands, such a Thásos, Límnos and Lésvós, and the Northern Sporades (Voriai Sporhadhes), situated off the eastern coast of Greece. In general, the islands are quite arid, hilly and stony with thin soils that are difficult to cultivate.

The mainland is divided into a number of different regions, comprising Macedonia in the north and northwest, Thrace in the far northwest, Epirus in the west, Thessaly in the east, central Greece and the Peloponnese Peninsula, which is joined to the rest of the mainland by the Isthmus of Corinth. The northwestern and central regions of mainland Greece are rugged and mountainous, the main chain being the Pindus Mountains (Pindos Oros). Westwards the hills gradually become lower with flatter land towards the coast of the Ionian Sea. A series of extensive plains interrupted by hills and mountains lie in the northeast while to the east of the Pindus Mountains lies the extensive plain of Thessaly, a fertile agricultural region. The southeastern 'finger' of mainland Greece consists of a series of hills, valleys and plains. The Peloponnese Peninsula is largely mountainous, with steep ridges and narrow valleys extending in a northwest–southeast direction, although there is some lower, flatter land in the west.

Lowland Greece has a Mediterranean climate with hot, dry summers and mild winters with most rainfall in the western coastal regions. In the north and in the mountains, winters are much colder and snow is plentiful at higher altitudes. Greece is not as densely forested as it was in the past, but both deciduous and pine forests occur on the hillsides with wild flowers, such as anemones and cyclamens, at higher altitudes around 1,220 metres or 4,000 feet. At lower levels and around the coasts, citrus fruits, olives, pomegranates, figs, dates and grape vines are grown. Greece has a variety of wildlife, particularly in the remoter, sparsely populated mountainous regions. Animals include bears, wild boar and chamois and among the birds are pelicans, storks and nightingales.

About 21 per cent of people are engaged in agriculture, mostly on small family farms of about 32–41 square kilometres or 8–10 acres. Soils are poor in many areas, and erosion and lack of water add to the difficult farming conditions. Crops grown include tobacco, maize, wheat, barley, fruit (peaches, nectarines, grapes, oranges), sugar beet, olives, potatoes and tomatoes. Livestock include poultry, sheep, goats, pigs and a relatively small number of cattle. Forestry and fishing are carried out on a small scale, and replanting schemes have been undertaken by the government to replace lost trees. The fish catch is for the home market only although sponges are harvested for export.

The country is relatively poor in mineral resources although it has significant oil and natural gas reserves in the Aegean Sea. Some deposits of lignite, iron ore, bauxite, copper, chromium, magnesium nickel, zinc, lead and silver also occur and are mined and processed on a small scale. Pollution, both of the air by emissions from industrial plants and vehicles and of the sea from sewage and industrial wastes, is a serious problem in many areas. Athens is affected by smog, which is damaging its archaeological heritage. Industries include oil refining, steel and metal production, chemicals, cement, machinery, textiles, shoes, clothing and food processing. Greece has traditionally been an agricultural country but it has undergone a rapid process of industrialisation since the Second World War. This received a fresh impetus when the country joined the European Union in 1981. Tourism and service industries are also very important to the economy.

GREENLAND (Kalaallit Nunaat) is the largest island in the world (discounting continental land masses). It lies mainly within the Arctic Circle, off the northeast coast of Canada. Its vast interior is mostly covered with a permanent ice cap that has a known thickness of up to 3,300 metres or 11,000 feet. The ice-free coastal strips are characterised by largely barren mountains, rising to Gunnbjorn at 3,700 metres or 12,140 feet in the southeast. Glaciers flow into deeply indented fjords which are fringed by many islands, islets and icebergs. Of the small ice-free fringe, only about a third (150,000 square kilometres or 58,000 square miles) can be classed as being inhabited – mainly in the southwest. The largely Eskimo (Inuit) population is heavily dependent on fishing for its livelihood and fish account for 95 per cent of exports. There is some sheep farming and mining of coal and mineral resources include iron ore, lead, zinc, uranium and molybdenum.

QUICK FACTS

Area: 2,175,600 square kilometres or
    840,000 square miles
Population: 58,200
Capital: Godthåb (Nuuk)
Form of government: Self-governing
    Region of Denmark
Religion: Lutheranism
Currency: Danish Krone

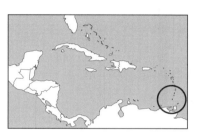

GRENADA is the most southerly of the Windward Islands chain in the Caribbean and its highest peak at 838 metres or 2,750 feet is Mount St Catherine. Its territory includes the southern Grenadine Islands to the north. The main island consists of the remains of extinct volcanoes and has an attractive wooded landscape. In the dry season, its typical climate is very pleasant with warm days and cool nights but in the wet season it is hot, day and night. Agriculture is the island's main industry and the chief crops grown for export are citrus fruits, cocoa beans, nutmeg, bananas and mace. Other crops grown are cloves, cotton, coconuts and cinnamon. Apart from the processing of its crops, Grenada has few manufacturing industries. It is a popular port of call for cruise ships and tourism is an important source of foreign revenue.

QUICK FACTS

Area: 344 square kilometres or
    133 square miles
Population: 92,000
Capital: St George's
Form of government: Independent State
    within the Commonwealth
Religions: Roman Catholicism, Anglicanism,
    Methodism
Currency: East Caribbean Dollar

GUADELOUPE consists of a small group of islands in the Caribbean lying in the middle of the Lesser Antilles islands, with some islands in the Leeward Islands and some in the Windward Islands. The two main islands of Basse-Terre and Grand-Terre accomodate 90 per cent of the population. Guadeloupe is an overseas department of France and has a warm and humid climate with rainfall heaviest between May and November. The country's main exports include bananas, sugar and rum.

QUICK FACTS

Area: 1,705 square kilometres or
    658 square miles
Population: 431,000
Capital: Basse-Terre
Other main town: Pointe-à-Pitre
Form of government: French Overseas
    Department
Religion: Roman Catholicism
Currency: Franc

GUAM is the most southerly and the largest of the Mariana Islands in the northwest Pacific Ocean. It consists mainly of a high coralline limestone plateau with some low volcanic mountains in the south of the island. Guam's climate is tropical with a rainy season from July to December. An unincoporated territory of the USA, its economy depends to a large extent on government activities and military installations account for some 35 per cent of the land area of the island. Exports include copra, palm oil and processed fish. The country has also become a financial centre, particularly for mainland and Asian banks, and tourism has come to play an important role in its economy.

QUICK FACTS

Area: 549 square kilometres or
    212 square miles
Population: 153,000
Capital: Agana
Form of government: Unincorporated
    Territory of the USA
Religion: Roman Catholicism
Currency: US dollar

GUATEMALA is situated between the Pacific Ocean and the Caribbean Sea, where North America meets Central America. It is a mountainous country with a ridge of volcanoes running parallel to the Pacific coast. Three of the volcanoes are still active and the country is also subject to earthquakes. In the northwest, there is a large, low-lying forested area called El Peten in which are located many archaeological remains of the Maya civilisation.

Guatemala has a tropical climate with little or no variation in temperature and a distinctive wet season. The Pacific slopes of the mountains are exceptionally well watered and fertile and it is here that most of the population is settled. Coffee growing on the lower slopes dominates the economy although bananas, sugar, cardamom, petroleum and shellfish are exported. The forested area of the country, about 36 per cent, plays an important part in the country's economy and produces balsam, cabinet woods, chicle (the main ingredient in chewing gum) and oils. There are also deposits of petroleum and zinc, while lead and silver are mined. Industry is mainly restricted to the processing of the agricultural products. Guatemala is politically a very unstable country and civil conflict has practically destroyed tourism.

QUICK FACTS

Area: 108,889 square kilometres or
    42,042 square miles
Population: 10,928,000
Capital: Guatemala City
Other cities: Cobán, Puerto Barrios,
    Quezaltenango
Form of government: Republic
Religion: Roman Catholicism
Currency: Quetza

GUINEA, formerly a French west African territory, is located at the 'bulge' in Africa's coastline. It is a lush, green, beautiful country about the same size as the United Kingdom. The Republic of Guinea is a country of varied topography crossed by many rivers including the upper reaches of the Senegal, Gambia and Niger. Its principal rivers are the Gambia and the Bafing. The coastal plain is about 50 kilometres or 30 miles wide before the land rises inland to form the central massif of the Fouta Djallon Highlands, a sandstone plateau dissected by deep valleys. The south of the country is occupied by the Guinea Highlands and between the two upland areas lies an area of the Sahel savannah grasslands extending northeastwards into Mali.

Mangrove forests blanket the area near the coast and the Guinea Highlands support dense tropical forest but trees have been cleared from parts of the Fouta Djallon. Wildlife is well represented and includes tropical birds, monkeys, leopard and many species of snakes. The rivers are home to crocodile and hippopotamus. A hot, humid, tropical climate prevails with plentiful rainfall during a rainy season which extends from May to November.

The majority of people are engaged in subsistence agriculture and the raising of livestock but Guinea has great agricultural potential and many of the coastal swamps and forested plains have been cleared for the cultivation of rice, cassava, yams, maize and vegetables. Further inland on the plateau of Fouta Djallon, dwarf cattle are raised and bananas and pineapples are grown in the valleys. Coffee and kola nuts are important cash crops grown in the Guinea Highlands to the southwest. Guinea is rich in mineral reserves, especially bauxite ore, iron ore and diamonds and has good potential for the development of hydroelectric power. Independence was achieved in 1958 and Guinea's political fortunes and its relationships with its neighbours have at times been strained.

GUINEA-BISSAU, formerly a Portuguese territory but granted independence in 1974, is located south of Senegal on the Atlantic coast of west Africa. The republic's territory includes over 60 coastal islands including the archipelago of Bijagós. It is a country of stunning scenery with a deeply indented and island-fringed coastline and a low, marshy plain, rising slightly to a plateau and hills on the border with neighbouring Guinea. Mangrove swamps and tropical jungle cover the land near the coast giving way to savannah-type grassland on the plateau.

The climate is tropical with abundant rain from June to November but hot, dry conditions for the rest of the year. The forests contain commercially valuable trees but the majority of the people are engaged in subsistence farming. The country's principal aim is to become self-sufficient in food and the main crops grown by its subsistence farmers are rice, groundnuts, cassava, sugar cane, plantains, maize and coconuts. Fishing is an important export industry although cashew nuts are the principal export. Peanuts, palm products and cotton are also a source of export revenue. Years of Portuguese rule and civil war have left Guinea-Bissau impoverished and it is one of the poorest states in west Africa.

GUYANA, the only English-speaking country in South America, is situated on the northeast coast of the continent on the Atlantic Ocean. Guyana was formerly called British Guiana but it achieved its independence in 1966. Prior to becoming a Crown colony, it was largely under the control of the Dutch West India Company. The Dutch were responsible for beginning an extensive land reclamation programme along the coast and, to this day, there is a narrow belt of fertile land with rich alluvial soils, protected from the sea by dykes and dams. Inland from Guyana's coastal belt, which nowhere exceeds 64 kilometres or 40 miles in width, there lies a densely forested region that covers about four fifths of the total land area. In the north and in the southwest, the forests give way to the high savannah of the Rapununi and Kanaku regions while in the western, central part of the country lie the Guiana Highlands and their table-top peaks.

The country's name means 'land of many waters' and Guyana is crossed by many important rivers. On one of these, the River Potaro, lie the spectacular Kaieteur Falls where the water drops 226 metres or 741 feet. The vast majority of Guyana's people live either in the capital city, Georgetown, or within the coastal belt.

It is on this narrow coastal belt that rice is grown and sugar is produced. Rice and sugar and its by-products are the mainstay of the country's economy, while tropical fruits and vegetables such as coconuts, citrus, coffee and corn are grown mainly for home consumption. Large numbers of livestock, including cattle, sheep, pigs and chickens, are raised in the savannah lands. Guyana's principal mineral is bauxite with gold, manganese and diamonds also being produced. There is potential for the production of minerals, hardwood and hydroelectric power in the forests of the southwest.

HAITI occupies the western third of the large island of Hispaniola in the Caribbean. It is a mountainous country consisting of five different ranges, the highest point being 2,680 metres or 8,793 feet at Pic La Selle. The mountain ranges are separated by deep valleys and plains. The climate is tropical but semiarid conditions can occur in the lee of the central mountains. Hurricanes and severe thunderstorms are a common occurrence. Only a third of the country is arable, yet agriculture is the chief occupation with around 80 per cent of the population concentrated in rural areas. Many farmers grow only enough to feed their own families. The export crops of coffee, sugar and sisal are grown on large estates. Severe soil erosion caused by extensive forest clearance has resulted in both a decline in crop yields and environmental damage. The country has only limited amounts of natural resources although deposits of salt, copper and gold exist. Haiti is the poorest country in the Americas and has experienced many uprisings and attempted coups.

QUICK FACTS

Area: 27,750 square kilometres or
  10,714 square miles
Population: 7,336,000
Capital: Port-au-Prince
Other towns: Cap-Haïtien, Les Cayes,
  Gonaïves
Form of government: Republic
Religions: Roman Catholicism, Voodooism
Currency: Gourde

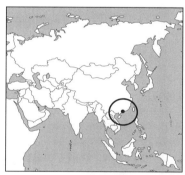

HONDURAS is a fan-shaped country in Central America which spreads out toward the Caribbean Sea at the Gulf of Honduras. Four fifths of the country is covered in mountains which are indented with river valleys running toward the very short Pacific coast. The highlands are covered with forests, mainly of oak and pine, while palms and mangroves grow in the coastal areas. There is little change in temperatures throughout the year and rainfall is heavy, especially on the Caribbean coast where temperatures are also higher than inland.

The country is sparsely populated and most people live in the west, in and around the capital, Tegucigalpa, and in the Cortes region in the north. Honduras is an agricultural country but only about 25 per cent of the land is cultivated. It was once the world's leading banana exporter and although that fruit is still its main export, agriculture is now more diverse. Grains, coffee and sugar are important crops, and these are grown mainly on the coastal plains of the Pacific and Caribbean. Forestry is one of the principal industries producing mahogany, pine, walnut, ebony and rosewood. Industry has increased in recent years, producing cotton, cement and sugar products for export.

QUICK FACTS

Area: 112,088 square kilometres or
  43,277 square miles
Population: 6,140,000
Capital: Tegucigalpa
Other cities: San Pedro Sula, La Ceiba,
  Puerto Cortés
Form of government: Republic
Religion: Roman Catholicism
Currency: Lempira

HONG KONG is a Special Autonomous Province of China. It is located in the South China Sea and consists of Hong Kong Island (once a barren rock), the peninsula of Kowloon and about 1,000 square kilometres or 386 square miles of adjacent land known as the New Territories. Hong Kong is situated at the mouth of the Pearl River about 130 kilometres or 81 miles southeast of Guangzhou (Canton). The climate is warm subtropical with cool, dry winters and hot, humid summers. Hong Kong has no natural resources and even its water comes from reservoirs across the Chinese border. Its main assets are its magnificent natural harbour and its position close to the main trading routes of the Pacific. Hong Kong's economy is based on free enterprise and trade, an industrious work force and an efficient and aggressive commercial system. Hong Kong's main industries are textiles, clothing, tourism and electronics.

QUICK FACTS

Area: 1,075 square kilometres or
  415 square miles
Population: 6,687,200
Form of government: Special Autonomous
  Province of China
Religions: Buddhism, Taoism, Christianity
Currency: Hong Kong Dollar

HUNGARY is a landlocked country sharing borders with Austria, Slovenia, Croatia, Yugoslavia, Romania and Ukraine. It is a region of plains ringed by the high mountain ranges of neighbouring countries. The main topographical feature is the Great Plain or Great Alföld which is situated east of the River Danube and extends southwards and eastwards across Hungary's borders. North of the Great Plain, near the Hungarian border, there are several upland areas. A smaller Little Plain or Little Alföld occurs in the northwest and continues into southern Slovakia.

The River Danube divides Hungary into two unequal halves. The Great Plain lies to the east while in the western, smaller portion, called Transdubnia, there is a generally more varied landscape with several upland regions, including the Mecsek Hills in the south and the Bakony Mountains just to the north of Lake Balaton. This lake is the largest in central Europe. The Danube and its tributaries, being navigable, form an important part of the country's transportation system and are the source of most of the country's water for domestic and industrial needs. Paradoxically, flooding of the rivers is also a problem and flood protection schemes are in place to try to limit the damage. Hungary has a continental type climate with hot, dry summers and cold winters, with most rainfall in the late spring and early summer. Parts of Hungary, particularly in the east, are subject to drought and irrigation is needed in order to sustain agriculture.

Since the collapse of communism, and especially during the last decade, farms have gradually been returning to private ownership. The government has invested money in improving agriculture by mechanising farms, using fertilisers and bringing new land under cultivation. Yields of cereals for bread-making and rice have since soared and large areas between the Danube and Tisza rivers are now used to grow vegetables. However, the use of artificial fertilisers has caused water pollution.

About 18 per cent of Hungary is covered with forest, and trees include broad-leaved types such as oak, beech,

QUICK FACTS

Area: 93,032 square kilometres or
  35,920 square miles
Population: 10,193,000
Capital: Budapest
Other major cities: Debrecen, Miskolc,
  Pécs, Szeged
Form of government: Republic
Religions: Roman Catholicism, Calvinism,
  Lutheranism
Currency: Forint

birch and lime as well as some coniferous species. Woodlands declined in the postwar years because of overexploitation but have recovered to a certain extent thanks to reforestation schemes and stricter controls on harvesting. Hungary's rivers and lakes, particularly Lake Balaton, are a source of freshwater fish that are harvested but stocks in some areas are affected by water pollution.

Pollution is a serious problem in Hungary, with both water and air being affected. The chemicals used in agriculture are the main culprits on the land with the run-off affecting the lakes and water courses. Emissions of sulphur dioxide from industries and vehicles cause acid rain, which in turn affects vegetation including the country's forests and also causes serious health problems for people. Hungary is endeavouring to address the problems caused by pollution.

Hungary is relatively poor in mineral resources but it does have substantial deposits of bauxite ore from which aluminium is produced. Other minerals include fairly modest reserves of natural gas, petroleum, coal and lignite, uranium, iron ore and manganese. The country is heavily reliant upon imports of oil and coal to supply its energy needs although over 40 per cent of electricity is now generated by nuclear power.

Hungary's economy has been transformed from one based almost entirely on agriculture to one with a sizeable industrial base. During the postwar communist years, most industries were state owned but, in the 1980s and more particularly in the 1990s, there has been a rapid move towards private enterprise. Industry in Hungary has always been dependent upon high levels of imported raw materials. Industries and manufacturing include the production of aluminium, chemicals, fertilisers, steel, cement, vehicles, pharmaceuticals, textiles, leather goods, plastics, electronic equipment and computers, agricultural products and foodstuffs. Tourism is a significant contributor to the economy, which has grown considerably since the demise of communism.

ICELAND is located in the North Atlantic Ocean about 298 kilometres or 186 miles east of Greenland and just south of the Arctic Circle. The island is roughly oval in shape with a deeply indented coastline and numerous fjords and bays. A large, broad peninsula projects from the northwestern corner of the island. Several small islands lie off Iceland's coast, notably Heimaey and Surtsey of the Verstmannaeyjar group of islands. Iceland is composed of volcanic rocks that have been pushed out from the Mid-Atlantic Ridge, an area where molten material is continually being extruded, pushing two of the Earth's crustal plates apart. Hence, not surprisingly, Iceland has numerous volcanoes and lies in an active earthquake zone. The centre of the island is a barren, uninhabited, high, rocky plateau composed of solidified lava from which rise volcanic mountains.

The inhabited lowlands of Iceland, comprising about a sixth of the total land area, occur in the coastal regions, especially in the southwest and southeast. Mount Hekla in the south (1,490 metres or 4,891 feet) is Iceland's most famous volcano and in the Middle Ages was regarded as being a 'gateway to hell'. It has erupted several times in the island's history, the last occasion being in 1980. Other signs of the volcanic activity lying just beneath the surface are provided by numerous geysers, bubbling mud pools, hot springs and heated geothermal pools with water that is rich in dissolved minerals. Strokkur and Geysir are two of Iceland's most famous geysers while the hot springs are used to heat most of the homes and businesses in Reykjavik.

Ice caps and glaciers cover about 11 per cent of the land surface at higher altitudes, of which Vatnajokull, covering 8,547 square kilometres or 3,300 square miles in the southeast, is the most extensive in Europe. Iceland has numerous lakes, fast-flowing rivers and waterfalls that are harnessed to generate the hydroelectric power that meets the electricity needs of the island. Trees are scarce and consist of a few birch and conifers while the main vegetation grows at lower levels and consists of lichens, mosses, heather and hardy grasses. Indigenous wild animals are quite limited with an absence of reptiles and amphibians although some animals (reindeer and rodents) have been either deliberately or accidentally introduced. A good variety of birds, some of which are migratory, inhabit Iceland. Seals and whales are common in Icelandic waters, as are the fish on which the country's economy depends. Salmon and trout are found in Iceland's lakes and rivers which are not affected by any form of pollution.

In spite of its northerly position, Iceland has a relatively moderate climate which is influenced by the warm waters of the North Atlantic Drift/Gulf Stream. Summer temperatures are mild to cool but it is cold in winter, especially in the north. Precipitation falls all year and is heavier in the south, with snow in the colder months on high ground and in the north. Strong winds are characteristic of the winter months but can occur throughout the year, causing occasional dust storms inland. Permanent daylight occurs for three months in summer and the beautiful Aurora Borealis (Northern Lights) can be seen from the end of August.

Very little of the land in Iceland can be cultivated and the main crops are root vegetables such as turnips and potatoes. The principal livestock are sheep, cattle, poultry and native Icelandic ponies. Dairy produce, eggs, milk, meat and wool are produced for home consumption. Fishing and fish processing are the mainstay of the Icelandic economy, with much of the catch being exported. Iceland has a 320-kilometre or 200-mile zone around its coasts from which foreign trawlers are excluded. The most important species include cod, haddock, herring and shellfish.

Iceland lacks exploitable minerals, apart from diatomite, and must import raw materials for its industries which do, however, benefit from the availability of cheap electricity. Aluminium and ferrosilicon, nitrates for fertilisers, cement and chemicals are produced for export. Other manufactured goods include paints, textiles, clothing, footwear and knitted products. Books and published material are also economically significant. Fish and fish products remain the most important aspect of the economy but tourism is of growing importance to the island.

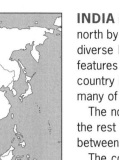

INDIA is a vast republic in South Asia which is dominated in the extreme north by the world's youngest and highest mountains, the Himalayas. The diverse Republic of India encompasses a huge variety of geographical features and human societies. It is the second most densely populated country in the world and is home to one in six of the world's population, many of whom live in conditions of extreme poverty.

The northeastern states, including Assam, are effectively cut off from the rest of India, connected only by a narrow corridor of land squeezing between the borders of Nepal and Bangladesh.

The country has three main geographical divisions: the high peaks of the Himalayas which dominate the northern border; the densely populated, fertile northern plains which are drained by the Ganges and Brahmaputra rivers; and the ancient Deccan Plateau region to the south which extends to the southern tip of the country.

The Himalayas form a massive mountain barrier which extends across the entire length of India's northern boundary – a distance of about 2,400 kilometres or 1,500 miles. Among the many massive peaks, including Mount Everest and K2, is Kanchenjunga, which at 8,598 metres or 28,208 feet is India's highest mountain and the third largest mountain in the world after Everest and K2. The northern plains region, which lies south of the Himalayas and extends into the northeastern states, is drained by the great River Ganges and its tributaries and by the River Brahmaputra in the east. It is a lowland, well-watered region of fertile alluvial soils. The Deccan Plateau is bounded on either side by the Western Ghats Mountains and Eastern Ghats Mountains. It is a ridged and rocky region, interrupted by low mountains and hills and dissected by deep valleys.

In general, India's climate is hot with monsoon rainfall between June and September but extremely cold winter conditions are experienced in the northern mountains. In central, lower regions, temperatures can fall to near freezing at night in winter. In many areas, high humidity and heat combine to make conditions unpleasant.

Natural vegetation varies greatly from tropical forests to desert plants in the arid northwest. Wildlife is equally diverse and includes some rare animals such as the tiger, Asian elephant, rhino, snow leopard, panther and clouded leopard. Several types of monkey, reptiles, antelope, deer, black bear, buffalo, ibex, wild goat and many bird species are also present.

About 70 per cent of the population depend on agriculture for their living and the lower slopes of the Himalayas represent one of the world's best tea growing areas. Rice, sugar cane and wheat are grown in the Ganges plain and there is a comprehensive system of irrigation to aid agriculture. India is self-sufficient in all of its major food crops and main exports include precious stones and jewellery, engineering products, clothes and chemicals.

India became a republic in 1950 and in its first half century of existence has continued to be troubled by internal dissent and external disputes, particularly with Pakistan over the status of Kashmir. To add to its problems, India is frequently subjected to famine and natural disasters such as devastating flooding and extremely severe cyclones.

INDONESIA is a republic made up of 13,677 islands, less than half of which are inhabited, scattered across the Indian and Pacific Oceans in a huge crescent and it is one of the world's most highly populated countries. Five main islands take up three quarters of Indonesia's total area and are home to 80 per cent of its people: Kalimantan (part of the island of Borneo), Sumatra, Java, Sulawesi (Celebes) and Irian Jaya (the western half of the island of New Guinea). Its largest landmass is the province of Kalimantan, which is part of the island of Borneo, while Sumatra is the largest individual island and Java is the dominant and most densely populated island.

The Indonesian islands have an extremely varied topography, ranging from high mountains to coastal plains and the southern ones occupy a volcanic belt containing 130 active volcanoes, 70 of which have erupted during the last 200 years. Natural vegetation varies according to the exact location and topography of each island but ranges from lowland tropical jungle to coastal mangrove swamps and upland mountain forest. An enormous variety of wildlife can be found throughout Indonesia with some species being unique to particular islands. Their number include the orang-utan, tapir, proboscis monkey, black gibbon, Komodo dragon (Komodo and Rinca islands), birds of paradise and cassowary.

Indonesia has a tropical climate which varies according to exact location. In many areas, the eastern monsoon causes a dry season between June and September while the western monsoon causes the main rains to fall between December and March. Rain and storms may, however, occur at any time of the year.

Rice, maize and cassava are the main crops grown. Indonesia has the largest reserves of tin in the world and is one of the world's leading rubber producers. Other mineral resources found are bauxite, natural gas, nickel and copper. Oil production is also important. Indonesia's resources are not as yet fully developed but the country's economy needs to expand if Indonesia is to create the two million jobs needed annually to keep pace with the growth in its population. Ongoing political instability and human rights abuse, such as occurred in East Timor in August 1999, have been condemned by the international community and are hampering this process.

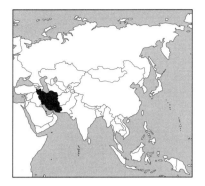

IRAN, ISLAMIC REPUBLIC OF, lies across The Gulf from the Arabian Peninsula and stretches from the Caspian Sea to the Arabian Sea. Since 1978/9, when Shah Muhammad Reza Pahlavi was overthrown by followers of Ayatollah Ruhollah Khomeini, Iran has been governed according to strict Islamic laws and has endured a costly war with Iraq (1980–88). It is a country of high mountains, plateaux and desert, notably the Zagros Mountains (Kuhha-ye Zagros) in the west, the Elburz (Reshten-ye-Kuhha-ye Alborz) range in the north and the sandy Dasht-e Lut and salty Dasht-e Kavir deserts of central and eastern Iran.

Although the climate is extremely hot and dry in summer, especially near The Gulf and in the desert, winters can be very cold, particularly in the Elburz Mountains. Rainfall is generally slight with most falling during the winter and early spring months, especially in the mountains. A range of trees and shrubs are able to grow in extensive forests in the more well-watered upland areas and there are also areas of steppe grassland on the plateaux. Elsewhere in the arid regions, only desert and scrub plants are able to survive. Wildlife is varied according to region but includes deer, ibex, porcupine, leopard, wolf and jackal. Birds are equally well represented including various predatory species and pelicans and flamingos along the shores of The Gulf.

Most of the population live in the north and west, where Tehran, the capital, is situated. The only good agricultural land is on the Caspian coastal plains, where wheat, barley, potatoes and rice are grown. Fresh and dried fruit are the country's main exports apart from petroleum. About 5 per cent of the population are nomadic herdsmen. Most of Iran's oil is in the southwest and other valuable minerals include coal, iron ore, copper and lead. Precious stones are found in the northeast. Main exports are petrochemicals, carpets and rugs, textiles, raw cotton and leather goods. There was a rapid expansion in the economy thanks to revenue from the petroleum industry. However, after the Islamic revolution in the late 1970s and a war with Iraq, the economy slowed dramatically and is only gradually beginning to pick up again.

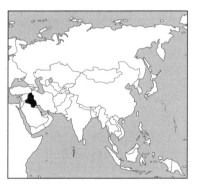

IRAQ is located in southwest Asia, wedged between The Gulf and Syria. The Republic of Iraq includes most of ancient Mesopotamia which lay between the Tigris and Euphrates, the two great rivers which are a dominant feature of Iraq. These two rivers flow through Iraq from northwest to southeast before finally uniting to form the tidal river of Shatt al Arab, which empties into The Gulf.

The lower part of this river courses through marshland while, west of the Euphrates, the land rises and grades into the semidesert and desert of Syria. The northeast of Iraq is mountainous with high peaks reaching elevations of 3,600 metres or 11,811 feet. The climate is arid with very hot summers and cold winters. Iraq has many ancient archaeological sites and Mesopotamia was the birthplace of such early civilisations as Sumer, Babylon and Assyria.

Although Iraq is primarily an agricultural country, the only fertile land is in the river basins of the Tigris and Euphrates where wheat, barley, rice, tobacco and cotton are grown. The world's largest production of dates also comes from this area and is the country's main export product. A variety of other fruits is grown such as apples, olives, figs, grapes and pomegranates.

Iraq profited from the great oil boom of the 1970s but, during the war with Iran, oil terminals in The Gulf were destroyed and the Trans-Syrian Pipeline closed. Internal and external conflict and economic sanctions imposed by the international community continue to have a severe effect upon Iraq's economy. The country is in a state of economic crisis with the health of the general population being low due to endemic diseases and poor sanitary conditions.

IRELAND, REPUBLIC OF, is one of Europe's most westerly countries and part of the British Isles. Situated in the Atlantic Ocean, it is separated from Great Britain by the Irish Sea and extends over four fifths of the island of Ireland. Much of the Republic of Ireland is low-lying and marshy but interrupted by a number of mountain ranges. These include the Wicklow Mountains in the east, the Caha and Boggeragh Mountains in the southwest, the Nephin Beg range in the west and the Derry Veagh Mountains in the north. The western coastline has numerous indentations and there are numerous lakes and peat bogs in the low-lying marshes inland, drained by such rivers as the Shannon. The climate is cool temperate with mild conditions and an even annual rainfall.

Ireland is famous for its green, rolling farmland. The richest soils are found in the south and southeast while those in the west are poorer and less productive. About 80 per cent of the land is under agriculture. The principal crops are wheat, barley, sugar beet, fodder crops and potatoes. Livestock includes cattle, sheep, pigs and poultry. Fishing is particularly important off the east coast. The rural population tend to migrate to the cities, and mainly to Dublin, which is the main industrial centre and the focus of radio, television, publishing and communications.

ISRAEL is a republic which was created in 1948 after the British withdrawal from Palestine, when the region was partitioned in accordance with a recommendation made by the United Nations. The new country was born into conflict, for the declaration of its existence by Jewish leaders led to immediate warfare with Arab neighbours – the first of five such ArabIsraeli wars. Israel won this first war (and all others since) and, as a result, immediately acquired new territory beyond that envisaged by the United Nations.

Following the Six Day War in 1967, Israel took control of East Jerusalem, the West Bank (the region between Jerusalem and the River Jordan, previously Jordanian), the Golan Heights (Syrian), the Gaza Strip (a narrow band of territory in southwest Israel beside the Mediterranean Sea administered by Egypt) and the Sinai Peninsula (also Egyptian). A degree of self-rule has since been awarded to Palestinian settlements in the West Bank. Israel has also withdrawn from the Sinai Peninsula (returned to Egypt) and the Gaza Strip (now administered by the Palestine Liberation Organisation and containing several vast Arab refugee camps).

Israel occupies a long narrow stretch of land in the southeast of the Mediterranean. Its eastern boundary is formed by the Great Rift Valley through which the River Jordan flows to the Dead Sea. The River Jordan, the Sea of Galilee and the Dead Sea occupy the Great Rift Valley which extends from beyond the source of the Jordan through the Gulf of Aqaba and the Red Sea and on into East Africa. The south of the country is made up of the triangular wedge of the Negev Desert which ends at the Gulf of Aqaba.

Israel has quite a varied topography of plains, hills, mountains and desert. Narrow coastal plains extend from north to south along the Mediterranean shores and are densely populated. The Plain of Esdraelon extends across the northern part of Israel from Haifa to the valley of the River Jordan and is reclaimed marshland which is intensively cultivated and settled. The Hills of Galilee occupy the northern part of Israel from the Sea of Galilee to the coast. The Judean and Samarian Hills extend in a northsouth direction behind the coastal plains throughout most of Israel.

Natural vegetation varies according to location and amount of rainfall but most plants are adapted to withstand drought. Wooded areas cover about 6 per cent of Israel and there has been an extensive programme to replant native species. Wildlife includes wolf, jackal, hyena, mongoose, porcupine and gazelle. The climate in summer is hot and dry and in winter mild with some rain but colder in the north. Tel Aviv (Tel Aviv-Yafo) is the country's capital and main commercial centre.

Israel's agriculture is based on collective settlements known as kibbutz. The country is virtually self-sufficient in foodstuffs and a major exporter of its produce. The Negev Desert has mineral resources, such as copper, phosphates and manganese, plus commercial amounts of natural gas and petroleum. Other assets are the vast amounts of potash, bromine and other minerals found in the Dead Sea. A wide range of products is processed or finished in the country and main exports include finished diamonds, textiles, fruit, vegetables, chemicals, machinery and fertilisers. Tourism also makes an important contribution to the economy.

ITALY is a republic in southern Europe, which comprises a large peninsula and the two main islands of Sicily (Sicilia) and Sardinia (Sardegna). The huge peaks of the Alps and the Dolomites form Italy's northern border with France, Switzerland, Austria and Slovenia. Towards the foothills of the mountains lie a number of large lakes of which the most famous are Maggiore, Como and Garda. The Adriatic Sea to the east separates Italy from the countries of former Yugoslavia. The fertile Plain of Lombardy lies to the south of the Alps. Numerous rivers rise in the northern mountains and many become tributaries of the great River Po which flows eastwards and drains the Lombardy Plain before emptying into the Adriatic Sea.

South of the Plain of Lombardy, lies the familiar long 'boot' of peninsular Italy, which comprises the majority of the country. The toe of the boot turns south and then southwest to 'kick' the island of Sicily from which it is separated by the narrow distance (3 kilometres or 2 miles) of the Strait of Messina. The Apennine Mountains extend down the length of the peninsula, the highest peak being Mount Corno (2,912 metres or 9,560 feet) which is situated west of Pescara in the central region. The principal rivers of the peninsula are the Arno, which flows through Florence (Firenze) and Pisa, and the Tiber (Tevere), which runs through Rome (Roma). Italy's climate is exceedingly varied according to both location and altitude but generally the country enjoys warm, dry summers and mild winters.

In the northern mountains, coniferous trees and Alpine flora as well as ibex, chamois, marmots and birds of prey can be found. In the Apennine Mountains, pine and fir trees grow at higher levels, with cypress, oaks and chestnut trees on the lower slopes. In lower and southern areas that have a Mediterranean climate, olive, date, orange, lemon, almond, fig and pomegranate trees can be found. In the hilly, densely wooded and sparsely populated southern part of Italy, wolves, wild boar and (very occasionally) bears are among the animal inhabitants.

Agriculture remains important to the Italian economy employing about 12 per cent of the workforce. Italy is one of the leading producers in Europe of wine and olive oil. Peaches, nectarines, oranges, lemons, pomegranates, almonds, melons, dates, figs, apples and tomatoes are among the fruits that are grown and exported. A variety of cereal crops are also grown and the dairy industry produces a number of famous cheeses, such as Parmesan and Gorgonzola. The coastal waters are rich in marine life and anchovy, sardine and tuna are of commercial importance.

The Italians transformed their economy after the Second World War, embarking upon a rapid process of industrialisation and the development of manufacturing from an entirely agricultural base. This has been a largely successful process and one that has been all the more noteworthy given that the country is poor in fossil fuel reserves. However, there is a considerable divide between the rich, developed and urban north and the poorer agricultural south and there has been rural depopulation to the more affluent towns and cities.

Although there is a lack of natural resources, almost 60 per cent of the land is under crops and pasture and there is an abundance of building stone, particularly marble. Industrial production includes textiles and cotton, leather goods and shoes, chemicals, foodstuffs, cars and electrical goods. Tourism is also an important contributor to the economy.

JAMAICA is an island state in the Caribbean Sea about 150 kilometres or 93 miles south of Cuba. The centre of the island comprises a limestone plateau and this is surrounded by narrow coastal flatlands and palm fringed beaches. The highest mountains, the Blue Mountains, are in the east of the island. The climate is tropical with high temperatures at the coast and slightly cooler and less humid conditions in the highlands. Jamaica suffers from severe earthquakes and thermal springs can be found in areas of the country. The island also lies in the middle of the hurricane zone. The traditional crops grown are sugar cane, bananas, peppers, ginger, cocoa beans and coffee while new crops, such as winter vegetables, fruit and honey, are being developed for export. There is also an illegal trade in cannabis. The mining of bauxite and alumina plays a very important part in Jamaica's economy and accounts for around 60 per cent of its total yearly exports. Industrialisation has been encouraged and clothing, footwear, cement and agricultural machinery are now produced. Tourism is a particularly important industry with over one million visitors annually.

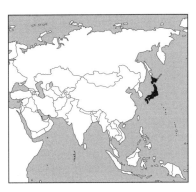

JAPAN, a constitutional monarchy, consists of a series of over 1,000 islands in East Asia. There are four principal, large islands running from north to south: Hokkaido, Honshu (the largest and known as the mainland), Shikoku and Kyushu. These four islands, all in close proximity to one another, make up 98 per cent of the total area of Japan.

In the north, the La Perouse Strait (Sea of Okhotsk) separates Hokkaido from the island of Sakhalin (Russia). In the northwest, Hokkaido is similarly separated from the Kuril Islands by the narrow Nemura Strait. (The Kuril Islands have been occupied by Russia since the end of the Second World War but are also claimed by Japan.) In the southwest, the Western Channel of the Korea Strait separates the Japanese island of Tsushima from South Korea. In the far southwest, the southernmost of the Japanese Ryukyu Islands lies about 201 kilometres or 125 miles east of Taiwan while the remainder are separated from China to the west by the broad expanse of the East China Sea.

All parts of Japan lie within fairly easy reach of the sea and the country has a very long coastline which is highly indented in places. The dominant topographical feature is a series of high mountains, hills and ridges interrupted by deeply cut valleys which occupy about 80 per cent of the total land area. Lower land is found only in some of the larger river valleys and coastal plains and is mostly intensely cultivated. The islands support a dense population, the great majority of whom live in crowded cities or towns.

The islands of Japan occur in a seismically active area of the Earth's crust and there are frequent earthquakes, two of which during this century, in 1923 and 1995 repectively, have had devastating effects and caused great loss of life. In addition, many of Japan's mountains are extinct or still active volcanoes and there are areas of obvious volcanic activity in the form of thermal springs and fissures emitting toxic gases. Among the active volcanoes are Asama-san and Bandai-san on Honshu and Sakurajima and Aso-san on Kyushu. Japan's highest mountain, Fuji-san (3,775 metres or 12,388 feet) is in eastern Honshu and is itself a dormant volcano whose last eruption was in 1707.

Most valleys on the islands are occupied by fast-flowing rivers or streams, which are not navigable but ensure an abundant supply of water and potential for the development of hydroelectric power. There are also numerous lakes, particularly in the mountainous regions. The most abundant trees in the north and on the mountain slopes are conifers, with the principal species being Japanese cedar (sugi), fir and spruce. In temperate regions and at lower levels, there are other trees such as beech, willow, poplar, alder and holly. Further south on southern Honshu, Shikoku and Kyushu there are subtropical forests of a variety of species including bamboo. Wildlife species include a large selection of mammals, reptiles, amphibians, fish and birds such as Japanese deer and the Japanese macaque.

Apart from Hokkaido and the subtropical south, most of Japan has a temperate climate with warm to hot summers and cool to cold winters with most rain falling in the summer although precipitation occurs throughout the year. Temperatures become cooler farther north and winters in Hokkaido are very cold with plenty of snow and summers are fairly brief. In the south, winters are mild and summers are moist and hot. Typhoons or tropical cyclones affect the Pacific coast from late August to October.

Only about 15 per cent of land in Japan is suitable for cultivation and this is done intensively with extensive use of fertilisers and modern technology (such as the development of bioengineered crops), so that maximum crop yields can be obtained. Cultivation is mainly of rice but wheat, barley, sugar beet, potatoes and other vegetables, soya beans and sweet potatoes are also grown. Fruits such as apples, cherries, peaches, oranges and pears are grown and some tea and tobacco cultivation takes place. The Japanese have also perfected the art of cultivating miniature trees (bonsai) and they are renowned for their cultivated flowers which include the lotus, chrysanthemum, tree peony and azalea. Mulberry bushes are cultivated for the raising of silkworms. There is little spare land for the raising of livestock although pigs, poultry and cattle are reared in some parts of Japan.

Much of Japan is covered with coniferous woodland which provides the basis for a considerable forestry industry although this is insufficient for domestic needs and the country has to import timber from elsewhere.

Fish, from the seas which surround Japan, have always formed the staple source of protein in the Japanese diet. Hence the country's fishing industry is highly important and well developed with fish being caught both for domestic consumption and for export. The fishing fleet is very large and while some boats operate far from home in international waters, others operate near the shore or within coastal waters.

Japan is lacking in mineral resources although it does possess some small reserves of lead, copper, zinc, natural gas and coal. Many raw materials must be imported. Heavy industries, such as iron and steel, shipbuilding, chemicals and petrochemicals, used to account for almost three quarters of Japan's export revenue but increasingly Japan has had to rely on the success of its manufacturing industry, which employs about one third of the workforce. Leading manufacturing industries produce cars, televisions, videos, electronic equipment, cameras, watches, clocks, robots and textiles. Japan's financial markets have experienced some problems in recent years which has introduced some uncertainty into what has hitherto been a very secure economy.

JORDAN, HASHEMITE KINGDOM OF, is almost landlocked except for a short coastline on the Gulf of Aqaba. It is bounded by Saudi Arabia, Syria, Iraq and Israel. Jordan is a predominantly arid country whose main topographical feature is a high, rugged plateau which rises up on the east side of the River Jordan. It reaches elevations of over 1,500 metres or 4,000 feet in the south of the country and is dissected by steep-sided gorges. The capital, Amman, is located at its northern end. The plateau loses height on its eastern side into a large area of semi-desert and desert. In general, summers are hot and dry and winters cool and wet with variations related to altitude. The east has a desert climate.

When Israel occupied the West Bank in 1967, Jordan lost most of its agricultural land and fertile, watered land is found only in the extreme west. Since under 5 per cent of the land is arable and only part of this is irrigated, crop production is insufficient for the country's needs. As a result, Jordan has to import some foodstuffs.

The manufacturing industry produces cement, iron, pharmaceuticals, processed food, fertilisers and textiles but the country's economy relies to a large extent on economic aid from rich Arab states, such as Saudi Arabia. The country has a modern network of roads which link the major cities. In 1994, an historic peace agreement was signed with Israel which ended 46 years of hostilities.

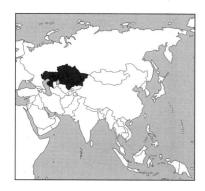

KAZAKHSTAN is a huge, central Asian republic, similar in size to India, which is bordered by Russia in the northwest and north, Mongolia (at one point) and China in the east, Kyrgyzstan in the southeast, Uzbekistan in the southwest and Turkmenistan in the south-southwest. The republic's western boundary is with the Caspian Sea.

Most of Kazakhstan consists of vast, arid plains or steppes with semidesert or desert characteristics. In the west, the land dips below sea level in the marshes beside the Caspian Sea and, in the east and southeast, the plains are interrupted by hills and high mountains in Kazakhstan's border regions. The Kazakh Highlands, containing several high mountain ranges, occupy the eastern, central part of the country and it is here that the large, mineral-rich Lake Balkhash is located. Along the southeastern borders with China and Kyrgyzstan, the mountainous areas include parts of the Tian Shan and Altai Mountains and some of the mountain peaks reach heights in excess of 4,876 metres or 16,000 feet. Nestling among them is the country's former capital and largest city, Almaty.

Much further west, the huge Aral Sea, which once straddled the border with Uzbekistan, is now reduced to two lakes, one in each country, which are still shrinking. The shrinkage has been caused by the siphoning-off of water for irrigation purposes from the rivers that feed the sea. This has been a disaster for the fishing communities which once relied upon the Aral Sea and has had severe environmental and health consequences for all the people in the region. Although some efforts are being made to reverse the process, if these are not successful, it is expected that the sea will dry up altogether in the next 10 to 15 years.

Kazakhstan has several major rivers which mainly arise in the mountains. Their number include: the Irtysh and Ishim, which continue across the northern border into Russia; the Syrdarya, which feeds the Aral Sea; the Emba flowing westwards into the Caspian Sea; and the Ural, which arises in Russia and flows southwards across the Caspian basin.

The natural vegetation of Kazakhstan varies according to location with specially adapted, water-conserving plants in the arid regions and trees in some of the hilly areas and river valleys. Animals include wolves, roe deer, ibex and gazelles. Lake Balkash supports a variety of fish species, particularly the large Balkash perch. As might be expected in such a large country, there is considerable climatic variation but in general it is hot and dry with very little rainfall. Snowfall occurs in the mountainous regions.

Parts of Kazakhstan, particularly the mountainous regions, are subject to earthquakes and the former capital, Almaty, has been largely rebuilt on two occasions following extensive damage. Almaty is the country's largest city and an important industrial and cultural centre but in 1997 the country's capital was moved to Astana, located north of the Kazakh Highlands in a more stable geological region. Pollution is a serious problem in parts of Kazakhstan, including radioactive fallout from Soviet nuclear tests.

Kazakhstan is a major producer of grain, particularly wheat, and the dry, steppe lands are used as pasture for sheep and goats. Fruits and vegetables are grown for local consumption in some areas. In the wooded mountainous regions, timber is cut for local construction purposes. Fishing is a small-scale activity carried out in the Caspian Sea and in rivers and lakes, especially Lake Balkhash.

Kazakhstan has valuable reserves of copper, tin, titanium, phosphorus, magnesium, chromium, lead, tungsten, zinc, coal, oil and natural gas. Mining of these minerals is the main economic activity and the industry was greatly developed during the Soviet period. Oil and gas reserves have yet to be developed to any great extent. Tourism is a small but growing industry in Kazakhstan with most visitors coming from Russia or other neighbouring countries.

Kazakhstan declared itself independent in 1991 and since then economic prospects have remained positive. However, environmental problems, such as the overdraining of the Aral Sea, remain as a legacy of past Soviet exploitation and have still to be tackled.

KENYA is a country of moderate size on the eastern side of the African continent. The Indian Ocean is to the southeast, with Tanzania to the south, Uganda to the west, Sudan to the northwest, Ethiopia to the north and Somalia to the east. The equator almost bisects the country in two and provides a dividing line between the deserts in the north and the savannah of the south. Highlands run north to south through central Kenya and are divided by the steep-sided Great Rift Valley. The highest peak is Mount Kenya at 5,200 metres or 17,000 feet.

A number of tree species are found in the distinct climatic regions including palm, mangrove, teak and sandalwood on the coast, acacia and others in the lowlands, bamboo in the rainforest and lobelias in the mountainous alpine areas. The variety in plant life is more than matched by a vast range of animals. Aided by the existence of several national parks, Kenya has many of the big game species, such as elephant, rhinoceros, lion, giraffe and zebra, as well as a large number and variety of birds and reptiles.

The coastal lowlands have a hot, humid climate but in the highlands it is cooler and rainfall heavier. In the east, it is very arid. The southwestern region is well watered with huge areas of fertile soil and it accounts for the bulk of the population and almost all of its economic production. Almost three quarters of the population live in rural areas but the capital, Nairobi, in the southwest of the country, has a population of well over one million and is a centre for industry and commerce and also for tourists coming to visit the country's game parks including the Nairobi National Park.

Agriculture is an important part of the economy and a wide variety of crops are grown for domestic consumption including wheat, maize and cassava. Tea, coffee, sisal, sugar cane and cotton are grown for export. Oil refining at Mombasa is the country's largest single industry but other mineral resources, including deposits of silver, lead and gold, are few or undeveloped. Kenya's many game reserves are a major attraction for visitors and tourism is an important source of foreign revenue.

KIRIBATI is a republic in Micronesia that comprises three groups of coral atolls and one isolated volcanic island spread over a large expanse of the central Pacific. The group includes the former Gilbert Islands, the Phoenix Islands (now Rawaki) and the southern Line Islands and, until independence from great Britain in 1979, was named the Gilbert and Ellice Islands. The capital, Bairiki, is located on an atoll, Tarawa, and the largest island is Kiritimati, formerly known as Christmas Island. The climate is maritime equatorial with a rainy season from October to March.

Ocean Island (Banaba) was a rich source of phosphate deposits (guano) but exhaustion of the reserves has left severe environmental damage causing most Banabans to resettle elsewhere. Agriculture and fishing are the main employers while coconuts and copra form the major commercial crops. Tourism is becoming increasingly important but overseas aid remains a vital part of the economy. As with the other states of Micronesia, Kiribati has significant strategic importance.

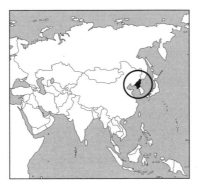

KOREA, or the **DEMOCRATIC PEOPLE'S REPUBLIC OF KOREA** (formerly North Korea), is located in eastern Asia and occupies the northern half of the Korean Peninsula. The Yalu and Tumen rivers form its northern border with China and the Russian Federation. The Korean Bay, which is an extension of the Yellow Sea, lies to the west with the Sea of Japan to the east. The Republic of Korea, formerly South Korea, occupies the southern part of the peninsula and is separated from the north by a buffer, demilitarised zone. Mountains are the dominant topographical feature of North Korea, occupying the whole of the northern part of the country and extending southwards in a broad band beside the coast of the Sea of Japan. The greatest range is in the northwest and North Korea's highest peak, Paektu-San (2,737 metres or 9,003 feet), is located on the border with China. The mountains in the north are rugged and forested and dissected by steep river gorges while those along the eastern seaboard consist mainly of bare, weather-beaten rock. Some flatter ground and lower-lying plains occur in the west and in the river valleys but this amounts to only about 20 per cent of the total land area. A number of rivers and streams rise in the mountains and empty either into the Sea of Japan or the Korean Bay. The largest and most important river is the Yalu which, for a considerable part of its course, forms the border with China. Many streams along the length of the country's rugged eastern coast descend steeply down the rocky mountain slopes into the sea.

The mountainous regions in the north of the country support large tracts of coniferous forest. In the lowland regions of the west, the deciduous forests have been cleared as this area provides the country's only cultivatable land. A variety of wildlife is found in the country, particularly in the sparsely populated mountains and forests. Large carnivores include tiger, leopard, wolf and bear but these are becoming increasingly rare. North Korea has a continental type of climate with hot summers and cold winters. The wet season is in the hottest months of July and August when most of the yearly average rainfall of 1,026 millimetres or 40 inches is experienced. Most people live in the flatter, western regions of the country and about two thirds of them in cities or towns, including the capital city of Pyongyang.

Flat land suitable for cultivation is at a premium in North Korea and soil improvement schemes, water conservation and irrigation, land reclamation and mechanisation are all very highly developed. This has resulted in improved food yields in recent years with the most important crops being rice, corn, potatoes, millet, soya beans, wheat, barley, sweet potatoes, vegetables and fruit such as apples. Livestock animals include pigs, cattle, sheep and poultry. Farms are run as collectives with a series of economic development plans in place which have mainly concentrated on mechanisation and technological improvements. Alternate floods and drought in the 1990s have resulted in crop failure and widespread famine in the country, necessitating international relief aid.

Wood is extracted from the forests mainly for home use in construction and a marine fishing fleet catches tuna, anchovy and mackerel. Seaweeds are also harvested. The country continues to fully exploit its fast-flowing rivers for the production of hydroelectric power which supplies about 60 per cent of its energy needs.

North Korea is richly endowed with a wide variety of minerals and mining is an important contributor to the economy. Of particular importance are coal and iron ore but there are also good reserves of copper, tungsten, lead, zinc, graphite, magnesite, gold, silver and phosphates. Industry is nationalised in North Korea and emphasis has been on heavy industrial developments including iron and steel, large machinery and engines, locomotives, rolling stock, trucks, construction equipment and vehicles. However, cement, fertilisers, textiles and clothing are also produced and there is some mineral refining.

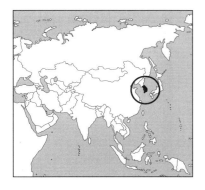

KOREA, REPUBLIC OF (formerly South Korea), occupies the southern half of the Korean Peninsula in eastern Asia. The country is bordered in the north by a demilitarised zone which acts as a buffer between the former South and North Koreas. The country has a considerable length of coastline bordering the Yellow Sea in the west, the Korea Strait in the south and the Sea of Japan in the east. Many islands lie off the western and southern coastline, the largest of which is Cheju.

Most of the country is hilly or mountainous. The most extensive range, the Taebaek-sanmaek Mountains, runs down most of the eastern coast from north to south but other hilly regions occur centrally and in the south. The highest peak, Mount Halla-san (1,944 metres or 6,398 feet) is on the volcanic island of Cheju. Several major rivers, such as the Han

and Naktong, rise in the Taebaek-sanmaek Mountains and flow generally westwards or southwards to empty into the Yellow Sea or the Korea Strait. Flatter land and plains that are quite densely populated constitute about 25 per cent of the total land area and occur mainly in the west and south and in the river valleys. The country's capital and largest city is Seoul (Soul).

Coniferous forests of fir, pine, cedar, spruce and larch occur in the mountainous regions, with deciduous woodlands, containing oak, maple, poplar, bamboo, aspen and laurel, found at lower levels. The forests have been extensively cut and cleared except in the more remote areas. Wildlife species are similar to those in the north but many have become rare due to habitat loss and hunting. The climate of South Korea is continental in nature with hot, wet summers, during which most of the yearly rainfall is experienced, and cold, dry winters.

About 23 per cent of the land is available for agriculture and most of this is under cultivation. Parcels of land were distributed after the Second World War but most farms are less than three acres in size. Rice, cereals (wheat and barley) and a wide variety of vegetables and fruit are grown. Non-food crops include soya beans, hemp and cotton. Silkworms are raised in some areas. The principal livestock animals are pigs, cattle, goats and poultry.

Forestry extraction and related activities are negligible in South Korea but the country has one of the largest deep sea fisheries in the world. Many species are exploited and fish processing is an important subsidiary industry resulting from the large annual catch.

South Korea is poor in mineral resources compared to North Korea but has small reserves of coal, zinc, tungsten, iron ore, graphite, lead, kaolin, silver and gold which are exploited. After the Second World War, South Korea concentrated on the development of light industries but has turned to heavy industrial development during the 1990s. A wide variety of goods are produced including ships, vehicles, machinery, iron and steel, electronic equipment and electrical goods, textiles, footwear, processed foods, toys, chemicals and fertilisers. Its people enjoy a reasonably high standard of living brought about by hard work and determination.

QUICK FACTS

Area: 99,373 square kilometres or 38,368 square miles
Population: 46,430,000
Capital: Seoul (Soul)
Other major cities: Pusan, Taegu
Form of government: Republic
Religions: Buddhism, Christianity, Confucianism, Chondogyo (a combination of Taoism and Confucianism) Unification Church
Currency: Won

QUICK FACTS

Area: 17,818 square kilometres or
   6,880 square miles
Population: 1,866,104
Capital: Kuwait City (Al Kuwayt)
Government: Constitutional Monarchy
Religions: Sunni Islam, Shia Islam
Currency: Kuwaiti Dinar

QUICK FACTS

Area: 198,500 square kilometres or
   76,641 square miles
Population: 4,575,000
Capital: Bishkek
Other major city: Osh
Government: Republic
Religion: Sunni Islam
Currency: Som

QUICK FACTS

Area: 236,800 square kilometres or
   91,429 square miles
Population: 5,035,000
Capital: Vientiane
Other major cities: Luang Prabang,
   Savannakhét, Paksé
Form of government: People's Republic
Religion: Buddhism
Currency: New Kip

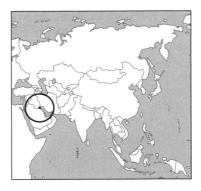

KUWAIT is a tiny Arab Emirate on The Gulf, comprising the city of Kuwait at the southern entrance of Kuwait Bay, a small desert wedged between Iraq and Saudi Arabia and nine small offshore islands. Most of the land is barren and consists of a gently undulating plain with no natural water courses. Desalination plants use seawater from The Gulf to supply Kuwait's freshwater needs. The climate is hot and humid in summer and cool to mild in winter with a small amount of rainfall.

There is little agriculture due to lack of water. The major crops produced are melons, tomatoes, onions and dates. Shrimp fishing is becoming an important industries. Large reserves of petroleum and natural gas are the mainstay of the economy although this wealth is limited. Kuwait has about 950 oil wells, 600 of which were fired during the Iraqi occupation in 1991. Apart from oil, the country's industries include boatbuilding and the production of plastics, petrochemicals, gases, cement and building materials.

Kuwait supported Iraq during the Iraq–Iran war in the 1980s but, after the conflict ended, the relationship between Kuwait and Iraq deteriorated, with disputes centred upon the price of oil, the shared Rumaila oilfield and non-repayment of loans owed by Iraq. The culmination of these disagreements was the Iraqi invasion of Kuwait in 1990 which led to international involvement and the Gulf War. Before being driven out of Kuwait, the Iraqi forces set fire to the country's oil wells resulting in devastating environmental damage. The war caused a period of political instability and repressive measures by the Kuwaiti government against people (mainly Palestinians) whom it considered to have collaborated with Iraq. Kuwait has also had to rebuild its shattered infrastructure and economy and make some attempt to repair the environmental damage.

KYRGYZSTAN is a central Asian republic which has been independent from the former USSR since 1991. It is bounded in the southwest by Tajikistan, in the west by Uzbekistan, in the north by Kazakhstan, and in the east and southeast by China. The land consists almost entirely of high, rugged mountains of outstanding natural beauty. The principal ranges are the Tien Shan Mountains (meaning the 'Celestial' or 'Heavenly Mountains') encompassing vast peaks and some of the largest glaciers on Earth. In the northeast of the country is the country's largest lake, Issyk Kul. Heated by volcanic action, this lake never freezes in winter. The main river system in the country is the Naryn which is a source of hydroelectric power. The capital and largest city is Bishek (formerly Frunze). The climate can be hot in summer but is very cold in winter with considerable snowfall and frosts.

In the north and at higher altitudes, conifers, particularly firs, are the main species of tree while willow and alder are found at lower levels. In the south and in the lower, drier regions, apple, maple, walnut and almond trees are among the trees that are able to grow. Kyrgyzstan is home to a variety of wildlife including snakes (boas), turtles, gophers, jerboas, hedgehogs, squirrels, ermine, martens, lynx, wild boar, wolves, foxes and brown bear. Birds include geese, black cock and vultures. Some rare species are considered to be unique to the region. Rivers and lakes support some 75 different species of fish.

Agriculture is the second most important economic activity and employs a large number of people. While only about 4 per cent of Kyrgyzstan is suitable for cultivation, there is other land which can be used for grazing and livestock rearing is the main aspect of farming. Animals include yaks, sheep, goats and horses with cereals, sugar beet, cotton and hay being grown on some farms. Fruit and nuts are harvested from orchards in the south. Soil erosion and degradation have occurred in some areas but measures are being taken to try and halt this process. Fish are caught for local consumption from rivers and lakes.

Forests cover about 4 per cent of the land area of Kyrgyzstan and are harvested for local use. There has been some reforestation but damage to trees, particularly from inappropriate felling and grazing cattle, remains a problem. Kyrgyzstan has valuable resources of oil, natural gas, coal, uranium and other mineral ores and mining is the principal contributor to the economy. Oil and gas have not, as yet, been developed and the country is dependent upon imports of fuel. Hydroelectric power supplies most of the country's electricity. Parts of Kyrgyzstan are threatened by environmental pollution caused by storage of toxic waste and radioactive material which are the by-products of mining, former nuclear tests and the overuse of chemicals, especially fertilisers. The government is making efforts to address the problem of pollution and of damage to the land caused by excessive grazing and tree-felling.

Tourism is at a low level at present with very few Western visitors. The government is actively encouraging foreign visitors and it is expected that climbers may be attracted to the country in the future to scale its mountains.

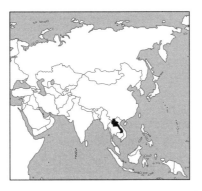

LAOS is a landlocked country in southeast Asia. It is ruggedly mountainous apart from the Mekong river plains along its border with Thailand. The Annam Mountains, which reach 2,500 metres or 8,203 feet, form a natural border with Vietnam. Like its neighbour, Myanmar, it has a wealth of plant and animal life. It has a tropical monsoon climate with high temperatures throughout the year and heavy rains in summer. Laos is one of the poorest countries in the world and its development has been retarded by war, drought and floods. Buddhism and spirit worship are the principal religions and religious activities play a very important part in the life of the people.

It is primarily an agricultural country with the principal crop being rice grown on small peasant plots. The mighty Mekong river provides the main means of transport and communication as well as irrigation for the rice paddies upon which the people's subsistence depends. Corn, potatoes and cassava are also grown. There is some export of timber, coffee, tin and electricity. All manufactured goods have to be imported and these are mainly food, machinery, petroleum products and electrical equipment. The capital and largest city, Vientiane, is the country's main trade outlet via Thailand.

LATVIA, a former constituent republic of the USSR, is a republic in northeastern Europe that shares borders with Estonia, Russia, Belarus and Lithuania. It is bounded in the west by the Baltic Sea and the Gulf of Riga, itself a large inlet of the Baltic Sea. Most of the country consists of a wooded lowland plain with numerous marshy areas and lakes. Inland and eastwards, there is some more hilly, forested country and towards the eastern border, there are more marshes, woodlands and lakes. Latvia is crossed by numerous rivers and streams, the most important of which is the Daugava and its tributaries. Latvia has cool, wet summers and long, cold winters. About 70 per cent of Latvians live in cities, towns or urban areas and there are numerous villages spread throughout the country. Riga, a large and important Baltic port, is Latvia's capital city and home to a third of its people.

Woodlands, which cover about a quarter of Latvia, consist of both coniferous and deciduous trees, including spruce, pine, birch, oak and aspen. The republic is home to a variety of wild animals and birds, particularly wetland species that flourish in the marshes and lakes. However, as a result of the rapid development of heavy industries in the postwar years, there is serious pollution in some areas, particularly of water courses.

Agriculture is an important part of the Latvian economy and employs about 20 per cent of the workforce. It consists mainly of the rearing of cattle for the meat and dairy industries but crops are also grown, including cereals (oats, barley, rye), sugar beet, potatoes and flax. The Latvian forests provide a valuable timber resource that is used in construction, paper and furniture-making. Latvia has an important marine fishery operating out of its Baltic Sea ports and the main species caught are cod and herring. In addition, there are many freshwater fish in the country's rivers and lakes that are caught for local consumption.

Latvia has abundant deposits of peat and gypsum but lacks other fossil fuels and minerals, which has made it heavily dependent upon imports of oil, gas and electricity. Hydroelectric plants on the Daugava river supply over half the republic's domestic production of electricity, which in total amounts to about 50 per cent of overall consumption. Latvia has experienced shortages of gas, oil and electricity because of disputes with its suppliers, particularly Russia and Estonia. It has a well-developed industrial base and produces electric railway carriages, electronic and electrical equipment (radios and refrigerators), paper, cement, chemicals, textiles, woollen goods, furniture and foodstuffs. Economic development was difficult in the early years following independence but the situation is gradually improving and Latvia is seeking full membership of the European Union.

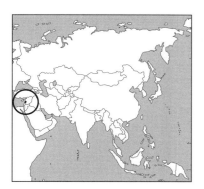

LEBANON is a small, troubled republic in the eastern Mediterranean. Throughout its long human history, it has seen the rise and fall of many civilisations and empires and its capital, Beirut (Beyrouth), has come to symbolise all the complex troubles of the Middle East.

A narrow coastal plain runs parallel to its 240-kilometre- or 149-mile-long Mediterranean coast and gradually rises to the spectacular Lebanon Mountains, which are snow-covered in winter. Running parallel to the Lebanon Mountains are the Anti-Lebanon Mountains, which form the border with Syria. Between the two ranges, lies the Beqaa Valley, through which flows Lebanon's only large river, the Litani. Very little natural forest remains other than isolated stands of trees in the mountains as deforestation has been taking place for thousands of years. The mountains provide a home for Lebanon's remaining wildlife which includes wolves, jackals, gazelles and wild donkeys.

Lebanon is an agricultural country, whose main regions of production are the Beqaa Valley and the coastal plain, although erosion is a common problem in the uplands. Main products include olives, grapes, bananas, citrus fruits, apples, cotton, tobacco and sugar beet. Industry is small scale and manufactured goods include cement, fertilisers and jewellery. There are oil refineries at Tripoli (Trablous) and Sidon (Saida). Lebanon's main economy is based on commercial services such as banking but civil war, invasion by Israel and factional fighting have created severe problems for the economy, causing high inflation and unemployment.

LESOTHO is a small, landlocked kingdom entirely surrounded by the Republic of South Africa. Snow-capped mountains and treeless uplands, cut by spectacular gorges, cover two thirds of the 'mountain kingdom'.

The climate is pleasant with variable rainfall. Winters are generally dry with heavy frosts in lowland areas and frequent snow in the highlands. Due to the mountainous terrain, only one eighth of the land can be cultivated and the main crop is maize. Yields are low because of soil erosion on the steep slopes and overgrazing by herds of sheep and cattle. Wool and mohair are exported but most of the country's foreign exchange comes from money sent home by Lesotho workers in South Africa. Tourism is beginning to flourish, with skiing and pony trails on hardy Lesotho ponies in the mountains two of the main attractions.

QUICK FACTS

Area: 64,600 square kilometres or 24,942 square miles
Population: 2,491,000
Capital: Riga
Other cities: Liepaja, Daugavpils
Form of government: Republic
Religion: Lutheranism
Currency: Lat

QUICK FACTS

Area: 10,400 square kilometres or 4,015 square miles
Population: 3,084,900
Capital: Beirut (Beyrouth)
Other important cities: Tripoli (Trablous), Sidon (Saïda),
Form of government: Republic
Religions: Shia Islam, Sunni Islam, Christianity
Currency: Lebanese Pound

QUICK FACTS

Area: 30,355 square kilometres or 11,720 square miles
Population: 2,078,000
Capital: Maseru
Form of government: Constitutional Monarchy
Religions: Roman Catholicism, other Christianity
Currency: Loti

LIBERIA is a republic located in west Africa. Founded in 1847 as a homeland for freed slaves from North America, Liberia is the only African country never to have been ruled by a foreign power. It has a treacherous coast with rocky cliffs and lagoons enclosed by sand bars, which stretches for 560 kilometres or 348 miles from Sierra Leone to Côte d'Ivoire. There is a low-lying, well-watered coastal plain with many mangrove swamps which rises inland to a densely forested plateau dissected by deep, narrow valleys. North of this, lie the Nimba Mountains which rise to a maximum height of 1,752 metres or 5,748 feet. The mountains are also forested and contain some beautiful waterfalls. The forests contain several commercially valuable species, particularly rubber trees, palms and mahogany. They are home to a wide variety of animals and birds including the pygmy hippopotamus, monkeys, chimpanzees and snakes.

Agriculture employs 75 per cent of the workforce and produces cassava and rice as subsistence crops and rubber, coffee and cocoa for export. The Nimba Mountains are rich in iron ore, which accounts for 70 per cent of export earnings and wood, rubber, diamonds and coffee are also exported. Liberia has a very large tanker fleet, most of which have foreign owners. Since its establishment in 1847, Liberia's history has at times been a turbulent one, culminating in a devastating civil war in the 1990s. The economy has suffered greatly as a result and the situation remains uncertain, leaving Liberia with considerable problems to overcome.

LIBYA is a large, north African country which stretches from the south coast of the Mediterranean to, and in some parts beyond, the Tropic of Cancer. The Socialist People's Libyan Arab Jamahiriyah is an oil-rich country but most of its territory is uninhabited, consisting of rocky or sandy desert with extensive 'sand seas'. The Sahara Desert covers much of the country extending right to the Mediterranean coast at the Gulf of Sirte. The only green areas are the scrublands found in the northwest and the forested hills near Banghazi. In general, Libya's terrain consists of undulating rocky plains with two areas of hills, one in the northwest and one in the northeast, and an outcrop of the Tibesti Massif across the border with Chad.

The climate is hot and dry although more moist on the coast where there is winter rainfall. Natural vegetation is very sparse and is confined to some coastal areas, hill slopes and oases. Wildlife species consist of animals able to survive the fairly harsh conditions, notably reptiles, rodents, gazelles, hyenas and vultures.

Most people live in the cities and urban areas along the north coast. Some people, however, still follow a seminomadic, traditional way of life. Many sheep, goats and cattle are reared and there is an export trade in skins, hides and hairs. The main agricultural region is in the northwest near Tripoli (Tarabulus) but this is dependent on rainfall. The main crops produced are wheat, tomatoes, fruits and barley. Libya is one of the world's largest producers of oil and natural gas and also produces potash and marine salt. Other industries include food processing, textiles, cement and handicrafts.

LIECHTENSTEIN, PRINCIPALITY OF, is a small independent state sandwiched between Switzerland in the north, west and south and Austria in the east. Liechtenstein is a hereditary, constitutional monarchy whose population shares many links with their near neighbours in Switzerland, Germany and Austria. German is the official language within the principality but a dialect called Alemannish is also in common use.

The upper reaches of the River Rhine flow along the western boundary of the principality while to the east and south lie the foothills of the Austrian Alps, reaching heights in excess of 2,438 metres or 8,000 feet. The highest peak, on the border with Switzerland, is Grauspitz (2,599 metres or 8,527 feet). Apart from the Rhine and its tributary streams, the second most important river is the Samina, which flows in a south–southeasterly direction from the mountains. The capital and principal town is Vaduz, situated in the west and centre of the principality overlooking the River Rhine.

Liechtenstein's small amount of farmland is mainly located within the Rhine valley and cereals, potatoes, vegetables and grapes (for wine) are the main crops grown. Goats, sheep and cattle are reared in small numbers and grazed in the traditional manner in Alpine meadows in the summer. The mainstays of the highly prosperous economy are international banking and financial services, sale of postage stamps and tourism. Many international businesses have set up companies in Liechtenstein because of extremely favourable tax regulations. Manufacturing has developed rapidly in the principality since the end of the Second World War and goods include precision tools and instruments, foods, pharmaceuticals, metal goods, pottery and furniture.

LITHUANIA is the largest of the three former Soviet Baltic Republics. Lithuania is bounded by Latvia, Belarus, Poland and Russia (Kaliningrad) with a Baltic Sea coastline to the west. Lithuania is a country of plains, broken by low hills with numerous rivers and lakes and many marshes and wetlands, some of which have been drained. The upland areas are generally to be found in the west while the majority of the lakes are in the southern and northeastern parts of the republic. The Neman river, with its tributaries, forms part of the border with Russia and supplies the country with hydroelectric power. Over two thirds of the country's people live in cities, towns or urban areas. Vilnius is Lithuania's capital and largest city.

Forests cover about a quarter of the country which is home to a range of wild animals, such as wolves and wild boar, and many birds, particularly wetland species. The rivers and lakes contain a variety of species of freshwater fish. Lithuania has a temperate climate but with generally more extreme and variable temperatures in the east. On the whole, summers are mild to warm and winters are cold or very cold, particularly inland, with considerable snowfall. Precipitation occurs throughout the year but especially in the summer months.

Lithuania was traditionally an agricultural country and although it underwent considerable industrialisation following the Soviet takeover in the 1940s, agriculture is still very important to the economy. Crops include cereals (rye and barley), sugar beet and potatoes. Cattle, sheep, pigs and poultry are among the livestock animals. Lithuania's forests, which cover about a quarter of the country, provide valuable timber resources. There is also a small but important fishing industry.

Lithuania lacks exploitable mineral reserves and the country is dependent upon imports of oil although it has some deposits of gypsum and small reserves of oil. Oil production has started from a small field at Kretinga in the west of the country some 16 kilometres or 10 miles north of Klaipeda. Nuclear power accounts for about half the country's energy needs with some additional power from hydroelectric schemes. The nuclear reactors are old, however, and subject to operational difficulties that are expected to continue to cause problems.

Considerable industrial development took place during the postwar communist years although adjustments have had to be made since the country has progressed towards a free market economy. Industries and manufacturing include shipbuilding, engineering, food processing, production of cement, machinery and electronic equipment. Amber is found along the Baltic coast and used by Lithuanian craftsmen for making jewellery. Financial scandals involving government members and banking institutions troubled the economy during the 1990s.

QUICK FACTS

Area: 65,200 square kilometres or 25,174 square miles
Population: 3,701,300
Capital: Vilnius
Other major cities: Kaunas, Klaipeda, Siauliai,
Form of government: Republic
Religion: Roman Catholicism
Currency: Litas

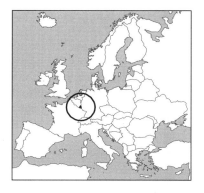

LUXEMBOURG, GRAND DUCHY OF, is entirely landlocked, bounded by France in the south, Belgium in the west and Germany in the east. The northern part of the country is a wooded plateau, known as the Oesling, rising to 550 metres or 1,804 feet. This region is a continuation of the forested hills of the Ardennes Plateau, where Luxembourg's highest peak, Buurgplatz (559 metres or 1,835 feet), is situated. The southern two thirds of the country consists of a lowland area of valleys and ridges and undulating wooded farmland, known as the Gutland. In the east, Luxembourg is bordered by the Moselle river in whose valley grapes are produced for wine.

Luxembourg is a wealthy and highly industrialised country whose citizens enjoy a very high standard of living. Partly because of its history, during which the duchy was ruled over or incorporated at various times into the territory of its European neighbours, Luxembourg has a cosmopolitan population and outlook. The capital, Luxembourg City, is the seat of the European Court of Justice. Northern winters are cold and raw with snow covering the ground for almost a month, but in the south winters are mild and summers cool.

Agriculture provides a small but important contribution to the economy with the production of grains, vegetables such as potatoes, fruits and grapes for wine. Pigs, cattle and poultry are among the animals that are reared. Luxembourg has rich (but declining) deposits of iron ore and the manufacture of iron and steel has traditionally been one of the two mainstays of the economy, the other being banking. Other manufactured goods include chemicals, machinery, paper and paper products, foods, plastics and rubber. Insurance services and tourism also play an increasingly important part in the country's economy.

QUICK FACTS

Area: 2,586 square kilometres or 998 square miles
Population: 412,000
Capital: Luxembourg City
Other cities: Esch-sur-Algette, Differdange, Dudelange
Form of government: Constitutional Monarchy (Duchy)
Religion: Roman Catholicism
Currency: Luxembourg Franc

MACAO or **MACAU**, formerly a Portuguese colony, reverted to China in 1999, becoming a special administrative region under Chinese sovereignty. China has promised 50 years of non-interference in its economic and social systems. One of the most densely populated places in the world, Macao consists of a rocky, hilly peninsula, connected by a sandy isthmus to China's Zhongshan (Tangjiahuan) island, and the two small islands of Taipa and Coloâne. A free port, it is a leading trade, fishing and tourist centre with gambling casinos and textile, clothing, toy, plastics, firework and food processing industries.

QUICK FACTS

Area: 18 square kilometres or 7 square miles
Population: 440,000
Capital: Macao
Form of government: Special Administrative Region under Chinese Sovereignity
Religions: Buddhism, Roman Catholicism
Currency: Pataca

MACEDONIA, FORMER YUGOSLAV REPUBLIC OF (FYROM), under the name of Macedonia, declared its independence from Yugoslavia in November 1991. The FYROM or Vardar Macedonia is one of the three parts of the ancient, historical kingdom of Macedonia, which also included Aegean Macedonia in Greece and Pirin Macedonia in Bulgaria. Vardar Macedonia only came into being as a republic of Yugoslavia, in 1946, following the victory of the communist forces of Josip Broz Tito. Its status was disputed at the time and this has continued to be the case. This controversy has been the cause of ongoing difficulties for the FYROM, mainly in gaining much needed international recognition since the collapse of the former Yugoslavia. The government of the FYROM has put into place several measures to encourage economic growth. It is hoped that, having now gained further international recognition, particularly from its neighbours since 1996, the country's economic situation will start to improve.

A landlocked country, Macedonia shares its borders with Albania, Bulgaria, Greece and Yugoslavia. The characteristic topographical features of the country are steep-sided, rugged hills and mountains dissected by deep valleys. There are numerous rivers and streams, the largest and most important of which is the Vardar. The Vardar river rises in the northwest and flows in a southeasterly direction, dividing the country into two halves. It continues through Greece (as the River Axiós) and eventually empties into the Aegean Sea. The FYROM's capital, Skopje, is located at the head of the Vardar river in the northwestern territory near the border with Yugoslavia. There are many freshwater lakes throughout the FYROM and these include Lake Ohrid ((Ohridsko Jezero) and Lake Prespa (Prespansko Jezero).

About 35 per cent of the country is forested, with both coniferous and deciduous trees being well represented and providing valuable timber resources.

The country is in a region that is seismically active, and the capital, Skopje, suffered a severe and destructive earthquake in 1963. A little over half the people live in the cities, particularly in Skopje. A continental climate prevails, with hot, dry summers, bitterly cold winters and a great deal of snow, especially at higher levels. The conditions are less extreme at lower levels and in the valley bottoms.

Agriculture is a very important part of the economy, with the other main activity being coal mining. Some of the country's natural resources include chromium, lead, zinc, nickel, iron ore and timber. There are some manufacturing, construction and service industries and forestry and freshwater fishing are also carried out. Tourism is a further contributor to the economy and is now starting to revive, having been badly affected by fighting in the region in the early 1990s.

MADAGASCAR is an island state in the Indian Ocean. It lies off the southeast coast of Africa and is separated from the mainland by the Mozambique Channel. There are a number of smaller islands. The main island is the fourth largest island in the world.

The centre of Madagascar is made up of high, savannah-covered plateaux. A chain of forested mountains fall steeply to the coast in the east while the land in the southwest falls gradually through dry grassland and scrub. The capital, Antananarivo, is situated at over 2,500 metres or 8,202 feet in the centre of the island. The climate becomes wetter moving north and the southern tip is semidesert.

Madagascar is a relatively poor country and most of the population work in agriculture although only a small proportion of the land is suitable for cultivation. The staple food crop is rice but cassava, potatoes, maize, beans and bananas are also grown. Some coffee, vanilla and sugar cane are grown for export. The hardwood forests have only been used thus far for local needs. Fishing is also a potential source of greater revenue while there are significant minerals deposits which are largely unexploited. These include offshore oil, chromite, salt and uranium. Due to Madagascar's isolation from mainland Africa, there are several species of plants and animals that are quite different from mainland species, such as the lemur. As a result, many tourists come to Madagascar to explore this aspect of the country's fauna and flora.

MALAWI lies along the southern and western shores of the third largest lake in Africa, Lake Malawi. It is bounded by Tanzania and Zambia to the north and northwest and Mozambique to the south and east. This narrow country is only a little over 800 kilometres or 496 miles long and up to 160 kilometres or 99 miles at its widest. It was formerly the British colony of Nyasaland ('Land of the Lake') and was given its name by the 19th century explorer, David Livingstone.

Its geography is dominated by Lake Malawi, which straddles the eastern border with Tanzania and Mozambique. To the south of the lake, the Shire river flows through a valley, overlooked by wooded, towering mountains. In general, moving from south to north the landscape changes from plateau to mountains. Malawi can boast most of the larger animal species found elsewhere in Africa as well as an abundance of birds, reptiles and insects.

The tropical climate has a dry season from May to October and a wet season for the remaining months. Malawi has an essentially agricultural economy and many Malawians live off their own crops. Exports include tea grown on the terraced hillsides in the south and tobacco grown on the central plateau plus peanuts, sugar and maize.

Lake Malawi supports a growing fishing industry. The country has bauxite and coal deposits but due to the inaccessibility of their locations, mining is limited. Hydroelectricity is now being used for the manufacturing industry but imports of manufactured goods remain high. Malawi's diverse landscape and enormous variety of wildlife have made it a popular tourist destination but it remains one of the poorest countries in the world.

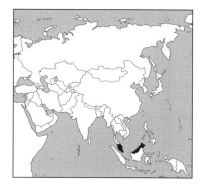

MALAYSIA is a federal constitutional monarchy which lies in the South China Sea in southeast Asia. It comprises eleven states located in the southernmost part of the Malay Peninsula which form West Malaysia and the two states of Sarawak and Sabah on the island of Borneo which form East Malaysia. Sarawak and Sabah are separated from the western part of the kingdom by 650 kilometres or 400 miles of the South China Sea.

Peninsular Malaysia has rugged mountains in the north and centre, reaching heights in excess of 2,100 metres or 7,000 feet, with a broad plain in the south and along each coast. Sarawak has a mainly low-lying and marshy broad coastal plain but with high mountain ranges in the east and along the border with Indonesian Borneo. Mountains are also the predominant feature of Sabah and Malaysia's highest peak, Kinabalu (4,094 metres or 13,455 feet), is located here.

The natural vegetation of Malaysia is dense, tropical rainforest and coastal mangrove swamps. The tropical jungles contain a wealth of plant and animal species, including the rare and beautiful orang utan, an arboreal ape which is found only in Borneo and Sumatra. However, the forests are threatened by logging and clearance for agriculture and few areas remain undisturbed except for those in designated national parks.

Malaysia is affected by the monsoon climate of south Asia. The northeast monsoon brings rain to the east coast of peninsular Malaysia in winter and the southwest monsoon brings rain to the west coast in summer. The climate is generally tropical and temperatures are uniformly hot throughout the year.

The kingdom is a leading producer of rubber, palm oil and tropical hardwoods. There is also some offshore oil and around the capital, Kuala Lumpur, new manufacturing industries are expanding and play an increasingly important role in the country's economy. Malaysia was hit by economic recession in 1997 and implemented a series of measures designed to restore confidence in its economy.

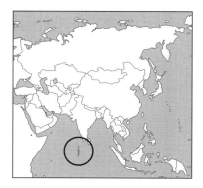

MALDIVES, the, is a republic consisting of 1,200 low-lying coral islands grouped into 12 atolls, lying 640 kilometres or 398 miles southwest of Sri Lanka in the Indian Ocean. Roughly 202 islands are inhabited and the highest point is only 1.5 metres or 5 feet above sea level. Independence was gained in 1965 with a republic being formed three years later. The climate is hot and humid and affected by monsoons from May to August. The islands are covered with coconut palms and some millet, cassava, yams and tropical fruit are grown. However, rice, the staple diet of the islanders, has to be imported. The most important natural resource is marine life and fishing is an important occupation. The chief export is now canned or frozen tuna but tourism has overtaken fishing as the major foreign currency earner.

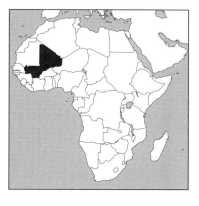

MALI is a landlocked republic in west Africa. Shaped somewhat like a butterfly with one wing larger than the other, it consists mainly of level plains interrupted by isolated groups of hills and mountains. It rises to 1,155 metres or 3,790 feet in the Adrar des Iforas Mountains in the northeast. The northern third lies within the Sahara Desert, which is slowly encroaching southwards, and life here revolves around the few oases. Southwest of the true desert lies a region of dry grassland called the Sahel and this gives way to better-watered land surrounding the Rivers Niger and Senegal and their tributaries.

The Niger flows in a semicircular arc through southern Mali and forms a marshy inland delta for part of its length. The Senegal waters the extreme west of Mali and both rivers provide water for irrigation, valuable agricultural land, a source of fish and a means of transportation. The Niger, in particular, is especially valuable to Mali as it is navigable throughout its entire length for most of the year.

Natural vegetation varies from dry grassland and thorn bushes to wooded areas in the south. Wildlife includes grazing animals, such as antelope, gazelle, giraffe and warthog, and their attendant large predators, lion, cheetah and leopard. Mali has a hot climate and is dry in the north but in the south there is enough rain for farming.

Most people live in the south and follow an agricultural or pastoral way of life. Rice, cassava and millet are grown for domestic consumption and cotton for export. The country's main exports include cotton, gold, foodstuffs, livestock and mangoes. Iron ore and bauxite have been discovered but have yet to be exploited. Independence was gained in 1960 and internal political power struggles, war with Burkina Faso and a damaging period of drought, have been among the problems that the new country has had to face. Mali appears to have entered a phase of greater political stability but remains an extremely poor land with many problems to overcome.

QUICK FACTS

Area: 316 square kilometres or
    122 square miles
Population: 376,513
Capital: Valletta
Form of government: Republic
Religion: Roman Catholicism
Currency: Maltese Pound

MALTA, situated in the Mediterranean Sea approximately 288 kilometres or 180 miles east of North Africa (Tunisia) and 93 kilometres or 58 miles south of Sicily, is an archipelago of three large inhabited islands and two small uninhabited ones, which together form an independent country of over 376,000 people.

Malta is the largest of the three inhabited islands, Gozo the second largest and Comino by far the smallest. Comino is sandwiched between Gozo in the northwest and Malta in the southeast. The Maltese islands are generally undulating, with low hills, terraced fields and no rivers. The coastline is rocky, with cliffs and sandy bays and Gozo has more rugged scenery with a greater covering of natural vegetation.

The capital of the islands, Valletta, stands on a rocky peninsula in the southwest of Malta beside the superb natural harbours of Grand Harbour and Marsamxett. It is the presence of these natural harbours, along with their strategic position, that has ensured that the islands have always been highly valued.

The climate is Mediterranean with hot, dry sunny summers and little rain. Since rainfall is limited and there are no rivers or lakes, desalination plants are needed to supply the islands with fresh water. There are also no mineral resources and few raw materials so Malta relies heavily upon imports, particularly of oil and foodstuffs. Industries include shipbuilding and servicing of vessels, the manufacture of clothing, textiles, electrical and electronic goods and equipment, plastics, chemicals, furniture and wooden goods, rubber, printing, publishing and food processing.

Some agriculture is carried out on the islands' terraced, hilly slopes with tomatoes, potatoes, grapes, onions, citrus fruits, melons and wheat being grown. A small number of sheep, goats, cattle, poultry and rabbits are raised. Tourism has boomed and the island has become popular as a place for retirement in the sunshine with low taxes.

QUICK FACTS

Area: 181 square kilometres or
    70 square miles
Population: 58,000
Capital: Dalap-Uliga-Darrit (on Majuro
    Atoll)
Form of government: Republic in free
    association with the USA
Religion: Protestantism
Currency: US Dollar

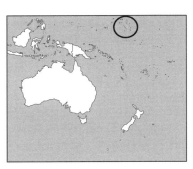

MARSHALL ISLANDS is an archipelago of over 1,000 atolls and islets in eastern Micronesia to the northwest of Kiribati in the western Pacific Ocean which were almost uninhabited until the 1880s. The climate is tropical maritime with little variation in temperature and rainfall is at its heaviest from July to October. The islands have undergone numerous changes of sovereignty. Germany bought them from Spain and then they fell under Japanese rule until the Second World War when the USA captured them. In 1947, they became a trusteeship of the USA and they achieved full independence in 1979. The republic remains in free association with the USA who have retained military bases on the islands (the Bikini Atoll was used as a nuclear testing area in 1946). Payment of rent by the USA contributes to the country's economy which otherwise depends upon agriculture and fishing, with copra as the main export. Attempts are being made to diversify the economy before US aid finishes in 2001.

QUICK FACTS

Area: 1,102 square kilometres or
    425 square miles
Population: 384,000
Capital: Fort-de-France
Form of government: Overseas
    Department of France
Religion: Roman Catholicism
Currency: French Franc

MARTINIQUE is one of the larger Windward Islands in the Lesser Antilles group in the southern Caribbean. It is administered as an overseas department of France. The Lesser Antilles group consists of the smaller islands to the east and south of the Caribbean, which are further divided into the Leeward Islands and the Windward Islands. Trinidad and Tobago, lying just off the coast of Venezuela, form the slightly larger tail end of this island group. The original inhabitants of Martinique were Arawak and Carib Indians but the establishment of the French colonies in the 17th century introduced Europeans and African slaves. In the later years of the 19th century, there was a further influx of people from India who came to work on the plantations.

The rocky, volcanic island of Martinique has sandy beaches of black, white and peppered sand, a mountainous interior and a tropical climate. Martinique's most famous peak is that of the volcano, Mount Pelee (1,448 metres or 4,750 feet). When this erupted in 1902, it destroyed the town of St Pierre, causing the death of 30,000 people. Martinique is periodically subjected to hurricanes that can cause considerable damage. The island's economy relies mainly on tourism with sugar, bananas, pineapples, citrus fruits, nutmeg and spices being grown in some parts of the island.

QUICK FACTS

Area: 1,025,520 square kilometres or
    395,956 square miles
Population: 2,351,000
Capital: Nouakchott
Other major cities: Kaédi, Nouadhibou
Form of government: Republic
Religion: Sunni Islam
Currency: Ouguiya

MAURITANIA or the **ISLAMIC REPUBLIC OF MAURITANIA** is nearly twice the size of France. Located on the west coast of Africa, almost the whole country lies within the sandy, stony wastes of the Sahara Desert. The only settlements found in this area are around oases, where a little millet, dates and vegetables can be grown. There are dry, Sahel grasslands in the south and a belt of fertile agricultural land along the northern side of the Senegal river valley. The River Senegal forms part of the country's southern border and its valley and the Sahel grasslands support some natural vegetation and wildlife. The climate is hot and dry with a rainy season that produces small amounts of rainfall in late summer and autumn but only in the south.

Most of the people follow a nomadic way of life centred around the herding of grazing animals but periods of severe drought in the 1970s killed about 70 per cent of the nation's animals forcing many people to settle along the River Senegal. As a result, vast shanty towns sprung up around all the main towns. The republic has rich deposits of iron ore and valuable Atlantic fish stocks, both of which are becoming important contributors to the economy. Mauritania finally achieved independence in 1960. However, as well as being severely affected by drought, it has also experienced some internal political unrest and been involved in disputes with its neighbours. Conditions appear to have become more settled in recent years with a new constitution adopted in 1991.

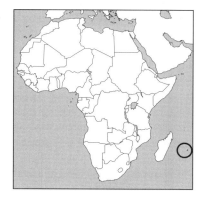

MAURITIUS is a beautiful island republic which lies in the Indian Ocean some 800 kilometres or 497 miles east of Madagascar. The islands of Rodrigues and Agalega are also part of Mauritius. Mauritius is a volcanic island with many craters surrounded by lava flows. The central plateau rises to over 800 metres or 2,625 feet then drops sharply to the south and west coasts. The climate is hot and humid with southwesterly winds bringing heavy rain in the uplands and the possibility of cyclones during December to April. The island has well-watered fertile soil, ideal for the sugar plantations that cover 45 per cent of the island. Although the export of molasses and sugar still dominates the economy, diversification is being encouraged. Other crops such as tea, tobacco, peanuts and vegetables are grown. The clothing and electronic equipment industries are becoming increasingly important and tourism is now the third largest source of foreign exchange.

QUICK FACTS

Area: 2,040 square kilometres or 788 square miles
Population: 1,160,000
Capital: Port Louis
Form of government: Republic
Religions: Hinduism, Roman Catholicism, Sunni Islam
Currency: Mauritian Rupee

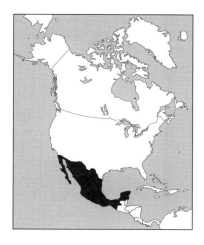

MEXICO is a large, densely populated country whose people are Spanish-speaking. It is bounded in the north by its long border with the USA. In the south, it shares a longer border with Guatemala and a shorter one with Belize. The Gulf of Mexico and the northern Caribbean Sea lie to the east, the Gulf of California to the northwest and the Pacific Ocean to the southwest. Mexico is a land of great geographical contrasts and includes most vegetational zones. It is dominated by a vast, central plateau that lies between two great mountain ranges running from northwest to southeast, the Sierra Madre Oriental in the east and the Sierra Madre Occidental in the west. In the south, they unite to form an impressive range of volcanic mountains, the Sierra Madre del Sur. In this area are situated Mexico's greatest peaks, some of which are still active volcanoes. The highest of these, Citlaltepetl, reaches a height of 5,699 metres or 18,697 feet. Mexico City, the capital, is also situated in this area.

QUICK FACTS

Area: 1,958,201 square kilometres or 756,066 square miles
Population: 96,578,000
Capital: Mexico City
Other major cities: Guadalajara, León, Monterrey, Puebla, Tijuana
Form of government: Federal Republic
Religion: Roman Catholicism
Currency: Mexican Peso

The northern part of the country is arid semidesert where cacti and yucca, wolves and coyotes can be found. The coastal plains, lower mountain slopes and the narrow neck or isthmus of Tehuantepec support lush, tropical vegetation and are inhabited by such animals as jaguars and peccaries. Higher up the mountain slopes, temperate forests of oaks and conifers, in which may be found bears and pumas, give way to sparse Arctic vegetation at the highest altitudes. The northwest coast along the Gulf of California is swampy, humid country and lies opposite the narrow, mountainous peninsula of Baja California. Similar conditions occur in the southeast along the coast of Campeche and Yucatan, where there are many lagoons.

Mexico has few rivers or lakes of any size except the Rio Bravo del Norte (Rio Grande) which runs from northwest to southeast along the border with the USA. Much of Mexico receives relatively little rainfall, with about 75 per cent falling in the regions east of the Sierra Madre Oriental, the Gulf coast and the Yucatan Peninsula. The isthmus of Tehuantepec also receives a reasonable amount of rain.

The arid and mountainous conditions mean that only about 15 per cent of the land is suitable for farming and this relies heavily on irrigation schemes. Crops include maize, sorghum, sugar cane, wheat, coffee, oranges, bananas, tomatoes, cotton and potatoes. The most important domestic animals are goats, sheep, horses, donkeys and mules and poultry. Forestry is an important natural resource, the exploitation of which is now strictly regulated. Mexico has valuable mineral reserves of industrial and precious commodities, including petroleum, natural gas, silver and gold. With over 6 million tourists a year visiting Mexico, tourism also makes an important contribution to the country's economy.

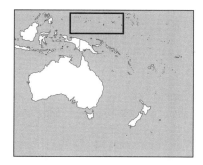

MICRONESIA, FEDERATED STATES OF, was formerly part of the US-administered UN Trust Territory of the Pacific, known as the Caroline Islands, and became independent in 1990. This self-governing republic consists of around 600 islands in the Caroline Islands Archipelago which lies scattered across the western Pacific Ocean roughly 4,025 kilometres or 2,500 miles southwest of Hawaii. There are four states: Yap, Chuuk (was Truk), Pohnpeé and to the extreme east, Kosrae. The climate is tropical maritime, with high temperatures and rainfall all year round but a pronounced precipitation peak between July and October. Independence from the USA was formally gained in 1990 but the decision to terminate their trusteeship was taken long before in 1978. However, Micronesia remains heavily dependent upon US aid and some of its natural resources – timber, tuna, minerals from the sea – are not used to their full benefit. There are significant phosphate deposits but the island's isolation restricts development. Tourism is a growing trade but the economy of the region remains fragile.

QUICK FACTS

Area: 702 square kilometres or 271 square miles
Population: 109,000
Capital: Palikir
Form of government: Republic
Religion: Christianity
Currency: US Dollar

QUICK FACTS

Area: 33,700 square kilometres or
    13,012 square miles
Population: 4,327,000
Capital: Chisinau
Other cities: Tiraspol, Tighina, Bel'tsy
Form of government: Republic
Religion: Russian Orthodox
Currency: Leu

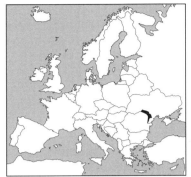

MOLDOVA (MOLDAVIA) is a landlocked, somewhat triangular-shaped republic in southeast Europe that from 1940 to 1991 was part of the USSR and was called the Moldavian Soviet Socialist Republic. It is bordered by Romania in the west and bounded on all other sides by Ukraine. The River Prut forms the whole of the western boundary with Romania while the River Dnister (Nistru) flows close to the eastern border and coincides with it in the northeast and southeast. Moldova is a predominantly hilly plain with an average height of around 150 metres or 500 feet. The Prut and Dnister and their tributaries are the main river systems but there are many smaller rivers and streams, all of them flowing generally southwards towards the Black Sea.

The natural vegetation is a mixture of grassland and woodland, a continuation of the steppe and wooded steppe of the Ukraine. Summers are warm to hot and winters are fairly cold with snow. The greatest amount of precipitation falls on the hills. Over 4 million people live in Moldova and the population density is quite high. Less than half the population reside in cities or towns and the majority live in rural areas and are engaged in agriculture.

Moldova's soils are very fertile and a variety of crops are grown, including cereals (wheat, barley, maize), sugar beet, soya beans, sunflowers, fruit, walnuts and tobacco. Cattle, sheep, pigs, poultry and horses are among the livestock raised and bees and silkworms are kept in some areas. Moldova is also a leading producer of rose oil for the perfume industry.

The economy suffered setbacks in the early 1990s following Moldova's declaration of independence and consequent serious ethnic divisions in two areas of the country that remain unresolved. However, it is slowly improving although the process of change is expected to be quite slow. Moldova's most important industries are in the area of food processing, particularly sugar refining, canned goods and the processing of tobacco and of sunflower seeds for oil. Other industries include metalworking, engineering and the manufacture of electrical equipment, farm machinery, refrigerators, construction materials, textiles and clothing.

QUICK FACTS

Area: 1 square kilometre or
    0.4 square miles
Population: 32,000
Capital: Monaco
Form of government: Constitutional
    Monarchy
Religion: Roman Catholicism
Currency: French Franc

MONACO is a tiny principality situated on the French Riviera. It comprises a rocky peninsula and a narrow stretch of coast with a coastline of just over two miles. It has mild, moist winters and hot, dry summers. The ancient fortified town of Monaco is situated on a rocky promontory and houses the royal palace and the cathedral. The Monte Carlo district has its world-famous casino and La Condamine has thriving businesses, shops, banks and attractive residential areas. Fontvieille is an area reclaimed from the sea where marinas and light industry are now located. Light industry includes chemicals, plastics, electronics, engineering and paper but tourism is the main revenue earner. The sale of stamps and tobacco and the insurance and banking industries also contribute to the economy. Well-known annual events, such as the Monte Carlo Rally and Monaco Grand Prix, are held in the principality.

QUICK FACTS

Area: 1,566,500 square kilometres or
    604,829 square miles
Population: 2,354,000
Capital: Ulaanbaatar
Other cities: Altay, Saynshand, Hovd,
    Choybalsan, Tsetserleg
Form of government: Republic
Religions: Buddhism, Shamanism, Islam
Currency: Tughrik

MONGOLIA is a large, central Asian republic which shares a long northern border with Russia and is surrounded on all other sides by China. The border with China extends for 4,670 kilometres or 2,901 miles. Mongolia consists mainly of a high plateau from which mountains rise in the west. The principal ranges are the Altai Mountains which extend southeastwards and the Hangayn Mountains in the central western area. The greatest peaks are to be found in the Altai Mountains. In the east and southeast, the elevation of the plateau is generally lower and arid, semidesert scrubland gradually gives way to the true desert of the Gobi which stretches across the southeastern portion of the country. A number of large lakes occur in Mongolia's mountainous regions and there are salt lakes and salt pans in the arid, desert regions. Several extensive rivers cross the country, arising mainly in the mountains. The principal rivers are the Selenge and its tributaries which flow northeastwards from the Hangayn Mountains, the Kerulen in the east and the Onhon in the north. Four vegetational zones can be recognised in Mongolia which grade into one another: coniferous forest in the mountains, forest-steppe, steppe and semidesert/desert.

Mongolia is a sparsely populated country whose people continue to adhere to a traditional, pastoral way of life based on the herding of grazing animals. Since the people live close to the land upon which their wellbeing depends, they have a great sense of respect for the natural flora and fauna of their country. Hence Mongolia preserves a wide range of species which have become rare in other parts of central Asia and the importance of conservation, particularly when set against the challenges of development, is well recognised by the government.

Mongolia has a dry continental climate with long, very cold winters and short, mild summers during which most of the yearly rainfall is experienced. Rain may not fall in parts of the desert for several years and, while daytime conditions can be searingly hot, the temperature may plunge at night to near freezing and, in winter, can fall as low as -20°C or -4°F. The capital and largest city in Mongolia is Ulaanbaatar. Although many of the people still follow a seminomadic way of life based on animal herding, some 58 per cent of Mongolians are classed as urban dwellers.

Agriculture, and more particularly the rearing and herding of livestock, is the main economic activity and source of employment in Mongolia. The principal animals are sheep, cattle, horses, goats and camels. Under Communism, all cultivation and livestock rearing was state-controlled or organised as collectives but Mongolia has now started to move towards a free market economy. Crops grown include cereals (wheat, barley and oats), potatoes and some other vegetables but cultivation is heavily dependent on irrigation. Mongolia has valuable reserves of iron ore, coal, copper, molybdenum, fluorspar, tungsten, uranium gold and silver. Ulaanbaatar is one of several industrial centres which were developed to exploit some of these minerals although others have yet to be extracted. Manufacturing industries are generally on a small scale and include the processing of wool, hides, leather, furs, meat and dairy produce, textiles, wooden goods, agricultural equipment and building products. The collapse of trade with the former Soviet Union has created severe economic problems for Mongolia and it is increasingly looking to Japan and China for trade and economic assistance.

MONTSERRAT is a British overseas territory and one of the Leeward Islands in the Caribbean Sea. The island is rugged, heavily forested and mountainous with active volcanoes. Many of Montserrat's inhabitants left the island between 1995 and 1998 because of a series of volcanic eruptions in the Soufrière Hills, which also caused the virtual destruction of the country's capital, Plymouth. The climate is tropical with low humidity and no well-defined rainy season. Tourism was the mainstay of the economy with tomatoes, peppers, manugactured goods,beef, cotton and cotton goods being the main exports.

QUICK FACTS
Area: 102 square kilometres or 39 square miles
Population: 4,500
Capital: Plymouth
Form of government: British Overseas Territory
Religion: Christianity
Currency: East Caribbean Dollar

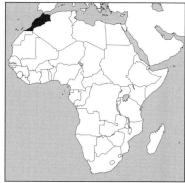

MOROCCO, in northwest Africa, is strategically placed at the western entrance to the Mediterranean Sea. Morocco lays claim to the territory of Western Sahara while the ports of Melilla and Ceuta are administered by Spain. It is a country of diverse topography, climate and human history whose ancient cities of Tanger, Fes, Marrakech and Casablanca have long held a fascination for Europeans. The country is split from southwest to northeast by the high, rugged Atlas Mountains, which dominate the landscape at over 4,000 metres or 13,000 feet. They give way to green, fertile coastal plains along the Atlantic coast while to the southeast the land falls away from the mountains to join the arid Sahara Desert. The Er Rif Mountains command the Mediterranean coast.

The coastal regions of Morocco have a Mediterranean type of climate with hot summers and mild winters. Inland, a more continental type of climate prevails with greater extremes of temperature and very cold conditions in winter in the mountains. Hot, dry conditions characterise the desert regions and rainfall occurs mainly in winter and is most plentiful near the coasts.

Once linked with Spain, Morocco's wildlife is a mix of both African and European species including Dorcas gazelles, Barbary apes and panther (African) and rabbits and squirrels (European). The Barbary lion, which was the subspecies used by the Romans in their bloodthirsty entertainments, is extinct in the wild. However, an ambitious project employing genetic screening along with selective breeding aims to try and reinstate this magnificent lion by breeding from captive animals which show strong Barbary characteristics.

The economy is very mixed. Morocco is mainly a farming country although agriculture accounts for less than 20 per cent of the land use. Wheat, barley and maize are the main food crops and it is one of the world's chief exporters of citrus fruit. Morocco's main wealth comes from phosphates, reserves of which are the largest in the world. Coal, lead, iron and manganese ores are also produced. Morocco is self-sufficient in textiles, it has car assembly plants, soap and cement factories and a large sea fishing industry. Tourism is a major source of revenue as are remittances sent home by Moroccans who work abroad.

QUICK FACTS
Area: 446,550 square kilometres or 172,414 square miles
Population: 27,623,000
Capital: Rabat
Other major cities: Casablanca (Dar el Beida), Fès, Marrakech, Tanger
Form of government: Constitutional Monarchy
Religion: Sunni Islam
Currency: Dirham

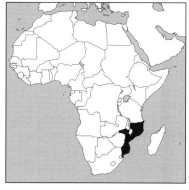

MOZAMBIQUE is a republic located in southeast Africa. It lies on the east coast of Africa, facing the island of Madagascar across the Mozambique Channel with Tanzania to the north, Malawi, Zambia and Zimbabwe to the west and South Africa and Swaziland to the south and southwest. The coastline of approximately 2,500 kilometres or 1,552 miles is fringed by lagoons, islands and reefs. A coastal plain covers most of the southern and central territory, giving way to highlands in the west and a plateau, including the Nyasa Highlands, to the north. The River Zambezi separates the high plateau in the north from the lowlands in the south before flowing into the Indian Ocean (Mozambique Channel).

The plateau contains some woodlands with stretches of steppe and the highlands to the north and west are forested in part with tropical rainforests, particularly in the river valleys. The country's wildlife is typically diverse. The major population centres are found in the coastal plain and productive river valleys. The country has a humid, tropical climate with highest temperatures and rainfall in the north. Normally conditions are reasonably good for agriculture but a drought in the early 1980s, followed a few years later by severe flooding, resulted in famine and more than 100,000 deaths.

The vast majority of the people are occupied with subsistence farming. Fishing, mainly lobster and shrimp, is an important source of export revenue. There are significant mineral resources to be exploited – diamonds, coal, titanium and others and forestry is another potential source of revenue which at the moment is largely untapped.

QUICK FACTS
Area: 799,380 square kilometres or 309,496 square miles
Population: 16,916,000
Capital: Maputo
Other towns: Beira, Nampula
Form of government: Republic
Religions: Animism, Roman Catholicism, Sunni Islam
Currency: Metical

A lot of industry was abandoned when the Portuguese left the country and, due to lack of expertise, was not taken over by the local people. The economy is now on the upturn although it has been negatively affected by floods, drought and civil war.

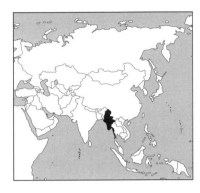

MYANMAR, UNION OF, (formerly Burma) is the second largest country in southeast Asia. The heartland of the country is the valley of the great Irawaddy river system. The north and west of the country are mountainous and the Shan Plateau runs along the border with Thailand in the east. The climate is equatorial at the coast, changing to tropical monsoon over most of the interior.

A combination of factors has ensured that the country has remained relatively underdeveloped and unspoiled and Myanmar retains large tracts of tropical forest containing commercially valuable species such as teak and rubber. Wildlife is abundant and includes some of the rarer Asian mammals such as tiger, leopard, rhinoceros, elephant, buffalo and gibbon. Elephants are used as pack and work animals and additionally there are many birds, reptiles, fish and insects. New species are still being discovered such as the smallest known type of Muntjac deer, called the 'leaf deer' by local people and measuring a mere 50 centimetres or 10 inches high at the shoulder. Although Rangoon (Yangon) is now the country's capital, it is Mandalay, its ancient royal seat, which is its cultural and spiritual heart. Buddhist pagodas, colourful traditional festivals, music, dance and theatre are all very much apparent in Myanmar.

Most of the people live in rural areas and are engaged in traditional occupations such as agriculture, fishing and forestry. The Irrawaddy river flows into the Andaman Sea, forming a huge delta area which is ideal land for rice cultivation. Rice is the country's staple food and accounts for half its export earnings. Tropical fruits, such as bananas, mangoes, citrus and guavas, grow well in the fertile coastal regions. Myanmar is rich in timber and mineral resources such as natural gas, petroleum, jade and natural rubies. However, because of poor communications, lack of development and unrest among ethnic groups, these resources have not been fully exploited which has at least contributed to the preservation of the country's natural environment.

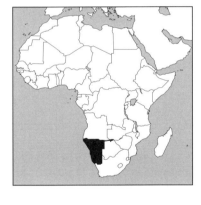

NAMIBIA is situated on the Atlantic coast of southwest Africa. This large country shares borders with Angola and Zambia to the north, Botswana to the east and South Africa to the east and south. There are three main regions in the country: the Namib Desert running down the entire Atlantic coastline; a central plateau of mountains, rugged outcrops, sandy valleys and poor grasslands to the east of the Namib; and further east and north, the Kalahari Desert. Also in the north of the country, is the Etosha Pan. The largest of Namibia's salt lakes, the Etosha Pan is surrounded by bush containing large numbers of Namibia's varied wildlife. The larger species include elephant zebra, giraffe and lion. Namibia has poor rainfall. Windhoek, the capital, has the highest amount of rain but even here it only amounts to 200–250 millimetres or 8–10 inches per year.

Namibia is essentially a stock-rearing country where sheep, cattle and goats are raised. The economy of Namibia reflects the split often seen in African countries: the bulk of the population involved in subsistence farming and fighting a losing battle against the encroaching desert while the country possesses some of the world's largest and richest diamond fields. Copper, uranium (Namibia has the world's largest uranium mine), tungsten and silver are among other minerals produced. One of Africa's richest fishing grounds lies off the coast of Namibia. Mackerel, anchovies and pilchards are exported although production has dropped in recent years due to overfishing.

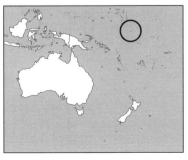

NAURU is the smallest of the states in Oceania and one of the smallest republics in the world, occupying just over 21 square kilometres or 8 square miles in the central Pacific. Formerly called Pleasant Island, it is a coral island with a population of around 11,000. The majority of the population live along a narrow coastal belt of fertile land where the main crops are pineapples, bananas and coconuts. The climate is tropical with a high and irregular rainfall. The country is rich, due entirely to the deposits of high quality phosphate rock in the central plateau which is sold for fertiliser to Australia, New Zealand, Japan and South Korea. Phosphate deposits are likely to be exhausted in the near future but the government is investing overseas and attempting to diversify to ensure the economic future of the country. Since around 80 per cent of the land will be uninhabitable once the mines are exhausted, considerable rehabilitation will be required.

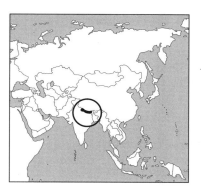

NEPAL, KINGDOM OF, is a constitutional monarchy with the Chinese autonomous region of Tibet lying on its northern, long side and surrounded by India on its other three sides to the west, south and east. The kingdom can be divided into three topographical bands running in a northwesterly to southeasterly direction: the high Himalayas which extend along the northern border with Tibet, the more modest ranges of the Himalayas and a narrow band of lower-lying land called the Tarai. The high Himalayas are the greatest of these bands, extending along the northern border with Tibet. The scale of the mountains is immense with average heights in excess of 4,560 metres or 15,000 feet. Eight of the world's highest peaks are located in Nepal or along its borders, including the greatest and most famous of all, Mount Everest (8,848 metres or 29,028 feet). South of these great mountains lies a band of the more modest ranges of the Himalayas, including the Siwaliks and the Mahabharat Lekh, where the average heights are in the region of 2,584 metres or 8,500 feet. These give way southwards to the narrow band of lower-lying land called the Tarai. This extends across Nepal's southern border into India to form the upper reaches of the plain of the Ganges river system. Most rivers in Nepal flow southwards to join the Ganges river system. A second area of lower ground is the basin, formed by a river valley in the lower Himalayas, where the kingdom's capital, and largest city, Kathmandu, is situated. Most of the population of about 21 million people live in or around Kathmandu or the Tarai region.

In the lower parts of Nepal, the climate is warm to hot in summer with monsoon-type rains, while winter is cool and dry. Spring and autumn are mild with some rainfall. Temperatures are cold in the Himalayas throughout the year with plenty of snowfall.

Nepal is one of the world's poorest and least developed countries. Most Nepalese are employed in agriculture which is the mainstay of the economy. Cultivatable land in Nepal, amounting to about 17 per cent of the total area, is found only in the Tarai and the Kathmandu Basin. The principal food crops are rice, wheat, millet and corn and also vegetables, including potatoes, fruit and sugar beet. Non-food crops are also grown especially cotton, jute and tobacco. Livestock animals include cattle, yak, sheep, goats and poultry. Animals are used for work and transport as well as being a source of meat.

Forestry is also an important industry in Nepal and provides raw materials for the pulp and paper industry and for export. However, it is estimated that 40 per cent of the natural forests clothing the lower mountain slopes have been removed during the second half of the 20th century. This overexploitation has led to erosion of the hillsides in some areas and poses an environmental problem for Nepal.

Some mineral deposits such as copper, iron ore, mica and ochre exist but, because of the country's inaccessible terrain, have not been completely charted. However, with Indian and Chinese aid, roads have been built from the north and south to Kathmandu. The construction of hydroelectric power schemes is underway although at a high cost. Nepal's main exports are carpets, foodstuffs, clothing and leather goods with the two principal sources of foreign revenue being tourism and Gurkha soldiers' foreign earnings.

Nepal has long been a popular destination for adventurous young people from the West but it now attracts thousands of visitors each year, many of whom belong to trekking and climbing expeditions. Although the visitors bring in much-needed foreign currency, a lot of rubbish is left by each expedition and since most rubbish does not rot easily in the rarefied air and cold temperatures of the mountains, it often remains in ugly piles next to the trekking trails and camps.

QUICK FACTS
Area: 147,181 square kilometres or 56,827 square miles
Population: 21,127,000
Capital: Kathmandu
Other city: Biratnagar
Form of government: Constitutional Monarchy
Religions: Hinduism, Buddhism
Currency: Nepalese Rupee

NETHERLANDS, also known as **HOLLAND,** forms one of the Benelux or Low Countries along with Belgium and Luxembourg. It is bounded in the north and west by the North Sea, in the east by Germany and in the south by Belgium. The Netherlands is a very low-lying country and slightly higher ground is found only in the southern extremity where the land rises towards the foothills of the Ardennes. The Netherlands has mild winters and cool summers.

Most of the North Sea coastline is marked by a narrow belt of huge sand dunes that are among the largest in Europe. These are carefully managed to preserve the marram grass and encourage the growth of other vegetation, including trees, wherever possible. These stabilise the dunes, which are important in providing protection for the low-lying farmland behind the coast since about 50 per cent of the country is below sea level. In the southwestern part of the coast, the mouths of several rivers create a delta region of estuaries and islands. This area suffered severe flooding during the winter storms of 1953, when an extremely high tide overwhelmed the defences and claimed the lives of 1,800 people. As a result of this tragedy, the Delta Plan was launched and a series of dykes, dams and canals with sluices and locks to control water levels were constructed to protect the area and prevent further flooding. Some islands were linked together and freshwater lakes created and the whole project was completed in 1986.

About 16 per cent of the Netherlands has been reclaimed from the sea. An ambitious reclamation project, to create land from an inlet of the sea called the Zuider Zee, was started earlier in the 20th century. A dyke was constructed across the mouth of the inlet, which was completed in 1932. Mechanical pumps and drainage schemes then began the work of removing the water to create about 2,250,000 square kilometres or 556,000 acres of reclaimed polder land. In addition to the new land, a large, freshwater lake has been created behind the dyke, which is called the Ijsselmeer. Beyond the dykes lies an enclosed area of sea, the Waddenzee, which is bounded by a long chain of islands, the West Frisian and East Frisian Islands.

QUICK FACTS
Area: 40,844 square kilometres or 15,770 square miles
Population: 15,517,000
Capital: Amsterdam
Seat of government: The Hague (s'Gravenhage)
Other major cities: Rotterdam, Eindhoven
Form of government: Constitutional Monarchy
Religions: Roman Catholicism, Dutch Reform, Calvinism
Currency: Guilder

The Netherlands are crossed by numerous rivers which include the Rhine and its tributaries and there are many navigable canals and lakes. The country also has highly developed road and rail networks. The majority of the population are Dutch but the Netherlands is a multicultural country with significant numbers of residents from other races and cultures. About 90 per cent of people live in cities or urban areas, such as the capital, Amsterdam. The main port of the Netherlands, Rotterdam, is the largest in the world.

There is very little natural landscape left in the Netherlands as the countryside has been greatly altered and managed by human beings for many hundreds of years. Efforts have been made to conserve and restore some areas and to plant trees, usually within national parks. Agricultural land is intensively farmed and managed and the lack of undisturbed areas has meant that many wild animals have disappeared, except from the national parks. The numerous man-made lakes, however, provide a useful habitat for many species of water-loving birds. The country suffers to some extent from pollution problems, particularly of its water courses, caused by intensive agriculture and heavy industry, and the government has initiated several environmental protection schemes.

Agriculture plays an extremely significant part in the Dutch economy and the land is intensively farmed and cultivated. Most farms are small, family-run businesses and are highly productive. Soils in the country are generally rich and fertile, particularly those of the reclaimed polders, although high use of fertilisers has led to problems with pollution. Among the crops grown are wheat and cereals, sugar beet, potatoes, vegetables and fruit. Other land is used for horticulture with bulbs and other flowers being grown for export. Animals reared include pigs, poultry and cattle, and the Netherlands is famous for its dairy produce and speciality cheeses such as Edam and Gouda.

Fishing has long been carried out from the North Sea coastal villages and the species landed include cod, herring, plaice and sole. There is very little forestry industry in the Netherlands as the amount of woodland cover is negligible and that which does exist is mainly within national parks or preserved for recreational purposes.

The Netherlands are poor in mineral resources although there were some coal deposits in the south in Groningen province which were mined until the early 1970s. For many centuries, the Dutch depended on peat for fuel and on wind energy driving numerous windmills to power machinery. As these were insufficient to provide for the rapid industrial development of the 19th and 20th centuries, the country had to import large quantities of coal and, later, petroleum and natural gas. After the Second World War, Rotterdam developed rapidly as a world centre for the refining of petroleum, much of which is exported. By the 1960s, extensive deposits of natural gas had been located around Groningen and have since been exploited to make the Netherlands a leading exporter of this commodity.

The country has a highly developed industrial and manufacturing base. In addition to natural gas and petroleum from the extensive deposits of natural gas located around Groningen, other important commodities include textiles and a wide range of light industrial and electronic goods.

NETHERLANDS ANTILLES consists of two sets of islands, the Southern Netherlands Antilles (Bonaire and Curaçao) and the Northern Netherlands Antilles (Saba, St Maarten and St Eustatius). Saba is the highest island in the group rising to 870 metres or 2,854 feet at Mount Scenery. The islands have a tropical climate. Oil refining and tourism are the most important economic activities.

NEW CALEDONIA or **NOUVELLE CALÉDONIE** is the most southerly of the Melanesian countries in the Pacific Ocean. It is a French overseas territory but there has been ongoing unrest in the country between the indigenous Melanesians and the French settlers over the question of independence. The main island, Nouvelle Calédonie, is 400 kilometres or 248 miles long and rises to a height of 1,639 metres or 5,377 feet at Mount Panie. The island is divided into two natural regions by the mountain range that runs down its centre – a dry west coast covered with gum tree savannah and a tropical east coast. It has a Mediterranean-type climate with rainfall at its heaviest between December and March.

The country is rich in mineral resources, particularly nickel, which accounts for 90 per cent of the country's exports. Other exports include coffee and copra. The main tourist resorts are on the east coast of Nouvelle Calédonie.

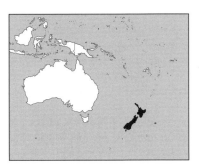

NEW ZEALAND lies over 2,000 kilometres or 1,242 miles south-east of Australia in the South Pacific. It comprises two major islands – North Island and South Island – Stewart Island and the Chatham Islands and many smaller islands. Features of the country vary from extensive grassland and alpine meadows to mountains, fjords and subtropical rainforests.

North Island is hilly with isolated mountains, active volcanoes, hot mineral springs and geysers. Earthquakes occur and in 1987 considerable damage was caused by one at Edgecumbe. On South Island, the Southern Alps run north to south and the highest point is Mount Cook at 3,753 metres or 12,313 feet. The Canterbury Plains lie to the east of the mountains while there are fjords and glaciers in the southwest of the island. The three main cities are Auckland and Wellington on North Island and Christchurch on South Island and the vast majority of the population live on North Island.

QUICK FACTS

Area: 800 square kilometres or
    309 square miles
Population: 207,333
Capital: Willemstad
Form of government: Self-governing Dutch
    Territory
Religion: Roman Catholicism
Currency: Netherlands Antilles Guilder

QUICK FACTS

Area: 18,575 square kilometres or 7,172
    square miles
Population: 189,000
Capital: Noumea
Form of government: French Overseas
    Territory
Religion: Roman Catholicism
Currency: Franc

QUICK FACTS

Area: 270,534 square kilometres or
    104,454 square miles
Population: 3,681,546
Capital: Wellington
Other major cities: Auckland, Christchurch,
    Dunedin, Hamilton
Form of government: Constitutional
    Monarchy
Religions: Anglicanism, Roman Catholicism,
    Presbyterianism
Currency: New Zealand Dollar

New Zealand enjoys very mild winters with regular rainfall and no extremes of heat or cold. The North Island tends to a sub-tropical climate while the South is more temperate. The wildlife is perhaps unusual in that many species have been introduced by man. Land mammals, including chamois, rabbit, hare, possum and deer, were brought in by Europeans to be used for their fur. In addition to a number of smaller mammals, there are the flightless kiwi and kakapo and many endemic bird species such as warblers, flycatchers, parrots, rails, penguins, shags and dotterels.

A number of marine mammals, including varieties of whale (killer, sperm) and dolphin (dusky, common, bottlenose), can be seen in the waters around New Zealand. The fur seal can be found all around the coast and although they were the focus, along with whales, of an entire industry in days gone by, numbers have now stabilised.

The country depends heavily upon its land for the major industries of agriculture, mining and forestry. Two thirds of New Zealand is suitable for agriculture with meat, wool and dairy goods being the main products. Forestry supports the pulp and paper industry and hydroelectric power produces cheap electricity for the manufacturing industry which now accounts for 30 per cent of New Zealand's exports. Mining is also an important industry with petroleum, natural gas, limestone, gold and iron ore being exploited.

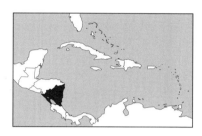

NICARAGUA is the largest of the central American countries. It lies between the Pacific Ocean to the west and the Caribbean Sea to the east, on the isthmus of central America, and is sandwiched between Honduras to the north and Costa Rica to the south. The dense forests and sandy beaches of the Mosquito Coast in the eastern part of the country are the wettest part of the island and home to a variety of wildlife including jaguar, monkey, puma and crocodile. The land rises inland to become mountainous with peaks rising to nearly 2,134 metres or 7,000 feet. The mountains are interspersed with fertile valleys. In the southwest, there is large basin that contains two vast lakes, Nicaragua in the south and Managua in the north. These are bordered in the north by volcanoes, many of which are still active. Nicaragua is subject to earthquakes and the capital, Managua, was severely damaged by tremors in 1931 and 1972.

Most of Nicaragua's people live in the region of the lakes or towards the Pacific coast in the west. Nicaragua is primarily an agricultural country and 65 per cent of the labour force work on the land. Coffee, cotton, bananas and sugar cane are grown, with cattle ranching in some of the upland areas. There are mineral deposits of gold, copper and silver with gold being of prime importance but the country's economy is largely dependent on foreign aid.

QUICK FACTS

Area: 130,668 square kilometres or
    50,193 square miles
Population: 4,663,000
Form of government: Republic
Capital: Managua
Other cities: Matagalpa, León, Granada
Religion: Roman Catholicism
Currency: Córdoba Oro

NIGER is a landlocked republic in west Africa, just south of the Tropic of Cancer. Over half of the country is covered by the encroaching Sahara Desert in the north while the drought-stricken Sahel grasslands lie to the south. In the extreme southwest corner, the River Niger, an important navigable waterway, flows southeastwards for 483 kilometres or 300 miles, cutting off Niger's far western territory. Lake Chad lies in the extreme southeast. The Ténéré Desert (part of the Sahara) is alternately stony and sandy and interrupted by plateaux and mountains rising to 2,022 metres or 6,634 feet. In the foothills of the mountains, in the heart of an oasis, lies the old city of Agadez which is still an important destination for Saharan traders.

The climate is hot and dry in the north but with heavy summer rainfall in the south. Southern and watered regions support a variety of vegetation, including forest trees, while the grasslands have some bushes but are mainly dry. Wildlife includes the large African species, such as elephant, giraffe, lion and buffalo, as well as reptiles and birds.

Almost all people are employed in subsistence agriculture, with the raising of livestock being the major activity. Niger has valuable mineral reserves, most of which have not been exploited and there is some small-scale manufacturing in the capital, Niamey. Niger has recovered from disastrous droughts and exports cotton and cowpeas, although uranium is its main export. More recently, there has been further unrest involving the Tuareg people who wish for an independent state.

QUICK FACTS

Area: 1,267,000 square kilometres or
    489,191 square miles
Population: 9,465,000
Capital: Niamey
Other major cities: Agadez, Maradi,
    Tahoua, Zinder
Form of government: Republic
Religion: Sunni Islam
Currency: CFA Franc

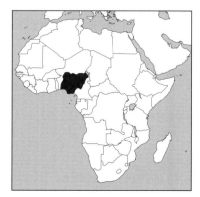

NIGERIA is a large federal republic in west Africa which extends from the Gulf of Guinea north to the border with Niger. It is not only the most densely populated country in Africa but also one of the most powerful and important.

Nigeria's topography, climate and natural vegetation vary considerably. The coastal belt is a region of sandy beaches, lagoons and swampy mangrove forests. Beyond this, lies a region of tropical rainforest with the land gradually rising towards extensive central and northern plateaux. Surrounding the plateaux are savannah plains which grade into semidesert and desert in the extreme north of the country.

Crossing the eastern border with Cameroon is the high Adamawa Plateau (Massif de l'Adoumaoua) where Nigeria's highest peak, Vogel (2,042 metres or 6,699 feet), is located. The Niger river system with its many tributaries drains the country and Lake Chad stretches across the far northeastern border. The climate varies from a humid, hot equatorial type in

QUICK FACTS

Area: 923,768 square kilometres or
    356,669 square miles
Population: 115,120,000
Capital: Abuja
Other major cities: Lagos, Onitsha, Enugu,
    Ibadan, Kano, Ogbomosho
Form of government: Federal Republic
Religions: Sunni Islam, Christianity
Currency: Naira

the south to more arid conditions with extremes of temperature in the north. The north is also affected by the dry harmattan wind from the Sahara. The rainy season varies according to area but there is considerably less rainfall in the north than in the south. Wildlife is diverse but animal numbers have declined in many areas due to human activity.

About 75 per cent of the land is suitable for agriculture and a wide variety of crops is raised by subsistence farmers. The main agricultural products are cocoa beans, rubber, groundnuts and cotton with only cocoa being of any export significance. The economy is heavily dependent upon the exploitation of large reserves of oil and natural gas but other mineral resources include extensive deposits of coal, iron ore and salt. Full independence was achieved by Nigeria in 1960 but due to several factors, including the complex ethnic make-up of the country, the country's progress has frequently been interrupted by strife and internal dissent.

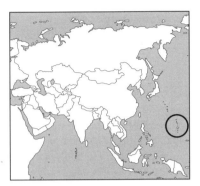

NORTHERN MARIANA ISLANDS are situated in the northwest Pacific Ocean. In 1986, the islanders voted for Commonwealth status in union with the USA and they were granted US citizenship. The country consists of mainly volcanic islands with coral limestone and lava shores. Tourism is the main industry.

QUICK FACTS

Area: 464 square kilometres or
   179 square miles
Population: 49,000
Capital: Saipan
Form of government: Commonwealth in
   union with the USA
Religion: Roman Catholicism
Currency: US Dollar

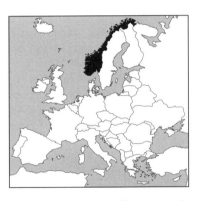

NORWAY, KINGDOM OF, is a constitutional monarchy occupying the western part of the Scandinavian Peninsula in northern Europe. Most of Norway's eastern boundary is shared with Sweden but in the northeast, the border is with Finland and, for a short distance, with Russia. In the far north, Norway's coastline runs along the Barents Sea, which is part of the Arctic Ocean, and the upper third of the country lies within the Arctic Circle. The country's long western coast is bounded by the Norwegian Sea or North Sea and, in total, the coastline extends for some 2,720 kilometres or 1,700 miles. In the southeast, the extension of the North Sea called the Skagerrak separates southern Norway from Denmark. Five political/geographical regions are recognised in Norway. These are North Norway, Trøndelag, Vestlandet, Sørlandet and Østlandet.

QUICK FACTS

Area: 323,877 square kilometres or
   125,050 square miles
Population: 4,445,460
Capital: Oslo
Other major cities: Bergen, Trondheim,
   Stavanger, Kristiansand, Tromsö
Form of government: Constitutional
   Monarchy
Religion: Lutheranism
Currency: Norwegian Krone

Norway is shaped like a long finger running from northeast to southwest which is narrow in the north but broadens out in the south. Nowhere in Norway is far from an inlet of the sea. Mainland Norway is dominated by high rugged mountainous terrain. This consists of a series of high plateaux, called vidder, which are themselves up to 1,067 metres or 3,500 feet above sea level, from which rise the mountain peaks. One of the most extensive areas is the Hardangervidda in the south. The highest mountain range, however, the Jotunheimen ('land of the giants') lies somewhat farther north above the Sogne Fjord and includes Glittertind (2,470 metres or 8,082 feet) and Galdhøpiggen (2,469 metres or 8,100 feet). The highest mountains are permanently covered in snow and ice, which includes a number of glaciers. Farther north, the mountains become lower but some of the most extensive glaciers in Europe are to be found in the Arctic region of Finnmark.

During the last Ice Age an ice sheet covered the whole of Scandinavia. The glaciers excavated and scoured the underlying valleys, creating the most famous feature of the Norwegian landscape, its spectacular series of fjords. Fjords extend along the whole length of the western coast.

Scattered close to the mainland throughout most of the length of the coastline are hundreds of islands known as the Skerryguard. These provide some shelter from the open sea and protection for the many boats upon which the seafaring Norwegians have always depended. The largest islands are the Lofoten and Vesterålen group in the north of the country. In addition, the Jan Mayen and Svalbard Islands in the Arctic Ocean, northeast of Iceland, and Bouvet Island in the South Atlantic, are also Norwegian territories.

Along the western seaboard, people live mainly in villages and towns built on the small areas of flat land available near the mouths and along the sides of the fjords and on the islands. In the southeast and east, the mountain slopes are more gentle and there are a series of long, deep valleys, the lower reaches of which provide more land for settlement and agriculture. North of the Jottunheim Mountains lies the Trøndelag or Trondheim region, centred on the Trondheim Fjord. Here there is a slightly greater area of flatter land available, making this an important area for farming and settlement.

North Norway is a large area of vidder, mountains and fjords lying within the Arctic Circle. It is a harsh region for human beings and is fairly thinly populated, with most of the people living along the coast or on the islands of the Lofoten and Vesterålen group. It includes the area of Finnmark, which is home to the Saami or Lapp people whose territory also extends into Sweden and Finland.

Also included in the legacy left by the last Ice Age are many glacial lake scattered throughout Norway, which were formed when the ice retreated and melted. The country is drained by numerous rivers and streams, and those in the west, descending the steep mountain sides, are short and fast-flowing with many spectacular waterfalls. The rivers in the east and south follow a gentler, generally more extended course, and it is here that Norway's longest river, the Glåma, is located. Almost 80 per cent of the rivers and lakes in southern Norway have been severely affected by acid rain caused by industrial pollution which originates in the British Isles and is carried eastwards by the prevailing winds. This is a cause of great concern to the Norwegians who themselves operate rigorous antipollution policies within their country.

Norway is fortunate in that, in spite of its northerly position, it lies in the path of the warm ocean currents of the Gulf Stream/North Atlantic Drift. These keep even its Arctic ports free of ice in the winter and have a considerable ameliorating effect on the climate. Most of the coastal areas have a temperate maritime climate with a relatively mild winter and cool summer although becoming colder in the north. Inland and in the south, a more continental type of climate is experienced with colder winters and hotter summers. In the north and in the high mountains, sub-Arctic conditions, with winter snowfall, prevail. Precipitation falls all year but more often in the summer and autumn and on the coast.

The capital and largest city is Oslo, located in the southeast, while second in size and importance is Bergen in the southwest. About half the Norwegian population live in the southeast, a quarter in Oslo itself and the rest in the other towns, villages or urban areas. Nearly all Norwegians live within easy reach of the sea, which has historically played an important part in the development of the country.

Because of the lack of suitable flat land, fairly unproductive soils and a short growing season in much of the country, agriculture is a small-scale enterprise in Norway. Only 3 per cent of the land can be cultivated and most of this is in the southeast and in the Trøndelag. Here some crops are grown and these include hay for fodder, cereals (rye, oats, barley, wheat), potatoes and some other vegetables. Most farms raise livestock and the principal animals are sheep, cattle and pigs. Dairy products and meat are produced for home consumption.

Productive forests are located mainly in the south and east of the country and Norway has many sawmills supplying an important wood pulp and paper industry. Fishing has always been an important part of the Norwegian economy and has remained strong despite the difficulties caused by declining fish stocks. Norway's fishing fleet operates far afield, particularly in the waters off Newfoundland, and among the most important species caught are mackerel, cod, herring, capelin and sand eels. Salmon, sea trout and prawns are also significant. In recent years, Norway has established many fish farms for the rearing of salmon and sea trout and the country is now a leading exporter, particularly of salmon. In spite of strong international opposition, Norway, as a traditional whaling country, continues to hunt a yearly quota of minke whales.

Norway has modest reserves of lead, iron, coal, copper and zinc that are extracted but the main area of production is in oil and natural gas, which were discovered in Norwegian waters during the 1970s and now form an important part of the economy. Norway has exploited its abundant potential for hydroelectric power to the full and is one of the leading producers of this form of electricity, some of which is exported. The availability of cheap electricity has enabled Norway to develop a major metallurgical industry and the production of aluminium, iron and steel is of particular importance. The country was traditionally a stronghold for heavy industries, particularly shipbuilding, but these have declined greatly. Many of the former yards have now diversified to produce equipment and machinery for the petroleum industry. Other manufactured goods include wood products and furniture, processed foods, advanced technology components, sports equipment and chemicals. Norway is also a popular tourist destination.

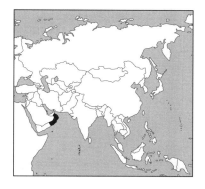

OMAN, or the **SULTANATE OF OMAN**, is an oil-rich state in the southern Arabian Peninsula. It has an additional enclave at the northern tip of the Musandam Peninsula which is separated from the rest of the country by the United Arab Emirates. Oman is a small country in two parts. It comprises a small mountainous area, overlooking the Strait of Hormuz, which controls the entrance to The Gulf, and the main part of the country, consisting of barren hills rising sharply behind a narrow coastal plain. Inland the hills extend into the unexplored Rub al Khali (The Empty Quarter) in Saudi Arabia.

Oman has very hot, dry summers and mild winters but there is high humidity along the coast. Some rainfall occurs during the winter months but amounts vary according to location. Natural vegetation, including the historically important frankincense trees in Dhofar, is able to grow in the non-desert regions. Wildlife species include a wide variety of birds and reptiles.

As a result of the extremely arid environment, less than one per cent of the country is cultivated, the main produce being dates and limes for export. The economy is almost entirely dependent on oil, which provides 90 per cent of its exports, although there are deposits of asbestos, copper and marble and a smelter at Sohar. Foreign workers make up over 15 per cent of the resident population. There are no political parties in Oman and the judicial system is centred on the law of Islam.

QUICK FACTS

Area: 309,500 square kilometres or 119,498 square miles
Population: 2,302,000
Capital: Muscat (Masqat)
Other towns: Salalah, Al Khaburah, Matrah
Form of government: Monarchy
Religions: Ibadi Islam, Sunni Islam
Currency: Rial Omani

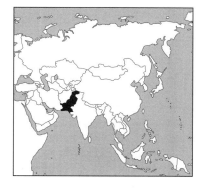

PAKISTAN, or the **ISLAMIC REPUBLIC OF PAKISTAN**, lies just north of the Tropic of Cancer and has the Arabian Sea as its southern border. The far north of Pakistan covers the disputed territory of Jammu and Kashmir which has been the cause of a serious conflict with India.

The Indus river system is the country's principal topographical feature. It splits the country into a highland region in the west and a lowland region in the east. The Indus enters the country in the northeast and is joined by four other major rivers, the Jelum, Cheenab, Ravi and Sutlej, which dominate the north central area before flowing southwestwards to the Arabian Sea. West of the Indus Valley lie the Baluchistan Highlands – an arid, rugged plateau interrupted by many mountain ranges which push southwards from the high Hindu Kush in the north. The north of Pakistan is dominated by the huge mountains of the Hindu Kush and the Karakorum range, containing K2 which, at 8,607 metres or 28,238 feet, is second in height only to Everest. In southeast Pakistan, the Thar Desert extends across the border into India.

QUICK FACTS

Area: 796,095 square kilometres or 307,374 square miles
Population: 134,146,000
Capital: Islamabad
Other major cities: Faisalabad, Hyderabad, Karachi,
Lahore, Rawalpindi
Form of government: Federal Islamic Republic
Religions: Sunni Islam, Shia Islam
Currency: Pakistan Rupee

A weak form of tropical monsoon climate occurs over most of the country and conditions in the north and west are arid. Temperatures are high everywhere in summer but winters are cold in the mountains. In most parts of the country, rainfall is light and falls in the summer months. Natural vegetation varies considerably from coniferous and evergreen forests to scrub and desert and there is a wide range of indigenous wildlife.

The alluvial plain of the Indus river system provides useful agricultural land but the cultivatable area is restricted because of waterlogging and saline soils. Most agriculture is subsistence, with wheat and rice as the main food crops and cotton and rice as the main cash crops. Pakistan's wide range of mineral resources has not been extensively developed and industry concentrates on food processing, textiles and consumer goods. Handicrafts include carpets and pottery. A lack of modern transport systems, due to the country's mountainous terrain, hinders further economic progress.

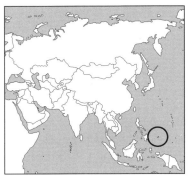

PALAU is a small republic in the Pacific Ocean, formerly called Belau or Beleu, which gained its independence from US trusteeship in 1994. It consists of a small number of volcanic islands and numerous coral atolls in the Caroline Group about 900 kilometres or 625 miles equidistant from New Guinea to the south and the Philippines to the west. A barrier reef to the west forms a large lagoon dotted with islands. Coral formations and marine life here are amongst the richest in the world. Most people live on Koror Island although eight other islands are inhabited – Babelthuap being the largest. Palau chose to become a republic in its own right when the Caroline Islands became part of the Federated States of Micronesia.

Farming and fishing provide a basic living and tourism is a growing export but the country remains very dependent on the USA for its economic survival.

PALESTINE is an ancient historic region on the eastern shore of the Mediterranean Sea, which is also known as 'The Holy Land' because of its symbolic importance for Christians, Jews and Muslims. It was part of the Ottoman Empire from the early part of the 16th century until 1917, when Palestine was captured by the British. In 1948, the UN partitioned the region between Jordan and the new state of Israel. This created hostility among Israel's Arab neighbours and Palestinians indigenous to the area, many of whom left. Since then, there has been a series of wars between the Arabs and Israelis and conflict between Israeli forces and the Palestine Liberation Organisation. The disputed territories are the West Bank, the Gaza Strip, the Golan Heights and Jerusalem. In 1994, limited autonomy of some of these disputed areas was granted to the appointed Palestinian National Authority and Israeli military forces began to withdraw from the area. However, the peace process has been compromised by ongoing violent conflict.

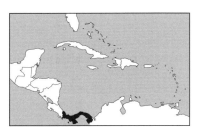

PANAMA is a narrow, S-shaped isthmus that links central America and South America. It is only about 177 kilometres or 110 miles across at its widest point. Most of the country is mountainous although the peaks are modest by central American standards. The climate is tropical with high temperatures throughout the year and only a short dry season from January to April. The economy depends on a wide variety of industries including the production of coffee, sugar cane, bananas, maize, beans, rice, some cattle ranching, fishing, timber production, manufacturing and oil refining. The economy is also heavily dependent on income from the Panama Canal which provides a route for ships between the Caribbean Sea, the Atlantic Ocean and the Pacific Ocean. The Canal has also ensured the strategic importance of Panama, particularly to its powerful neighbour, the USA.

PAPUA NEW GUINEA in the southwest Pacific, comprises the eastern half of the island of New Guinea and a number of archipelagoes and islands including New Britain, the Bismarck Archipelago and New Ireland. The other half of New Guinea is Irian Jaya, part of Indonesian territory. The main island has a mainly low-lying coast and southern half but from the centre to the north there are spectacular and rugged mountains which form the Highlands. The mountain chain extends for well over 1,000 kilometres or 621 miles and individual peaks and ridges are separated from each other by fertile valleys. Lower slopes are cloaked in dense tropical rain forests and the forbidding landscape has meant that many local tribes have remained isolated from each other and undiscovered for hundreds of years. The highest peak is Mount Wilhelm at 4,500 metres or 14,765 feet. Major rivers include the Fly, Purari, Sepic and Ramu. The climate is tropical with high temperatures and heavy rainfall.

Many of the smaller islands are volcanic in origin with dramatic mountains. Some volcanoes on the north coast and smaller islands are active. The rough and inaccessible countryside means travelling is difficult and in places road building is impossible. There are a modest number of roads but no rail system and a light plane is often the only mode of transport which can reach remote villages.

Subsistence farming is the main economic activity although some coffee, cocoa beans and copra are grown for cash. Timber is cut for export and fishing and fish processing industries are developing. The country's wildlife is plentiful and varied while the coastal waters support an abundance of sea life. Minerals such as copper, gold, silver and oil form the mainstay of the economy. The country still receives valuable aid from Australia from whom it gained its independence in 1975.

PARAGUAY is a small landlocked country in central South America. It is bordered by Bolivia, Brazil and Argentina and is divided into two distinct regions by the River Paraguay. Paraguay Occidental is the larger region to the west of the river. It consists of a marshy, alluvial plain which is also part of the Gran Chaco. In the south and east, much of this area is water-logged swamp but the land rises gradually and gives way to grassy areas and arid, scrub forest towards the northwestern border.

Paraguay Oriental lies to the east of the River Paraguay and consists mainly of an upland plateau called the Parana Plateau. Paraguay has a subtropical climate and much of the Oriental region is covered with thick forests containing numerous varieties of plants and animals. The River Parana itself flows through the plateau and forms the country's eastern and southern border, joining with the River Paraguay at the southwestern corner. Almost 95 per cent of the population live east of the river.

The western edge of the Parana Plateau falls away to form grass-covered hills before flattening down towards the valley of the River Paraguay. A third large river, the Pilcomayo, flows southwest, forming the border with Argentina. The country's capital, Asunción, is on this border at the confluence of the Pilcomayo and Paraguay rivers.

The country's economy is largely dependent upon agriculture with cotton, sugar cane, soya beans, cassava, wheat, bananas, oranges and sweet potatoes among the crops grown. Cattle, pigs, sheep and horses are reared in the grassland areas. Forestry and its products are also important to the country's economy but Paraguay lacks the mineral wealth of other South American countries. With three important rivers, the Paraguay, Parana and Pilcomayo, the country has many impressive waterfalls, such as the Guaira Falls. In cooperation with its neighbours, it has developed its potential for hydroelectric power to the full and is able to meet all its energy needs. Developed with Brazil and opened in 1991, the Itaipu Hydroelectric Dam on the (Alto) Parana river is the largest dam in the world. Other hydroelectric schemes include the Yacyreta Dam, developed with Argentina and opened in 1994.

QUICK FACTS

Area: 406,752 square kilometres or
    157,048 square miles
Population: 4,955,000
Capital: Asunción
Other major cities: Concepción, Ciudad del
    Este, Encarnación
Form of government: Republic
Religion: Roman Catholicism
Currency: Guaraní

PERU is located just south of the Equator, on the Pacific coast of South America. The country has four topographical regions that run largely north to south: the Costa, the high Sierra, the Montana and the Selva.

The Costa is a narrow, coastal belt that varies in width between about 56–160 kilometres or 35–100 miles. It is mainly a dry desert region except where it is traversed by rivers flowing westwards to the Pacific. The valleys of these rivers are cultivated for rice, cotton and sugar cane.

Behind the coastal belt, the land rises to the high Sierra of the Andes, whose main ranges are the Cordillera Occidental, the Cordillera Central and the Cordillera Oriental. This Sierra region has peaks that average 3,657 metres or 12,000 feet in height but it is also cut by steep-sided gorges interspersed with plateaux. Most of Peru's native Indian peoples live in this region. On the lower western slopes of the Andes, some cultivation is possible, notably maize and potatoes, and the higher regions provide grazing for llamas, alpacas, guanacos and vicunas.

On the eastern side of the Andes, lies the Montana region, an area of subtropical jungle and cloud forest that remains virtually impenetrable in some places. To the east and north, the land flattens to form the Selva, a part of the Amazon river basin covered with dense tropical jungle.

Most large-scale agriculture is in the oases and fertile, irrigated river valleys that cut across the coastal desert. Sugar and cotton are the main exports. Sheep, llamas, vicunas and alpacas are kept for wool. The fishing industry was once the largest in the world but recently the shoals have become depleted. Anchovies form the bulk of the catch and are used to make fish meal. Minerals, such as iron ore, silver, copper and lead as well as natural gas and petroleum, are extracted in large quantities and are an important part of the economy. Peru is not yet a fully industrialised country but the majority of its 22 million population have moved to urban areas in the hope of finding work and live there in extreme poverty. The economy in the late 1980s was damaged due to the declining value of exports, inflation, drought and guerrilla warfare which made the government introduce an austerity programme in the 1990s.

QUICK FACTS

Area: 1,285,216 square kilometres or
    496,225 square miles
Population: 25,015,000
Capital: Lima
Other major cities: Arequipa, Callao,
    Chiclayo, Cuzco, Trujillo
Form of government: Republic
Religion: Roman Catholicism
Currency: Nuevo Sol

QUICK FACTS

Area: 300,000 square kilometres or
115,831 square miles
Population: 71,899,000
Capital: Manila
Other cities: Cebu, Davao, Quezon City,
Zamboanga
Form of government: Republic
Religions: Sunni Islam, Roman Catholicism,
Animism
Currency: Philippine Peso

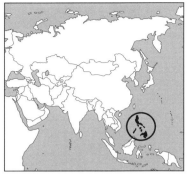

PHILIPPINES comprise a group of 7,107 islands and islets in the western Pacific which are scattered over a great area and form the northernmost group of the Malay Archipelago. There are four main groups: Luzon and Mindoro to the north, the Visayan Islands in the centre, Mindanao and the Sulu Archipelago in the south and Palawan in the southwest. Manila, the capital, is on Luzon. The great majority of the islands (6,647) are less than 2.6 square kilometres or 1 square mile in area and uninhabited and only 11 are of a large enough size to accommodate the bulk of the population. These are Luzon and Mindanao (the two largest islands), Mindoro, Samar, Masbate, Leyte, Cebu, Bohol, Negros, Panay and Palawan.

Most of the islands are mountainous with larger coastal or river valley plains occurring only in Luzon and Mindano. The Philippines are part of a chain of volcanic mountains and some 20 volcanoes are still active. The islands are also subject to fairly frequent earthquakes. Typhoons, which occasionally strike the Philippines from July to October, are another natural hazard.

Over a third of the islands are wooded and forests contain, among others, palms, rubber trees and banyan. There are many varieties of wild flowers and plants, such as orchids and the fibrous abaca or Manila hemp, from which Manila envelopes were originally made. Mammal species are poorly represented in the Philippines but there are a good number of birds and reptiles and abundant marine life, especially shellfish. Pearls, harvested from oysters found around the Sulu Archipelago, are highly prized on the world market. The islands have a tropical climate but are cooled by sea breezes on the windward coasts. The rainy season is from July to October with a distinct dry season between January and April and moderate rainfall in May and June and November and December.

Rice, cassava, sweet potatoes and maize are the main subsistence crops and coconuts, sugar cane, pineapples and bananas are grown for export. Agriculture employs around 42 per cent of the workforce. Fishing is of major importance and there are sponge fisheries on some of the islands. Mining is an important industry and its main products include gold, silver, nickel, copper and salt. Other prime industries include textiles, food processing, chemicals and electrical engineering.

QUICK FACTS

Area: 5 square kilometres or 2 square miles
Population: 54
Form of government: British Overseas
Territory
Religion: Seventh Day Adventism
Currency: New Zealand Dollar

PITCAIRN ISLANDS are a British overseas territory situated in the southeast Pacific Ocean. They are volcanic with high lava cliffs and rugged hills. The islanders are direct descendants of the HMS Bounty mutineers and their Tahitian wives. Subsistence agriculture produces a wide variety of tropical and subtropical crops but the sale of postage stamps is the country's main revenue earner.

QUICK FACTS

Area: 323,250 square kilometres or
124,808 square miles
Population: 38,628,000
Capital: Warsaw (Warszawa)
Other major cities: Gdansk, Kraków, Lódz,
Poznan, Wroclaw
Form of government: Republic
Religion: Roman Catholicism
Currency: Zloty

POLAND is situated on the North European Plain with a Baltic Sea coastline. It shares borders with Germany to the west, the Czech Republic and Slovakia to the south, Russia (Kaliningrad) to the north and Belarus and Ukraine to the east.

Poland consists mainly of lowlands. In the north, a low-lying narrow coastal plain of sandy beaches and dunes forms most of the Baltic Sea coastline. The low-lying wooded hills and valleys of the Baltic Heights region lie further inland and then come the extensive central lowlands, which are crossed by numerous rivers and streams in a series of shallow valleys. In the south, there is a region of uplands and valleys and then the land rises more steeply to form the Sudeten Mountains and ranges of the Carpathian Mountains. The Plain of Silesia lies in the southwest beyond the Sudeten Mountains.

Poland is drained by numerous rivers, most of which empty into the Baltic Sea. The most important are the Oder (Odra) in the west, which forms the boundary with Germany, and the Vistula (Wisla), which flows through Warsaw (Warszawa) and empties into the Gulf of Danzig (Zatoka Gdanska). Both have many important tributaries and, together with canals, they go to make up the country's 4,000 kilometres or 2,500 miles of navigable waterways. There are numerous freshwater lakes, particularly in the Masuria region in the northeast.

The northwestern coastal parts of Poland experience generally more temperate conditions than the inland areas where an eastern European climate prevails. Summers are generally warm to hot and winters can be very cold inland and in the mountains but are milder on the coast. Rainfall occurs throughout the year, particularly in summer, and there is considerable snowfall in the mountains.

Poland's capital and largest city is Warsaw, situated on the River Vistula in the central part of the country. About 62 per cent of Poles live in cities or towns, where problems caused by high levels of unemployment, social deprivation and poverty make life difficult for many people. Conditions were particularly difficult in the early 1990s during the transition to a market-style economy but are now slowly improving.

Agriculture plays an important part in the country's economy with almost two thirds of the land area suitable for farming and over one quarter of the labour force involved in agriculture. Most of the farms are small, family-owned enterprises but many are in need of modernisation and lack basic equipment. Crops grown include cereals (rye, wheat, oats, barley), vegetables (especially potatoes and sugar beet), fruits (blackcurrants, raspberries, strawberries and apples), tobacco and rapeseed. Livestock animals include cattle, sheep, pigs, poultry and horses. Poland's forests cover over a quarter of its land area and provide valuable timber resources for its paper and furniture industries.

There are both marine and freshwater fishing industries. The main species caught are cod, pollock, herring, sprat and squid. The freshwater fishing industry has declined in recent years because of a drop in fish stocks caused by pollution. Fish processing is quite an important industry and about 12 per cent of the total catch is exported. The country has valuable reserves of both hard coal and lignite, sulphur, copper, silver, iron ore, lead, zinc, magnesium, gypsum and rock salt but it has very little oil or natural gas so is heavily dependent upon imports to supply its domestic needs.

Industry and manufacturing were taken under state control during the communist years and expanded, with particular emphasis on iron and steel. These enterprises are now being returned to private ownership. Other industries include food processing, engineering, shipbuilding, textiles and chemicals. The country has serious environmental problems due to factors such as untreated sewage, industrial discharges, air pollution and soil contamination although some progress has been made to rectify matters. Tourism is of increasing importance to the country's economy.

PORTUGAL, in the southwest corner of Europe, makes up about 15 per cent of the Iberian Peninsula. It includes the island groups of Madeira and the Azores in the Atlantic. Lying to the west of Spain, mainland Portugal has a long Atlantic coastline and is mountainous only in the north, where the mountain ranges are lower extensions of those in Spain. The highest peaks occur north of the River Tejo (Tajo in Spain) in the Sierra da Estrela, reaching a height of 2,000 metres or 6,562 feet. South of the Tejo river, lie the wheat fields and cork plantations of the extensive plains of the Alenteja region. These are broken by a range of hills that divide them from the coastal plain of the Algarve, with its beautiful groves of almond, fig and olive trees.

The Iberian Peninsula is traversed by several large rivers that rise in Spain and flow on across Portugal, often through deep gorges cut through the rocks of the mountains. They flow along a generally westerly or southwesterly course before emptying into the Atlantic Ocean. The most important are the Tejo (Tajo in Spain), with Lisbon (Lisboa) at its mouth, the Douro (Duero), with Porto (Oporto) at its mouth, the Guadiana, which forms part of Portugal's southeastern border with Spain, and the Minho (Miño), which forms a part of the northwestern border. As agricultural methods remain traditional in many areas, wild animals and birds are able to flourish relatively undisturbed in Portugal.

The climate varies widely throughout the Iberian Peninsula. In general, appreciable amounts of rain and temperate conditions prevail in the coastal regions of the Bay of Biscay and Atlantic Ocean. In the Algarve, in the south of Portugal, summers are hot and dry and temperatures are usually mild in winter. The northeast of Portugal has hot summers and cold winters and is generally dry.

Manufacturing has assumed greater importance as the country slowly moves away from a largely agriculture-based economy but about 25 per cent of people are still engaged in farming and live outside the main cities in small rural villages. Crops include maize, wheat, rye, potatoes, tomatoes, olives and grapes (for wine-making). Portugal's Port and Madeira wine are renowned and the country is a main exporter of olive oil. Cattle, pigs, sheep and poultry are the most common farm animals.

Over two thirds of Portugal is wooded and the country is a leading exporter of cork oak and manufactures other wood products and paper. The long coastline has meant that Portuguese fishermen have always enjoyed ready access to the Atlantic fishing grounds. Many species are caught, including mackerel, cod, hake, sardines, halibut, tunny and anchovy. Shellfish are also harvested from the shallower, inshore waters, particularly oysters.

Portugal has some valuable mineral resources that were underdeveloped until comparatively recently. These include copper ores, wolframite (from which tungsten can be produced), coal (although of rather low quality), kaolin, gold, tin and iron ore. Food processing (especially sardines), textiles, paper and wood products, chemicals, ceramics, iron and steel, machinery, glass and fertilisers are among the items produced by the country's manufacturing industry. A petrochemical plant and oil refinery is located near Lisbon and hydroelectric power has been developed in recent years. Portugal is also renowned for certain high quality craft products, especially lace, pottery and tiles.

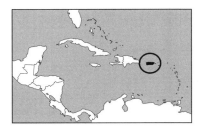

PUERTO RICO is the most easterly of the Greater Antilles Islands and lies in the Caribbean Sea between the Dominican Republic and the US Virgin Islands. It is a self-governing commonwealth in association with the USA and its people are US citizens. The country includes the main island, Puerto Rico, the two small islands of Vieques and Culebra and a fringe of smaller uninhabited islands. The climate is tropical, modified slightly by cooling sea breezes. The main mountains on Puerto Rico are the Cordillera Central, which reach 1,338 metres or 4,390 feet at the peak of Cerro de Punta. Dairy farming is the most important agricultural activity but the whole agricultural sector has been overtaken by industry in recent years. Tax relief and cheap labour encourage American businesses to be based in Puerto Rico. Products include textiles, clothing, electrical and electronic goods, plastics, pharmaceuticals and petrochemicals. Tourism is another developing industry and there is the prospect of oil exploration both on and offshore. San Juan is one of the largest and best natural harbours in the Caribbean.

QUICK FACTS

Area: 11,000 square kilometres or
    4,247 square miles
Population: 558,000
Capital: Doha (Ad Dawhah)
Form of government: Absolute Monarchy
Religion: Wahhabi Sunni Islam
Currency: Qatar Riyal

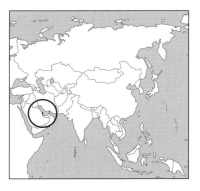

QATAR, an oil-rich emirate which lies halfway along the coast of The Gulf, is an absolute monarchy. A former British Protectorate, it became fully independent in 1971. It comprises a low barren peninsula and a few small islands. Apart from some low hills in the northwest, it consists of low-lying, arid, stony desert and salt flats. The climate is hot and uncomfortably humid in summer and the winters are mild with rain in the north (less than 127 millimetres or 5 inches a year). Vegetation and wildlife species are limited and adapted to desert conditions.

Most fresh water comes from natural springs and wells or from desalination plants. Some vegetables and fruit are grown but the herding of sheep, goats and some cattle is the main agricultural activity. The country is famous for its high quality camels. The discovery and exploitation of oil has resulted in a high standard of living for the people of Qatar with some of the revenue being used to build hospitals and a road system and to provide free education and medical care for its citizens. The Dukhan oil field has an expected life of 40 years and the reserves of natural gas are enormous. In order to diversify the economy, new manufacturing industries, such as iron and steel, cement, fertilisers and petrochemical plants, have been developed.

QUICK FACTS

Area: 2,510 square kilometres or
    969 square miles
Population: 664,000
Capital: St Denis
Form of government: French Overseas
    Department
Religion: Roman Catholicism
Currency: Franc

RÉUNION is a French overseas department in the Indian Ocean, south of Mauritius. The island is mountainous and has one active and several extinct volcanoes. Most people live on the coastal lowlands and the economy is dependent upon tourism and the production of rum, sugar, maize, potatoes, tobacco and vanilla. French aid is given to the country in return for its use as a French military base.

QUICK FACTS

Area: 238,391 square kilometres or
    92,043 square miles
Population: 22,520,000
Capital: Bucharest (Bucuresti)
Other major cities: Brasov, Constanta,
    Galati, Iasi, Timisoara, Craiova, Brâila,
    Arad, Ploiesti
Form of government: Republic
Religions: Romanian Orthodox, Roman
    Catholicism
Currency: Leu

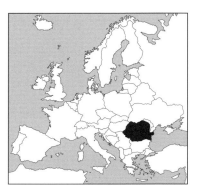

ROMANIA is located in southeast Europe and bordered by Ukraine, Moldova, Bulgaria, Yugoslavia (Serbia) and Hungary. In the southeast, the republic's coastline stretches for approximately 200 kilometres or 125 miles along the shores of the Black Sea. The Carpathian Mountains run through the north, east and centre of Romania and dominate most of the country. The Carpathians are geologically unstable and Romania periodically experiences severe earthquakes.

In the centre of the country, almost enclosed by the mountains, is Transylvania, a high and extensive plateau of uplands and forests. There is a continuation of the Hungarian Plain or Great Alföld in the west while further plains lie to the east, southeast and south of the mountains. The eastern region is called Moldavia and the southern area, Walachia. The southeastern region, bordering the Black Sea and containing the delta of the River Danube, is called Dobruja. Large areas of the steppe are highly fertile and intensively cultivated, particularly the 'black earth' soils in the west and central regions.

Alpine flowers and plants grow in the mountain pastures above the treeline while lower down there are coniferous forests, mainly of spruce and pine. At still lower levels, deciduous trees are able to grow and species include oak, birch, beech and alder. The natural vegetation of the Romanian plains is a mixture of woodland and steppe but this has been extensively cleared to provide land for farming.

The Danube, with its tributaries, is Romania's most important river. It forms part of the western border with Yugoslavia and most of the border with Bulgaria before turning north and then east to flow along the southern boundary with Ukraine. The delta of the Danube occupies the northeastern corner of the Dobruja region where there are also numerous lakes and lagoons. Many of Romania's other important rivers are connected to the Danube system, and these include the Mures, Olt, Jiu, Siret and the Prut, which forms the eastern border with Moldova.

Pollution, both of air and water, is a serious problem in parts of Romania, mostly as a legacy of industrial development during the communist era. Efforts are now being made to clean up the environment and reduce the amount of pollutants that are being released.

Romania was traditionally an agricultural country until after the Second World War when, during the communist period, the emphasis was on industrial development and farms were state-run or operated as collectives. During the 1990s, most farmland (about 43 per cent of the total land area) was returned to private ownership. The cultivated areas are mainly on the plains, particularly in the Danube river basin, and the most important crops are cereals (wheat, maize, barley, rye), some of which are exported, and sugar beet, vegetables (especially potatoes) and fruits. Orchards of fruit trees and vineyards for Romania's wine industry flourish on the more sheltered lower hill slopes. Wine is produced for export as well as for the domestic market. A variety of livestock animals are reared including cattle, pigs, sheep, poultry and horses. Horses are still used for work on many farms. Drought can severely affect agricultural production in Romania. Romania's extensive forests cover about 30 per cent of its land area, providing valuable timber that is harvested for construction purposes and used in paper and furniture manufacturing. The forests and the forestry industry are owned by the state. Romania has both a freshwater and offshore fishing industry although fish stocks have been affected by pollution in some areas. The fish that are harvested include herring, flounder, sturgeon and salmon and the main marine fishery is in the Atlantic Ocean. Sturgeon (for caviar) are caught in the Black Sea and Danube delta.

Romania has enjoyed the benefit of having considerable exploitable reserves of petroleum and natural gas although the former is now rapidly becoming exhausted. Processing of petroleum is carried out mainly in the city of Ploiesti. Other mineral reserves include coal, lignite, iron ore, lead, copper, aluminium (bauxite) and zinc. Electricity is generated from oil, coal, gas, hydroelectric and nuclear facilities and a small amount is exported. A large hydroelectric scheme, operated jointly with Yugoslavia, is centred on the Iron Gate, a deep gorge cut by the Danube in the border region between the two countries. The post-communist government has worked hard to bring about changes and improve the economy. The principal industries produce petroleum, gas, petrochemicals, cement, construction materials, iron and steel, machinery, vehicles, electrical equipment, textiles, furniture and wood products, clothing, footwear and processed foods.

RUSSIA or the **RUSSIAN FEDERATION** is the largest single country in the world extending into two continents and around almost half of the globe. Mainland Russia extends from the Gulf of Finland in the west to the shores of the Pacific Ocean in the east and from the Arctic Ocean in the north to the Caucasus in the south. Russian territory also includes several large islands and the enclave of Kaliningrad (bordering the Baltic Sea, Poland and Lithuania).

The Russian coastline is longer than that of any other country in the world. In the north, the coastline borders extensions of the Arctic Ocean namely, from west to east, the White Sea, Barents Sea, Kara Sea, Laptev Sea, East Siberian Sea, Chukchi Sea and Bering Strait. Russian islands include the Komandorskie Islands in the Bering Sea between the Aleutian Islands and the east coast of the Kamchatka Peninsula. The elongated Sakhalin Island (Ostrov Sahalin) lies in the Sea of Okhotsk, an extension of the Pacific Ocean which forms most of the coastline of eastern Russia. This island separates the Sea of Othotsk from the Sea of Japan which forms the coastline of southeast Russia. The Kuril Islands (Kurilskiye Ostrova) arch in a long chain from the southern tip of the Kamchatka Peninsula to just a few miles from the coast of Japan and form a barrier between the Sea of Okhotsk and the open waters of the Pacific Ocean. They are mainly volcanic mountains with 30 active volcanoes. The Russian coastline also borders the Sea of Azov, the Black Sea and the Caspian Sea. The Black Sea is a tideless sea with its sole outlet to the Mediterranean through the narrow Bosporus Strait. The Caspian Sea is a saline lake and the largest of its kind in the world. It is made salty by evaporation and the slow accumulation of minerals. It is the habitat of the sturgeon, the roe of which is the source of Russian caviar.

The Ural Mountains (Uralskiy Khrebet) divide the country into two unequal parts, the smaller European Russia in the west and Asian Russia in the east. Most of European Russia is an eroded, undulating plateau that is part of the North European Plain. It has been worn away by the action of ice, wind and water and, in general, does not exceed about 182 metres or 600 feet in height. Apart from the Ural Mountains and the Caucasus (Kavkaz) Mountains, the only other mountains in this region are to be found in the far northwest in the Kola Peninsula (Kol'skiy Poluostrov). The Urals form an ancient, eroded mountain chain which extends roughly 2,415 kilometres or 1,500 miles from north to south, from the Arctic coast to the border with Kazakhstan. The Caucasus Mountains belong to a different geological time period being much younger and situated in an active earthquake zone. The highest mountain in Europe, the extinct volcano, Mount Elbrus (5,642 metres or 18,510 feet), is located here.

There are several broad, marshy areas in European Russia, occurring mainly in the north and an extensive region of lakes in the northwest called the Great Lakes. The largest of these are Lake Lagoda (Ozero Ladozhskoye) north of St Petersburg and Lake Onega (Ozero Onezhskoye) slightly farther to the west. Both lakes and marshes are features of the last Ice Age and were left when the ice melted and retreated. Other glacial land forms include moraines (mounds of debris deposited by ice) and broad U-shaped valleys excavated by the glaciers which once covered the mountains.

The principal river system of European Russia is the Volga and its tributaries. The Volga is the longest river in Europe and flows for 3,692 kilometres or 2,293 miles, arising in the Valdai Hills northwest of Moscow and running east and south to its delta in the Caspian Sea. The Volga has several important tributaries and is dammed in places to create several large lakes. The river, which is navigable for almost its entire length, has been used as a means of trade and communication for many centuries and today is also a source of hydroelectric power. Other major rivers in the region include the Divina, Pecora and Don.

Asian Russia is essentially a vast plain which has a large central plateau and is fringed by mountains in the south, east and northeast. The huge, low-lying West Siberian Plain is a marshy, poorly drained area of swamps situated east of the Ural Mountains. It continues southwards to the border with Kazakhstan and also southeastwards, until the land begins to rise towards the southern mountains. In the east, the plain is interrupted by the great mass of the Central Siberian Plateau which varies in height between about 486–699 metres or 1,600–2,300 feet above sea level. It is an area of rolling uplands with deeply dissected river valleys and, in places, spectacular gorges eroded by the action of water on the surrounding rocks. The plain continues to the north of the plateau as the North Siberian Lowland and also to the east although here the land is slightly higher and less marshy. High mountain ranges in the northeastern corner of Kazakhstan and most of Mongolia continue across the southern border of Asian Russia.

QUICK FACTS

Area: 17,075,400 square kilometres or 6,592,850 square miles
Population: 146,100,000
Capital: Moscow (Moskva)
Other major cities: St Petersburg (Sankt Peterburg), Nizhniy Novgorod, Novosibirsk, Samara
Form of government: Republic
Religions: Russian Orthodox, Sunni Islam, Shia Islam, Roman Catholicism
Currency: Rouble

A broad swathe of the region is mountainous and the ranges include the Altai, Zapadnyy Sajan, Vostochny Sayan, Yablonovyy Khrebet and, in the east, the Stanovoy Khrebet. In the far southeast, flanking the Sea of Japan north of Vladivostok, there are the ranges of the Sikhote-Alin Khrebet. The mountains continue northwards to occupy most of Eastern Siberia. Asian Russia contains several rivers which flow for hundreds, if not thousands, of miles. They include the River Lena (4,271 kilometres or 2,653 miles), the Irtysh and Ob rivers (a collective length of 5,413 kilometres or 3,362 miles) and the River Yenisey (Enisej) which arises in Mongolia and flows northwards to empty into the Kara Sea. There are numerous lakes in the marshy, low-lying plains of Asian Russia but the most famous one of all, Lake Baikal, is located in the mountains of the south. Lake Baikal is the deepest freshwater lake in the world, filling a rift valley and having a greatest depth of about 1,737 metres or 5,714 feet and a surface area of about 31,491 square kilometres or 12,159 square miles. It has the largest collection of surface fresh water on the Earth and is the source of the River Angara, the main tributary of the River Yenisey.

Most people live in European Russia and three quarters of the population inhabit the cities or urban areas. Moscow is the capital and largest city but there are many other important cities and towns including St Petersburg (Sankt Peterburg), Nizhniy Novgorod, Novosibirsk and Samara.

Although there are considerable variations, most of Russia experiences very cold winters and summers which may be mild, warm or hot, depending upon the location and prevailing air masses. Rainfall is generally greatest in the summer months although, in most of the steppe region, conditions tend to be dry and this can pose problems for agriculture. Snow can accumulate in considerable amounts even at lower levels but is a particular hazard in the mountains.

Agricultural land is found in a broad band which includes most of European Russia but narrows eastwards across the Southern Urals and tapers out towards the southern mountains. Beyond this zone, agriculture is mainly restricted to some sheltered valleys and areas in the far southeast. Cultivation is only possible in the dry, southwestern parts of Russia with the aid of irrigation and elsewhere, in most of Siberia, the climate is too cold with frozen or waterlogged soil and a very short growing season. During the communist period, agriculture was centred on large-scale collective or state-run farms occupying thousands of acres. Today, most farms are still run as cooperatives although there are a growing number of privately owned holdings that are all on a much smaller scale.

Agriculture experienced a considerable decline in the early 1990s due to the economic uncertainties which accompanied the collapse of communism. Recovery has been slow but agriculture remains a very important part of the economy with most of the output being produced for the home market. Many different types of crops are grown including the major cereals (wheat, barley, rye, oats), rice, soya beans, millet, sunflower seeds, sugar beet, buckwheat, maize and vegetables, especially potatoes and peas. Fruits of various kinds, including apples, pears, cherries and grapes, are grown in suitable areas. Cattle, sheep, pigs, poultry and horses are all important livestock animals.

Forestry is of great importance to Russia which has about 50 per cent of the world's coniferous forests. Many of the more accessible forests containing the most valuable trees are located in European Russia and these have now been harvested quite heavily. Remaining forests are situated in the more remote areas of Siberia where the predominant species is larch. The remoteness of the terrain has meant that, so far, the forests have not been subjected to intensive felling. Cut timber is exported in addition to being used in other industries such as pulp and paper but the forestry industry as a whole was severely affected by the economic upheaval which accompanied the collapse of communism in the early 1990s. It seems likely that recovery will be slow but that forestry will remain an important sustainable natural resource if it is harvested carefully.

The Russian fishing industry is the fourth largest in the world. Fishing is of great importance to Russia not only for economic reasons but also because fish is a mainstay of the national diet. Traditional fishing was concentrated in the coastal waters of neighbouring seas and also in the inland seas, freshwater lakes and rivers. However, as fishing technology has improved, the Russian fleet has begun to venture farther afield and now operates in most international fishing grounds. In addition, fish farms have been established in suitable waters in order to increase the catch. The greatest proportion of the marine catch is harvested from the Pacific Ocean, the Sea of Okhotsk and the Bering Sea, with Vladivostok in the far southeast being the major fishing port. In the west, the main Baltic Sea fishing activities are centred off the Russian enclave of Kaliningrad and at St Petersburg on the Gulf of Finland.

Russia has valuable and abundant reserves of many precious mineral resources and these include both fossil fuels and metallic and precious ores. The most important regions are Siberia, the Ural Mountains and the Kola Peninsula and deposits include coal, oil, natural gas, iron ore, nickel, gold, tin, aluminium, diamonds, zinc, lead, manganese and copper. In general, oil and coal production have declined in the last decade, mainly because the more accessible reserves have become depleted. The costs of beginning new mining operations in the more remote areas of Siberia, where large fuel-bearing deposits are known to exist, have so far been prohibitive for the hard-pressed Russian economy.

Russia has a wide range of industries and manufacturing output. In the communist period, the emphasis was on heavy industrial development and engineering, including the production of all types of machinery, railway rolling stock, shipbuilding, agricultural equipment, military equipment and weapons, aerospace and space technology. Other areas of production now include computers and technological equipment, textiles, leather goods (especially footwear), electrical equipment and foods. Industries have also suffered greatly as a result of the break-up of the old USSR and the change over to a more Western-style economy. The Russian Federation is beset by many economic problems at the present time and recovery is likely to be a long and difficult process. However, one of the factors in the country's favour is its abundance of energy supplies, which include renewable sources and in particular hydroelectric power, and this should stand it in good stead in the years that lie ahead.

Russia, with its spectacular and varied scenery and rich cultural, historical and architectural heritage, has always been a magnet for tourists. The proportion of Western visitors has increased considerably since the collapse of communism and tourism provides a welcome boost for the economy.

RWANDA is a small, landlocked republic in the heart of central Africa. Its predominant feature is a central high plateau with an average elevation of about 2,000 metres or 6,000 feet from which streams flow west to the River Congo and east to the River Nile. High mountains rising to 4,507 metres or 14,786 feet dominate the north and west of the country sloping downwards to the basin of Lake Kivu on the western border. East of the plateau, the land drops downwards to a region of marshes and lakes surrounding the River Kagera.

Although lying in the tropical zone, temperatures in Rwanda are moderated by the high altitude of most of the country, making it warm rather than extremely hot. Temperatures can be cold in the mountains, especially at night and rainfall comes mainly in two rainy seasons. The country was once thickly forested but much of this has now been cleared and is confined to the mountain slopes. Wildlife is varied but it has suffered from the effects of human activity and warfare.

The soils are not fertile and subsistence agriculture dominates the economy. Staple food crops are sweet potatoes, cassava, dry beans, sorghum and potatoes. Soil erosion, overgrazing and drought leading to famine make the country very dependent on foreign aid. The main cash crops are arabic coffee, tea and pyrethrum. There are major reserves of natural gas under Lake Kivu in the west but these are largely unexploited.

Rwandans comprise three ethnic tribes: the Hutu (90 per cent), the Tutsi (9 per cent – a ruling, élite class) and the Twa (1 per cent – believed to be the original people of the country). The Hutu had settled in Rwanda by the Middle Ages but themselves came to be dominated by the Tutsi who conquered the region a short time later. Tutsi society was organised around an absolute monarch, supported by a number of subordinate chiefs, each in charge of a kingdom. It was a feudal system in which the Hutu eventually became a subclass of serfs – a situation which also existed in Burundi. In the late 19th century, Rwanda became a German-administered territory and was later passed to the Belgians after the First World War. Independence was gained in 1962 but throughout much of the 20th century there have been serious ethnic divisions between the Hutu and Tutsi and many acts of violence.

Matters came to a head once more in 1994 with the outbreak of a civil war which caused thousands of deaths (mainly of the Hutu) in a series of massacres. Many other Rwandans fled to neighbouring Zaire and Tanzania, living in refugee camps in appalling conditions which swamped the international community's capacity to help. Although the war is now over, Rwanda faces huge problems in restoring stability. The UN War Crimes Tribunal is seeking to bring to trial those accused of war crimes and, in the long term, progress depends upon the Rwandan people being able to coexist peacefully together.

ST HELENA is a volcanic island in the south Atlantic Ocean. It is a British overseas territory and an administrative centre for the islands of Tristan da Cunha to the south and Ascension Island to the north. The main exports are fish, timber and handicrafts.

ST KITTS AND NEVIS lies in the Leeward Islands in the eastern Caribbean Sea. In 1983, St Christopher (popularly known as St Kitts) and Nevis became a sovereign democratic federal state with the British monarch as head of state. St Kitts consists of three extinct volcanoes linked by a sandy isthmus to other volcanic remains in the south. Nevis, 3 kilometres or 2 miles south of St Kitts, is an extinct volcano. The highest point is Mount Liamuiga (1,315 metres or 4,314 feet) on St Kitts and the islands have a tropical climate. Around most of the island of St Kitts, sugar cane is grown on fertile soil covering the gentle slopes. Sugar is the chief export crop but market gardening and livestock are being expanded on the steeper slopes above the cane fields. Some vegetables, coconuts, fruits and cereals are grown. Industry includes sugar processing, brewing, distilling and bottling. St Kitts has a major tourist development at Frigate Bay and tourism is the country's main source of income.

ST LUCIA is one of the Windward Islands in the eastern Caribbean. It lies to the south of Martinique and to the north of St Vincent. It was controlled alternately by the French and the British for some 200 years before becoming fully independent in 1979. St Lucia is an island of extinct volcanoes and the highest peak is 950 metres or 3,117 feet. In the west, the twin volcanic peaks of Gros and Petit Piton rise directly from the sea to over 750 metres or 2,461 feet. The climate is tropical with a rainy season from May to August. The economy depends on the production of bananas and, to a lesser extent, coconuts and mangoes. Production, however, is often affected by hurricanes, drought and disease. There are some manufacturing industries, which produce clothing, cardboard boxes, plastics, electrical parts and drinks, and the country has two airports. Tourism is increasing in importance and the capital, Castries, is a popular calling point for cruise liners.

QUICK FACTS
Area: 26,338 square kilometres or 10,169 square miles
Population: 5,397,000
Capital: Kigali
Other major city: Butare
Form of government: Republic
Religions: Roman Catholicism, Animism
Currency: Rwanda Franc

QUICK FACTS
Area: 122 square kilometres or 47 square miles
Population: 5,157
Capital: Jamestown
Form of government: British Overseas Territory
Currency: St Helena Pound

QUICK FACTS
Area: 261 square kilometres or 101 square miles
Population: 41,000
Capital: Basseterre
Other major city: Charlestown
Form of government: Constitutional Monarchy
Religions: Anglicanism, Methodism
Currency: East Caribbean Dollar

QUICK FACTS
Area: 622 square kilometres or 240 square miles
Population: 144,000
Capital: Castries
Form of government: Constitutional Monarchy
Religion: Roman Catholicism
Currency: East Caribbean Dollar

Area: 388 square kilometres or
150 square miles
Population: 113,000
Capital: Kingstown
Form of government: Constitutional
Monarchy
Religions: Anglicanism, Methodism, Roman
Catholicism
Currency: East Caribbean Dollar

Area: 61 square kilometres or
24 square miles
Population: 25,000
Capital: San Marino
Other towns: Borgo Maggiore, Serravalle
Form of government: Republic
Religion: Roman Catholicism
Currency: Lira

Area: 964 square kilometres or
372 square miles
Population: 135,000
Capital: São Tomé
Form of government: Republic
Religion: Roman Catholicism
Currency: Dobra

Area: 2,149,690 square kilometres or
830,000 square miles
Population: 18,836,000
Capital: Riyadh (Ar Riyād)
Other major cities: Ad Dammam, Mecca
(Makkah), Jeddah(Jiddah), Medina (Al
Madinah)
Form of government: Monarchy
Religions: Sunni Islam, Shia Islam
Currency: Riyal

ST VINCENT AND THE GRENADINES achieved its independence from Britain in 1979. St Vincent is one of the Lesser Antilles Islands situated in the eastern Caribbean between St Lucia and Grenada. It is separated from Grenada by a chain of some 600 small islands known as the Grenadines, the northern islands of which form the other part of the country. The largest of these islands are Bequia, Mustique, Canouan, Mayreau and Union. St Vincent is mountainous and a chain of volcanoes runs up the middle of the island. One of these volcanoes, Soufrière (1,234 metres or 4,049 feet), is active and last erupted in 1979. The climate is tropical with very heavy rain in the mountains. Farming is the main occupation on the islands although tropical storms are always a threat to crops. Bananas for the UK are the main export and the country is the world's leading producer of arrowroot starch. There is little manufacturing and unemployment remains high. The government is trying to promote tourism.

SAN MARINO is a tiny landlocked republic in central Italy, lying in the eastern foothills of the Apennine Mountains. It is one of two small, independent enclaves (the Vatican City being the other), entirely surrounded by the country of Italy, which have survived from the time when the region consisted of autonomous city states. Given the turbulent history of Italy and the fact that the larger, more powerful states tended to swallow up the smaller ones, San Marino's survival is truly remarkable. According to legend, a stonecutter called Marinus, who had embraced Christianity, was forced to hide on San Marino's mountain because he was being persecuted for his faith. He founded a Christian community that survived and grew to become the independent state of San Marino, which was officially recognised as such by the Pope in 1291. Since 1862, as the rest of Italy moved towards unification, San Marino has maintained treaties of friendship with its all-embracing neighbour. The country's main topographical feature is the three-peaked, rugged hill of Mount Titano (739 metres or 2,424 feet). Wooded mountains and pasture land cluster around Mount Titano's limestone peaks. The country has a mild Mediterranean climate.

Most people work on the land or in forestry. Wheat, barley, maize, olives and vines are grown and dairy produce is the main agricultural export. The other main exports are wood machinery, chemicals, wine, textiles, tiles, varnishes and ceramics. Many tourists visit the country each year and much of the country's revenue comes from the sale of stamps, postcards, souvenirs and duty-free liquor. Italian currency is in general use but San Marino issues its own coins. In 1992, San Marino became a member of the United Nations and it is a full member of the Council of Europe.

SÃO TOMÉ AND PRÍNCIPE are volcanic islands which lie off the west coast of Africa. The islands were colonised in the 15th century by the Portuguese, who developed a slave trade, grew sugar cane and settled convicts and other exiles on the islands. São Tomé is covered in extinct volcanic cones reaching heights of 2,024 metres or 6,641 feet. The coastal areas are hot and humid. Príncipe is a craggy island lying to the northeast of São Tomé. The climate is tropical with heavy rainfall from October to May. Some 70 per cent of the workforce work on the land, mainly in state-owned cacao plantations which were nationalised in 1975 after independence. The other main agricultural products are coconuts, melons, copra, bananas and melons. Since the crops grown are primarily for export, about 90 per cent of the country's food has to be imported. Small manufacturing industries include food processing and timber products.

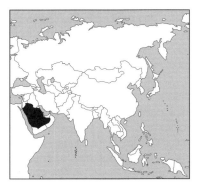

SAUDI ARABIA is a monarchy whose government and laws are based on the sacred teachings of Islam. The country plays a leading role in both the politics of the Middle East and on the international stage. It occupies over 80 per cent of the Arabian Peninsula and most of its territory is desert. The largest expanse of sand in the world, Rub al Khali (the Empty Quarter), is found in the southeast of the country – a harsh, uninhabited region hardly ever visited by man. Behind the narrow coastal plain of the Red Sea in the west, rise a series of plateaux and mountains which reach a height of over 3,000 metres or 9,800 feet in the south. Along The Gulf, there is a second fertile coastal plain and it is in this region (Al Ahsa) that Saudi Arabia's great reserves of oil are to be found.

The climate is hot and dry with light rainfall confined to the winter months making Saudi Arabia one of the world's most arid countries. Some areas have had no precipitation for years. Winter temperatures are generally mild to warm except in the mountains where there can be frost and snow. Temperatures may also plunge below freezing in the desert at night. Saudi Arabia has no permanent lakes, rivers or streams due to its extreme aridity and many watercourses or waddies are only briefly filled during the winter rains.

Oases are thinly distributed throughout the country in all but the Empty Quarter and provide much-needed cultivatable land and water. Natural vegetation is scarce but desert plants spring to life after rainfall and rapidly complete their life cycle. Oases provide another area where plants can grow but these are often under cultivation. Wildlife varies according to location (mountain or desert) but includes gazelle, antelope, ibex, wildcat, desert fox, hyena, various birds and reptiles.

The government has spent a considerable amount on reclamation of the desert for agriculture and the main products are dates, tomatoes, watermelons and wheat which are grown in the fertile land around the oases. Saudi Arabia exports wheat and shrimps and is self-sufficient in some dairy products. The country's prosperity, however, is based almost entirely on the exploitation of its vast reserves of oil and natural gas. Industries include petroleum refining and the production of petrochemicals and fertilisers. As a result of the Gulf War in 1990–91, 460 kilometres or 285 miles of the Saudi coastline has been polluted by oil, threatening desalination plants and damaging the wildlife of saltmarshes, mangrove forest and mudflats.

SENEGAL is a former French colony in west Africa which extends from the most western point in Africa, Cape Verde, to the border with Mali. The Republic of Senegal consists mainly of a low-lying savannah plain with higher ground only in the extreme southeast. The Fouta Djallon Mountains in the south rise to 1,515 metres or 4,971 feet. The River Senegal forms the northern boundary and other rivers further south include the Gambia.

Senegal has a hot, tropical climate. It is dry in the north but becomes progressively wetter towards the south. Natural vegetation in the north of the country consists of Sahel savannah grassland with some thorny bushes and isolated trees. Further south, with the greater amounts of rainfall, vegetation becomes much more lush and there are areas of dense tropical forest. Wildlife is very diverse and includes large grazing mammals, monkeys, hippopotamus, reptiles and many bird species. The most densely populated region is in the southwest.

Agriculture accounts for almost 80 per cent of the workforce. Peanuts and cotton are grown for export and millet, sugar cane, maize, rice and sorghum as subsistence crops. Increased production of crops such as rice and tomatoes has been encouraged in order for the country to achieve self-sufficiency in food. The country's economy is largely dependent on peanuts but there is a growing manufacturing sector including food processing and the production of cement, chemicals and tinned tuna. Tourism is also expanding.

QUICK FACTS

Area: 196,722 square kilometres or
   75,955 square miles
Population: 8,572,000
Capital: Dakar
Other major cities: Kaolack, Thiès, St Louis
Form of government: Republic
Religions: Sunni Islam, Roman Catholicism
Currency: CFA Franc

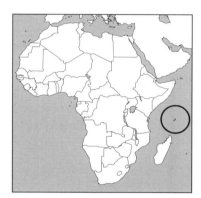

SEYCHELLES are a group of volcanic islands which lie in the western Indian Ocean about 1,200 kilometres or 746 miles from the coast of east Africa. About 40 of the islands are mountainous and consist of granite while just over 50 are coral islands. The climate is tropical maritime with heavy rain. About 90 per cent of the people live on the island of Mahé which is the site of the capital, Victoria. The staple foods are coconut, imported rice and fish and some fruits are grown for home consumption. Tourism accounts for about 90 per cent of the country's foreign exchange earnings and employs one third of the labour force. Export trade is based on petroleum (after importation), copra, cinnamon bark and fish. The only mineral resource is guano. The Seychelles were a one party socialist state until 1991, when a new constitution was introduced. The first free elections were held in 1993.

QUICK FACTS

Area: 455 square kilometres or
   175 square miles
Population: 76,000
Capital: Victoria
Form of government: Republic
Religion: Roman Catholicism
Currency: Seychelles Rupee

SIERRA LEONE, a republic on the Atlantic coast of west Africa, is bounded by Guinea to the north and east and by Liberia to the southwest. The country possesses a fine natural harbour where the capital and major port of Freetown is situated. A range of mountains, the Sierra Lyoa, rise above the capital on the Freetown Peninsula but, elsewhere, the coastal plain is up to 110 kilometres or 70 miles wide rising to a plateau and then mountains which are part of the Guinea Highlands Massif. The highest mountains are just under 2,000 metres or 6,562 feet. Eight rivers and many streams descend from the higher ground.

Natural vegetation varies from mangrove swamp near the coast to savannah in the north and jungle, containing commercially valuable trees such as palm, teak and mahogany, in the southeast. Wildlife includes varieties of monkey, chimpanzees, hippopotamus, tropical birds, porcupine, bushpig and reptiles. The climate is tropical with heavy rain during a rainy season lasting from May to November. During the dry season, an arid, dust-laden wind called the harmattan blows in from the Sahara Desert.

Most people are engaged in either agriculture or mining. The country's main food is rice and this is grown in the swamplands at the coast by the subsistence farmers. Other crops grown include sorghum, cassava, millet, sugar and peanuts. In the tropical forest areas, small plantations produce coffee, cocoa beans and palm oil. In the plateau region, much of the forest has been cleared to grow groundnuts.

Most of the country's revenue comes from agriculture and mining, principally of rutile, although bauxite is produced in significant quantities. Diamonds are also mined but in much-reduced amounts and there are deposits of iron ore with some gold and platinum. The country gained independence in 1961 and was troubled by political unrest and civil strife during the early 1990s.

QUICK FACTS

Area: 71,740 square kilometres or
   27,699 square miles
Population: 4,297,000
Capital: Freetown
Other city: Bo
Form of government: Republic
Religions: Animism, Sunni Islam,
   Christianity
Currency: Leone

SINGAPORE is a small island republic located just off the southern tip of the Malay Peninsula in southeast Asia. It became a British Crown Colony in 1867 and attained full independence in 1965 when it separated from Malaysia. One of the world's smallest yet most successful countries, it comprises the larger Singapore Island, much of which is occupied by the city of Singapore, and 58 islets. Singapore Island is mainly low-lying and flat but with small central hills rising to 176 metres or 577 feet. The natural tropical jungle and swamp vegetation has all been cleared apart from one small, hilly region and a considerable area of marshland has been drained and reclaimed. Singapore has a hot, humid, tropical climate with plenty of rainfall all year but especially between November and January.

A modern, vibrant and wealthy kingdom, Singapore's economy is based on trade which is carried out through the city of Singapore – one of the most important port cities in the world. Only 1.6 per cent of the land area is used for agriculture and most food is imported. The country's flourishing manufacturing industry also relies heavily on imports. Products traded in Singapore include machinery and appliances, petroleum, food and beverages, chemicals, transport equipment, clothes, paper products and printing. Shipbuilding, international banking and tourism are also important sources of foreign revenue.

SLOVAKIA, or the **SLOVAK REPUBLIC**, is a small, landlocked central European republic that came into being as a new independent nation in January 1993, following the dissolution of the 74-year-old Federal Republic of Czechoslovakia. It shares its borders with the Czech Republic to the northwest, Austria to the west, Hungary to the south, Poland to the north and Ukraine to the east. Slovakia is a mountainous country dominated by the Carpathian Mountains which occupy most of the northern and central part of the republic. There are several Carpathian ranges, the greatest of which are the High Tatry Mountains in which Slovakia's highest mountain, Gerlachovsky Stit (2,655 metres or 8,711 feet), is located. The Bohemian Forest stretches across the whole length of the southwestern border and is a region of mountains, hills and extensive woodlands. Flatter land is mainly confined to the Danubian lowland basin in the southwest but also to a strip along the southern border and in the east between the mountains. Elsewhere, river valleys and the foothills of the mountains provide some lower-lying land suitable for farming.

The main river is the Danube (Dunaj) which flows eastwards into Slovakia from Vienna and for a distance of about 120 kilometres or 75 miles forms the border with Hungary. There are many other rivers and numerous freshwater lakes in the mountains. Over a third of Slovakia is forested with firs and coniferous species on the higher slopes and deciduous trees, such as the oak and birch, at lower levels. Rare animals in the wilder mountain areas include bears and wolves although neither is commonly seen. A continental type of climate prevails with cold, dry winters and hot, moist summers. Snow persists in the mountains for much of the year.

As a legacy of the inefficient industrialisation of the old régime, Slovakia has many economic and environmental problems, in particular with atmospheric and water pollution. Nearly 60 per cent of the people live in urban areas, particularly in and around the capital, Bratislava. In the early 1990s, unemployment increased and inflation was high, resulting in a general lowering in people's standard of living.

Cultivatable land is located mainly in the Danubian lowlands, in the south and west and in the river valleys. Crops grown include cereals (wheat, corn and barley), sugar beet, vegetables, especially potatoes, grapes for wine and some tobacco. Pigs, cattle, sheep and poultry are among the animals reared.

Slovakia is heavily dependent upon imports of oil and gas to supply its energy needs and its petroleum industry. However, hydroelectric power schemes supply some of the country's energy needs. Slovakia has reserves of iron ore, lead, copper, manganese, zinc and lignite, all of which are exploited although many mines have closed in recent years.

During the communist years the country became an important producer of heavy machinery and iron and steel, much of it for armaments. Military equipment and weapons are still produced although on a lesser scale. Other manufactured goods include processed foods, dairy produce such as sheep's cheese, textiles, ceramics, chemicals and petroleum products and arts and crafts. There has been a slow change from state to private ownership of the old industries, many of which require substantial modernisation. Modern, privately owned service and technical companies have been formed since the collapse of communism. Tourism is a growing contributor to the economy. Visitors come to Slovakia for skiing and mountain pursuits as well as to enjoy the historical and cultural attractions of the towns and cities.

SLOVENIA is a small republic that prior to 1991 was part of the former Yugoslavia. It is a mountainous country, bounded by Croatia in the southwest, Hungary in the east, Austria in the north and Italy in the west. Slovenia also has a short stretch of coastline (45 kilometres or 28 miles) bordering the Adriatic Sea where the port of Koper is located. Most of Slovenia is situated in the Karst Plateau and in the Julian Alps (Julijske Alpe). The Julian Alps are in the densely forested, northwestern part of the country and contain the country's highest mountain, Mount Triglar (2,863 metres or 9,393 feet). The Julian Alps are renowned for their scenery and the Karst Plateau contains spectacular cave systems. Slovenia's capital, Ljubljana, is situated fairly centrally within the upland region.

About half of Slovenia's people live in small, rural farming communities where cattle and sheep rearing are particularly important but crops are also grown. The northeast of the republic is famous for its wine production. Mineral resources include oil, coal, lead, uranium and mercury, while iron, steel and aluminium are produced. Although farming and livestock raising are the chief occupations, Slovenia has also been successful in establishing many new light industries and this has given the country a well-balanced economic base for the future with unemployment lessening and industrial output increasing. Tourism is also an important industry.

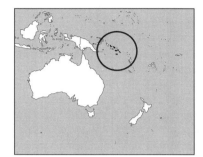

SOLOMON ISLANDS is an archipelago of several hundred islands in the southwest Pacific Ocean. Formerly a British Territory, the Solomon Islands became an independent state in 1978. The six main islands have rainforest-covered volcanic mountains, deep narrow valleys and coastal belts lined with coconut palms and ringed by reefs. Most of the smaller islands are coral atolls in various stages of development. The climate is equatorial. Most people live in small settlements along the coast of the large islands and rely on subsistence farming with taro, rice, bananas and yams being the main crops. Agriculture, including forestry and fisheries, is the mainstay of the economy and the main exports are timber, fish, copra and palm oil.

SOMALIA is a republic lying on the horn of Africa's east coast. It is bounded in the north by the Gulf of Aden and in the south and east by the Indian Ocean, and its neighbours are Djibouti, Ethiopia and Kenya.

Hills and mountains, rising between 915–2,135 metres or 3,000–7,000 feet, dominate the north behind the coastal plain, while most of the southern interior comprises a dry and rugged plateau. Two rivers, the Jubba and the Shebele, enter southern Somalia from Ethiopia and their valleys provide useful agricultural land.

The country has a hot, dry climate with lower temperatures in the northern mountains. There is a rainy season from April to June but amounts are slight in many areas. Natural vegetation consists of tough grasses, bushes and some trees, particularly on the mountain slopes and in the south. However, trees have been extensively cut down for fuel and this, coupled with overgrazing, has led to environmental degradation. Wildlife includes many of the larger African species such as lion, elephant, giraffe and zebra and various reptiles and snakes.

Most people live in the mountains and river valleys and there are a few towns on the coast. The country has little in the way of natural resources but there are deposits of copper, petroleum, iron, manganese and marble. Main exports are live animals, meat, hides and skins. A few large-scale banana plantations are found by the rivers. Civil war in the 1980s and early 1990s resulted in a huge loss of life and widespread famine. International UN peacekeeping forces were deployed and humanitarian aid given to try to avert a catastrophe but these withdrew in 1995. The situation remains unresolved although there has been some recovery in agriculture and food production.

SOUTH AFRICA is a republic that lies at the southern tip of the African continent. It has a huge coastline to the west on the Atlantic Ocean and to the east on the Indian Ocean, while Namibia, Botswana, Zimbabwe, Mozambique and Swaziland lie to the north of the country.

It is a diverse country with a wide variety of landscapes, rich animal and plant life and a vibrant economy which has developed after some difficult years because of apartheid and the consequent application of trade sanctions by most of the outside world. Most of the country lies below the Tropic of Capricorn and it can be divided into three main topographical regions - a vast central plateau, mountains, and a coastal belt. The high central plateau consists of grassland (the highveld) at heights of 1,200-1,800 metres or 3,937–5,905 feet and it is ringed to the east, south and west by escarpments which rise above the plains. The highveld ends to the north in a ridge called the Witwatersrand and beyond this is bushveld. The highest peaks can be found in the Drakensberg Mountains in the east which rise to just over 3,000 metres or 10,000 feet. The highest point is Champagne Castle at 3,375 metres or 11,072 feet. The coastal fringes merge into the plateau via steps or steep slopes and some smaller plateaux, such as the Great and Little Karoo.

Towering above Cape Town on the southern coast, is the famous Table Mountain, an isolated flat-topped peak reaching just under 1,100 metres or 3,609 feet. The major rivers are the Limpopo, the Vaal and the Orange, which is the longest. A rich mix of animal life and habitat means that South Africa can boast several national parks, the largest of which is the Kruger Park in the northeast of the country. The climate in South Africa is generally mild and temperate with plenty of sunshine and relatively low rainfall. This varies with latitude, distance from the sea and altitude.

Some 58 per cent of the total land area is used as natural pasture although soil erosion is a problem. The main crops grown are maize, sorghum, wheat, groundnuts and sugar cane. A drought-resistant variety of cotton is also now grown. South Africa's extraordinary mineral wealth, which includes gold, coal, copper, iron ore, manganese, diamonds and chrome ore, overshadows all its other natural resources. Since the dismantling of apartheid in 1994, the country has once again become an active and recognised member of the international community.

SPAIN is located in southwest Europe and occupies the greater part of the Iberian Peninsula, which it shares with Portugal. It includes the Balearic Islands (Islas Baleares) in the Mediterranean Sea, the Canary Islands (Islas Canarias) in the Atlantic Ocean and the enclaves of Ceuta and Melilla on the coast of Morocco in north Africa.

Spain is the second most mountainous country in Europe, surpassed only by Switzerland. Two of the principal mountain ranges are the Pyrenees, which rise to over 3,400 metres or 11,155 feet and stretch for about 400 kilometres or 250 miles along the border with France, and the Sierra Nevada, which run roughly west to east behind the Mediterranean coast. The dominant topographical feature of Spain is a large, elevated central plateau or tableland called the Meseta, which has an average height of 607 metres or 2,000 feet above sea level. This is dissected by a series of mountain ranges that include the Sierra de Guadarrama, the Montes de Toledo and the Sierra Morena. Further ranges occur in the northwest and west, notably the Montes de León and the Cordillera Cantabrica, behind the north coast of the Bay of Biscay.

The Iberian Peninsula is traversed by several large rivers that rise in Spain and flow on across Portugal, often through deep gorges cut through the rocks of the mountains. They flow along a generally westerly or southwesterly course before emptying into the Atlantic Ocean. The most important are the Tajo (Tejo in Portugal), the Duero (Douro) and the Guadiana, which forms part of Spain's southeastern border with Portugal, and also the Miño (Minho), which forms a part of the northwestern border with Portugal.

The climate varies widely throughout the Iberian Peninsula. In general, appreciable amounts of rain and temperate conditions prevail in the coastal regions of the Bay of Biscay and Atlantic Ocean. In the Mediterranean regions of Spain, summers are hot and dry and temperatures are usually mild in winter. The Meseta Plateau has hot summers and cold winters and is generally dry.

Because of the generally dry conditions, forests are not abundant in Spain and those that occur are usually found on the lower mountain slopes and in the wetter regions. Deciduous and evergreen oaks, cork oak, beech, poplar, chestnut, elm and pine trees can all be found and cork bark is harvested for commercial use. In the drier regions, scrub bushes, aromatic plants and grasses may be found and one particular type, Esparto Grass, is harvested for its fibre which can be used in paper-making. Considerable areas of Spain are relatively wild and uninhabited and are home to some of Europe's rarer animals. These include the wolf, lynx, wildcat, fox, mountain goat, wild boar, deer, eagle and other large birds of prey. Freshwater fish are abundant in rivers, streams and lakes.

Until the 1970s, Spain was a largely agricultural country and farming continues to be a significant factor in the country's economy. Technological advances and investments, particularly since the country joined the European Union, have brought about great improvements and modernisation. Cultivation depends upon locality and climate but grapes (for an important wine-producing industry), olives, cereals (wheat, maize, barley, rye, oats, rice), citrus and other fruits, almonds, vegetables and sugar beet are grown. In addition, cotton, flax, jute and hemp are grown to provide raw materials for the textile industry. Sheep are the most important animals to be reared, particularly the Merino breed, which is native to the country and produces a fine wool, but also pigs, goats, cattle and horses.

Spain formerly had one of the largest fishing fleets in the world and, although it is smaller today, the industry remains an important part of the economy. Tuna, sardines and hake are among the fish caught and also mussels and squid. The main forestry product is cork, of which Spain is a major world producer along with Portugal. Other timber operations are on a small scale and Spain has to import wood and pulp to supply its domestic needs.

Spain has poor fossil fuel reserves although it does produce some coal and petroleum. Electricity is generated from hydroelectric schemes, nuclear power and through the burning of (mainly imported) fossil fuels. Other minerals are well represented and the country has useful reserves of iron ore, copper, lead, zinc, mercury, gypsum and silver. Also, titanium, manganese, sulphur and potassium salts are worked in small amounts.

Traditional industries such as shipbuilding, iron and steel and textiles have declined although they still remain important. There has been considerable expansion in new areas such as information technology and electronics and also food processing, chemicals, shoes and clothing, cement production and manufacture of motor vehicles.

Spain welcomes numerous visitors each year who come to enjoy its Mediterranean coastal resorts, historical cities and the largely unspoiled towns and villages of the interior. The Balearic and Canary Islands, which belong to Spain, are also major tourist attractions and tourism makes a significant contribution to the country's economy.

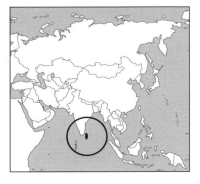

SRI LANKA is an island republic lying in the Indian Ocean just off the southeastern tip of India, from which it is separated by the Palk Strait. Until 1948, when it achieved independence, it was under British rule and called Ceylon. The shallow Palk Strait is itself interrupted by a chain of reefs and islands known as Adam's Bridge which almost links the two coasts. The island is dominated by a central, southern mass of hills and mountains (rising to a maximum height of 2,524 metres or 8,281 feet) which are surrounded by lower, coastal plains.

The climate is equatorial with a low annual temperature range but it is affected by both the northeast and southwest monsoons. Rainfall is heaviest in the southwest of the country while the north and east are relatively dry. Sri Lanka has a rich variety of natural vegetation including tropical jungles and forests containing many types of trees and plants such as mahogany, satinwood, ebony, cypress and eucalyptus. Equally varied are the wildlife species which include many rare animals and birds.

Agriculture engages 47 per cent of the work force and the main crops are tea, rubber, coconuts and rice. Some rice, sugar and wheat have to be imported. Sri Lanka has long been famous for its tea plantations and tea is one of the mainstays of the economy. Among the chief minerals mined and exported are precious and semiprecious stones. Graphite is also important. The main industries are food, beverages and tobacco, textiles, clothing and leather goods, chemicals and plastics. Attempts are being made to increase the revenue from tourism.

Politically, Sri Lanka has been afflicted by ethnic divisions between the Sinhalese and Tamils. In the 1980s, attempts by Tamil extremists to establish an independent homeland brought the northeast of the country to the brink of civil war and the situation remains extremely volatile.

SUDAN is the largest country in Africa, lying just south of the Tropic of Cancer in northeast Africa. The Republic of the Sudan divides naturally into three main regions: desert in the north; dry grasslands and steppe in the centre; and marshland, giving way to tropical forest and mountains, in the south. Cutting through the country and forming a fourth major and life-sustaining feature, is the great river system of the Nile. Its two main headwaters, the White Nile, arising in the south in Uganda, and the Blue Nile, which has its origins in the highlands of Ethiopia to the east, unite at Sudan's capital, Khartoum (El Khartum). Most of Sudan's cultivatable land lies in this central belt, south of Khartoum, between the Blue and White Nile rivers.

An upland mountainous plateau, the Janub Darfur (3,038 metres or 10,131 feet), rises near the border with Chad in the west, and the Red Sea Hills lie behind the coast in the northeast. Mountains straddle the border with Uganda and Sudan's highest peak, Kinyeti (3,187 metres or 10,456 feet), is located here. North of these mountains and traversed by the many tributaries of the White Nile, lies a huge area of marshland called the Sudd. This area is subjected to regular flooding and is the home of cattle-rearing tribal peoples.

Sudan has a hot, tropical climate with high temperatures in summer and cooler ones experienced only in the desert on winter nights. There is virtually no rainfall in the desert regions of the north but amounts increase southwards, with a distinct summer rainy season from June to September in the equatorial regions of the south.

Natural vegetation varies from desert plants to steppe grasslands to tropical forests containing commercially valuable species such as castor oil plants, rubber, ebony and mahogany trees. Wildlife is equally varied and includes some of the large African mammals, reptiles, such as crocodiles, and many species of snake and tropical birds. Disease-bearing, biting insects such as the tsetse fly and mosquito are a threat to human health in some areas.

Sudan is an agricultural country and subsistence farming accounts for 80 per cent of production. Livestock is also raised. Cotton is farmed commercially and accounts for about two thirds of Sudan's exports. Sudan is the world's greatest source of gum arabic which is used in medicines, perfumes, processed foods and inks. Other forest products are tannin, beeswax, senna and timber. Due to the combination of ongoing civil war and drought, Sudan has a large foreign debt estimated to be three times its gross national product.

SURINAME, formerly Dutch Guiana, is a republic in northeast South America, bordered to the west by Guyana, to the east by French Guiana and to the south by Brazil. The country, formerly a Dutch colony, declared independence in 1975. Suriname, which nowhere exceeds 80 kilometres or 50 miles in width, is primarily a country of upland plateaux and highlands that are covered with forests and traversed by numerous rivers and streams, many of which are important navigable waterways. The mangrove swamps of the coastal plain give way inland to a strip of sandy savannah. The central area is occupied by a low plateau region with savannah and forest. In the south, the land becomes mountainous and is covered with tropical jungles. The climate is tropical with heavy rainfall mainly from December to April.

Agriculture remains fairly underdeveloped. Crops cultivated include rice, bananas, citrus fruits, sugar cane, coffee and cacao. Molasses and rum are produced along with some manufactured goods and there is an important coastal shrimp fishery. Suriname's economy is based on the mining of bauxite, which accounts for 80 per cent of its exports, and on the production of alumina and aluminium. The country has important mineral reserves of iron ore, nickel, copper, platinum and gold. Suriname's natural resources also include oil and timber, and forestry is an expanding industry. However, the country is politically unstable and in need of financial aid to develop its resources.

SWAZILAND is a landlocked hilly country almost entirely within the borders of the Republic of South Africa but with a short border in the east with Mozambique. The mountains in the west of the country rise to almost 2,000 metres or 6,562 feet then descend in steps of savanna toward hilly country in the east. The climate is subtropical moderated by altitude. The land between 400–850 metres or 1,312–2,789 feet is planted with orange groves and pineapple fields, while on the lower land sugar cane flourishes under irrigation.

Most of the population work on the land raising livestock or growing crops such as cotton, maize and fruits. Forestry is an important industry with production centred mainly on pine since it matures extremely quickly due to Swaziland's climate. Coal is mined and also asbestos although in lessening amounts due to its associated health risks. Manufacturing includes fertilisers, textiles, leather and tableware. Tourism is a growing industry, with the country's game reserves, spas and casinos proving popular destinations for visitors.

SWEDEN is a constitutional monarchy which occupies the larger and longer eastern section of the Scandinavian Peninsula. It is bordered by Norway in the west and northwest and Finland in the northeast, while its eastern and southern boundary is formed by its long coastline which extends for a distance of some 7,520 kilometres or 4,700 miles. In the south and southeast, the coastline borders the Baltic Sea and it is here that the Swedish islands of Oland and Gotland are located. In the north-east, the coastline borders the Gulf of Bothnia, an arm of the Baltic Sea, while in the far southwest the narrow Öresund separates Sweden from the Danish island of Sjælland. The remaining part of Sweden's coastline borders the Kattegat and Skagerrak, which are extensions of the North Sea. Apart from the larger inhabited islands of Oland and Gotland, many thousands of small islets line Sweden's western coast, particularly in the region of Stockholm.

Sweden is less mountainous than neighbouring Norway although the great mountain ranges that are such a dominant feature of the Scandinavian Peninsula extend across much of Sweden's western boundary. The highest mountains are in the north of the country, with Mount Kebhekaise (2,111 metres or 6,926 feet) reaching the greatest elevation. Glaciers occur at some of the higher levels. East of the mountains, there is a plateau region with the land sloping gradually eastwards towards the sea. The southern part of Sweden consists mainly of lowland plains interrupted only by an isolated upland region, called the Smaland Highlands, which reaches a height of 380 metres or 1,250 feet. In the far south and southeast, there is a low-lying area called the Plain of Skane or Scania. Most of the population live in southern Sweden, the great majority in cities, towns or urban areas.

Among the most striking features of the Swedish landscape are the numerous lakes, numbering more than 96,000, which are a relic of the last Ice Age. In the lowland areas in the east and south, many lakes were left when the ice retreated and the largest of these are Mälaren near Stockholm, Vättern to the south and Vänern. The country is crossed by numerous rivers and streams, the largest of which are used as a source of hydroelectric power. They include the Torne, Skellefte, Osterdal and Ume. Sweden is also fortunate in retaining many of its natural forests, which extend over about 60 per cent of the country. These are mainly of conifers that grow below the treeline in all but the far north and south of the country, the main species being pine and spruce. At higher levels, there are some scrub birch and willow trees that give way to moorland vegetation and then bare rock on the high mountain summits. The far north of Sweden lies within the Arctic Circle and contains the Swedish part of Lapland. Here, there are no trees but an Arctic/tundra type of vegetation with lichens and mosses and specialised plants that are adapted to a short growing season. In the south, which is a region of farmland interspersed with woodland areas, deciduous trees are able to grow although some of the wooded areas have been cleared for farming.

The climate is relatively moderate in view of the northerly position of Sweden with considerable variations between north and south. In the south, the Gulf Stream and prevailing westerly winds have an ameliorating effect on temperatures but, farther north, the mountains, higher altitudes and proximity to the Arctic Circle block these influences. In winter, Sweden is affected by cold air from Russia and the east and temperatures, even in the south, are often below freezing. The northern part of the country within the Arctic Circle experiences two months of perpetual daylight in the summer and a similar period of continual darkness in the winter, with these effects gradually lessening towards the south. Because of its position on the eastern side of the peninsula's mountains, precipitation is moderate in Sweden, except in the southwest and in the mountain regions, and rainfall is greatest in late summer and early autumn. There is considerable snowfall in winter, particularly at higher altitudes.

Swedes take pride in the natural beauty of their country and are a very environmentally conscious people. Of considerable concern is the fact that a proportion of Sweden's lakes and forests have been affected by acid rain caused by industrial pollution generated in the British Isles. Also, algal blooms off the southwestern North Sea coastline and the decimation of the seal population by a virus have been cause for further alarm. Environmental concerns are high on the agenda of the Swedish government. The country intends to close its nuclear power stations and is actively engaged in the research and development of renewable energy sources.

The best soils and most favourable conditions for agriculture are found in the south of Sweden. Most agricultural production is for the home market and Sweden is more or less self-sufficient in dairy products, grains and vegetables. Livestock rearing, particularly for the production of dairy produce, is the most important aspect of farming. The principal animals are cattle, pigs, poultry and sheep. Mink are also reared for their fur. Fields are intensively fertilised and cultivated to produce a range of different crops that include cereals (wheat, oats, barley, rye), sugar beet and vegetables, especially potatoes.

Sweden makes full use of its extensive forests to produce large quantities of cut timber for export and as a basis for its wood pulp and paper industries. Most of the mills are located on the coast of the Gulf of Bothnia and lumber is extracted from forests on the mountain slopes, with rivers being used for transport and as a source of hydroelectric power.

Sweden has an important marine fishing industry that supplies the domestic market. The most important species is herring but mackerel, cod, sprats and sea trout are also caught. Göteborg is the principal fishing port. In addition, there is a variety of freshwater species in good numbers in Sweden's lakes and rivers.

Sweden lacks oil or coal reserves and is particularly dependent upon imported petroleum but it has fully exploited its potential for hydroelectric power, which supplies about 47 per cent of the country's electricity needs. A further 40 per cent is provided by nuclear power, although the plan is to phase this out gradually. Iron ore, uranium, silver, lead, copper, gold and zinc are among the minerals that are extracted. Manufactured goods include paper, furniture, wood products, iron and steel, machine products, vehicles and vehicle parts, electrical goods, chemicals and textiles, as well as fine crafts such as glassware, ceramics, silverware and items made from stainless steel.

Sweden attracts many tourists each year and the country's excellent road, rail, canal and ferry networks make it easy for visitors to travel to even the more remote parts of the country.

SWITZERLAND is a landlocked country in central Europe, sharing its borders with France, Italy, Austria, Liechtenstein and Germany. It is dominated by the Alps, which occupy over 60 per cent of the total land area. A second lower mountain range, the Jura Mountains, occurs in the west of the country. These two main east–west mountain chains are divided by the Rhine and Rhone rivers and between them lies a plateau region at a height of about 396 metres or 1,300 feet above sea level. Switzerland has many spectacular lakes, most of them nestling at the foot of the mountains and some quite large. They include Lake Geneva (Lac Léman), Lake Lugano and Lake Constance, which straddle neighbouring borders, and Lake Lucerne, Lake Zurich, Lake Neuchâtel and Lake Thunersee. Northern Switzerland is the industrial part of the country and where its most important cities are located. The climate is either continental or mountain-type. Summers are generally warm and winters cold and both are affected by altitude.

Coniferous forests cover the lower mountain slopes while deciduous trees flourish in the valley bottoms and around the lakes. In all, about a quarter of the total land area is forested, and timber is a valuable natural resource although some woodlands have been adversely affected by air pollution. Above the tree line, alpine flowers grow in spring and summer in high meadows that traditionally provide summer grazing for cattle, goats and sheep.

Much of Switzerland is unsuitable for agriculture, however, and most farms are fairly small, family-run enterprises that receive government subsidies. Cattle, sheep, goats, pigs and poultry are reared and grapes, apples, barley, potatoes, wheat and sugar beet are among the fruits and crops grown. Dairy products, particularly chocolate and Emmenthal and Gruyère cheese, are valuable export products. The grapes are used to produce about 125 million litres or 33 million gallons of wine each year. Freshwater fish, particularly salmon and trout, are abundant in Switzerland's lakes, rivers and streams and are harvested annually.

Switzerland has few mineral resources but its lakes and rivers enable it to generate abundant hydroelectric power. Most raw materials and food have to be imported. Switzerland is an affluent country whose people enjoy a high standard of living. It is renowned for the excellent quality of its manufacturing, particularly of watches and clocks, precision tools and machines and engineering products. Pharmaceuticals, textiles, handcrafted products, service industries and tourism are other important areas of the economy. It is as the premier centre for international banking, however, that Switzerland is perhaps most respected and renowned, with Zürich being the main city involved in this activity.

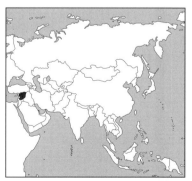

SYRIA, or the **SYRIAN ARAB REPUBLIC**, as it is officially called, is a country in southwest Asia which borders on the Mediterranean Sea in the west. Much of the country consists of arid plateau lands and plains which grade into desert in the southeast. There is a narrow, fertile coastal plain alongside the Mediterranean shore but this soon gives way to a belt of hills running north to south which rise to form the higher Anti-Lebanon Mountains extending across the border with Lebanon. The River Euphrates enters the country from Turkey in the northwest and flows southeastwards into Iraq, while a second major river, the Orontes, flows northwards from the Anti-Lebanon Mountains across western Syria.

The country experiences hot, dry summers and fairly cold winters with light to moderate rainfall. The coastal region has a more pleasant climate with mild, moist winters but most of Syria suffers from water shortages. Natural vegetation is fairly sparse, consisting of low bushes and thin grasses but with forests of Aleppo pine, oak and firs on the slopes of the mountains. There are relatively few mammal species but their number include porcupine, deer and wildcat. The desert regions have specialised wildlife, such as reptiles, which have adapted to the harsh conditions.

Agriculture employs some 20 per cent of the workforce. Sheep, goats and cattle are raised and cotton, barley, wheat, tobacco, grapes, olives and vegetables are grown although some land is unused due to lack of irrigation. Syria's resources include oil, hydroelectric power and fertile land. Reserves of oil are small compared to neighbouring Iraq but there is enough to make the country self-sufficient and provide three quarters of the nation's export earnings. Manufacturing industries such as textiles, leather, chemicals and cement have developed rapidly in the last 20 years with the country's craftsmen producing fine rugs and silk brocades. Foreign revenue is gained from tourism and also from countries who pipe oil through Syria. The country is dependent on the main Arab oil-producing countries for aid.

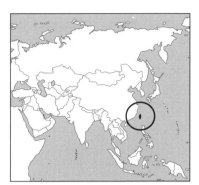

TAIWAN, REPUBLIC OF CHINA, was formerly known to the West by its Portuguese name of Formosa, 'Beautiful Island'. It is the largest of a group of islands located in the Pacific Ocean about 161 kilometres or 100 miles off the southeast coast of mainland China, across the Taiwan Strait. Taiwan's independence, resulting from the island's seizure by nationalists in 1949, is not fully accepted internationally and China lays claim to the territory. An additional 78 islands make up Taiwan province, including those called the Pescadores ('Fishermen's Islands') by the Portuguese but known as Penghu to the Chinese. Other islands, such as Quemoy (Jinmen) and Maju, lie closer to the coast of the mainland.

Mountains dominate the island covering three quarters of the land area and absent only from western, coastal regions. Most of the mountains are high with more than 60 peaks attaining heights of 3,040 metres or 10,000 feet. However, the highest of all is the Jade Mountain (Yu Shan) which stands at 3,940 metres or 12,960 feet high. The mountain slopes are mostly covered with coniferous trees (cedar, pine, larch) at higher levels and broadleaved evergreen species (Chinese cork oak and camphor) at lower levels. A variety of wildlife is indigenous to Taiwan but many species are now confined to remote mountain regions where there is less disturbance from humans. Their number include the Formosan black bear, Formosan sambar, sika and Chinese Muntjac deer, Formosan rock monkey, green turtle, Taipei tree turtle, Formosan salamander, black-faced spoonbill and Formosan landlocked salmon.

The climate of the island is subtropical with hot, wet summers and mild winters. About 20 million people, almost all of whom are Chinese, live on the island of Taiwan and the population density is high. The capital and largest city is T'aipei. Low-lying land in the west of Taiwan is fertile and heavily cultivated with a variety of crops including rice, sugar cane, tea, coffee, cashew nuts, sweet potatoes, bananas, pineapples, tobacco, cotton, sisal and cloves. Forestry is carried out in Taiwan to supply a plywood industry and numerous fish species are harvested from the surrounding seas, providing an important food source.

Taiwan's relatively few resources include gas, marble, limestone and small coal deposits. Taiwan is a major international trading nation based on its broad range of manufactured goods and has some of the most successful export-processing zones in the world, accommodating both domestic and overseas companies. Exports include 'high tech' goods, machinery, electronics, textiles, footwear, toys and sporting goods.

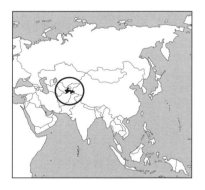

TAJIKISTAN is a republic of the former USSR, which declared itself independent in 1991. This central Asian country is bounded by China in the east, Afghanistan to the south, Uzbekistan to the west and Kyrgyzstan to the north. It also includes the autonomous region of Gorno-Badakh Shan. The southeast is occupied by the Pamir Mountains, whose snow-capped peaks dominate the country. More than half the country lies over 3,000 metres or 9,840 feet. Pastoral farming of cattle, sheep, horses and goats is important. Some yaks are kept in the higher regions. The lowland areas are irrigated so that cotton, mulberry trees, fruit, wheat and vegetables can be grown. The Amudarya river is used to produce hydroelectric power for industries such as cotton and silk processing. The republic is rich in deposits of coal, lead, zinc, oil and uranium, which were previously exploited. There has been a continuing civil war in which tens of thousands of people have been killed or made homeless.

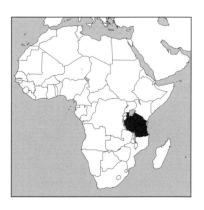

TANZANIA, a republic on the east coast of central southern Africa, comprises a large mainland area and the islands of Pemba and Zanzibar. Tanzania lies east of the Democratic Republic of Congo and Zambia, south of Kenya and north of Mozambique with the Indian Ocean in the east. The mainland consists mostly of coastal plains, a central plateau rising to high grasslands and mountain ranges and the eastern branch of the Great Rift Valley. The coastal strip is rich in tropical vegetation while the other areas consist of savannah, semidesert and bush cover. The climate is very varied and is controlled largely by altitude and distance from the sea. The coast is hot and humid, the central plateau drier and the mountains semitemperate.

Some 80 per cent of Tanzanians make a living from the land,

QUICK FACTS

Area: 35,742 square kilometres or
  13,800 square miles
Population: 21,854,273
Capital: T'ai-pei
Other major cities: Kao-hsiung, T'ai-nan,
  Chang-hua, Chi-lung
Form of government: Republic
Religions: Taoism, Buddhism, Christianity
Currency: New Taiwan Dollar

QUICK FACTS

Area: 143,100 square kilometres or
  55,251 square miles
Population: 5,919,000
Capital: Dushanbe
Other major city: Khujand
Form of government: Republic
Religion: Shia Islam
Currency: Tajik Rouble

QUICK FACTS

Area: 938,000 square kilometres or
  362,162 square miles
Population: 30,799,100
Capital: Dodoma
Other towns: Dar es Salaam, Zanzibar,
  Mwanza, Tanga
Form of government: Republic
Religions: Sunni Islam, Roman Catholicism,
  Anglicanism, Hinduism
Currency: Tanzanian Shilling

producing corn, cassava, millet, rice, plantains and sorghum for home consumption. Cash crops include cotton, tobacco, tea, sisal, cashews and coffee. Fishing is an important activity, particularly in inland waters. Pemba and Zanzibar produce the bulk of the world's cloves. Diamond mining is an important industry and there are also sizeable deposits of iron ore, coal and tin. Although Tanzania is one of the poorest countries in the world, it has a wealth of natural wonders, such as the Serengeti Plain and its wildlife, the Ngorongoro Crater, Mount Kilimanjaro and the Olduvai Gorge, where fossil fragments of early humans have been found, all of which attract large numbers of tourists, making a significant contribution to the country's economy.

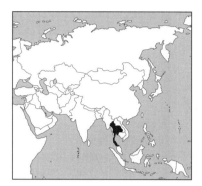

THAILAND, formerly known as Siam, is a constitutional monarchy located in southeast Asia and the only country in the region to have escaped being made into a European colony (although it was occupied by Japanese troops during World War II). It is a tropical country of mountains and jungles, rainforests and green plains. Central Thailand consists of the densely populated, fertile plain and valley of the country's principal river, the Chao Phraya. The mountainous Isthmus of Kra joins southern Thailand to Malaysia and the country has an extensive coastline surrounding the Gulf of Thailand (South China Sea). Thailand has a tropical climate with heavy monsoon rains from June to October, a cool season from November to February and a hot season from March to May.

The natural vegetation of the coastal region is tropical forest which is home to a variety of animals including tiger, leopard, Asian rhinoceros, gibbon, water buffalo, crocodile, snakes and birds. As in other parts of southeast Asia, elephants are used as work animals, particularly in the northern, upland forests where commercially valuable trees such as teak are extracted. Buddhism is the principal religion. Followed by 95 per cent of the population, it exerts a strong influence on everyday life.

Thailand is rich in many natural resources, such as mineral deposits of gold, coal, lead and precious stones, with rich soils, extensive areas of tropical forests and natural gas offshore. The central plain of Thailand contains vast expanses of paddy fields which grow enough rice to rank Thailand as one of the world's leading producers. The narrow southern peninsula is very wet and it is here that rubber is produced. Other crops grown are cassava, maize, pineapples and sugar cane. Fishing is an increasingly important industry with prawns being sold for export.

TOGO is a tiny republic with a narrow coastal plain on the Gulf of Guinea in west Africa. It is a narrow 'fingerlike' country, pushing inland and north-wards from the Gulf of Guinea and sandwiched between Ghana and Benin.

The country nowhere exceeds 125 kilometres or 75 miles in width and extends for about 500 kilometres or 312 miles from north to south. The main feature is a central range of low mountains, the Togo Highlands (700–986 metres or 2,300–3,235 feet), which extend northeast–southwest. High plateaux, mainly in the more southerly ranges, are heavily forested with teak, mahogany and bamboo. Northeast of these, lie the Oti plateau and plain which is covered by savannah grassland and drained by the Oti river. There is a region of coastal marshes and lagoons with thick mangrove forest in the south and an area of tropical jungle in the southwest. Beyond this to the north, savannah grassland is the main type of vegetation.

Wildlife species are varied and include birds, monkeys, snakes, crocodiles, hippopotamus, antelope and lion. Togo has a tropical climate with a major rainy season from March to July and a minor one from October to November. The north is affected by the dry harmattan wind from the Sahara during December and January. Over 80 per cent of the population is involved in subsistence farming with yams, cassava, sorghum and millet as the principal crops. Minerals, particularly phosphates, are now the main export earners along with raw cotton, coffee, cocoa beans, cement and palm kernels.

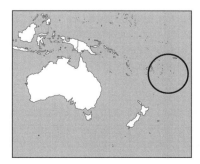

TONGA is situated about 20° south of the Equator and just west of the International Date Line in the Pacific Ocean. It comprises a low limestone chain of islands in the east and a higher volcanic chain in the west. There are 170 islands but only about 40 of them are inhabited. The climate is warm with heavy rainfall and destructive cyclones are likely to occur every few years. The government owns all the land and males can rent an allotment for growing food. Yams, cassava and taro are grown as sub-sistence crops while fish from the sea supplement the islanders' diet. Pumpkins, bananas, vanilla and coconuts are exported. The main industry is coconut processing. About 70 per cent of the workforce is occupied in either fishing or agriculture while many Tongans are employed overseas. Tourism, foreign aid (from countries such as the UK, Australia and New Zealand) and the income sent home from overseas workers all contribute to the country's economy.

QUICK FACTS

Area: 5,130 square kilometres or
   1,981 square miles
Population: 1,297,000
Capital: Port of Spain
Other towns: San Fernando, Arima
Form of government: Republic
Religions: Roman Catholicism, Hinduism,
   Anglicanism, Sunni Islam
Currency: Trinidad and Tobago Dollar

QUICK FACTS

Area: 162,155 square kilometres or
   62,592 square miles
Population: 9,092,000
Capital: Tunis
Other major cities: Sfax, Bizerte, Sousse
Form of government: Republic
Religion: Sunni Islam
Currency: Dinar

QUICK FACTS

Area: 774,815 square kilometres or
   299,158 square miles
Population: 62,697,000
Capital: Ankara
Other major cities: Istanbul, Izmir, Adana,
   Bursa
Form of government: Republic
Religion: Sunni Islam
Currency: Turkish Lira

TRINIDAD AND TOBAGO forms the third largest British Commonwealth country in the West Indies. The islands, situated off the Orinoco Delta in northeastern Venezuela, are the most southerly of the Lesser Antilles group. Trinidad consists of a mountainous range in the north and undulating plains in the south. It has a huge, asphalt-producing lake, Pitch Lake, which is approximately 42 hectares or 104 acres in size. Tobago is actually a mountain that is about 550 metres or 1,800 feet above sea level at its peak. The climate is tropical with little variation in temperature throughout the year and a rainy season from June to December. Trinidad is one of the oldest oil-producing countries in the world. Output is small but provides 90 per cent of Trinidad's exports. Sugar cane, cocoa beans, citrus fruits, vegetables and rubber trees are grown for export but imports of food now account for 10 per cent of total imports. Tobago depends mainly on tourism for revenue. A slump in the economy in the 1980s and early 1990s saw widespread unemployment but economic growth has improved in recent times.

TUNISIA is a country in north Africa which lies on the south coast of the Mediterranean Sea. It is bounded by Algeria to the west and Libya to the south. Several islands, notably Djerba and Kerkennah, lie near the shore. Northern Tunisia consists of hills, plains and valleys. Inland, the foothills of the Atlas Mountains project into the northwestern part of the country, rising from 610–1,520 metres or 2,000–5,000 feet. To the south and southeast, the land descends to a region of salt lakes and salt pans (called chotts), some of which lie below sea level. Beyond these, are the fringes of the Sahara Desert, occupying two fifths of the country's total land area. Fertile, cultivatable valleys and plains occur in the north and along the coast although output is regulated by fluctuations in water supply. These regions also support a variety of vegetation including woodlands and grasslands which are inhabited by a number of wildlife species. Desert animals include reptiles such as horned vipers and cobras.

The northern coastal regions have a Mediterranean-type climate of hot summers and mild winters with moderate rainfall. Conditions are much hotter and drier in the south with very little rainfall in the desert regions. Agriculture produces wheat, barley, olives, grapes, tomatoes, dates, vegetables and citrus fruits and a growing fishing industry produces mainly pilchards, sardines and tuna. About 26 per cent of the workforce is engaged in these two occupations but overall there is a general lack of employment. The mainstays of Tunisia's modern economy are oil from the Sahara, phosphates, natural gas and tourism on the Mediterranean coast.

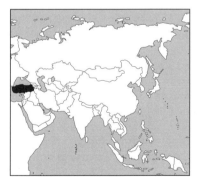

TURKEY spans the continents of Europe and Asia and guards the sea passage between the Mediterranean Sea and the Black Sea. The modern republic of Turkey came into being in 1923 following the collapse of the Ottoman Empire and the Turkish War of Independence (1918–23).

European Turkey, known as Thrace, is a fairly small, fertile area comprising some 3 per cent of the total area of the country. It is separated from the much larger region of Asiatic Turkey, known as Anatolia, by the narrow straits of the Bosporus (Istanbul Bogazi), the Dardanelles and the intervening, broader Sea of Marmara (Marmara Denizi).

Asiatic Turkey is bordered to the north by the Pontine Mountains (Kuzey Anadolu Daglari) and to the south by the Taurus Mountains (Toros Daglari). It is largely a region of plateaux, highlands and rugged mountains dominated by a central plateau. The highest mountains are in the east and the greatest of them is Mount Ararat (Agn Dagi) at 5,165 metres or 16,854 feet. According to the Biblical account, Noah's ark made landfall after the Great Flood on the summit of Mount Ararat. The two great rivers, the Tigris and Euphrates, upon which the ancient civilisations of Mesopotamia to the south so much depended, both arise in eastern Turkey.

The Mediterranean and Aegean regions of Turkey have hot summers and mild winters during which most of the yearly rainfall is experienced. Along the Black Sea, temperatures are similar but it is generally more humid, with greater rainfall, while a continental climate prevails inland with hot, dry summers and cold winters.

Vegetation varies from Mediterranean-type bushes to olive and citrus trees, from woodlands along the shores of the Black Sea to grasslands and coniferous forests in upland regions inland. Alpine plants are found on the higher slopes and towards the summits of the mountains. Wildlife is well represented, especially in remote regions, and includes bears, wolves, jackals, wild cats, lesser-spotted eagles and falcons. Turkey occupies an area in which seismic activity is a frequent occurrence and the country regularly experiences devastating earthquakes.

Agriculture employs almost half the workforce with the major crops being wheat, sugar beet, cotton, tobacco, barley, fruit and nuts, maize and oil seeds. Turkey is self-sufficient in most foodstuffs. The country's main mineral resources are chromium, iron ore, coal, magnetite, zinc and lead. Hydroelectric power is supplied by the Tigris and Euphrates rivers. A growing manufacturing industry produces mainly processed foods, chrome, iron and steel, textiles, motor vehicles and Turkey's famous carpets. The country's main exports are chrome, iron and steel, cotton, dried fruits, tobacco, textiles, leather clothes and carpets. Tourism is a fast-developing industry and plays an increasingly important role in the economy.

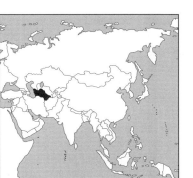

TURKMENISTAN, a central Asian republic of the former USSR, declared itself a republic in 1991. It is bounded in the west by the Caspian Sea, in the northwest by Kazakhstan, in the north and northeast by Uzbekistan, in the southeast by Afghanistan and in the southwest by Iran. All but about 20 per cent of the land consists of the arid 'black sands' of the Karakum Desert. In the central and northern part of the country lies the Adzhakya Basin where the land descends to some 80 metres or 265 feet below sea level. Hills and the Kopet Dag Mountains rise in the south and east and some peaks exceed 3,040 metres or 10,000 feet in height. These ranges extend for over 1,449 kilometres or 900 miles and straddle the border with Iran and Afghanistan.

The only major rivers are the Amudarya which forms the border with Uzbekistan and the Murgab which rises in Afghanistan. The Amudarya has been diverted to form the important Kara Kum Canal which is one of the longest canals in the world and provides irrigation and drinking water for the southeastern parts of the country. The Kara Kum is the largest of the many other canals which are vital for the country's existence.

Turkmenistan is an extremely dry country where surface water of any kind is scarce. The country has environmental problems relating to its basic lack of water and poor water quality. Most water is not fit to drink and this causes serious health problems. Also, the lack of water sometimes causes food shortages and infant mortality is high.

The climate of Turkmenistan is desert/continental with extremely hot summers, bitterly cold winters and very little precipitation. Most of the precipitation is in the mountains, falling as snow at higher levels. Conditions are pleasant to tolerable in spring and autumn but uncomfortable in summer and winter. In most of Turkmenistan, the natural vegetation consists of species adapted to desert or extremely arid conditions but greener plants are able to grow around the scattered oases which, for centuries, have been so important to the way of life of the nomadic Turkmen people. The republic is sparsely populated with about four and a half million inhabitants. The capital and largest city is Ashgabat ('City of Love').

Agriculture remains one of the most important activities in Turkmenistan and employs about 45 per cent of the workforce. Traditional breeding and rearing of livestock continues to be prominent and the most notable animals are the renowned Akhal-Tekke horses, cattle, camels and Karakul sheep. Under Russian rule, irrigation schemes were put in place for the growing of cotton and this remains the most important crop. In addition, wheat and a variety of fruits and vegetables are cultivated where conditions are suitable. Silkworms are raised for silk which is used in the traditional clothing still commonly worn by the Turkmen.

Turkmenistan has valuable and extensive reserves of oil, natural gas, sulphur, copper and coal. The mining and processing of fossil fuels are the principal industrial activities. Oil and natural gas have long been exported through Russian-controlled pipelines but since independence, Turkmenistan has been developing new partnerships with other countries for the exploitation of its fossil fuels. Other industries include food processing, cotton and textiles, especially silk but also wool for the manufacture of the traditionally patterned red carpets and rugs for which the Turkmen are renowned. These carpets are very much a part of the culture of the Turkmen as each tribe, in addition to having its own dialect, costume and jewellery, also has its own individual carpet styles and patterns. The rugs and carpets (called 'Bukhara rugs' simply because they were usually sold in Bukhara in neighbouring Uzbekistan) are produced for export and provide valuable revenue for the country. Other industries are mainly small-scale enterprises for local needs.

QUICK FACTS
Area: 488,100 square kilometres or
    188,456 square miles
Population: 4,569,000
Capital: Ashkhabad (Ashgabat)
Other cities: Chardzhou, Mary,
    Turkmenbashi
Form of government: Republic
Religion: Sunni Islam
Currency: Manat

TURKS AND CAICOS ISLANDS are two island groups which form the southeastern archipelago of the Bahamas in the Atlantic Ocean. Only six of the islands are inhabited. A British Crown Colony, the country's economy relies mainly on tourism and the export of shellfish to the UK and the USA. The climate is subtropical cooled by southeast trade winds which blow all the year round.

QUICK FACTS
Area: 430 square kilometres or
    166 square miles
Population: 23,000
Capital: Grand Turk
Form of government: British Crown Colony
Religion: Christianity
Currency: US Dollar

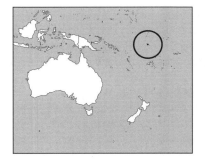

TUVALU, located just north of Fiji in the South Pacific, consists of nine coral atolls. The group was formerly known as the Ellice Islands and the main island and capital is Funafuti. Tuvalu became independent in 1978. The climate is tropical, with an annual average rainfall of 3,050 millimetres or 120 inches. Coconut palms are the main crop and fruit and vegetables are grown for local consumption. Sea fishing is extremely good and largely unexploited although licences have been granted to Japan, Taiwan and South Korea to fish the local waters. Revenue comes from copra, the country's only export product, foreign aid, the sale of elaborate postage stamps to philatelists and income sent home from Tuvaluans who work abroad. English and Tuvaluan are both spoken by the Polynesian population and there is an airport situated on Funafuti Atoll.

QUICK FACTS
Area: 26 square kilometres or
    10 square miles
Population: 10,000
Capital: Funafuti
Form of government: Constitutional
    Monarchy
Religion: Protestantism
Currency: Tuvalu Dollar/Australian Dollar

QUICK FACTS

Area: 241,038 square kilometres or
  93,065 square miles
Population: 19,848,000
Capital: Kampala
Other cities: Entebbe, Jinja, Soroti, Mbale
Form of government: Republic
Religions: Roman Catholicism,
  Protestantism, Animism, Sunni Islam
Currency: Uganda Shilling

UGANDA is a landlocked republic in east central Africa. The Equator runs through the south of the country and for the most part it is a richly fertile land, well-watered with a pleasant climate. Uganda is a country of plateaux, mountains, lakes and plains, presenting a great variety of landscapes and vegetation.

Almost half of Lake Victoria lies within Uganda's territory while the country's western border extends along the Great Rift Valley, in which lie Lake Albert and Lake Edward. Other smaller lakes include George, Kyoga and Kwania. The White Nile flows from Lake Victoria across the northern part of the country. High mountains, including Mount Elgon (an extinct volcano), arise on or near the eastern border, while the southwest is occupied by the massif of the snow-capped Ruwenzori Mountains which reach heights of 5,109 metres or 16,762 feet. Tropical forests clothe the lower slopes of the Ruwenzori Mountains, which also support tea plantations. Elsewhere, natural vegetation varies from savannah grassland to marshland and scrubland in the more arid areas. The lowlands around Lake Victoria, once forested, have now mostly been cleared for cultivation. A good variety of African wildlife can be found in Uganda including chimpanzee, lion, elephant, leopard and rhinoceros.

Thanks to its high elevation (averaging 900 metres or 3,000 feet above sea level) equatorial Uganda enjoys a relatively temperate climate with warm rather than extremely hot conditions. Temperatures on the mountain peaks are cold with snow. Elsewhere, rainfall is greatest in the south, becoming progressively lighter towards the north. Most people are engaged in agriculture and the main subsistence crops are plantains, cassava and sweet potatoes. Coffee is the main cash crop and accounts for over 90 per cent of the country's exports although cotton and tea are also important.

Forestry is also of importance and the major export is mahogany but the bulk of the country's wood is used as fuel. Virtually all of Uganda's power is produced by hydroelectricity with the plant on the Victoria Nile being of major importance. Copper mining used to be important but has declined and other mineral reserves have not yet been exploited. However, attempts are being made to expand the tea plantations in the west, to develop a copper mine and to introduce new industries to Kampala, the capital. Since 1986, Uganda has slowly been rebuilding its shattered economy in spite of some resurgence of earlier violence.

QUICK FACTS

Area: 603,700 square kilometres or
  233,090 square miles
Population: 51,094,000
Capital: Kiev (Kiyev)
Other major cities: Dnepropetrovsk,
  Donetsk, Khar'kov, Odessa, Lugansk,
  Sevastopol (in the Crimea)
Form of government: Republic
Religions: Eastern Orthodox, Roman
  Catholicism
Currency: Rouble

UKRAINE, formerly a Soviet socialist republic, declared itself independent of the former USSR in 1991. An eastern European country, it shares borders with Moldova, Hungary, Slovakia, Poland, Belarus and Russia. Within Europe, it is surpassed in size only by Russia. The Crimean Peninsula in the south (Crimea), which borders the Black Sea and the Sea of Azov, has been an autonomous region within the Ukraine since 1996.

Most of the country is an elevated continuation of the Russian plains with a swathe of higher ground in the west and a smaller area in the southeast around Donetsk. The Carpathian Mountains cut across the extreme western portion of the Ukraine. The Crimean Mountains occupy the extreme south of the peninsula. The plains are generally lower-lying in the east and south while in the northwest there is a region of marshes.

The Ukraine encompasses four vegetational zones which, from south to north, are Mediterranean, steppe, forest-steppe and forest. In the forest region, the main species are pine and oak in the northwest and spruce, pine and other conifers in the northeast. In the west, beech trees predominate but in the mixed area of forest and steppe various species including oak can be found. The steppe or grassland region for which the Ukraine is famous occupies the southern one third of the country, giving way to a narrow strip of Mediterranean-type vegetation in the Crimean Peninsula. Large areas of the steppe are highly fertile, particularly the 'black earth' soils in the west and central regions, and are intensively cultivated. The steppe becomes much drier in the far south and hence less useful for agriculture.

The Ukraine is drained by numerous rivers, mainly flowing southwards towards the Black Sea and the Sea of Azov, of which the most important is the Dnieper (Dnipro) and its tributaries. As well as being Europe's third longest river, it is an important source of hydroelectric power. The forests and steppes of the Ukraine provide a habitat for a variety of wild animals and birds. These include wolves, brown bears, lynx, elk, beavers, wild boar, musk rats, deer, eagles and vultures. Many colourful wild flowers adorn the valleys and hillsides of the Ukrainian countryside. People, wildlife and vegetation have, however, all suffered as a result of pollution problems that affect parts of the Ukraine. The most serious incident was the accident at the Chernobyl nuclear power plant in the northern part of the country which caused death and devastation over a wide area and the effects of which continue to be felt today.

Most of the Ukraine has a continental-type climate with warm or hot summers and cold winters, especially in the east. There are considerable variations, with conditions being generally more severe in the east and in the mountains. Rain is usually more frequent in summer and there may be considerable snowfall in parts of the Ukraine in the winter months. In the Crimea, a Mediterranean climate prevails with moist, mild winters and dry, hot summers. The capital and largest city is Kiev (Kiyev).

The Ukraine has some of the most fertile soils in Europe and has been called 'the bread basket of Europe' as a result. The main farming region is in the west and, during the period of union with Russia, the Ukraine was responsible for a quarter of all agricultural production. Wheat, corn, sugar beet, soya beans, potatoes, flax, tobacco and hops are the main crops, while cattle, pigs, sheep, oats, horses and poultry are the animals raised. Most farms are still organised as collective or state-run enterprises although some are privately owned. The Ukraine has valuable reserves of timber that can supply domestic needs and a small-scale fishing industry.

The Ukraine is rich in natural mineral resources, especially coal, iron ore and manganese. It has the highest production of manganese in the world and is the second greatest producer of iron ore. Industry and manufacturing were greatly developed during the Soviet period and the country became highly industrialised, especially in the east. Since the collapse of communism, however, many industries have struggled to compete on the world market and are greatly in need of reinvestment to modernise their technology and production methods. Industries and manufacturing include iron and metals, heavy machinery, chemicals, refining of oil and gas, and food processing.

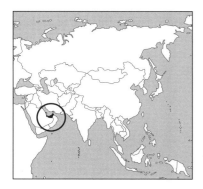

UNITED ARAB EMIRATES (UAE) is a federation of seven oil-rich sheikdoms located in The Gulf. The Emirates have loosely defined boundaries and occupy a region that was formerly known as the Pirate Coast and later, the Trucial States. The largest is Abu Dhabi while the others are Dubai (Dubayy), Sharjah, Ras al Khaymah, Al Fujayrah, Ajman and Umm al Qawayn. As well as its main coast on The Gulf, the country has a short coast on the Gulf of Oman. The land is mainly flat, sandy desert except to the north on the peninsula where the Hajar Mountains rise to 2,081 metres or 6,828 feet. The summers are hot and humid with temperatures reaching 49°C or 120°F but from October to May the weather is warm and sunny with pleasant, cool evenings. Rainfall is, at best, very light.

The only fertile areas are the Emirate of Ras al Khaymah, the coastal plain of Al Fujayrah and the oases. Vegetation and wildlife are limited and adapted to desert conditions with virtually no cultivation possible. Abu Dhabi and Dubai are the main industrial centres and, using their wealth from the oil industry, they are now diversifying industry by building aluminium smelters, cement factories and steel-rolling mills. Education is compulsory for 12 years from the age of six. Prior to the development of the oil industry, traditional occupations were pearl diving, growing dates, fishing and camel breeding. Dubai is the richest state in the world.

QUICK FACTS

Area: 83,600 square kilometres or
   32,278 square
miles
Population: 2,260,000
Capital: Abu Zabi (Abu Dhabi)
Other major cities: Dubai (Dubayy),
   Sharjah, Ras al
Khaymah
Form of government: Monarchy
Religion: Sunni Islam
Currency: Dirham

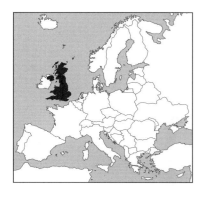

UNITED KINGDOM OF GREAT BRITAIN AND NORTHERN IRELAND (UK) is situated in northwest Europe and comprises England, Wales, Scotland and the six counties of Northern Ireland. The latter are an historical and political entity rather than a geographical one. Also belonging to the United Kingdom are several hundred islands, many of them off the Scottish coast and some of which are large and inhabited while others are little more than rocky outcrops battered by stormy seas.

England is bounded in the north by Scotland and to the west by the Irish Sea. The English Channel and the North Sea separate it from mainland Europe. It is a country of rolling, green hills and rich farmland but with large, industrialised cities. The most densely populated parts of England cover the major urban areas of Greater Manchester, Merseyside, South Yorkshire, Birmingham, West Midlands and Greater London. England is divided from Scotland in the north by a boundary that runs from the Solway Firth in the west to the mouth of the River Tweed in the east. In parts of England, intensive agricultural and urban developments have posed a threat to wildlife and some species are now quite rare. Principal industries include motor vehicles, electronics and electrical engineering, textiles and clothing, aircraft and consumer goods. Tourism is also an important industry.

The small kingdom of Wales, which includes the island of Anglesey, is largely a country of mountains, uplands and moorlands. The Cambrian Mountains, which extend from north to south, form the backbone of the country but others are the Snowdon range in the northwest and the Brecon Beacons in the southeast. The upland region of Blaenau Morganwy in the south is dissected by a series of steep-sided glaciated valleys, such as the Rhondda and Taff, where coal was discovered in the 19th century. Several fairly large rivers flow through Wales, including the Dee and the Wye. Most of Wales is relatively sparsely populated and there are significant areas of National Park so animals and birds in these areas are able to thrive fairly free from human interference. Nearly two thirds of the population live in the south, where industry developed around the coalfields. The coalfields of South Wales were once the most important coalfields in the world but coal mining has declined dramatically and light industry is now much more important. Tourism is one of Wales's chief industries thanks to the beautiful scenery of its National Parks and some flourishing resorts around the coast.

Scotland is largely a country of mountains, rolling hills and lochs and is renowned for the beauty of its scenery. It can be divided into three distinct topographical regions – the Southern Uplands, the Central Lowlands and the Highlands. The Highlands occupy about half the total land area and yet this is the most sparsely populated region. The Scottish coastline is deeply indented and there are hundreds of offshore islands. The largest island groups are the Western Isles, which consist of the Outer Hebrides and the Inner Hebrides off the west coast, and the Orkney and Shetland Islands in the far north. Another feature of the Scottish landscape is its numerous lochs, of which Loch Lomond and Loch Ness are the two most famous. The Central Lowlands are the industrial heartland of the country and its most densely populated area. It is here that the capital, Edinburgh, and the largest city, Glasgow, are situated.

Ireland is a large island located to the west of the British mainland, which is divided politically into two different

QUICK FACTS

Area: 244,101 square kilometres or
   94,248 square miles
Population: 58,784,000
Capital: London
Other major cities: Birmingham,
   Manchester, Glasgow,
Liverpool, Edinburgh, Cardiff, Belfast
Form of government: Constitutional
   Monarchy
Religions: Anglicanism, Roman Catholicism,
Presbyterianism, Methodism
Currency: Pound Sterling

unequal parts. These are Northern Ireland, Ulster or the Six Counties, which have been an integral part of the United Kingdom since 1920, and the Republic of Ireland or Éire, which comprises the majority of the country and has been independent since that date. Northern Ireland is situated in the northeastern part of the island. The central part of this area is low-lying and contains the largest lake in the British Isles, Lough Neagh. A second marshy area in the southwest contains two other sizeable lakes which are Lower and Upper Lough Erne. There are three upland areas – the mountains of Antrim in the northeast, the Mourne Mountains in the southeast, in which the region's highest peak, Slieve Donard (852 metres or 2,796 feet), is located and the Sperrin Mountains in the northwest.

The UK is primarily a highly urbanised industrial and commercial country. Only 2 per cent of the workforce are employed in agriculture and, although production is high thanks to modern machinery and scientific methods, the UK still has to import one third of its food. Major crops include barley, potatoes, sugar beet and wheat, while livestock raised includes sheep, cattle, pigs and poultry. Fishing is also an important industry. The UK has to import most of the materials it needs for its industries as it lacks natural resources apart from coal, iron ore, oil and natural gas. Many of the older industries, such as the coal, textiles and heavy engineering industries, have declined significantly in recent years while service industries play an increasingly large part in the UK's economy as does tourism.

QUICK FACTS

Area: 9,158,960 square kilometres or
   3,536,278 square miles
Population: 270,298,524
Capital: Washington DC
Other major cities: New York, Chicago,
   Detroit, Houston, Los Angeles,
   Philadelphia, San Diego,
   San Francisco
Form of government: Federal Republic
Religions: Protestantism, Roman
   Catholicism, Judaism, Eastern Orthodox
Currency: US Dollar

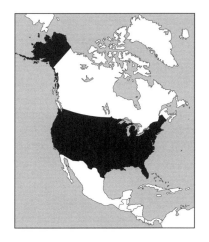

UNITED STATES OF AMERICA (USA) is the fourth largest country in the world. It stretches across central north America, from the Atlantic Ocean in the east to the Pacific Ocean in the west and from Canada in the north to Mexico and the Gulf of Mexico in the south. The world's most developed nation, the USA consists of fifty states, including outlying Alaska, northwest of Canada, and Hawaii in the Pacific Ocean. There are two great mountain ranges dominating the country, the Rocky Mountains in the west and the Appalachian Mountains in the east. Between them lie the Great Plains – fertile, flat lands crossed by many rivers. The largest of these rivers is the Mississippi and together with its main tributary, the Missouri, it is the third longest river in the world. The Great Lakes (Superior, Michigan, Huron, and Erie) in the northeast form part of the border with Canada.

The climate in the USA varies a great deal and weather patterns can shift quite dramatically mainly due to the westerly winds sweeping across the country from the Pacific. In the south, during the wetter summer months, one or two hurricanes a year can rage across Florida and, on a more local scale, tornadoes or 'twisters' can cut a narrow path of destruction in the wake of a spring or summer thunderstorm.

Although agricultural production is high, it employs only a small percentage of the work force primarily because of its advanced technology. The USA has a wealth of natural resources, including vast mineral reserves of oil, gas, coal, copper, lead, uranium, gold, tungsten and timber. Iron and steel, chemicals, motor vehicles, aircraft, telecommunications, information technology, electronics and textiles are the main industries. The USA is the richest and most powerful nation in the world.

QUICK FACTS

Area: 177,414 square kilometres or
   68,500 square miles
Population: 3,203,000
Capital: Montevideo
Other major cities: Salto, Melo
Form of government: Republic
Religions: Roman Catholicism,
   Protestantism
Currency: Peso Uruguayos

URUGUAY is one of the smallest countries in South America. It lies to the south of Brazil on the east coast of the continent and is bordered by the Uruguay river to the west, the waters of the Rio de la Plata to the south and the Atlantic Ocean to the east. Uruguay consists of low plains and plateaux. In the southeast, the grass-covered, rolling hills rise to 500 metres or 1,641 feet. There is a plateau with hills rising to 377 metres or 1,237 feet in the northwest and a second area of higher ground along the Atlantic coast with a maximum elevation of 501 metres or 1,645 feet. The Negro river, which rises in Brazil, crosses the country from northeast to southwest, dividing Uruguay almost into two halves. It joins with the Uruguay river in the southwest before opening out into the large Rio de la Plata estuary. The climate is temperate and rainfall plentiful, and the natural vegetation is prairie grassland. Some of the river valleys are wooded but Uruguay lacks the dense forests of other parts of South America.

About 90 per cent of the land is suitable for agriculture but only about 8 per cent is cultivated. The rest of the land is used to graze the vast herds of cattle and sheep which provide over 35 per cent of Uruguay's exports in the form of wool, hides and meat. Stock-rearing is the mainstay of Uruguay's economy. Cultivation is on a fairly small scale but crops grown include corn, wheat, rice, sugar cane, vegetables, potatoes, sorghum and fruits. Fishing is important to the economy. Uruguay has few mineral reserves and oil has to be imported. Hydroelectric power supplies most of Uruguay's energy needs. Industrial activities include cement and steel production, food processing and the manufacturing of textiles, aluminium, electrical goods and rubber.

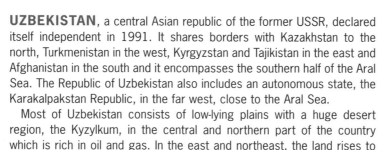

UZBEKISTAN, a central Asian republic of the former USSR, declared itself independent in 1991. It shares borders with Kazakhstan to the north, Turkmenistan in the west, Kyrgyzstan and Tajikistan in the east and Afghanistan in the south and it encompasses the southern half of the Aral Sea. The Republic of Uzbekistan also includes an autonomous state, the Karakalpakstan Republic, in the far west, close to the Aral Sea.

Most of Uzbekistan consists of low-lying plains with a huge desert region, the Kyzylkum, in the central and northern part of the country which is rich in oil and gas. In the east and northeast, the land rises to form the foothills and peaks of ranges that merge with the Pamirs and Tien Shan Mountains of Tajikistan and Kyrgyzstan. The greatest peaks in this region are about 4,560 metres or 15,000 feet high. The whole region is seismically active and subject to quite frequent earthquakes.

The Aral Sea is a large inland sea, which once straddled the border with Kazakhstan but now forms two separate seas, one in each country. The Amudarya, the principal river of Uzbekistan, flows into the southern part of the Aral Sea within the republic. The Syrdarya, which crosses northeastern Uzbekistan but flows for most of its course through Kazakhstan, enters the northern part of the Aral Sea in Kazakhstan. Both these rivers have had large volumes of water diverted for irrigation purposes and this has been responsible for the shrinkage of the Aral Sea. As a result, both the environment and health of the people, as well as the local economy, have been severely affected. Uzbekistan and neighbouring republics have now joined forces to try and repair some of the damage and to prevent the disappearance of the Aral Sea, which the gloomiest prediction states could occur in as little as 15 years.

Water is scarce in Uzbekistan and there is very little rainfall. As a result, many reservoirs and artificial lakes have been created, particularly in the east where most of the population is concentrated. The capital and largest city is Tashkent in the northeast of the country. The city of Tashkent had to be substantially rebuilt following an earthquake in 1966. A continental climate prevails with hot summers and cold winters and most precipitation occurs in the mountains, falling as snow at higher levels.

Agriculture is the most important economic activity but Uzbekistan still has to import many of its basic foodstuffs. The land is so dry that agriculture can only be practised in the east and northeast with the aid of irrigation. Cotton is the most abundant crop and much of it is exported but other crops include cereals (wheat and barley), rice and many different types of fruits and vegetables. Livestock includes goats and sheep, especially Karakul sheep, which are reared for their wool and meat. Another more unusual activity is the raising of silkworms for the production of silk. Forestry and fishing are small-scale activities in Uzbekistan.

Uzbekistan has valuable reserves of gold, oil and natural gas and produces farm machinery and equipment for the textile industry, aircraft, textiles, cotton, natural gas and gold. Economic growth has been checked by concerns about political instability. The country has significant reserves of natural gas but the oil industry is, as yet, underdeveloped and imports of fuel are needed for domestic and industrial use. Hydroelectric schemes supply much of the republic's electricity needs.

QUICK FACTS

Area: 447,400 square kilometres or
  172,742 square
miles
Population: 24,000,000
Capital: Tashkent
Other cities: Urgench, Nukus, Bukhara,
  Samarkand
Form of government: Republic
Religions: Sunni Islam, Eastern Orthodox
Currency: Soum

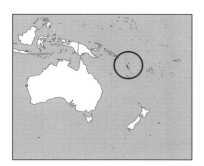

VANUATU is a parliamentary republic which has been independent since 1980. It was formerly known as the New Hebrides and jointly held by France and Great Britain. It consists of some 12 islands and 60 islets in the southwest Pacific Ocean. Most of the islands are volcanic and densely forested, with raised coral beaches and fringed by coral reefs. The climate is tropical. Cultivated land is generally restricted to the coastal plains and the main cash crops are copra, cocoa beans and coffee. Meat and fish are also exported and light industries include food processing and handicrafts for an increasing tourist industry.

QUICK FACTS

Area: 12,189 square kilometres or
  4,706 square miles
Population: 169,000
Capital: Vila
Form of government: Republic
Religion: Roman Catholicism
Currency: Vatu

VATICAN CITY lies in the heart of Rome in Italy on a low hill on the west bank of the River Tiber. It is the world's smallest independent state and headquarters of the Roman Catholic Church. The Vatican City was formally created in 1929 and is the last of the Papal States – territories that once came under the direct control of the Pope. It is a walled city with six gates and consists of the Vatican Palace, the Papal Gardens, St Peter's Square and St Peter's Basilica as well as museums, a library and about a thousand rooms and offices. The state has its own police, newspaper, telephone and telegraph services, coinage, stamps, radio station and railway station. The radio station, 'Radio Vaticana', broadcasts a service in 34 languages from transmitters within the Vatican City. Its outstanding museums have collections of antiquities and works by Italian masters and the Vatican Library's collection of ancient manuscripts is priceless. The Pope exercises sovereignty and has absolute legislative, executive and judicial powers.

QUICK FACTS

Area: 0.44 square kilometres or
  0.2 square miles
Population: 1000
Capital: Vatican City
Form of government: Papal Commission
Religion: Roman Catholicism
Currency: Vatican City Lira

VENEZUELA forms the northernmost crest of South America. Its northern coast lies along the Caribbean Sea and it is bounded to the west by Columbia, to the south by Brazil and to the southeast by Guyana.

Venezuela has four distinctive topographical regions. The Guiana Highlands in the south occupy about half the total land area while north of these are the plains known as the Llanos which are drained by the River Orinoco. This is a region of grassy plains used mainly for cattle ranching. The Maracaibo Lowlands occupy a basin in the northwest of the country and include Lake Maracaibo, which is an inlet of the Gulf of Venezuela or the Caribbean Sea. The lowlands separate two mountain ranges called the Venezuelan Highlands in the north and northwest, in which the country's highest peak, Pico Bolivar (5,007 metres or 16,427 feet), is situated.

Over two thirds of Venezuela is forested, providing a home for animals such as anacondas and boa constrictors, crocodiles, ocelots, jaguars, monkeys, bears, deer, sloths, armadillos and anteaters. The climate ranges from warm temperate to tropical and rainfall is plentiful.

Agricultural activities include cattle ranching in the Llanos area and the rearing of pigs, sheep and goats. Crops include sugar cane, bananas, oranges, maize, sorghum, rice, plantains, coffee and cassava. There are also rich fishing grounds around the coast and off Venezuela's 72 islands. Venezuela's economy is built on its oilfields located in the Maracaibo region but it also has other important mineral reserves including bauxite, iron ore, coal and precious metals and stones, such as gold, silver, platinum and diamonds.

VIETNAM is a long narrow socialist republic in southeast Asia which runs down the coast of the South China Sea. It incorporates the ancient kingdoms of Cochin China, Annam and Tonkin. The country was formerly divided into a Communist north and a republican, Western-backed south but the two parts were reunited in 1976 at the close of the Vietnam war. Vietnam has a varied topography which includes mountains, the broad plains of river deltas and coastal plains. It has a narrow central area which links broader plains centred on the Red (Hong) and Mekong rivers. This narrow zone, now known as Mien Trung, is hilly and makes communication between north and south difficult.

About two fifths of Vietnam is wooded, mainly with tropical rainforest which contains a variety of trees including the commercially important teak and bamboo. However, parts of Vietnam have suffered severe erosion due to the indiscriminate cutting of forest trees, mainly for fuel, and the government imposed a ban on timber exports in the early 1990s as a conservation measure. Vietnam has a wide range of wildlife including rare and spectacular Asian mammals such as the tiger, leopard and elephant. Several previously unknown mammal species have been discovered in the remoter regions of Vietnam in recent years, including a new type of okapi.

Hanoi, the former northern capital, is the capital of the unified Vietnam but Ho Chi Minh City (formerly Saigon) in the south remains the country's largest city. Most people live in rural villages on the plains. The climate is humid with tropical conditions in the south and subtropical in the north. The far north can be very cold when polar air blows over Asia.

Agriculture, fishing and forestry employ around 74 per cent of the workforce. The main crop is rice but cassava, maize and sweet potatoes are also grown for domestic consumption. Soya beans, tea, coffee and rubber are grown for export. Major industries are food processing and the manufacturing of textiles, cement, cotton and silk. Fishing, also an important export trade, is conducted mainly on the South China Sea although there is some fish farming in flooded inland areas. Vietnam is still recovering from the ravages of many wars this century and it remains underdeveloped as a result.

VIRGIN ISLANDS, BRITISH, lie at the northwestern end of the Lesser Antilles in the Caribbean Sea. They are a British overseas territory and comprise 4 large islands and 36 islets and cays. Only 16 of the islands are inhabited. Most of the islands are hilly and wooded and the climate is subtropical moderated by trade winds. Agriculture produces livestock, coconuts, sugar cane, fruit and vegetables, but only a small percentage of the land available to agriculture is under cultivation. The main industries are tourism, construction and rum distilling. Tourism is the mainstay of the economy.

VIRGIN ISLANDS, US, are part of the Virgin Islands group in the northwest of the Lesser Antilles in the Caribbean Sea. A self-governing US territory, this group of 50 volcanic islands are rugged and mountainous with a subtropical climate. Agriculture is not well developed and most of the country's food has to be imported. There is a small manufacturing industry but tourism is the mainstay of the economy with many cruise ships calling at the island of St Thomas in particular because of its natural deep-water harbour.

QUICK FACTS

Area: 347 square kilometres or
   134 square miles
Population: 106,000
Capital: Charlotte Amalie
Form of government: Self-governing US
   Territory
Religion: Protestantism
Currency: US Dollar

WALLIS AND FUTUNA ISLANDS, in the southern central Pacific Ocean, is the smallest and poorest of France's overseas territories. The two island groups are 230 kilometres or 142 miles apart. The climate is warm and humid with a cyclone season between October and March. Subsistence farming and fishing are the main activities with copra the only important export.

QUICK FACTS

Area: 200 square kilometres or 77 square
   miles
Population: 15,000
Capital: Mata-Uru
Form of government:
Religion: Roman Catholicism
Currency: Franc

WESTERN SAHARA is a disputed west African territory with a coastline on the Atlantic Ocean. A thinly populated desert country of rocky plains and plateaux with low hills in the extreme northeast, it is rich in phosphates. Formerly Spanish Sahara, the entire territory has been claimed and administered since 1979 by Morocco, against the wishes of an active separatist movement, the Frente Polisario. In 1976, they declared the existence of the Saharawi Arab Democratic Republic which has been recognised by most African and Arab states. Moroccan sovereignty is not universally recognised and the UN has attempted unsuccessfully to oversee a referendum to try and resolve the problem of who should have control of the country. It is a poor country with most of the population following a nomadic existence. The bulk of its food has to be imported. Phosphates comprise two thirds of the country's meagre exports.

QUICK FACTS

Area: 266,000 square kilometres or
   102,703 square miles
Population: 266,000
Capital: Laâyoune (El Aaiún)
Form of government: Republic (de facto
   controlled by Morocco)
Religion: Sunni Islam
Currency: Moroccan Dirham

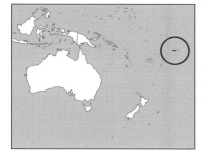

WESTERN SAMOA lies in the Polynesian sector of the Pacific Ocean about 720 kilometres or 447 miles northeast of Fiji. It consists of seven small islands and two larger volcanic islands, Savai'i and Upolu. Savai'i is largely covered with volcanic peaks and lava plateaux. Upolu is home to two thirds of the population and the capital, Apia. The climate is tropical with high temperatures and very heavy rainfall. The islands have been fought over by the Dutch, British, Germans and Americans but they now have the lifestyle of traditional Polynesians. Subsistence agriculture is the main activity and copra, cocoa beans and coconuts are the main exports. Many tourists visit the grave of the Scottish writer, Robert Louis Stevenson, who died here in 1894 and whose home is now the official home of the king. There are some light manufacturing industries, including clothing, and a car components factory which is now the largest private employer and a major export industry.

QUICK FACTS

Area: 2,831 square kilometres or
   1,093 square miles
Population: 166,000
Capital: Apia
Form of government: Constitutional
   Monarchy
Religion: Protestantism
Currency: Tala

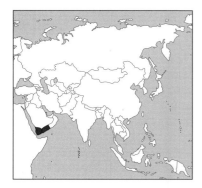

YEMEN is a republic bounded by Saudi Arabia in the north, Oman in the east, the Gulf of Aden in the south and the Red Sea in the west. The republic was formed after the unification of the previous Yemen Arab Republic (North Yemen) and the People's Democratic Republic of Yemen (South Yemen) in 1990. Several large islands, notably Socotra in the Indian Ocean, Perim in the Bab el Mandeb and Kamaran in the Red Sea, belong to Yemen. The Hanish Islands in the southern Red Sea are claimed by both Yemen and Eritrea in Africa which lies opposite Yemen across the narrow straits of Bab el Mandeb.

   Most of Yemen consists of a high plateau which becomes gradually lower eastwards and northwards until it merges with the desert lands of the Empty Quarter (Rub al Khali) which extend into Saudi Arabia. In the west, high mountains extend in a north–south direction and west and south of these lies an arid, coastal plain called the Tihama. The mountains are dissected by steep-sided wadis through which water is channelled during the summer monsoonal rains.

   The climate of Yemen is hot and dry on the coastal plains and in the desert but with lower winter temperatures in the uplands and mountains. Rainfall is scarce and erratic and falls mainly in the summer months in the

QUICK FACTS

Area: 527,968 square kilometres or
   203,850 square miles
Population: 15,919,000
Capital: San'a
Commercial capital: Aden (Adan)
Other cities: Al Hudaydah, Ta'izz
Form of government: Republic
Religions: Zaidism, Shia Islam, Sunni Islam
Currency: Riyal

mountains where some percolates down to collect in underground aquifers. This water, in the north and central parts of Yemen, allows cultivation to be carried out, much of it on terraced fields cut into the mountain slopes.

The country is almost entirely dependent on agriculture even though a very small percentage of the land is fertile. The main crops are coffee, cotton, wheat, vegetables, millet, sorghum and fruit. Fishing is an important industry with mackerel, tuna, lobster and cod caught and some canning factories along the coast. Other industry is on a very small scale, consisting mainly of a manufacturing industry which produces textiles, plastic, rubber and aluminium goods, paints and matches. Modernisation of industry is slow because of lack of funds.

QUICK FACTS

Area: 102,173 square kilometres or
   39,449 square miles
Population: 10,574,000
Capital: Belgrade (Beograd)
Other cities: Nis, Novi Sad, Pristina
Form of government: Federal Republic
Religions: Eastern Orthodox, Islam
Currency: New Dinar

YUGOSLAVIA (FRY) was created in 1918 and became a single federal republic after World War II under the leadership of Marshal Tito (1892–1980). The six constituent republics were Serbia, Croatia, Slovenia, Bosnia–Herzegovina, Macedonia and Montenegro. The Federal Republic of Yugoslavia now consists of only Serbia and Montenegro, which are the largest and the smallest of the six republics of the former Yugoslavia.The other republics, beginning with Slovenia and Croatia in 1991, have all declared their independence from Yugoslavia.

The bulk of the country (86 per cent) is occupied by Serbia with Montenegro forming a smaller region in the southwest. In addition, there are two ethnic enclaves within the territory of Yugoslavia: Kosovo, in the south near the border with Albania, where Muslim Albanians, who make up about 17 per cent of the total population of Yugoslavia, have been in ongoing conflict with Serbia over their status; and Vojvodina, in the north, which is home to people of Hungarian descent who constitute about 3 per cent of the total population. Ownership of some of the neighbouring territory is disputed and the Serb Republic in Bosnia-Herzegovina together with Serb-held lands in Croatia in effect extend the jurisdiction of 'Greater Serbia'. Yugoslavia was recognised as an independent republic by the European Union in 1996 but the country has been slow to gain further international recognition because of its role in the wars in the region in the 1990s.

The northern part of Serbia consists of fertile, low-lying plains drained by the River Danube (Dunav) on which the capital, Belgrade (Beograd), is situated. In the east, the land rises to form the ridges and hollows of a limestone plateau while mountains and hills predominate in the southeast. Dense forests cover much of the southern part of upland Serbia. Montenegro is also mountainous and has a 192-kilometre or 120-mile stretch of coastline along the Adriatic Sea providing the republic with its main port of Bar. Here the vegetation is more typically Mediterranean, with citrus fruit trees, palms, olives, figs, grape vines and pomegranates.

Before 1991, Serbia was the most densely populated and Montenegro the most thinly populated of the states of the former Yugoslavia and this remains the case today. About 50 per cent of the people live in rural areas while the rest reside in or near the larger cities or towns, especially in the capital, Belgrade. The economy was severely affected by the war and by the imposition of sanctions by the international community during the early 1990s. Economic sanctions were lifted in 1995 and the situation improved slightly but many ecomomic activities were again affected by NATO's bombing of the country in 1999.

The economy is largely agricultural and produce includes wheat, maize, grapes and citrus fruit. Forestry is also important to the economy. Yugoslavia, and more especially Serbia, contains important mineral reserves, with copper, antimony, lead, bauxite, coal, petroleum, natural gas, zinc, chromium and gold all being present. Other economic activities include mining and the manufacturing of iron and steel, chemicals, machinery, electronic equipment, textiles and clothing.

QUICK FACTS

Area: 752,618 square kilometres or
   290,587 square miles
Population: 8,275,000
Capital: Lusaka
Other cities: Kitwe, Ndola, Mufulira
Form of government: Republic
Religions: Christianity, Animism
Currency: Kwacha

ZAMBIA, located in central southern Africa, is essentially a massive plateau surrounded by Mozambique, Zimbabwe, Botswana, Namibia, Angola, the Democratic Republic of the Congo and Tanzania. Bordering it to the south is the River Zambezi and to the southwest, the Kalahari Desert. It has some other large rivers, including the Luangwa and the Kafue, and some lakes, the largest of which is Lake Bangweulu.

The Muchinga Mountains in the northeast reach a little over 2,100 metres or 6,890 feet with the plateau averaging between 100–1,4000 metres or 328–4,593 feet in height. The plateau is covered with grasslands and some trees and is home to a typically diverse array of African wildlife. There are large game parks on the River Luangwa and River Kafue.

The climate is tropical, modified somewhat by altitude. About two thirds of the population work in farming at a subsistence level. Agriculture is underdeveloped and vulnerable to weather variations which can lead to food shortages and the need for large quantities of imported food. The principal subsistence crops grown are corn, sugar cane and cassava. Zambia's economy relies heavily on the mining of copper, lead, zinc and cobalt. The poor market prospects for copper, which will eventually be exhausted, make it imperative for Zambia to develop her vast agricultural potential. The majority of the country's power is provided by the Kariba Dam on the River Zambezi and there is potential for further hydroelectric development.

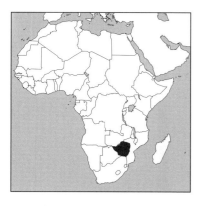

ZIMBABWE is a landlocked country in southern Africa. Bounded to the west by Zambia and Botswana, to the north and east by Mozambique and to the south by South Africa, Zimbabwe is a country with spectacular physical features, teeming with wildlife. It is bordered in the north by the River Zambezi, which flows over the wide Victoria Falls before entering Lake Kariba. In the south, the River Limpopo marks its border with South Africa. Most of the country is over 300 metres or 984 feet above sea level and a great plateau between 1,200–1,500 metres or 3,937–4,922 feet in height occupies the central area. Massive granite outcrops, called kopjes, also dot the landscape. Only one third of the population lives in towns and cities, the largest of which is the capital, Harare. The climate is tropical in the lowlands and subtropical in the higher land.

About 75 per cent of the workforce are employed in agriculture. Tobacco, sugar cane, cotton, wheat and maize are exported and form the basis of processing industries. Zimbabwe is rich in mineral resources such as coal, chromium, nickel, gold, platinum and precious metals and mining accounts for around 30 per cent of foreign revenue. Tourism has the potential to be a major growth industry as Zimbabwe has many tourist attractions, such as the Victoria Falls and Great Zimbabwe – the ruins of a settlement that flourished during the 13th and 15th centuries and was the work of a Shona-Karanga society – and several wildlife parks. However, there has been ongoing dissatisfaction within the country at the very high inflation rate and the economy has declined rather than prospered.

QUICK FACTS

Area: 390,757 square kilometres or
 150,872 square miles
Population: 11,908,000
Capital: Harare
Other cities: Bulawayo, Mutare, Gweru
Form of government: Republic
Religions: Animism, Anglicanism, Roman
 Catholicism
Currency: Zimbabwe Dollar